THE EXPECTATION

OF JUSTICE

THE EXPECTATION OF JUSTICE

FRANCE, 1944–1946

Megan Koreman

DUKE UNIVERSITY PRESS

Durham and London

1999

© 1999 Duke University Press
All rights reserved

Frontispiece: The liberation of Rambervillers,
30 September 1944. (Courtesy of J.-C. Kempf)
Typeset in Carter & Cone Galliard by Tseng Information Systems, Inc.
Library of Congress Cataloging-in-Publication Data appear on the last
printed page of this book.

For my parents

CONTENTS

Maps ix

Acknowledgments xvii

List of Abbreviations xix

Introduction 1

CHAPTER 1 Three Towns, Three Liberations 8

CHAPTER 2 Living in the Aftermath of War 48

CHAPTER 3 Legal Justice and the Purge of Collaborators 92

CHAPTER 4 Social Justice and the Provisioning Crisis 148

CHAPTER 5 Honorary Justice and the Construction of Memory 189

CHAPTER 6 Popular Justice or Republican Legitimacy? 229

Conclusion 258

Notes 265

Bibliography 321

Index 337

OCCUPIED FRANCE

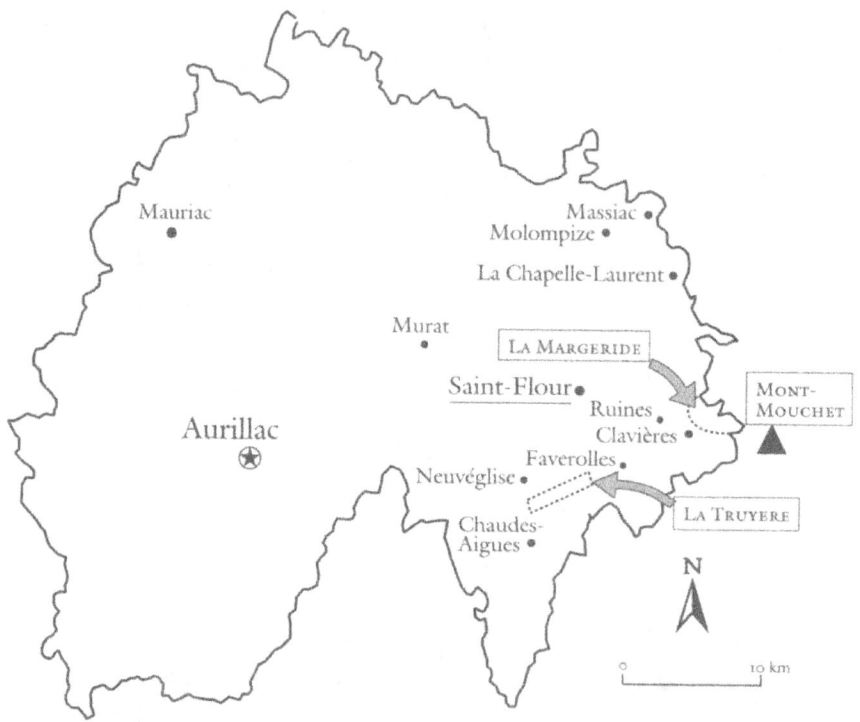

CANTAL

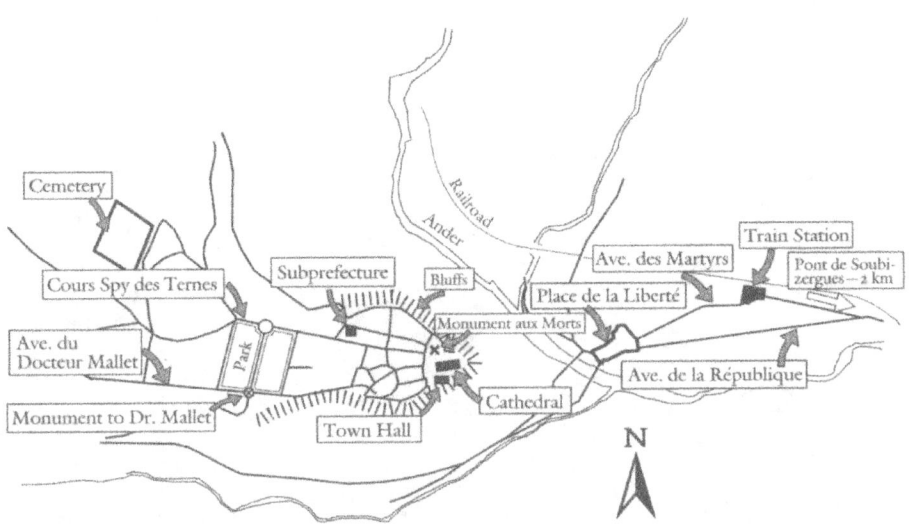

SAINT-FLOUR

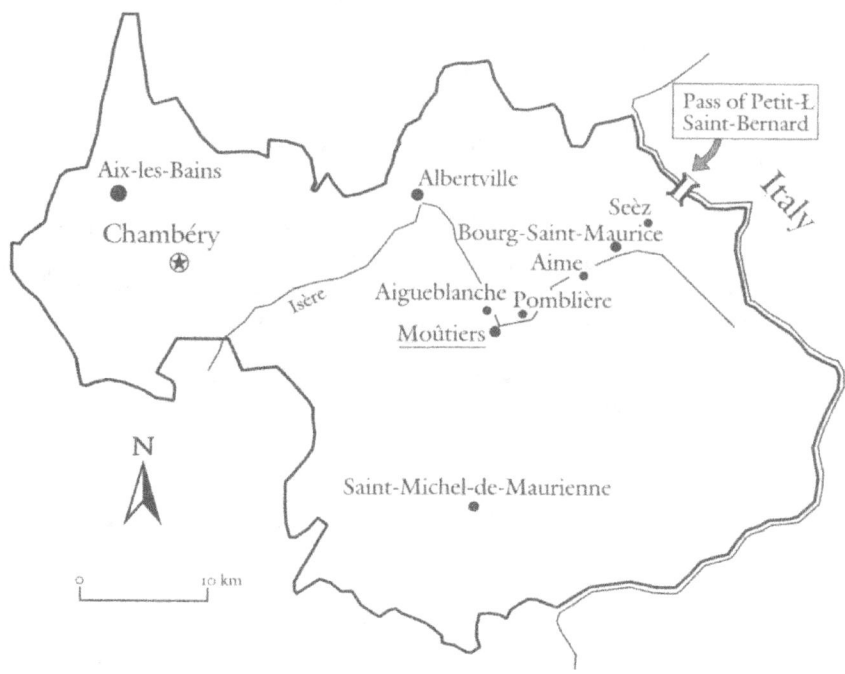

SAVOIE

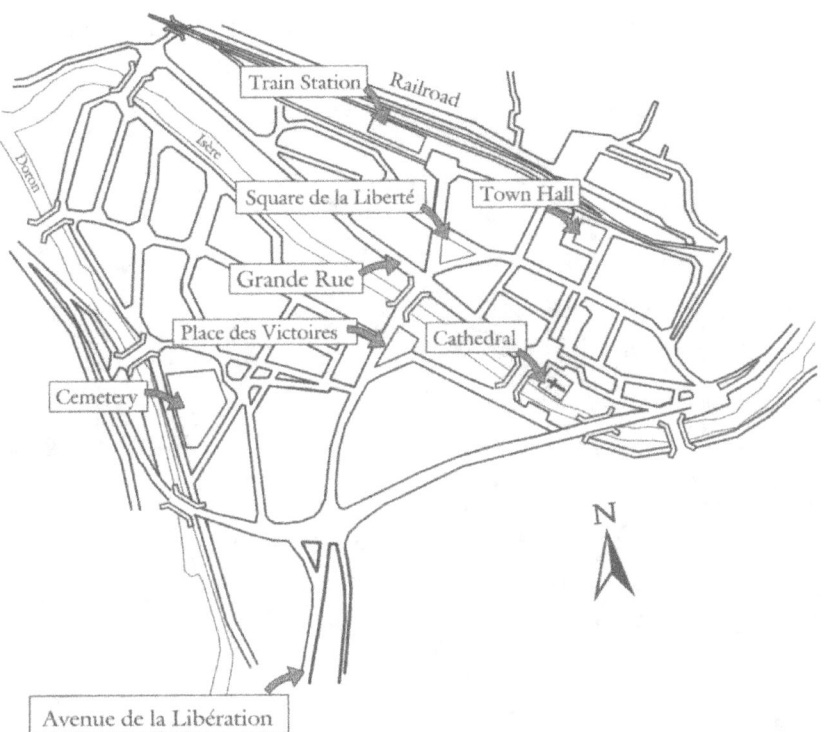

MOÛTIERS

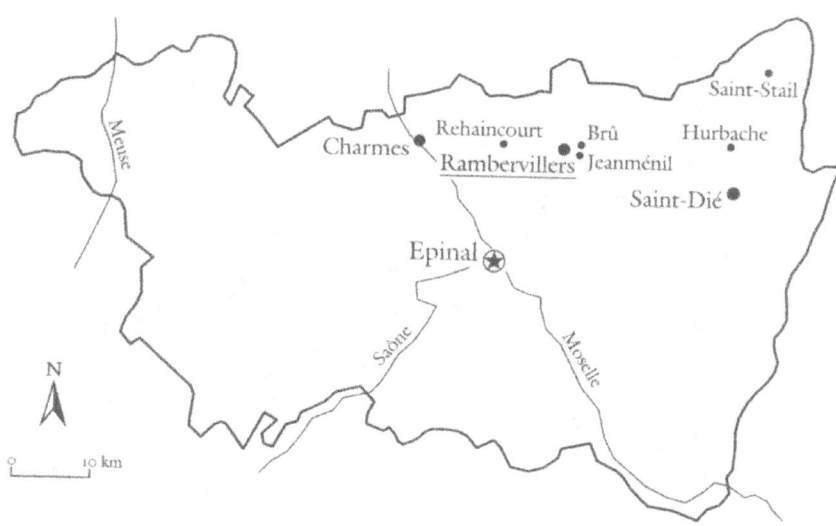

VOSGES

Maps xv

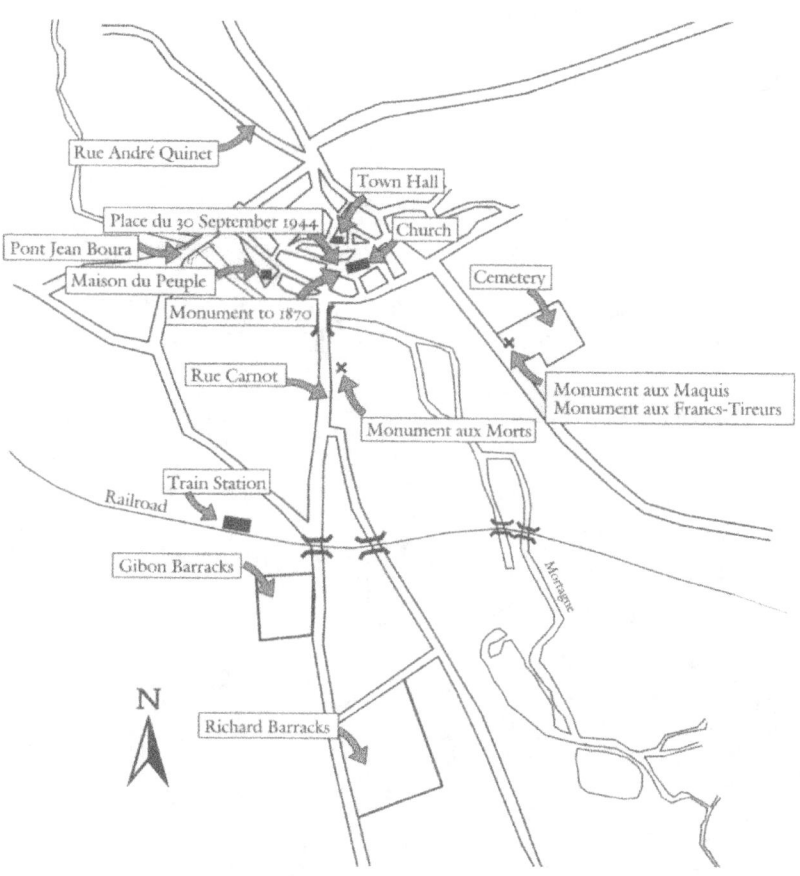

RAMBERVILLERS

ACKNOWLEDGMENTS

Having begun this project as a dissertation, I have collected a number of debts of gratitude to many people for their generous assistance over the years.

The funding for the dissertation came through a Peace Scholar award from the United States Institute of Peace, which does not in any way share in the findings or opinions expressed in this book, a Humanities Graduate Research Grant from the University of California at Berkeley, and a Mellon Dissertation Fellowship in the Humanities.

While doing the research, I benefited from the generous assistance of Madame Danielle at the Versailles annex of the Bibliothèque nationale and the directors and staffs of the section contemporaine of the Archives nationales, the departmental archives of Cantal, Savoie, and the Vosges, the Service historique de l'Armée de Terre, the Hoover Institution Archives, and the National Archives and Records Administration. I would also like to thank the mayors of Moûtiers, Rambervillers, and Saint-Flour for opening the municipal archives to me.

The people of Rambervillers have earned my particular gratitude for their extraordinary enthusiasm and generosity in digging up documents of every sort for me, especially M. Jean-Claude Kempf, Mayor Chevrier, and Deputy Mayor Fevotte. To all those in Rambervillers and elsewhere who shared their recollections of the war and liberation with me, especially M. and Mme. Vouaux and Abbé Hudry, I express my thanks and my hope that I have done justice to their achievements and their memories.

While in Berkeley, I benefited immensely from the support and constructive criticism of my committee, Professors Susanna Barrows, Gerald Feldman, and Stanley Brandes, and from the members of Professor Barrows's dissertation seminar, especially David Barnes, Doug Mackaman, Vanessa Schwartz, Regina Sweeney, and Tami Whited.

The subsequent development of the project owes a great deal to the help of colleagues at Texas Tech University and elsewhere, especially Sarah Fishman, Nancy Green, John Howe, Rod Kedward, John Merriman, M. Catherine Miller, John Sweets, and David Troyansky. I would also like to thank all those who have commented upon and questioned my conference papers, particularly Omer Bartov, Francis Murphy, Tyler Stovall, Rebecca Ullrich, and Krystyna von Henneberg.

I would further like to acknowledge the assistance and support given to the final stages of making this into a book by Valerie Millholland and the staff at Duke University Press and by Texas Tech University and the history department there. My thanks also to Susan Tomlinson for drawing the maps. Unless otherwise noted, all translations are my own.

Of course, any such lengthy project also owes a great deal to the patience and support of friends. In this regard I would particularly like to thank my family, Case and Joyce Koreman, Elizabeth, Neil, Paul, and Margaret. For their friendship and willingness to run monumental errands and to act as dictionaries for me, I am indebted to Sue Peters, Gregg Williams, Tami Whited, and Jean-Yves Boulard. I will always be grateful for the friendship and encouragement given me by Paul Friedland, Page Herrlinger, Ann, John, Joe, Tom, and Anna Howe, and John McGreevy.

Any errors or misinterpretations are, of course, wholly my own. It is my hope that amid the facts and anecdotes I have managed to convey both the terror and tremendous hope that came out of the maelstrom of the Second World War and the burning necessity for justice in building peace.

LIST OF ABBREVIATIONS

AAS	Anciens de l'Armée secrète (Moûtiers)
AC	Archives départementales du Cantal
AN	Archives nationales de France
AS	Archives départementales de la Savoie
AS	Armée secrète
AV	Archives départementales des Vosges
AVAD	Association vosgienne d'anciens détenus
BCRA	Bureau central de renseignements et d'action
CEA	Centre d'entr'aide
CAL	Comité d'arrondissement de libération
CCL	Comité cantonal (or communal) de libération
CDL	Comité départemental de libération
CFLN	Comité français de libération nationale
CLL	Comité local de libération
CDLR	Ceux de la Résistance
CE	Contrôle économique
CFTC	Confédération française des travailleurs chrétiens
CGT	Confédération générale du travail
CM	Conseil municipal
CNR	Conseil national de la Résistance
CRR	Commissaire régional de la République
FFI	Forces françaises de l'intérieur
FN	Front national
FTPF	Francs-tireurs et partisans français

GPRF	Gouvernement provisoire de la République française
MLN	Mouvement de libération nationale
MP	Milices patriotiques
MRP	Mouvement républicain populaire
MUR	Mouvements unis de résistance
NARA	National Archives and Records Administration (USA)
PGA	prisonniers de guerre de l'Axe
PCF	Parti communiste français
POW	prisoner of war
RG	Ravitaillement général
SFIO	Section française de l'Internationale ouvrière
STO	Service du travail obligatoire
UFF	Union des femmes françaises

INTRODUCTION

Imagine yourself in Europe in the closing days of the Second World War. Millions have died or been forced from their homes as refugees, soldiers, prisoners, or slave laborers, and economic and political structures have begun to collapse. The clash of ideologies and a swarm of subsidiary civil wars have left little common moral ground to the survivors. Peace has not yet officially arrived, although you have been liberated from enemy occupation and the battle has moved on to other territory. How would you and your neighbors regather yourselves into a community in the wake of such a cataclysm? How would you bridge the gulf between war and peace to embark on social, cultural, and political reconstruction?

More specifically, imagine yourself in France during the *après-libération*, the liminal period between the liberation of most of the country in the summer of 1944 and the January 1946 resignation of Charles de Gaulle from the presidency of the Gouvernement provisoire de la République française (Provisional Government of the French Republic, GPRF).[1] Although for the most part spared the full brunt of the war, France emerged from it in a state of political and social fragmentation and of economic disrepair caused by government collaboration and the depredations of German occupation. Nazi Germany had defeated France in 1940 in a matter of weeks, leading to the division of the country into several occupation zones and to the creation of the collaborationist Etat français of Marshal Philippe Pétain, better known as Vichy France. When the Allied armies invaded Normandy and Pétain retreated with the Germans in 1944, however, the Resistance, in the form of de Gaulle and the GPRF, was able to step into Vichy's place.

But the new government faced immense challenges. If the antagonism between Resistance and Collaboration served as the primary domestic fault line of the après-libération, the Vichy-era division of the country into five occupation zones created a dense network of fissures and crevasses. As a nation, the French had no common experience of the Second World War. From the atmosphere of repression to the availability of food, the daily realities of occupation varied so wildly across the zones that they might as well have been separate countries. Everyday life in those few departments annexed to Nazi Germany or one of its administrative creations, for instance, held vastly different problems and terrors than those experienced in the relatively untouched Vichy zone. The pattern of liberation that required full-scale industrial battle in some towns but looked like nothing so much as a village fete in others further complicated the French experience of the war. In the summer of 1944, the differences among occupation and liberation zones, the destruction of the communications and transportation networks, and the abeyance of central authority temporarily shattered France into an archipelago of detached local communities.[2]

To compound this political crisis, the economy actually deteriorated even further after the liberation. By 1945, for example, 20 percent of the building stock had been destroyed and only 40 percent of railroad lines still functioned. French rations allotted 35 percent less meat, 65 percent less fats, and 62 percent less sugar than British rations, which were not themselves particularly generous. The prospects for improvement looked dim because the 1945 wheat harvest registered only half the prewar average. Ominously, the franc lost five-sixths of its value between 1938 and 1946.[3]

The Gaullists in the Provisional Government looked at this situation from the perspective of national and international politics, with particular attention to France's reputation among the Allies and its position in the postwar world. They accordingly gave top priority to legitimating the new Resistance government in the eyes of its citizens and of the world by establishing a republican legitimacy that would be demonstrated by the reimposition of central authority and by the early election of democratic representatives. The new government in Paris therefore reinforced the power of the bureaucracy and police, held municipal and national elections, and convened a constituent assembly.[4]

But the divisions created by the war were so deep and complex that elections alone would convince neither world nor domestic opinion that France was a unified country standing solidly behind its new republican government. For that, de Gaulle used the Resistencialist myth. That myth, best described by Henry Rousso, claimed that all the French had stood united in the (Gaullist) Resistance and had fought together against the foreign enemy, who had only a handful of collaborators.[5] The truth was that in 1940 the great majority of the French supported the collaborationist Vichy government, only slowly turning to the Resistance under the pressure of food shortages and the threat of forced labor. Until the Allied armies landed in Normandy, about an equal number of activists supported Resistance as supported Collaboration.[6]

The truth, though, did not serve de Gaulle's purpose of claiming equal status with the victorious American, British, and Soviet allies. Nor would it help him to reimpose central authority within France. The myth, however, did both these things by denying any significant French involvement with the soon-to-be-defeated Germans. In the international arena, the myth suggested that the French were more to be pitied than blamed for events under the occupation; indeed, they were to be admired for their gallant resistance. In the domestic arena, it implied that the French had no cause for division, because, according to the myth, almost everyone had been a resistant and therefore could have no reason to quarrel with his or her neighbor, who was also a resistant. This "nationalization" of the Resistance, to use Pieter Lagrou's term, bought unity at a high price, only one aspect of which was the sudden loss of the well-deserved moral elitism of authentic resistants.[7] More important, it required instant amnesia from people who were only slowly realizing the full consequences of what had really happened.[8]

In the long term, of course, the Resistencialist myth enjoyed such tremendous success that it shaped postwar French national identity and politics. But in the short term it ran into sometimes violent opposition in the provinces because it offended provincials' often sorrowful memories of the war and betrayed their expectations of a Resistance-led future, the long-promised *lendemains qui chantent* (singing tomorrows). Indeed, opposition to the myth symbolized a much more fundamental conflict between the people and the new regime. If the Gaullists of the Provisional Government approached the après-libération from the perspective of national and international politics, the people of small-town France reacted to the wholly local circumstances of what had happened to particular people in a particular place. While the Gaullists in Paris noticed the collapse of the franc and the emerging balance of power in the Allied command and the United Nations, ordinary men and women noticed the decline in the size of the bread ration and the continuing, agonizing absence of the political deportees.

Even in the most sheltered places where the Germans never set foot, the occupation and liberation had upset family life, often by the forced absence of one or more family members, had brought the anxiety of food shortages, and had given the local community more than usual autonomy from the failing central government. Even the best of circumstances had given men and women ample cause to consider the proper relationship between a government and its citizens as well as the proper organization of society. Indeed, the Second World War created the unusual situation in which ordinary people thought about the social contract and had an opportunity to renegotiate it. In après-libération France, the general consensus of the people in the provinces was that the new, postwar society should be based on justice. The promises of the clandestine press led many to expect that the new Resistance regime would take the path of popular legitimation by providing that justice.[9]

But what did the French mean by justice as they emerged from the wreckage of the Second World War? The closest thing to a widely held definition was the CNR Charter, a programmatic statement of the shape of the postwar just society. Signed by the Conseil national de la Résistance (National Council of the Resistance, CNR) on 15 March 1944, the charter promised a social and economic democracy. Its main provisions called for the reestablishment of the Republic; the punishment of traitors and collaborators; the confiscation of war and black market profits; the reestablishment of universal suffrage and civil liberties; and reforms to create greater social and economic equality, including the nationalization of important financial and industrial concerns and the implementation of comprehensive social security measures.[10] The CNR Charter provided a common vision of the just society for resistants at all levels, from the very highest to the most obscure. Indeed, the public consensus of the après-libération, which excluded only collaborationists, favored the charter's provisions for the reestablishment of the republic, a purge of collaborators, and social justice.[11]

The CNR Charter, however, only indicated the type of legislative measures that citizens expected the new regime to effect in pursuit of the just society. The conception of justice that shaped the events and tensions of the après-libération went far beyond the questions of wage distribution and civil liberties in the charter to embrace the moral and practical principles that would reconstruct the local and national community on just foundations. It might, indeed, be understood as an economy, or circuit, of justice that shares out not only goods but also honor among the living and the dead. While this economy divides some things, such as bread, equally among all the members of a community, it bestows or withdraws others, such as good repute, according to each individual's merit. Because it is thoroughly rooted in and bounded by the community, the configuration of an economy of justice shifts over time and place to respond to local circumstances.

Such a community-based conception of justice recognizes three spheres or realms—legal justice, social justice, and honorary justice—without necessarily separating them out from each other. Legal justice holds men and women to the written and customary laws of the state and the codes of conduct of the community. More than merely the legal code, the prescriptions of legal justice also evoke a community's standards of moral respectability and, an important consideration at the end of the Second World War, solidarity. It therefore encompasses both the state's judicial courts and the informal courts of neighborhood opinion. A person falling afoul of legal justice might be hunted by the police and/or shunned by his or her neighbors. Given the ideological context of the war and the fratricidal conflict between the French Resistance and Vichy, during the après-libération issues of legal justice inevitably swirled around the questions of collaboration and betrayal.

The better-known concept of social justice refers to the fair distribution of goods among the community. In the penury of the après-libération, the exact details of that distribution constituted a concrete, daily concern for every citizen, most notably in the form of food rations. There is nothing abstract about social justice in a country with absolute food shortages and a dysfunctional rationing system. Any schoolchild can explain it; indeed, waiting in a food line would give him or her ample time to elaborate an entire theory of it.

Even less tangible than social or legal justice, honorary justice apportions honor among the living and the dead of a community. Because honor depends on opinions and attitudes rather than concrete goods or published rules, honorary justice stirs the most controversy within communities. The townsfolk might disagree over who should be honored, particularly in troubled times such as the liberation when a victory makes yesterday's official heroes into tomorrow's traitors. They might also disagree over how fallen heroes should be honored, some interpreting the demands of honorary justice as a license for violent vengeance and others seeing those demands as imposing a memorial duty.[12] During the après-libération, both monument builders and vigilantes responded to the call of honorary justice.

Although legal justice most properly pertains to the purge of collaborators, social justice to the rationing system, and honorary justice to commemorative politics, the three realms constantly overlapped in the daily life of the après-libération. Food rations, for instance, clearly belonged in the realm of social justice, but the food rations of a patriotic hero such as a political deportee repatriated from a concentration camp also evoked honorary justice. Likewise, the purge of collaborators involved questions of honorary as well as legal justice, especially in the minds of vigilantes. Nevertheless, the relative weight that a community or faction within a community gave to each realm depended on its particular experiences and circumstances. The type and intensity of collaboration in an area, for instance, affected how people there defined collaboration, how seriously they thought it should be punished, and how they thought its victims should be honored. Indeed, local understandings of justice could be remarkably flexible and subtle; in 1945 crowds in the purge courts were known to cheer acquittals as well as death sentences.

During the après-libération, the economy of justice acted as more than a dream of a "pure and strong France" that would punish traitors, feed everyone, and honor the righteous. It also informed the relations between the new Resistance government and the small-town citizenry. To a certain extent, it provided a common ground for the new regime and the people because the national government ratified many popular ideas of justice. The very fact of a rationing system meant that the government endorsed the concept of social justice, and the decision to give repatriated deportees double rations indicated that it shared the general notion of honorary justice. The government similarly acknowledged the need for legal justice with the purge of collaborators.

Nonetheless, the expectation of justice created by the circumstances of the Second World War and the seeming consensus among the citizenry and the Resistance government of the après-libération also acted as a wedge driving apart the people and the new regime. The people of the small towns of France wanted justice and expected it from the Gaullist government. The Gaullists, however, followed a path of republican legitimation that not only placed other considerations above the popular conception of justice but often brought the central government into direct conflict with those popular notions. When the authorities in Paris scheduled municipal elections before the POWs and deportees could return to take part in them, for example, people in the provinces took it as an insult to honorary justice more than as a reassurance of republican order. Similarly, when de Gaulle pardoned locally notorious collaborators, he outraged the local sense of legal and honorary justice more than he smoothed over divisions. And when the government failed to control the black market, it proved its inability to provide social justice.

Ironically, at the very moment in late 1945 when the Gaullists achieved their understanding of legitimation through republican order by holding general elections for a constituent assembly, they lost any hope of gaining the popular legitimation given to those who provide justice because they toyed with the bread ration. On the superficial terms of restoring order, reimposing central authority, and even of plastering over public antagonisms, the Resistance government navigated the transition from war to peace successfully. But on the deeper levels of resolving resentments and popularly legitimating the Fourth Republic, it failed through its neglect of the demands of justice. Indeed, the peace following the Second World War disappointed many in France because it was built on weariness and fear rather than on justice.

CHAPTER ONE

THREE TOWNS, THREE LIBERATIONS

Photojournalism and myth have created an image of the liberation of France as a day on which joyously tearful men and women crowded around an Allied tank or maquisard car, pressing wine and kisses on their liberators while Allied flags flew bravely in the background. Later that same day, the maquisards, bristling with submachine guns and the cross of Lorraine, shaved the heads of collaborationist women in a square filled with howling onlookers, perhaps also marking them with swastikas of tar and parading them through the streets.[1] The stereotype makes a good story: the soldiers heroically free the people; the people gratefully thank their saviors; the patriots sternly punish the traitors. Any regrettably excessive emotions are understandable and limited to one overwhelming day. The good guys win; the bad guys are punished. Justice is served.

It is a nice story and it fits well with Gaullist myth, but it is not especially representative.[2] France was not liberated on a single day in a single manner, but over the course of ten months and in as many ways as there are towns and villages in France.[3] In parts of the north, liberation came with death and destruction on the heels of mechanized warfare. In large areas of the south, the Germans simply withdrew, while in other areas, particularly in the southeast, they retreated under maquisard fire. Neighboring towns could have had completely different experiences, one being torn apart by executions, deportations, and arson, while the other escaped untouched.[4] Some towns faced severe food shortages; others held public feasts.

The emotional clichés of maquisards and head shavings further obscure the essential fact that the liberation was primarily a transfer of power between French regimes. Over the course of the previous 156 years, of course, the French had had considerable experience with not only rapid changes in governors but with profound alterations in forms of government and political ideologies. But although previous transfers of power had occurred during wars and revolutions, none had involved quite such complicated circumstances as the liberation. In 1944 the new regime came to France from exile to join mostly unknown colleagues in the metropole while two foreign armies battled out a world war on French soil. In a certain sense, the Gaullists' seizure of the apparatus of power from Vichy may have been the easiest task facing the GPRF at the liberation.[5] Even before the Allies landed in Normandy, they infiltrated an embryonic administration into France through the metropolitan resistance networks so that during the liberation eighteen Commissaires régionaux de la République (Regional Commissioners of the Republic, CRRs), all proven resistants, exercised full and extraordinary powers up to that of granting pardons in their regions. They remained in their uneasy positions between the Resistants of the central government and the increasingly alienated local resistants in the provinces until the dissolution of the commissariat in March 1946.[6]

As the representatives of the national Resistance and the GPRF in regions that would be cut off from Paris for an undetermined period, the CRRs governed through a dual bureaucracy. On the one hand, they installed resistants as prefects and mayors in the traditional offices of the highly centralized French state. On the other, they also worked with the new committees of liberation that had grown out of the Resistance itself and that represented the people of the grass-roots Resistance movement rather than the state. The density, composition, activity, and influence of liberation committees varied widely across the country, but every department had a Comité départemental de libération (CDL) representing Resistance networks, political parties, trade unions, and other groups such as women or POWs. Smaller areas had a Comité d'arrondissement de libération (CAL), Comité local de libération (CLL), or Comité cantonal (or communal) de libération (CCL). In the first days, even months, of an area's liberation, the liberation committees exercised considerably more influence there than the central government. But as the government regained its power and the means of asserting its authority, the liberation committees found themselves steadily excluded from real influence. Although resistants staffed both bureaucracies, it became increasingly clear that they represented different interests (national or local) and different visions of a Resistance France.

If every new regime must find some form of popular acceptance, the nature of the Resistance made the matter especially complicated at the liberation. On the one hand, all branches of the Resistance supported the return of the Republic, which implied elected rather than self-proclaimed representatives. If resistants could not win popular endorsement through elections, they would have to either step aside or betray their own ideals. On the other hand, other than Charles de Gaulle few resistants had a public reputation on which to build an electoral campaign. Resistants based their claims to postwar power on the moral qualities of their stand against the Nazis and their collaborators, yet those legitimating acts of resistance had had to be kept secret for fear of the Gestapo and the Milice. Resistants therefore had to prove their resistance all over again after the liberation. The contemporary wave of refashioning and whitewashing caused even more problems for authentic resistants; recruits rushed into the Resistance once the Allies had landed in Normandy, and even confirmed collaborators began touting themselves as undercover resistants (as some actually were).[7]

The confusion created by the necessary secrecy of the authentic resistants and the need for elections meant that the political transfer of power extended over a much longer time period than the military liberation. In fact, the transfer of power showed even greater variations in its implementation than the military liberation because it operated on so many levels and because over the months the recipient of power, the Resistance, broke apart and, in some places, turned on itself. If on the national level the reins of power fell remarkably easily from Vichy to de Gaulle's Resistance GPRF, they got terribly tangled on the local level. Some towns were happy to see the Resistance take over the national government but did not want local resistants to take over the local government. In other towns local resistants joined the rest of the community in opposing the new Resistance government. And, of course, there were also towns that accepted and supported both the national and local Resistance and where the local resistants never objected to the policies of their Gaullist colleagues in Paris. It would indeed be far more accurate to speak of the liberations rather than the liberation of France.

Yet even with the inherent variation of the liberation, the French experiences of the transition from war to peace, from the Etat français to the Fourth Republic, did have enough similarities to bear reduction into broad patterns. Those patterns can best be represented through the experiences of communities of three to seven thousand inhabitants, which can be taken to speak for the France of 1944–45 for several reasons. First, in 1946 about half the French people lived in towns of similar size.[8] Second, such towns often served as cultural, economic, and political centers for much larger areas, meaning that events and opinions that took place or were expressed there reflected the experiences and views of the farmers and villagers from the outlying areas as well as of the town dwellers. In less populated departments, a town of five thousand might house the courts, markets, and newspaper used by a much larger number of people scattered in the surrounding countryside. In more populated departments such a place might provide employment in small factories or shops to people living in nearby villages. Such towns served and therefore spoke for more than their own inhabitants. Third, because such towns were small enough to engage in community-wide disagreements but too large to do so merely by word of mouth, the divisions there took public form in newspapers, ceremonies, and elections.

Fourth, small market towns offered natural centers for local Resistance groups. The printing presses needed by the intellectual Resistance, for example, were found in towns large enough to support a newspaper. Similarly, the doctors who issued false medical certificates to maquisards often lived in towns and traveled to patients in the countryside and vice versa, again linking the small town with its hinterland. Although the resistance groups in such towns often belonged to the major Resistance networks, they remained small and obscure enough to represent a local resistance more than the national Resistance. Fifth, small towns drew only a moderate interest from the central government; the authorities cared enough to document events and opinions in such a place, but not enough to expend scarce resources on influencing them. Indeed, the breakdown of the communications network meant that during the *après-libération* such communities enjoyed even more autonomy than usual. This combination of local importance and national unimportance meant that small towns were big enough to develop coherent discussions and positions on contemporary events and small enough to be allowed to do so without much interference from the national authorities.

The fragmentation of the country by occupation zones and liberation battles, however, temporarily reshuffled the French into new groupings arranged according to war damage and food shortages rather than those traditionally defined by religious or political affiliations. Only a comparison of small towns from different occupation and liberation zones can speak for France of the après-libération. Saint-Flour (Cantal), Moûtiers (Savoie), and Rambervillers (Vosges) serve the purpose well because in normal circumstances they would have been very similar. They were all *chefs-lieux* of their districts, which were all predominantly rural, although Rambervillers and the Vosges were more industrialized than Cantal or Savoie. Furthermore, they shared the cultural cohesion of belonging to regions known for their Catholicism.[9]

The geography of war, however, gave these otherwise similar towns wildly different experiences of the après-libération. As the capital of eastern Cantal in Auvergne in the Massif Central, Saint-Flour enjoyed the relative safety of the Vichy zone. Except for a few traumatic weeks in the summer of 1944, for the Sanflorains the war rumbled threateningly but distantly on the horizon. Moûtiers, on the other hand, endured three different occupation regimes as the capital of an Alpine valley close to the Italian border. For the Moutiérains, the war mostly took the form of a low-scale, guerrilla-style civil war between Vichy and the irregular Resistance army, the Forces françaises de l'intérieur (French Forces of the Interior, FFI), who liberated the area. In even greater contrast, Rambervillers, a market town in Lorraine, suffered one of the harshest occupation regimes in France, that of the reserved zone. The Rambûvetais experienced the war as the clash of mechanized armies, especially during the fall of 1944 when the German garrison gave way to American troops and the town huddled on the front line for a month. Because the war meant very different things to the Sanflorains, Moutiérains, and Rambûvetais, so did the liberation. Taken together, their experiences broadly represent the French transition from war to peace.

SAINT-FLOUR

Founded by a fourth-century bishop, Saint-Flour perches on a rocky outcropping of the old volcanic highlands of the Massif Central in Auvergne. On three sides the town ends abruptly in cliffs almost nine hundred meters high pointing over the River Ander. The ancient cathedral sits at the eastern point, while the rest of the old town crowds into narrow, crooked streets leading to the elongated square in front of the cathedral and the town hall. The subprefecture and a spacious, shady park lie across the western entrance. By the twentieth century, Saint-Flour had expanded beyond its natural fortress, both westward into the plateau and downward into the new town at the base of the cliffs. The railroad station sits in the new town, but the old town remains the heart of Saint-Flour: in front of the cathedral stands the First World War Monument aux Morts.

In 1945 the community of 5,590 inhabitants still preserved some of its honors as the traditional capital of Haute-Auvergne and eastern Cantal.[10] As the seat of a bishopric, the subprefecture, and the Cour d'assises, it was more than just a regional market town. As the home of eastern Cantal's newspaper, it also served as an information center and cultural trendsetter. During the après-libération, transportation difficulties and severe freezes isolated the town and its region for weeks on end, further reinforcing Saint-Flour's importance.

Compared to other parts of France, Saint-Flour and the department of Cantal had a relatively uneventful war until the summer of 1944. Because Cantal lies south of Vichy, the department spent the first two years of occupation in the privileged free zone. Certainly, the Cantaliens suffered from shortages and economic hardship as much as, if not more than, people in other parts of the country. The volcanic heights are amenable to dairy cattle, sheep, and crops such as lentils but very little else. Yet if the terrain made it difficult to import goods, it also made the department unappealing to the Germans. Even after November 1942, when they occupied southern France, the Germans had little inducement to invest this sparsely populated region. A small unit garrisoned the departmental capital of Aurillac and, after July 1943, used Saint-Flour as a stopover, permanently renting some rooms and a garage. Resistants, on the other hand, recognized the hilly, wooded area's potential as a site for parachute drops, radio relays, and maquis units. By 1943 the arrondissement of Saint-Flour had its own maquisard unit of four to six hundred men, some of whom had come from more crowded places to hide in the hills of Auvergne. Other networks also operated in the area, including judges at the Cour d'assises who hid weapons in the courthouse.[11] Nevertheless, according to the historian of the department during the war, Eugène Martres, Cantaliens on the whole supported Vichy's National Revolution.[12]

The situation in Cantal changed abruptly with the Allied invasion on 6 June 1944, when the Resistance mobilized and an infamous German division began to make its bloody way from the south toward Normandy. The exact chain of events in the department remains confused and controversial today. As of 6–7 June, the Resistance controlled the region of Mauriac, northwest of Saint-Flour, although neither Vichy nor the Germans realized it for some time. By 8 June, 1,800 Cantaliens had left their homes to join the maquis in the FFI redoubts of Mont-Mouchet and La Truyère. Mont-Mouchet being only thirty-five kilometers from Saint-Flour, 150 men from the subprefecture and its northern arrondissement, including the entire gendarmerie brigade, reported there.

On 10 June, the Germans attacked the maquis camp at Mont-Mouchet from three sides, sparking off a month of guerrilla fighting throughout the department that left behind 350 French and 50 to 60 German victims.[13] The Germans responded with a bloody trail of reprisals, including the deportation of 115 persons from the small commune of Murat, only 30 of whom survived the Nazi concentration camps, and the execution of 25 hostages at the Pont de Soubizergues two kilometers west of Saint-Flour.[14]

The German forces in Cantal, which had increased from two hundred men in April to one thousand by 10 July, made Saint-Flour their headquarters for the repression of the maquisard uprising. In July the *Kommandantur* closed off the town to all men between the ages of eighteen and fifty and required anyone else to show a laissez-passer. Food began to run short in the besieged town; on 15 July the daily bread ration was reduced to two hundred grams.[15] By 12 August the only Germans left in Cantal were the 300 to 350 camped in Saint-Flour and surrounded by FFI units, including some American parachutists. The German commander rejected an ultimatum on 20 August by raining machine-gun fire down from the old town, but in the smallest hours of the stormy night of 23–24 August the Germans retreated. Saint-Flour and Cantal were liberated.¹⁶

That day the Sanflorains celebrated in the streets while the Resistance's "home guard," the Milice patriotique (MP), publicly shaved the heads of four or five women. Over the following days, the MP arrested about a dozen men and nine women for collaboration.¹⁷ The town officially celebrated its liberation three days later with an elaborate ceremony honoring the twenty-five men executed on 14 June at the Pont de Soubizergues. The other communities that had suffered in the Germans' June rampage also held memorial ceremonies soon after their liberations, setting a pattern in the region of associating the liberation with grief and the Resistance with the cult of the heroic, patriotic dead.

For the first two weeks of its liberation, power in Saint-Flour appears to have been in the hands of the seven Resistance leaders on the liberation committee, the CAL, who considered matters ranging from public security to the harvest. The CAL, however, soon lost any real power that it might have had to a special delegation appointed by the prefect to act as a municipal council until elections could be arranged. The fourteen men and two women on it were chosen for their Resistance activity or their relation to a resistant.¹⁸ Indeed, being in the resistance was such an important qualification that one of the new councillors was away fighting with the FFI and three were in German captivity and could as easily have been presumed dead, as one already was. After an expansion in October, the special delegation included another two women taking the places of a husband or brother who were political prisoners.¹⁹ The members of the special delegation, like those of the CAL, therefore, were all resistants, but, unlike the CAL members, they derived their power from the central government. That government appeared locally in the form of a new subprefect, Louis Licheron, who had also won his post through service to the Resistance.

The confusion over the exact source of authority at the liberation—the national government or the local community—complicated the elaborate installation of the subprefect and special delegation in mid-September. The appointed representative of the central government, the prefect, inducted the subprefect in the subprefecture, but the representatives of Cantal's Resistance, the CDL, presented the special delegation to the prefect across town in the town hall. Any tensions between the center and provinces, however, were screened by a heavy use of patriotic symbolism, from Allied flags to wreaths laid at the Monument aux Morts and a common attachment to the Resistance and the republic. The new mayor, for example, promised to work impartially to "make [the people] love the republican regime which has returned to them the Liberty of which they were deprived, alas!, for too long."[20]

Once installed, the town council only rarely paid attention to what might be considered "resistance" issues, dealing instead with the traditional problems of a municipal council magnified by wartime conditions. The school buildings requisitioned by German troops during the summer of 1944, for example, could not be properly repaired for lack of building materials.[21] Indeed, the town lacked some basic tools, such as a drum for the town crier, who was reduced to using a child's trumpet.[22]

But if the resistants on the council became swamped by the details of running a town, those on the CAL, freed from any real power or responsibility, focused on more utopian projects and a more aggressive defense of what they considered to be Saint-Flour's rights. In early 1945 the CAL changed its name to the CLL (local rather than arrondissement) and expanded to include members of every acceptable (i.e., noncollaborationist or right-wing) group as part of a national effort to shore up the waning popularity of the committees of liberation.[23] It met once a month and issued petitions covering matters from the fate of pigs requisitioned in the arrondissement, to a proposed amnesty for looters, to raising funds for the Remembrance Committee by selling a calendar honoring the Sanflorain martyrs of the liberation.[24] Other than rile the department's bureaucrats, however, the CLL appears to have played a mainly ceremonial role.

In terms of provisioning crises or military alarms, Saint-Flour enjoyed a calm après-libération. But the citizens compensated for the benefits of a quiet life in the former Vichy zone with a full ceremonial calendar and active political rivalries. With one notable exception, local factions fell into the same configurations as before the war, now reclothed in the rhetoric of collaboration and resistance.[25] Indeed, more than elsewhere, in Saint-Flour local politics during the après-libération seemed to be rehashing Third Republic politics, especially the hoary argument between clericals and anticlericals.

For most of the après-libération, René Amarger spoke for the local Resistance establishment as a founding member of the local Resistance, officer of the CDL, member of the national bureau of the Socialist Party (SFIO) and, most important, owner and editor of the Sanflorain newspaper *La Margeride*. Openly a Resistance paper and named for the site of partisan fighting in June 1944, *La Margeride* appeared twice a week to cover all the arrondissement's news, with a heavy emphasis on the exploits of the local resistance and ceremonies held to honor it. The newspaper also actively defended the local resistance from rumors or from attacks launched by the Catholic paper. Indeed, on the pages of *La Margeride* the Resistance often bore a remarkable similarity to the Socialist Party.

But Amarger's long-standing political rival was even more thoroughly stuck in prewar political battles. The reactionary right, whose voice was stifled in most of the rest of the country by the Resistance's near monopoly on the press, spoke in Cantal through Abbé Lissorgues' *La Voix du Cantal*. The abbé's claims that he was a truly authentic resistant, and his protestations that he had sheltered a Jew at great risk to himself when no one else would, failed to win the sympathy of any of his journalistic colleagues or of the authorities. Indeed, the Ministry of Information investigated *La Voix du Cantal* as a blatant continuation of the occupation-era *La Croix du Cantal*, which had been suppressed under the law regarding the collaborationist press.[26] For political reasons, the ministry allowed Lissorgues to continue publishing but begged the bishop of Saint-Flour to convince him to moderate his polemics.[27] The abbé nonetheless continued his scurrilous attacks against those he called the "profiteers of the Resistance," such as the editors of *La Margeride* and the CDL's *Le Cantal libre*. His accusations became so scandalous that the prefect worried that "their most obvious result is that [Lissorgues] risks detaching Catholic resistants from the Church and the Catholic parties."[28] Indeed, the rest of the Cantalien press published letters from Catholics across the country denouncing Lissorgues.[29]

Despite a concerted press and legal campaign against him, there are some indications that a number of Cantaliens shared the abbé's nostalgia for Vichy and his skepticism about the department's Resistance establishment. Certainly, the department saw some suspicious anti-Resistance activities in the fall of 1944, and enough people sprang to the defense of collaborators that in its frustration the CDL announced that anyone intervening in the legal purge on behalf of a defendant would also be investigated.[30] More significant, in October 1945 the department elected a formerly high-ranking Vichy official to the Constituent Assembly of the Fourth Republic.

The new actor on the Sanflorain stage at the liberation was the local section of the Communist Party. Despite its controversial wartime record, the Communist Party (PCF) claimed to be the Resistance party par excellence, the "party of 75,000 *fusillés* [executed]." Having been outlawed in August 1939 because of the Nazi-Soviet Pact, the PCF did not officially join the Resistance until after the German invasion of the Soviet Union in June 1941. By the après-libération, Vichy's virulent anticommunism, the spectacular exploits of the Communists in the Resistance, and the heroism of the Red Army had won the PCF a great deal of sympathy.[31] Chambéry even celebrated a "Red Army Day."[32] The leftist trend of Resistance thought shown in the CNR Charter also inclined opinion toward communism, as did the noticeable activity of local PCF sections.[33] Indeed, provincial administrators often ranked the Communists as the most active party in the provinces.[34] Everywhere the PCF or its offshoot the Union des femmes françaises (Union of French Women, UFF) claimed the honor of speaking for the people's grievances over food and other material distresses.[35] The unprecedented support won by the PCF during the occupation and the liberation translated in 1945 into a quarter of the popular vote and three cabinet ministries but did not eliminate anticommunism. Public opposition to the UFF centered around the disputed fact of its allegiance to the PCF, communism apparently being much more dangerous when directed toward women.[36]

Drawing on its Resistance credentials rather than any prewar power base, the Sanflorain PCF attended ceremonies, ran in elections, and maintained a column in *La Margeride*. That column reprinted the section's continual petitions on everything from the state of the municipal baths to the inconveniences of regional train travel and occasionally tackled such thorny issues as whether one could be both a good Christian and a good Communist (entirely possible in the Communists' view).[37] The town did not, however, have a chapter of the UFF until quite late: September 1945. But that delay may have had more to do with the shape of local discontent over food shortages than with local political sympathies.

One of the most successful Communist sections in the country, the

Sanflorains echoed the PCF leadership's emphasis on republican order and legality.[38] They also went to great lengths to establish their respectability.[39] This emphasis on respectability and order served the Sanflorain Communists well in their attempts to create a place for themselves in local politics. Indeed, both sides of the old prewar rivalry of anticlericals and clericals preferred to support the Communists rather than their old opponents. The Abbé Lissorgues actually recommended the PCF's candidate in the cantonal elections, describing him as a person, "who, for a communist, is no less a good (*brave*) man."[40] The CRR interpreted the even more surprising fact that Cantal elected a Communist to the Constituent Assembly as a vote against the right rather than one in support of the left.[41]

By the legislative elections in October 1945, Saint-Flour's politicians had very much resumed their traditional battles, merely using the special conditions of the après-libération to give a contemporary gloss to politics as usual. The atmosphere of political infighting and intrigue in Saint-Flour may be seen in a ration-ticket scandal that engulfed the town in the late summer of 1945. The details remain unclear, but it appears that a woman working in the town hall was caught with the highly irregular number of 174 ration tickets. She claimed that the tickets belonged to friends who did not want to stand in line to renew them, but she failed to account for thirty to fifty of the owners.[42] The rumors implicating persons in influential positions so agitated public opinion that the subprefect ordered an official investigation.[43]

The affair threw Saint-Flour into turmoil because to steal a ration card meant to purloin only the right to buy sugar, or meat, or bread in a shop, not to seize any actual goods. Stealing ration cards was not so much theft as it was an attempt to short-circuit the just economy that apportioned scarce goods equally among all citizens. It was therefore an offense against a very basic justice. The local section of the PCF called a public meeting to demand that the guilty parties be exposed, no matter who they were, and continued to make that demand in the press. Predictably, *La Voix du Cantal* accused a "resistance 'Mafia'." *La Margeride* hinted at the involvement of former municipal councilors and POWs but spent most of its energy defending the Resistance against Lissorgues' attacks. Even the bishopric was implicated.[44]

René Amarger turned out to be responsible for thirty of the rogue

20   The Expectation of Justice

cards. He had used them during the occupation to feed the maquis and continued to use them after the liberation, he claimed, to help old comrades in need. His explanation, however, did not satisfy the resistants of Saint-Flour, causing Amarger to resign from the leadership. By this time the scandal had become so politicized and overladen with local rivalries and ambitions that the rhetoric would have drowned out any explanation, no matter how well-meaning. Indeed, the prefect interpreted the Communists' persistence in the matter as a political maneuver meant to defeat the Socialists in the upcoming election.[45]

Because its isolated location in south central France spared Saint-Flour from the worst effects of the occupation and liberation, except, of course, for the fighting and reprisals of June and July 1944, the war's greatest influence on Saint-Flour during the après-libération lay in the way it shaped local political culture. The Resistance struggle gave politicians a new rhetoric with which to maneuver, and the tragedies of the liberation gave the town and its leaders the cause and rhetoric of an active commemorative politics that engaged the Sanflorains and their neighbors throughout the period.

MOÛTIERS

Built as a crossroads rather than a safe haven, the town of Moûtiers lies at the confluence of the rivers Isère and Dorons, surrounded by the majestic peaks of the Alpine valley of the Tarentaise, the inhabitants of which are known as the Tarins. The railroad, built in 1893, enters the town from the departmental capital, Chambéry, and the *chef-lieu d'arrondissement,* Albertville, at lower altitudes to the north. Between this modern iron river and the waters of the Isère sit the modern town hall and the cathedral, which was begun in the fifth century. The town continues westward by means of four bridges across the Isère into a v-shaped plain formed with the Doron. The local economy depends on the sodium chloride mines of Salins, two kilometers to the south, and the hydroelectric and timber industries. Such agriculture as is possible emphasizes wheat and pasturage.[46] Formerly the ancient capital and seat of the archbishopric of the Tarentaise, during the après-libération Moûtiers played a more vital role as a commercial and cultural center to its inaccessible valley than was usual for a *chef-lieu de canton* of 3,105 people.

Moûtiers' position at 480 meters' elevation in the Alps and close to the Italian border made the war years more eventful there than in much of France.[47] From June 1940 to November 1942, Moûtiers lay in Vichy's free zone. From November 1942 until September 1943 it belonged to the Italian zone of occupation, despite the Savoyards' firm conviction that they had not been defeated by the Italians.[48] After that, it passed under German control, at which point the Savoyards could also think of themselves as occupied by Vichy's paramilitary forces, which had been drawn there by Resistance activity. During the final battles leading to the German retreat in 1944, Savoie and the region dependent on Lyon came as close to a civil war between resistants and collaborators as anywhere in France, leading to liberation by the FFI rather than by the Allied armies or by German withdrawal.

This wartime history gave Moûtiers' après-libération some distinctive characteristics. The first was an anti-Italian sentiment not found in Cantal or the Vosges; the second was a strong attachment to the FFI and a thoroughgoing Resistance administration. The anti-Italian feeling grew out of the long history of complex exchanges between French and Italians in this border region that had not joined France until 1860, when Italian nationalists traded it to France for support for Italian unification. Before the war, approximately 1,700 Italians worked in Savoie, of whom three hundred worked in Tarin industry, adding economic competition to nationalist rivalries and fueling the violent hostility to *"macaronis"* and other foreigners seen throughout France in the 1930s.[49]

After the liberation the bitterness of "unearned" occupation and competition for jobs in a department whose economy had virtually stopped during the fighting of 1944 fused to produce an open *"Italianophobie."*[50] In early 1945 the Radical-Socialist Party of Albertville sparked a long discussion of the matter by publishing an anti-Italian manifesto in Moûtiers' paper. Citing such infractions as the use of Italian by Italian priests during Mass in Savoyard churches and the prewar creation of summer camps for the children of Italian immigrants, the manifesto railed against the "attempt at Italian colonization of this dear province" and recommended stringent measures against Italian nationals. In particular, it called for the revision of all naturalizations of Italians dating after October 1922 and a ban on Italian ownership of businesses in Savoie or Haute-Savoie.[51] The manifesto suggested these measures without any apparent awareness of how they mimicked Vichy's treatment of the Jews and how they clashed with the ideals of liberty and justice so loudly proclaimed on every other topic.

The first response in Moûtiers, where a number of Italians lived and worked with or without the proper papers, came from a naturalized Italian who identified the racism of the manifesto as what it was. Explaining the logical consequences of such divisions, he pleaded "that all the '*macaronis*' not be put in the same pot."[52] Over the next few weeks the paper published letters and articles for and against Italian immigration. Some recalled the friendly behavior that certain Italians in Moûtiers had shown toward the Italian soldiers of occupation, "occupying a country they had not conquered," or the destruction wrought by that army; others argued for economic cooperation as the means to peace.[53] For their part, the antifascist Italians of the canton of Moûtiers created a Comité italien de libération in January 1946. But they may have faced deep opposition; only a year earlier a similar initiative in Haute-Savoie had been quashed by the prefect, and the mayor of Albertville had been severely criticized by his municipal council for accepting a donation of 800 francs for the POWs' savings books from Italian workers.[54]

Anti-Italian sentiment, however, was only a minor undercurrent in Moûtiers' après-libération compared to the town's emotional and social investment in the military resistance. During the occupation, Savoie's mountains made it possible for young men to hide from the security forces or labor recruiters and for army officers to hide weapons and later train the irregular fighters of the FFI to use them. Organized since 1942, the Savoyard FFI, combining units of the Armée secrète (AS) and the Communist Francs-tireurs et partisans français (FTPF), harassed the Germans and their collaborators by sabotaging factories, power lines, and locomotives.[55] After a disastrous attempt to create an FFI redoubt on the Glières plateau in Haute-Savoie in February 1944, Savoie endured the intense and most unwelcome attentions of Vichy's paramilitary forces, particularly the expressly anti-Resistance Milice. A number of those Miliciens were Savoyards; indeed, the subprefecture of Albertville alone contributed a hundred men to the Milice or its forerunner at a time when the more populous department of the Vosges contributed only fifty.[56] In the summer of 1944, however, that same arrondissement of Albertville, including Moûtiers, produced three thousand volunteers for the FFI.[57] Both the FFI and the Milice drew men from throughout France into Savoie and pitted them against each other in a guerrilla combat of ambushes and reprisals.[58]

As resistants did throughout France, on 6 June 1944 the Savoyard FFI mobilized and engaged German troops before quickly pulling back on orders from London. They continued their harassing actions until a second general mobilization in early August; indeed, they prevented any electrical power from leaving the department. The Resistance rebellion and the department's location on the escape route to northern Italy in August 1944 brought ten thousand German troops into the region. Determined to protect their retreat, the Germans joined the Milice in their war against the insurgents and, by extension, the general populace.

On 6 August 1944 the FFI of the Tarentaise engaged the German garrison of Moûtiers in bloody fighting in the streets of the town. By evening, forty-five Germans were holed up in the Hotel Terminus. Frightened enough to believe the resistants' claim that the town was surrounded by five hundred FFIs (a gross, but convincing, exaggeration), the Germans surrendered.[59] Moûtiers was free, but only for a week. Because of its strategic importance on the road to Italy, the Germans retook the town, obliging all men between the ages of seventeen and thirty-five to report to barracks. In marked contrast to their behavior elsewhere in the department, the Germans did not destroy anything in Moûtiers when they evacuated it on 24 August. But they did take twenty-one men and boys with them as hostages, pledging to treat them as POWs in the same way that the FFI had treated their forty-five German prisoners earlier that month.

To their great pride, the Resistance of the Tarentaise and of Savoie liberated themselves from the Germans and their collaborators with only minimal assistance from regular North African troops and a few Allied soldiers (mostly American and Czech). But they did so at considerable cost. The Savoyards suffered all the terror and losses, and harvested all the bitterness, of a fratricidal guerrilla war. Over the course of the occupation and liberation, the department of 234,000 inhabitants saw 318 persons executed as hostages or resistants and lost 205 combatants and 378 civilians in battle, including 195 killed during air raids. It saw 512 persons deported to the Third Reich, including 140 Jews and 36 Spanish republicans. Of these, almost half, 243, never returned, including almost all the Jews (111) and 108 resistants. Furthermore, 2,170 buildings were damaged, in many cases in reprisals during which entire villages were put to flames.[60] One of the men who died in battle was a twenty-nine-year-old priest serving with a Communist FTPF unit.[61] His story indicates that in Savoie the Resistance ideal of a union of all in the good fight, even Communists and Catholics, was more than mere propaganda.

But while liberated on 24 August, Moûtiers, unlike Saint-Flour, was hardly free of the war. In late August the FFI and regular North African troops chased the Germans to the Italian border through the neighboring valley of Maurienne, where German reprisals drove over a thousand refugees from their homes. The front line stabilized over the bitterly cold winter along the spine of the Alps a mere twenty-five kilometers from Moûtiers. The mountainous nature of those twenty-five kilometers kept the town safe from actual danger, but the presence of so many local men on the line kept it in the town's attention. Indeed, Moûtiers remained in a war zone, albeit a quiet one, until May 1945.

As of 20 December 1944, Moûtiers belonged to the "Alpine security zone." This area of severely restricted travel stretched for four departments along the length of the Italian border and meant that Moutiérains who wished to travel only as far as the subprefecture in Albertville, or even outside the commune, needed a laissez-passer from the gendarmerie (office open weekdays 10–11 A.M. and 3–4 P.M.). Anyone living outside the zone but wishing to travel into it needed a laissez-passer from the military authorities in Chambéry or one of the other departmental capitals. The end of the war lessened but did not eliminate these restrictions.[62]

Such security impositions only reinforced an isolation that had already been created by the battle for liberation. The repairs on the railroad bridge at Notre-Dame-de-Briançon that resistants blew up in June 1944, for example, lasted until September, meaning that no supplies could be brought in by train to Moûtiers, which had already run out of stocks of wheat and groceries in June.[63] Passenger service between Moûtiers and Chambéry was not reestablished until after March 1945, leading Moûtierains to complain of being "abandoned."[64] Furthermore, the Savoyard postal service did not resume normal operations until late September 1944; in December Moûtiers lost its regular express service for lack of gasoline for the carrier. Telephone connections were also difficult because of sabotage during the liberation, heavy snowfall that snapped the lines, and the requirement that a log be kept of anyone using a public phone.[65]

Some of those signing the logbook would have been FFIs on temporary leave from the front.[66] Although Moûtiers' newspaper patriotically welcomed the few regular troops who moved through the barracks in 1944–45, the town's heart belonged to its own irregular soldiers.[67] Moûtiers loudly proclaimed its attachment to its Resistance fighters in an elaborate fete on 1 October 1944 called "FFI Day" in honor of the partisans of the four cantons of Moûtiers, Bourg-Saint-Maurice, Bozel, and Aime. After speeches on the men's heroism and the army's future, a parade led by three bands and representing every FFI unit of the Haute-Tarentaise, including the medical staff, wound through the flag-bedecked town past cheering crowds to the reviewing stand, which held civil and military authorities from the local, departmental, and national levels of government as well as the bereaved relatives of fallen maquisards.

At 11:30 A.M. the Abbé Hudry, professor at the seminary and FFI officer, celebrated Mass in the cathedral. In his sermon the abbé drew the lesson from what he had learned while working and talking with his comrades in the FFI. What such patriots wanted and what France needed, he explained, was not individualism, "egotism," or the factionalism of political parties, but the union of fraternity forged in the terrible days of fighting and the joyous days of liberation. Their comrades had died for the ideal of such a union, leaving them to realize it. However, "the ideal for which they died must not be realized in hatred, but in unity, in charity." Emphasizing the sterility of hate, the abbé ended with a warning that "our political life has been infested by numerous opportunists without scruples, who consider only their personal interest, not the country's interest. It is up to you to eliminate [those] whom I would call politicians and to choose statesmen."[68] A short wreath-laying ceremony at the Monument aux Morts separated the Mass from a banquet set for 1,300 people. The day did not end, however, until after representatives of departmental Resistance organizations spoke on the future tasks to be accomplished.[69]

26   The Expectation of Justice

In the same issue of the local paper that reported on FFI Day, the commander of the Tarin FFI recruited men for the FFI Alpine Division that guarded the frontier. Despite their amalgamation into the regular French army, the FFI division was the poor cousin of the Allied effort. Men held the mountain passes without winter clothes, warm boots, or even, in some cases, helmets. Not surprisingly, the local soldiers attracted the particular charitable attentions of their friends and neighbors in Moûtiers and throughout Savoie. The Anciens de l'Armée secrète (AAS) of Moûtiers, for instance, organized Christmas collections of food: "eau-de-vie, fruits and vegetables (beans, cabbage, chards, carrots, lettuce, etc.) (except potatoes, the troops having had only those on the menu for more than a month)."[70] In fact, so many groups competed to help the FFIs that the CDL intervened to coordinate their efforts. The new Comité des œuvres de guerre de Tarentaise, under the honorary presidency of the Archbishop of Moûtiers, represented men and women of all the region's Resistance movements, syndicates, social services, and schools. The committee particularly adopted a company that was made up almost completely of Tarins and commanded by a former schoolteacher from Moûtiers.

The grassroots support for the Resistance in Savoie was also evident in the ease and comprehensiveness of the seizure of political power at the liberation. Indeed, the CDL of Savoie took power during the summer of 1944 with such determination that it rejected the first prefect nominated by the national Resistance government, despite its own identification of de Gaulle and the CNR as the source of its authority.[71] The CDL also promised the Savoyards a fair and impartial purge that would strike without pity against collaborators and "all those who have not hesitated, at a time when the French people were hungry, to make immense profits on the misery of the people. The profiteers of the black market [would] answer to the nation," with the death penalty if necessary.[72] By March 1945, however, the prefect could describe the CDL as little more than an organizer of charities and critic of the national government.[73]

Such was not the case with the Comité de libération de Haute-Tarentaise, sometimes also known as the CLL Moûtiers.[74] The CLL that took control in the Tarentaise during the liberation gave power to fifteen men, including a priest representing the abbé who had been taken hostage by the Germans. The commander of the Tarin FFI doubled as president of the

CLL, underscoring the military nature of the local resistance. In the first issue of the town's new newspaper, significantly named *La Résistance savoyarde*, the CLL established its authority by announcing that it acted in the name of General de Gaulle and the government in Algiers and urged citizens to strive for unity, discipline, and order. It further promised: "We will take all appropriate measures to encourage respect for justice and liberty. Glory to our brothers who have fallen on the field of honor at home and abroad. Long live France! Committee of Liberation." A longer article entitled "Resistance! Liberation! Who are these Men?" rehearsed the patriotism and struggle of the Tarin Resistance in pursuit of the goals of helping the Allies, liberating France, and placing the nation under de Gaulle's leadership.[75]

The CLL took over administrative power in the Tarentaise to an impressive degree, including an active involvement in the provisioning of the town.[76] It nominated a special delegation for the municipal council composed of one woman and twenty men, six of whom also served on the CLL. The occupation mayor Marius Collomb, who was credited with helping to preserve the town from even worse treatment at German hands, continued as mayor after the liberation until he resigned for reasons of health in April 1945.[77] Although the special delegation fulfilled its obligations as municipal council, it stood in the shadow of the CLL. Indeed, when the subprefect visited in early September and the prefect visited in early October, it was Commandant Lungo of the Tarin FFI in his capacity as president of the CLL who introduced Mayor Collomb to these representatives of central authority.[78]

The CLL could exercise such power because it controlled the local press and its own police force. As the official "organ of the committee of liberation," *La Résistance savoyarde* showed a preference for the Resistance point of view, although that did not mean unqualified support for de Gaulle's government in Paris, especially as the months wore on. But as a matter of principle, because resistants had risked their lives for liberty, the editors opened their columns to all shades of opinion, "always on the condition that the pursued end contribute through its inspiration to the search for an improvement in the current moral, material, and spiritual conditions." Anonymous submissions and, one presumes, those blatantly supporting collaboration, were not accepted.[79] More important for an organization with aspirations as sweeping as the CLL's, it had not only its own police force (MP) but also a Purge Commission. During the first three months of liberation, the Purge Commission investigated 117 cases and the MP performed at least 153 related operations.[80]

The Tarin Resistance establishment could be found at its headquarters in Moûtiers' Hotel Terminus, which housed the CLL, the MP, the Purge Commission, and the local resistance's social service, which was devoted to assisting all war victims and their families. As of December 1944, the organized resistance could also be found in the AAS, a group of FFI veterans who concerned themselves with remembering their fallen comrades and aiding their survivors. Unlike the resistants of Saint-Flour, those of Moûtiers enjoyed excellent relations with the local clergy because the Tarin Resistance was much more a creation of wartime events than a continuation of prewar political factions along new rhetorical lines. The presence of Savoyard priests in the FFI and among the region's hostages guaranteed the clergy a place in the postwar resistance, even if it did not shield certain members of the hierarchy from criticism.[81] The same easy coexistence between Catholic and secular organizations appeared in the après-libération merger of local unions into the CFTC-CGT of the Haute-Tarentaise.[82]

Accordingly, the installation of a new archbishop involved the entire community. The authorities requested that the inhabitants decorate the main street, and both the CLL and the municipal council attended the ceremony in the cathedral as well as officially welcoming Archbishop Jauffrès at the town hall. During the ceremonies the prelate spoke on the need for unity "if one does not want the world to drown in chaos." *La Résistance savoyarde* approved the celebration as "a fine example of concord."[83]

The Catholicism of the Savoyards and their resistance may help to explain the unusual fact that a joint meeting of all the movements of the Resistance held in Moûtiers on 1 October 1944 did not include the Communists on the grounds that the PCF was a political party. It might also have reflected a tendency in the Resistance to hope to transcend the discredited party politics of the Third Republic. Whatever the reasons, the Communist Section of the Tarentaise naturally objected that the PCF was indeed a Resistance movement as well as a political party, though the section had very little voice in the region, especially compared to their Sanflorain comrades.[84] Other than holding an informational meeting in October and a general assembly in February 1945, during which the section endorsed the party's national platform, the Moutiérain Communists did very little to draw attention to themselves.[85] The town did, however, have a section of the UFF a full year before Saint-Flour did.

Indeed, the women of Moûtiers took an active voice in local politics, mostly through the UFF and the women's section of the Resistance network, the Mouvement de libération nationale, the Comité d'action féminine–MLN (AF-MLN). The two groups often met together and sent their joint complaints to the CLL, CDL, and prefect. Provisioning, or more correctly the lack thereof, stood as the groups' first priority, but they also considered issues such as the shortage of housing and public baths in Moûtiers and voter registration of women.[86] None of this activity, however, translated into political positions for women in Moûtiers. The town had no women at all on its CLL and only one on its special delegation, despite the important and well-acknowledged service that women had rendered to the Tarin Resistance. Indeed, one local woman won a posthumous medal of the Légion d'honneur for her work as a liaison agent, and another received the Croix de guerre avec étoile d'argent because her house had served as headquarters for the AS.[87]

Although Moûtiers was clearly a Resistance town in sentiment as well as government, certain hints arose that some people in town suspected that the official Resistance establishment represented those "opportunists without scruples" who worried the Abbé Hudry rather than authentic resistants. *La Résistance savoyarde* occasionally hinted at arguments among resistants and among official Resistance organizations and others over events during the summer of 1944 that cast doubt on the Resistance establishment's claims to leadership.[88] Indeed, in late 1945 accusations of financial impropriety created so much trouble that the militants of the Tarin Resistance requested a police investigation in order to put an end to the "grotesque . . . calumnies . . . [that] . . . tend to throw discredit on all of a movement that paid for the Liberation with its blood, hunger, [and] limitless fatigue."[89] However, the detectives' determination that the allegations had absolutely no foundation did not put an end to malicious gossiping.[90] The only certain fact to fall between the lines of this discreet printed feuding was that the quarrel within the local resistance was an open secret in town. The surprising fact that the Resistance slate lost the municipal

30   The Expectation of Justice

elections of April 1945 suggests that the local Resistance establishment's opponents enjoyed considerable support in the wider community. In every realm other than electoral politics, however, the Moutiérains stood united behind their idea of the Resistance, even to the point of violent protest against the national government's policies. Indeed, the war so profoundly affected this small community that it reshaped its identity during the après-libération in terms directly related to the conflicts of 1940–45.

RAMBERVILLERS

Although also an ancient settlement, Rambervillers enjoys none of the natural defenses of Saint-Flour or Moûtiers. Straddling the River Mortagne where the plain butts up against the foothills of the Vosges, Rambervillers has been a crossroads of armies for centuries. Completely sacked and burned in 1557, the town was occupied by Cossacks in 1814 and served as the site of fierce resistance to the Prussians in 1870. The Germans faced such strong opposition in the area again in 1914 that Rambervillers won the Croix de guerre 1914–1918 to accompany its Légion d'honneur for 1870. But that proud history appeared sadly reversed in 1940 when the Rambûvetais watched thousands of French soldiers surrender themselves and their equipment to the victorious Wehrmacht.

As a *chef-lieu du canton* only twenty-seven kilometers from the departmental capital of Epinal, Rambervillers acted as a market town for the surrounding farms and a small industrial center with textile mills, sawmills, a quarry, a glassworks, a paper mill, and a pottery works. The 1946 census counted 6,097 inhabitants. Because it lies on the eastern edge of the old Duchy of Lorraine close to the disputed Franco-German border, only a hundred kilometers from Strasbourg, the town has two barracks. During the Second World War that location spared Rambervillers the Alsatian fate of annexation to the Third Reich but trapped it and the whole department of the Vosges in the reserved zone of occupation. To Vosgiens the "reserved" (*interdite*) label seemed to be an attempt to separate them from France. Travel to and from the rest of the country required considerable paperwork; the refugees who had fled south in 1940 and who included, by order of the government, many men of military age were not allowed to return until 1945.[91]

A more serious consequence of being in the reserved zone came from the heavy presence of the German conquerors. Already in June 1940 two civilian men were executed, for no reason apparent to their neighbors other than their being French.[92] In December 1942, the Feldgendarmerie of the town's Kommandantur surrounded the football stadium, evacuated the spectators at gunpoint, and arrested the Rambûvetais team as well as a few others. After rifling the building and cash box of the sports club, the Germans imprisoned about twenty of the young sportsmen in Epinal before deporting them to the concentration camp at Buchenwald. As far as the Rambûvetais could divine, the Germans did this in retaliation for patriotic graffiti proclaiming confidence in an eventual French victory.[93]

Resistance was particularly difficult and dangerous under such conditions; yet by 1942 Rambervillers had a Resistance group connected to London through Ceux de la Résistance (CDLR) and led by a local lawyer and a schoolteacher from a nearby village who was also an army lieutenant. Although active all that summer, the Maquis of Rambervillers—202 men in the field, including the town's gendarmes, and another 129 in town— formally mobilized on 26 August 1944. In the following days, the maquis' three units received several parachute drops of weapons and special agents. They made it a top priority not to bring reprisals on the civilian population, even going so far as to hide the corpse of a German soldier someone else had killed.[94]

Meanwhile, several men, women, and girls remained in Rambervillers to provide the maquisards with supplies and information. That work grew increasingly dangerous as the battlefront moved eastward.[95] Although the Rambûvetais could hear the roar of the fighting, it bogged down to the west through the month of September. Tension also mounted among the Germans who retreated into Rambervillers. On 4 September 1944 the Kommandantur put Rambervillers under a state of siege and ordered the inhabitants not to leave town, gather in groups of more than three, or be outside between the hours of 8 P.M. and 7 A.M. It later confiscated all radio sets, made a list of ten hostages, and sent around a town crier with threats to burn the town and deport the inhabitants. On 13 September the Germans blew up the railway depot, destroying five locomotives, two railcars, and all the equipment.

Those left in town had more reason to worry with each day. On 16 September a panicky unit of German soldiers and French Miliciens seized thirteen local men who happened to be in front of the town hall, mostly as part of a forced work detail ordered to build defenses. After a tense hour of negotiations, the German lieutenant in charge managed to forestall the execution of his workers. Around the same time, other troops blew up all but one of the bridges over the Mortagne, which they mined in order to explode it under the feet of the Americans. They also blew up some of the town's electrical pylons. On 18 September the Germans barricaded themselves in town and mined the roads leading out of it. As of 21 September Rambûvetais needed an *ausweis* to go from the town proper to the *faubourg,* usually a negligible distinction. Two days later the town was completely isolated, making it extremely difficult to supply the maquis or anyone else. The municipality suppressed the bread card in favor of a blanket ration of 250 grams per person per day, provided one could get it.

For the last few rainy weeks of occupation, the Rambûvetais had very little food, no electricity, light, or radio, but an overabundance of rumors. One such rumor, recorded by a woman on 26 September, held that Rambervillers would be easy to take, but that the Allied military authorities were hesitating for fear that the Germans would kill the inhabitants and destroy the city. It was no idle threat. After the premature liberation of Charmes, thirty kilometers to the west, the Germans took numerous hostages and shelled the town. They also burned most of the village of Rehaincourt, halfway between Charmes and Rambervillers, in reprisal for the death of a German officer.[96] The concussions of the guns to the west and the flights of bombers overhead underscored the fearful rumors and the tension in the town.

On 28 September, American artillery shelled Rambervillers, killing a woman and her child. There was more shelling on the twenty-ninth, but, then, on the morning of 30 September, the FFI, the American 45th Infantry division, and the French 2ème DB (Division blindeé, tank division) liberated Rambervillers. According to the report of the town's maquis commander, Jean Meuth, the loss of Rambervillers cost the Germans twenty-three deaths, several wounded, and over 250 prisoners, some of whom threw down their weapons quite willingly. The FFI suffered only one severe casualty.[97] The maquis, however, were not the only valiant Rambûvetais that day; the mines on the remaining bridge over the Mortagne were cut by two men acting separately. Faced with a petition in support of the heroism of an electrician as well as a police report testifying to that of a farmer, the town council later decided to honor both men for saving the bridge and the neighborhood.[98] Over two years later, the municipal council also decided to honor a woman with an award of one thousand francs for her unspecified "courageous conduct during the bombardments of 1944."[99]

The question as to whether the FFI or the American army liberated the town still provokes controversy today, perhaps because the liberation of Rambervillers offers an almost classic example of how participants in the same event experience and understand it in radically different ways according to their physical and social perspectives. The official U.S. Army 157th Infantry report of the liberation of Rambervillers mentions the "softening up" shelling of the town and heavy fighting, but not the FFI.[100] Yet the official FFI reports describe how maquisards waded the Mortagne to take German machine-gun nests and over two hundred prisoners. Civilian diaries suggest that the Rambûvetais certainly thought they were being liberated by the FFI; when Mme. Auger's family discovered a hidden lair of Germans, for example, they alerted the FFI as well as the Americans.

To complicate the matter further, the liberation of Rambervillers became politicized almost immediately. The 5 October 1944 issue of the department's daily newspaper carried a long article on "the glorious role of the FFI in the liberation of Rambervillers" and described in detail "this magnificent victory achieved by the FFI alone, supported by American artillery," as justification of the honor conferred on, and the final word to counter any criticisms of, the Vosgien FFI. Rambervillers became known as the only town in the Vosges liberated by the FFI. From there it was but a small step to make the liberation a touchstone of local politics. The resistants and their supporters, who based much of their legitimacy on their heroic exploits in September 1944, would claim that the FFI alone had liberated the town, with only a little help from the Americans, who were in the neighborhood anyway. Those who opposed the resistants' later influence would strike at the base of their authority by insisting that even if the FFI were running around town on 30 September, they only lived to tell about it because American tanks parked in the streets kept the Germans at bay. Others implied that the FFI owed their success to divine patronage.

Still others appear to have viewed the FFI's fighting as foolhardiness rather than heroism. For example, a Rambûvetais published a signed, scathing rebuke of a woman who was overheard at a Resistance funeral to say, "One doesn't quite know why they fought." Blaming the woman's incomprehension on the fact that she had a wallet in place of a heart, the author explained that the youth of France had joined the maquis out of the same noble instinct that motivated their fathers in 1914–18. The point of their fighting, he wrote, was to save the ungrateful woman's two sons from being deported and herself from being a refugee.[101] Yet in the circumstances, the woman might be forgiven for thinking that the Americans would have liberated the town with or without the FFI and that the maquisard's death was therefore unnecessary. She apparently needed more than ceremonies and speeches to persuade her to accept the Resistance's interpretation of the immediate past.

To some degree or another, the FFI and the American army worked together to liberate Rambervillers. If the Americans had tanks and artillery, the FFI had a detailed map of all the German emplacements and minefields. More significant, by 3 P.M. on 30 September, the FFI had taken power, installed a liberation committee (CCL) and a special delegation, set a guard around the town, and begun arresting collaborators. Also around 3 P.M. of the same day, the Germans shelled the town, killing two men. By 5 P.M., however, the Rambûvetais had put out the Allied flags and were celebrating with the FFI and the Americans. Snapshots taken that day show the classic pose of liberation: happy men, women, and children mobbing an American tank. The crowds had also demolished the barricades that the Germans had so laboriously built at the entrances to town. By 7 P.M. a woman living in town could write that "one ate tranquilly," but things were far from tranquil on the outskirts of town.

The Germans may have been displaced from Rambervillers on 30 September, but they did not go far; the front line stalled for a month not more than four kilometers to the northeast. While the U.S. 45th Infantry and elements of the French 2ème DB used the town as a base, the Germans shelled it almost daily. The worst attack took place on the morning of 3 October, just prior to the funeral of the two men killed on the afternoon of liberation. The large crowd and the nonchalance shown by the Rambûvetais toward being shelled—a nonchalance that amazed an American officer—led to the loss of some seventeen civilian lives and perhaps thirty seriously wounded.[102] At this point some of the Rambûvetais lost their sangfroid and retreated to safer havens behind the American lines, which might in any case be expected to provide more than 250 grams of bread a day as well as some electricity. On 5 October, as her family was evacuating southward, Mme. Auger noted in her diary: "Poor Ramber [sic], almost all the buildings on the main street have been damaged by shells, it's mortally sad; not a single civilian! Some American vehicles, that's all."[103]

For the rest of the month those who stayed continued to endure the sleep-shattering sound of German shelling and the American response. The situation remained uncertain; on 15 October German patrols returned to the outskirts of town. Finally, on 26 October the neighboring village of Jeanménil was liberated, but at the cost of the "transfer" of most of its population behind German lines and the destruction of most of its buildings. Rambervillers itself was shelled for the last time on 31 October, leaving over a hundred buildings partially or completely destroyed. The men of the U.S. 45th Infantry division then left Rambervillers on 11 November to push the attack through the Vosges at heavy cost to themselves and to the civilian population trapped in the German scorched-earth policy.[104]

The situation in Rambervillers itself improved once the shelling stopped and supplies increased. Mme. Frachet made a terse note of the improvement: "Good news: 750 grams of bread instead of 250 grams. What a conquest."[105] But heavy rains prolonged the town's troubles. A U.S. Army photograph taken on 8 November shows several heavy trucks fording Rambervillers' main street, up to their military axles in flood waters.[106] Although safe from German attack after October 1944, the Rambûvetais could not forget their precarious position. After all, if they stood on their rooftops in November, they could see Saint-Dié burning for three days and nights thirty kilometers to the east.[107] Or they could talk to the refugees from the fighting in the mountains who passed through the town's U.S. Army refugee "holding center" for civilians evacuated from the battle zone or the Entr'aide française's welcome center and canteen for refugees and war victims.[108] There were also other disruptions of the normal routine that attested to the continuing state of war. The schools, for example, did not begin their fall semester until 8 December, two full months after schools in Saint-Flour and Moûtiers, because the Americans had requisitioned the buildings.[109] Rambervillers also had a reduced electrical power schedule and both a curfew (9:30 P.M. to 5:30 A.M.) and a blackout (7:30 P.M. to 6:00 A.M.).[110]

The fighting in the Vosges lasted until February 1945. One quarter of the department's population emerged from their liberation as *sinistrés* (those whose homes had been damaged), deportees, or prisoners.[111] In Rambervillers' arrondissement of Epinal alone, the Germans killed or executed 324 persons, either directly or through the slow torture of the concentration camps, and committed four mass war crimes.[112] The exact numbers of victims for Rambervillers itself are not clear. Perhaps the most dependable figures can be found on the town's citation for the Croix de guerre avec étoile d'argent, which lists 155 deportees, fifty-one dead, forty-seven wounded, and ten hostages.[113] The unspecified category of "dead" probably includes the five men executed by the German authorities during the occupation; the men, women, and children killed by artillery fire; individuals killed while in German captivity; and men and women killed in combat. The 155 "deportees" probably combine what are now called political deportees, racial deportees, and labor deportees, although such distinctions were not made at the time.

In addition to the cost in human lives, the Vosges paid a high price in the destruction of the department's infrastructure and economy. The German scorched-earth policy in the mountains and the fighting on the plain shattered the communications network. The department had no regular telephone or postal connections with the rest of the metropole until April 1945; communications between the regional capital of Nancy and the departmental capital of Epinal, only seventy-five kilometers apart, were not reliably reestablished until February 1945.[114] American military restrictions, together with the damage to the rail system, made it extremely difficult for anyone to go anywhere in the Vosges through the spring of 1945. Individuals, including government officials, needed passes to move more than six kilometers from their residences, and a curfew stopped all legal movement during the night. Furthermore, the American army blocked several major roadways to civilian traffic even after they had been repaired and cleared of mines.[115]

These restrictions might have been circumvented by resourceful individuals, but they stifled the revival of a departmental economy already flattened by war. The gravest consequences occurred in the realm of provisioning. American civil affairs officers calculated that the average diet of adults in the Vosges had decreased from 1,570 calories per day in October 1944 to 1,483 in November 1944, considerably below U.S. War Department estimates of 2,000 calories per day needed by individuals to maintain minimum health.[116] The Americans helped with the flour shortage caused by the destruction of the grain mills in Epinal by loaning trucks to the provisioning authorities.[117]

The detritus of war posed another serious problem. As a region, the Vosges ranked second in the number of land mines sown. By 31 December 1945, over a year after most of the department's liberation, the rural corps of engineers had cleared forty thousand hectares of more than 417,500 explosives, at the cost of almost three hundred civilians, bomb-disposal experts, and volunteer German prisoners of war dead, and two hundred more wounded.[118] Before this dangerous work could be accomplished, however, all those explosives made people afraid even to walk, let alone work, in their fields or forests.

Tragically, many of the civilian casualties were children. The CRR at Nancy reported in March 1945 that in the previous six months 150 people had been killed and 190 wounded by mines in the Vosges. As 40 percent of the victims were children, "this question *profoundly upsets (émeut)* the population."[119] Indeed, the departmental daily ran a regular column, "The murderous explosives," that reported deaths and injuries by mines. Rambervillers appeared in it twice in March 1945 alone—once when a twelve-year-old girl triggered a mine, which caused severe wounds from which she died the next day, and once when a teenage girl was wounded while tossing grenades.[120] But the paper did not cover all such accidents, particularly those that occurred during the fighting. On 15 October 1944, for example, a Rambûvetais boy was indelibly struck by the sight of one of his playmates arriving home by jeep cradled in the arms of an American soldier after being torn apart by a grenade he had found in the school playground.[121]

Although the use of prisoners of war for dangerous work such as clearing land mines was illegal under international treaties, it was not only done during the après-libération, it was popular.[122] In the Vosges, even the moderate Catholic newspaper that consistently championed Christian charity and forgiveness argued that German prisoners should clear the mines.[123] Similarly, the prefect of Creuse reported that his constituents supported such use of defeated enemy labor: "The Creusoise population is hostile to any consideration of international laws concerning the work of prisoners of war. The Germans, they say, did not worry whether our POWs and deportees were doing work authorized by international regulations. It would be absurd if we, in our turn, worried about such legislation."[124]

Rambervillers' location in a war zone, then, gave the town's après-libération a profoundly different shape than Moûtiers' or Saint-Flour's. Neither of the other towns was shelled by artillery; neither served as an American base. Still, the basic pattern of social reconstruction in Rambervillers followed that of the other towns. It, too, got a new administration at the liberation; it, too, saw its civic groups realign themselves along the contemporary rhetorical lines of collaboration and resistance.

During the afternoon of 30 September 1944, Captain Mueth of the Rambervillers Maquis installed himself in the police station and the CCL in the town hall. The liberation committee, composed of twenty-five men and one woman, officially derived its power from the decision of General Cochet, commander of the FFI-OS, who was himself authorized by the Gaullist Resistance. As a first order of business, it "rendered emotional and grateful homage to the valiant FFI who have chased the invader from our walls, as well as to the glorious American troops who came to support them and consolidate their gains."[125] The committee functioned as a municipal council until 27 October 1944, after which it faded from the scene. Like the departmental CDL, the town's CCL played its most active role as an investigator for the legal purge, by gathering information and compiling dossiers.

The new municipal council nominated by the prefect of the Vosges, Robert Parisot, a man of impeccable Resistance credentials, gave Rambervillers considerable administrative continuity with the prewar period. Sixteen members of the new council, including Mme. Poirot, had also served on the CCL; five were either maintained or reinstated in the position to which they had been elected in 1936. Only three had neither been elected before the war nor appointed to the CCL; only Mayor Albert Bodson had both been elected in 1936 and appointed to the CCL. During their first meeting, while Rambervillers was still under sporadic German bombardment, the municipal council unanimously voted to send a message to Charles de Gaulle in which it "assure[d] him of its unwavering confidence in the destiny of immortal France, which he liberated from teutonic brutality, and congratulate[d] him on his attachment to republican institutions."[126]

The new Resistance government in Rambervillers faced three challenges not seen in Saint-Flour and Moûtiers: significant physical damage, refugees, and the American army. The German bombardment of 3 October that killed seventeen Rambûvetais and sparked a voluntary evacuation did sufficient material damage to cause the new prefect to visit the town two days later and present a check for ten thousand francs to take care of the most pressing needs.[127] Such public buildings as the church, town hall, schools, library, dispensary, slaughterhouse, and shooting range, however, would have to wait until 1946 or after to be repaired. In addition, the difficulties in finding capital and materials to repair private residences created such a long-term housing shortage that two years later, in October 1946, the municipal council formed a special committee to study the matter.[128]

In the meantime, the municipal council helped families whose homes had been damaged (sinistrés) or pillaged (pillés) to negotiate with the Ministry of Prisoners, Deportees, and Refugees, with the social services, or with charitable organizations such as the Committee Bourbonnais-Lorraine for the Relief of War Victims. Rambervillers itself officially claimed 4 families whose homes had been totally destroyed, 70 families whose homes had been partially destroyed, and 150 families whose homes had been pillaged. All of these people needed food, clothing, household goods, and possibly shelter. Some of them might also have needed to replace the formidable array of identification cards and ration cards required of private citizens at the time. The municipality also faced the difficulties of hosting refugees in a time of serious shortages. An official list from mid-1945 names 95 families staying in town, many from as close as the neighboring but utterly destroyed village of Jeanménil, but others from as far away as Paris or Perpignan.[129]

The presence of refugees and damaged buildings merely intensified the anxieties about war and displacement that haunted all France. What made Rambervillers' experience unusual was the additional revolving presence of thousands of American troops bivouacked in the town itself and in the fields all around it. Accustomed as they were to soldiers on their streets, even the Rambûvetais must have been struck by the arrival of the American army and all of its fabled wealth. Indeed, in October 1944, they had cause to think of their liberation as a second, much happier, occupation. The Americans not only changed the landscape, but their presence so saturated town life that it altered the local economy, interfered with the children's education, affected public ceremonies, and worried the authorities.

While the American advance stalled east of town, Rambervillers served as a command center for the 45th Infantry Division. For the five weeks that Rambervillers huddled just behind the front line, the men of the 157th Infantry Regiment spent eight days on the line and then four days back in regimental reserve on the roadblocks in and around town. They could find some relaxation in the barracks near the railroad station or the elementary school where Special Services had set up hot showers, a reading room, a cinema, and a cafeteria and bar with the best drinks available. After the line moved east on 11 November, fighting units such as the 191st Tank Battalion passed through the town within a matter of days. But the support services remained for weeks, providing recreational facilities to GIs, housing a refugee holding center in November, or acting as a main supply dump for units such as the 36th Engineer regiment. Even after the 20th Special Services company moved out of Rambervillers on 2 December, it continued for months to operate showers and two movie theaters there. The American Red Cross also maintained an outpost in town.[130]

Rambervillers' location and barracks also brought medical units and thousands of French, German, and American military and civilian patients to town. One young Rambûvetaise found herself actively involved in caring for the wounded almost by accident one Sunday in November 1944 when she came across some tents marked with red crosses. Because she had had a year of nursing school, Germaine Kempf began working with the U.S. 10th Field Hospital the next day and later transferred to the larger 93rd Evacuation Hospital.[131]

Then, on the night of 31 December 1944, the 9th Evacuation Hospital pulled back into Rambervillers in the face of the Ardennes offensive. Relegated to one of the old barracks, the unit recruited a hundred civilians to help clean it out and set up the medical facilities. In the first three weeks of January 1945, the 750-bed hospital admitted 1,619 patients, of whom 483 were French or American battle casualties. The official nurses' history remembers the conditions in Rambervillers as difficult; the damaged four-story building was cold and very hard to navigate with stretchers and food. The nurses themselves lived in a dilapidated, drafty house, with four to six women sharing a bedroom. The "bitterly cold winter"—it was four degrees Fahrenheit when they arrived—did not help the situation. Amenities were as short for the medical staff as for their civilian hosts. Indeed, food formed a leitmotif of the unit's reports, provoking comments like: "Rations were not as adequate in quantity and variety as in December, items such as spam, corned beef, string beans and peas being issued twenty-two times in thirty-one days."

The situation generally improved in February when the fighting eased and the 9th Evacuation Hospital began to serve as a station hospital for the 45th Division, which had pulled back to rest in the area. The highlight of the month came on 28 February with the award of the Meritorious Service unit plaque to the 9th Evac. The ceremony was held in the courtyard of the barracks turned hospital, which had been outfitted with a public address system to allow the three hundred or so civilian spectators to hear. The commanding officer awarded the plaque, honored twenty-five French civilians for their work with the unit since August 1944, and introduced and thanked the mayor of Rambervillers and the president of the CCL for their cooperation with the hospital's activities over the previous two months. The hospital moved eastward on 11 March, but the town remained a minor American base through the summer of 1945.[132]

The Americans moved into the town's economy as well as its buildings. In November 1944 the American commander in Rambervillers advertised for men between the ages of eighteen and forty-four to work as civilians.[133] On an informal level, civilians took in the GIs' laundry in exchange for canned food or money until the prefect regulated the prices for such work.[134] Homeowners could also lodge and board American soldiers at government expense.[135] One Vosgien even wrote to the prefect suggesting that he encourage Americans to take vacations in the department's villages because the notorious way that Americans wasted food would benefit everyone in the community.[136] Precisely that American reputation for careless wealth created a realm of less than legal relations with Americans and their goods. Certain business people were accused of unpatriotically overcharging Americans for wine or bread.¹³⁷ On the other hand, there were surely many unrecorded negotiations between Rambûvetais and friendly GIs who looked the other way while civilians took food from the loosely guarded crates of rations stacked along the sidewalks, or between Rambûvetais and unscrupulous GIs engaged in black marketeering.

At least from the perspective of the American civil affairs staff, relations between the Rambûvetais and the GIs were satisfactory, given the circumstances of the time. Unlike other towns in the vicinity, Rambervillers does not appear in the American records as either the recipient of emergency supplies of food, fuel, or water purification tablets, or as the site of any remarkable interallied tension over the attitudes of civilians or the military use of buildings.¹³⁸ Indeed, in January 1945 the general commanding the American troops stationed in Rambervillers officially thanked the municipality and the citizens for the "friendly welcome given to his soldiers."¹³⁹

Officially, the American troops acted as good citizens of the town, helping to put out fires on at least two occasions.¹⁴⁰ And American officers participated in public celebrations and in a Christmas party for two hundred children of POWs and war victims.¹⁴¹ Indeed, public ceremonies in the Vosges during the après-libération were noteworthy for their internationalism. American troops participated in all French holidays, and the Vosgiens celebrated the American holidays of Memorial Day and Independence Day. In Rambervillers the three-thousand-man American garrison celebrated the Fourth of July with a parade past their own officers and the local authorities that incorporated the rituals of French patriotism, with the mayor giving a wreath to the commander and the whole company observing a minute of silence at the Monument aux Morts. The military band naturally played the "Marseillaise" as well as the "Star Spangled Banner."¹⁴²

Despite these positive relations, there were some unfortunate incidents in Rambervillers. A French Resistance officer who parachuted in to fight with the local maquis, for example, reported that in early October 1944 an American officer responded to a maquisard request to continue working with the U.S. Army by giving them the job of checking for land mines. When the French officer remarked to the American that the Germans had used pigs for that job, the American replied, "We're paying them," leading the Frenchman to reflect that "the moderate sympathy that one may feel in regard to certain allies should not make one forget the sacrifices of tens of thousands of others."[143] A couple of months later, a completely drunk paratrooper of the 82nd Airborne on leave after the fiasco in the Netherlands entered a home and demanded, at gunpoint, to buy a one-and-a-half-year-old girl. The family fled to the attic while four other Americans who had been across the street at the Red Cross arrested the paratrooper, who returned the next day to apologize.[144] Both these incidents might be attributed to the stress of battle. Given its exposure to so many soldiers, it is remarkable that no incidents of a more serious nature appear to have happened in Rambervillers.[145]

French estimations of Franco-American relations were mixed, ranging from adulatory to disgusted. The Americans made a good impression as generous liberators when they first arrived in Rambervillers. Mme. Auger noted in her diary that the Americans posted in her family's barn at the liberation gave them cigarettes, chocolate, and preserves, and that some joined their celebration by singing the French, American, and British anthems after a champagne toast. However, she found other Americans who showed up in the following days to be "phlegmatic" and sure of themselves and their matériel in their impressive little jeeps.[146] Half a century after the liberation, the first person in town to see a GI, who was motioning to Liliane Vouaux to take cover early on 30 September 1944, still vividly remembered how she went out to greet the liberators, only to be scooped into their tank during German shelling, and how a laughing GI took her home on the crossbar of a bicycle.[147] Men who were then children remembered the smiling GIs giving them chocolate and that mysterious candy called chewing gum, and how they loved French fries and liked to "do a little trading and business" with the children.[148] Local history buffs have collected and cataloged the scraps the Americans left behind: the gas cans, the helmets, the artillery shells, and the soap that they gave to their French friends, who considered it too precious a gift to use.

The behavior of the GIs and the tolerance of the French in the Vosges however, deteriorated markedly after the German surrender. In June 1945, for instance, a departmental paper pleaded with the American commander to order his soldiers to at least blow their horns before careening through Epinal's intersections.[149] Of much more serious consequence, in July 1945 a fourteen-year-old girl was injured by an unidentified American in Rambervillers.[150] The report did not elaborate on the circumstances of the injury;

it could have been a traffic accident or a brutal rape. Surprisingly, the relations between the women of Rambervillers and the American GIs left no trace in the documents, although there must surely have been a romance or two. The French authorities certainly considered such Franco-American relations enough of a threat to do everything in their power to keep French girls out of sight.[151] Whether or not they were chasing the town's women, the GIs clearly began to disturb Rambervillers' peace beyond an acceptable level. In August the mayor banned the sale of alcohol to American soldiers "with the goal of stopping the incidents that happen every day and in order to reestablish good order in town."[152]

Underneath the tide of transient refugees and soldiers, the Rambûvetais reconstructed the town's civic life according to the demands of life in a battle zone. Indeed, the town had an unusually high number of charitable groups designed to help or represent the many categories of war victims, from refugees to widows to forced laborers. Being less than thirty kilometers from the capital of a department short of everything but misfortune, Rambervillers did not have its own newspaper. It did, however, have its own column in the departmental papers. The Vosges had one daily paper, *Le Démocrate de l'Est,* that changed its management and its name to *La Liberté de l'Est* in March 1945 because of a scandal over collaboration.[153] Although all members of the press identified themselves as Resistant, only *La Liberté de l'Est* took a deliberately nonpartisan stance. The multiplicity of perspectives—Catholic, Socialist, Communist, or veteran—allowed a wider range of direct voices from Rambervillers than from the other towns, making it appear to be a more bitterly divided community. Yet a handful of correspondents to departmental papers are not necessarily more representative of a whole community, nor as responsible to it, than an editorial staff living and working in the town. Indeed, the continual browbeating of their neighbors by correspondents to papers belonging to political parties for what the correspondents considered to be inappropriate attitudes suggests a certain alienation between the majority of Rambûvetais and their journalistic representatives. The easy success of the Resistance slate in the municipal elections further suggests that the community supported a local resistance that did not correspond to the political parties' vision of the Resistance.

The Rambûvetais Resistance had been mostly a military affair focused on the liberation of the town; it did not play as large a political role after the liberation as either the resistants in Moûtiers, who ran their region through the CLL of Haute-Tarentaise, or those of Saint-Flour, who controlled the local press through René Amarger. The local resistants did, however, organize themselves as the former FFIs of Rambervillers and surrounding communes and later merged with the CDLR veterans.[154] This combined association, the "CDLR (*anciens* FFI) of Rambervillers," held regular meetings, organized the distribution of blue cards of clandestinity and FFI cards to authentic resistants, and worked on the arrangements for the celebration of the first anniversary of the town's liberation. By September 1945, however, their meetings attracted only half as many participants as they had a year earlier.[155]

As happened elsewhere, the local resistants did not always agree with each other on a number of matters, including what constituted a resistant. For example, when the local section of the Association vosgienne d'anciens détenus (Vosgien Association of Former Prisoners, AVAD) formed in the late summer of 1945, the correspondent for the Socialist paper took exception to their choice of president, accusing him of being a Pétainist and a collaborator. The AVAD responded with a unanimous vote of confidence in their president and a counter suggestion about inappropriate "political or confessional activity."[156] The controversy is interesting because as well as exposing dissension within the town, it challenges the prevailing hierarchy according to which deportees were, a priori, the purest sort of resistants. Apparently, not everyone agreed that the experience of deportation alone absolved persons of their previous Pétainist sins. It also confirms the feeling among some resistants that the prewar confrontational style of political parties had no place in the Resistance or its "pure and strong France."

At least in the eyes of these same correspondents, all of whom claimed to speak for the Resistance, the local reaction or collaboration hid behind the skirts of Catholicism during the après-libération. Unlike Cantal's Abbé Lissorgues, however, the Vosges' Catholic newspaper deserved no such accusations. Indeed, the moderately left and wholeheartedly Resistant *La Croix de Lorraine* shared its name, as everyone knew, with the symbol of the Gaullist Resistance.[157] Yet popular Catholicism would have been an excellent place to build an opposition in the Vosges. The CRR at Nancy often commented on the Catholicity of the Vosgiens in their choice of affiliations and public events.[158] Indeed, in 1945 the whole department celebrated the feast of their local saint, Joan of Arc, at the same time as the German surrender, despite the saint's association with Vichy. Furthermore, in September 1945, the departmental capital commemorated its liberation with a "pious pilgrimage of the Virgin" in honor of the *morts pour la France*. When a few cinema owners refused to close their doors for three hours that afternoon despite personal phone calls from the mayor, they received extraordinary citations. The official Resistance felt strongly enough about this insult to "our martyrs and their families" to publish a rebuke in the departmental daily.[159] Rambervillers itself still supported a confraternity of Saint-Eloi, founded in 1615, and convoked 120 members for its 1945 banquet.[160] If Moûtiers enjoyed better relations between clergy and resistants, its townspeople did not practice such a deep level of almost medieval piety and devotion to the saints as did the Rambûvetais.

Given this widespread and even official Resistance involvement, popular Catholicism was bound to get caught up in local politics, especially at a time of death and destruction that called for public religious rituals. In Epinal the Resistance may have joined the devout in a public pilgrimage, but those correspondents who claimed to speak for the Resistance in Rambervillers read a threat in the direction of popular piety. In particular, they objected to a day of prayer and an effort to restore a chapel in thanksgiving to the town's patron saint for her protection during the liberation. Without the correspondents' protests that all this devotion was meant to discredit the FFI, the episode would have passed unremarked as an example of the religiosity with which many European communities reacted to the destruction and chaos of the Second World War.[161] Instead it turned into a divisive quarrel that recast the conflict between Resistance and Collaboration along religious lines.

The people of Rambervillers, however, did not all uphold the newspaper correspondents' configuration of their differences. In September 1945 the town council adopted the unusual step of taking a secret ballot in response to a request that the municipality give the same assistance to needy students in the Catholic school as to those in the public school. The council voted twelve to eight to subsidize the students of both schools equally.[162] Although secret, the balloting makes it clear that a number of councilors who had been elected as resistants voted to support the Catholic school. It therefore discredits any facile division of Rambervillers into "resistants" and "Catholics," as the Socialist and Communist press tried to do. Clearly, some resistants also considered themselves Catholics and vice versa. What Rambervillers most probably offers is an example of the transposition of well-worn prewar animosities (anticlerical and clerical, left and right) onto new categories (resistance and collaboration), and the attempted manipulation of both those categories and popular culture for specific political ends. In the former war zone of Rambervillers, however, the pressing practical needs created by land mines, power cuts, and food shortages almost wholly submerged the relatively unimportant maneuverings of local electoral politics.

CHAPTER TWO

LIVING IN THE AFTERMATH OF WAR

The instability of daily life created by the industrial devastation and ideological frenzy of the Second World War lingered long into the *après-libération*. Even the towns spared actual physical ruin lived in an atmosphere of implicit violence manifested by the presence of armed men both in and out of uniform. Economic insecurity flowed from the same source as physical insecurity: the armies' great need for men and matériel shattered the European economy, leaving millions without sufficient food, clothing, or shelter, and putting everyone at risk of epidemic disease and famine. In addition, the construction and collapse of Hitler's New Order destabilized not only governments, but also their underlying social orders. In France, the transfer of power from Vichy to the Resistance went smoothly, but it opened troubling questions about the social order, the moral order, and gender relationships. All of these insecurities came into play in the French reaction to the drama of the displaced persons that engulfed Europe when the Allies opened the Nazi concentration and slave labor camps.

During the liberation, the sense of danger seeped beyond the areas of immediate military activity into every corner of France in the form of a perceived breakdown of law and order fostered by the Resistance's clandestine struggle and the everyday use of the black market that had habituated the French to illegality. The Resistance's victory over Vichy did not instantly reinstate an automatic respect for the law or its officials; in fact, that victory undercut the cause of order by throwing the French police into a crisis of confidence. Crime, then, appeared both more possible and more prevalent.[1] Indeed, the occupation and liberation opened entirely new arenas of criminality, including pillage, forgery, illegal dancing, theft from the U.S. Army, and black marketeering.

The uncertainty of the times also created new guises for old crimes. Confidence men, for instance, preyed on the anxieties of the families of missing persons.[2] And brigands known as faux-maquis robbed people, they claimed, in the name of the Resistance. Such bandit faux-maquis switched their covers as local circumstances changed. For example, on 28 June 1944 a gang of two farming brothers in their twenties, a fifty-one-year-old farmer, and a twenty-year-old servant robbed a farm near Saint-Flour by claiming to be Germans. A month later, in early August when the Germans were evacuating the department, the gang robbed three more farms, but this time under the guise of being the maquis. At their trial, the prosecutor pleaded successfully "with the jury to punish severely those who spread terror among our good peasant women by covering themselves in the cloak valiantly worn by those who have liberated our country."[3] Similar bands of what the French always referred to as *les gangsters* operated throughout the country.[4]

The temporary retreat of the police augmented the feeling of increased vulnerability. The liberation created a severe shortage of trained and reliable officers because policemen who had seriously compromised themselves under Vichy had to be replaced.[5] The Return of the Absents (deportees) in the summer of 1945 increased the shortage by revealing that agents who had been widely believed to be patriots at the liberation were actually implicated in the arrests and deportations of resistants during the occupation.[6] And if police forces did not lose officers to the purge, they lost them to the army. Indeed, according to the prefect, the police were "close to nonexistent" in Saint-Flour.[7]

The CRR at Clermont-Ferrand complained repeatedly about the ineffectiveness of the police in his region, saying that the new agents recruited from the Resistance were only interested in assignments relating to the purge and that the old agents were too afraid of being purged themselves to come to any hard decisions.[8] It surely did not help the self-confidence of the police in the region that they were literally under attack by resistants, such as the group of 100 to 150 FFIs who stormed a police barracks in Le Puy in October 1944, took the agents' weapons, broke the furniture, and rifled the archives to avenge a comrade who had been arrested and roughed up by the police.⁹ Such blatant hostility was exceptional, but suspicion hampered the police's effectiveness and the citizenry's security everywhere.

The doubts cast on the police only magnified other, less easily manageable fears than those provoked by lawlessness. Rumor, of course, accompanies any great upheaval, whether it be war or revolution.¹⁰ In 1944–45, the collapse of fascist or collaborationist regimes freed Europeans from the lies of propaganda machines and from the fear of public discussions, leaving them, as Roger Absalom has noted for Italy, "intoxicatingly at liberty to discover or invent news and to discuss it without let or hindrance."¹¹ In France the rumors flourished so profusely that an editorial in *La Résistance savoyarde* compared them to poisonous mushrooms.¹² Feeding on odd bits of fact and reasonable speculations, French rumor particularly fretted over the possibility of a collaborationist fifth column bent on counterliberation.¹³ Were enemy soldiers operating behind the lines? Were saboteurs planted among the civilian population intent on ruining the economy and discrediting the Republic? Was there a sort of counter-Resistance, a "maquis blanc," whose name evoked the eighteenth-century counterrevolution?

The fears of a fifth column found some basis in the fact that a few collaborators actually did return to France secretly, apparently in coordination with the Ardennes offensive. In December 1944 and January 1945 the national gendarmerie arrested nineteen Frenchmen of Vichy's Milice who had parachuted back into France from Germany and an undisclosed number of "individuals belonging to antinational groups" who had allegedly parachuted into the departments of Manche, Sarthe, Eure-et-Loir, Seine-et-Marne, Lot, and Tarn with weapons, explosives, and radio transmitters.¹⁴ Some provincial authorities undoubtedly added to the speculation by encouraging unarmed civilian patrols to guard the roads, although others discouraged any such efforts.¹⁵

The rumored fifth column, however, was not confined to military agents preparing for a return invasion. For its part, the gendarmerie blamed fifth columnists for rumors about losses to French troops, the devaluation of the franc, air raids, V-1 bombs, secret weapons, the possible defection of the USSR from the alliance, and Allied designs on French colonies.¹⁶ The man in the street also suspected that collaborators were gathering in the hills to fight the new Resistance regime. Again, police investigations into suspected "maquis blanc" lent some of the rumors a foundation, particularly in the Loire, where some farms had been put to flames.[17] Accordingly, the prefect of Cantal requested immediate investigations by national intelligence and security units after receiving near-simultaneous reports of the discovery of a letter addressed to a German soldier, some mysterious lights in a hilly area, and clandestine meetings against the Resistance held in a garage in Saint-Flour.[18] The speculation regarding the lights in the hills reached such a pitch that *La Margeride* felt obliged to publish a warning against false alarms over the matter.[19] Nor did the German surrender put an end to fears of fifth columnists. In May 1945, the prefect of Savoie suggested to the government that all persons condemned to national degradation by the purge courts be identified by a red mark on their identity cards in order to help the police monitor possible fifth column activity.[20]

The climate of fear and suspicion fueled by rumors of faux-maquis and fifth columnists led to tragic mistakes such as the death of a thirty-two-year-old wine merchant from Moûtiers who had gone with his wife to visit friends in Tarbes. A friend had taken the couple for a drive at night when soldiers out of uniform, probably suspecting black market activity, signaled them to stop. The driver, fearing an attempt to steal his van, continued on. The soldiers responded with shots that killed the merchant and seriously wounded his wife and friend.[21] In a similar case, the moderate *La Liberté de l'Est* attributed the murder of a detective mistaken for a Milicien to the violent and unstable atmosphere of the times: "We are living in a dangerous time when nervous tension inclines the individual to commit a thousand excesses that, in good conscience, he would have previously reproved. That which previously made one indignant, scarcely astonishes today. It becomes natural to insult, to curse, to slander, to calumniate, as it becomes natural to pillage, to steal, to punish, or to kill. There is a furor to harm that surpasses the imagination. Human wickedness has settled into our mores and exercises its ravages in complete liberty."[22]

The presence of armed men engaged in a war only underscored the prevailing sense of peril. Except in the northern corridor and major cities that hosted the Allied armies, the most common soldiers in France during the après-libération were the irregular Resistance units that had come out of hiding across the country during the battle for liberation. In the summer of 1944, the FFI dominated the social landscape of France as the great heroes of the liberation. These romantic figures, pictured as young men with bandoliers slung over their shoulders, grenades dangling from their pockets, and rifles grasped in their fists, zoomed about in commandeered vehicles painted with the cross of Lorraine.[23]

In the fall and winter of 1944–45, some FFI units that neither disbanded nor followed the fighting to the frontiers encountered criticism for lacking discipline and exceeding their authority. Complaints ranged from FFI rowdiness—"they fire their pistols a little too freely in the streets at night"—to illegal arrests and requisitions.[24] The poorly equipped FFIs who did continue to fight the enemy, however, benefited from the charitable solicitude of their countrymen. National, regional, and local organizations successfully appealed for material and emotional support for the serving FFI. One of the most popular charities during the winter of 1944–45 asked girls and women to knit fifteen- by fifteen-centimeter squares of odd wool to be sewn together into blankets for the FFIs. The initiative, which appeared throughout the country, enjoyed the support of both Catholic and Communist women's groups. Indeed, it turned into a competition in the region of Saint-Flour, where the girls of different schools and the women of different associations publicly vied with one another to see who could knit the most squares and collect the most woolen garments.[25] The FFI, then, acted as both a source of controversy and an object of charity in their communities.

But the national authorities took a different view of the country's local heroes. In pursuit of its policies of consolidating central authority and distrusting the Communists, the new Resistance government tried to amalgamate all armed resistants into the regular police and army as quickly as possible. De Gaulle's provisional government showed particular concern over the unhappily named Milices patriotiques (MP), which should not be confused with Vichy's paramilitary anti-Resistance Milice. The MP had been created during the occupation as a sort of FFI home guard to secure the FFI's rear from counterattack and sabotage. In June 1944, for example, the CDL of Savoie recruited eight hundred generally older, well-established men as a nonpartisan (neither AS nor FTPF) MP.[26] If a local MP did not disband at the liberation, it filled the gap left by the regular police. Although the MP of Bourg-Saint-Maurice (Savoie) fined people for jaywalking, most

MP units focused on what they saw as their mandate to search out and arrest collaborators and other traitors, especially black marketeers.

De Gaulle, however, suspected the MP as a Trojan horse of revolution and dissolved it on 31 October 1944. The CDL of Cantal protested de Gaulle's order of dissolution on the grounds that the MP was a much needed anticollaborator police force without which it would not be able to fulfill its promises to punish traitors and traffickers.[27] But such protests had little effect or even much public backing. For the most part, the men of the Milices patriotiques submitted calmly to their dissolution or transfer to other duties such as guarding an internment camp for collaborators in Cantal.[28]

A more obvious reminder of the continuing dangers of war came from the uniformed men (and women) of the regular armies engaged in France. The French army itself caused little comment in the provinces other than complaints about the 1945 draft and remarks about the army's less than sterling performance in 1940.[29] Indeed, if the French army had a presence in 1944–45, it was the ghostly one of the approximately one million POWs held prisoner in Germany until the end of the war. The Allied and German armies, on the other hand, captured French attention. Indeed, although few Americans traveled beyond the narrow invasion corridors between the beaches of Normandy and Provence and Germany, the reputation and goods of the American army spread throughout the country.

French gratitude for American assistance in their liberation did not stifle all criticisms of their sometimes exasperating guests. The French, or at least French administrators, feared that the Americans saw them as a conquered people. As Dominique Veillon has phrased it, "The German occupation was succeeded by another occupation based on chewing gum and jazz."[30] An incident in the war zone of Courcelles-Chaussy (Moselle) between an American captain and the local gendarmerie illustrates why the French might have felt this way. Despite the gendarmes' protests, the captain personally broke the locks on a villa and installed himself there. When criticized, he replied that "he hadn't come five thousand kilometers for 'the French to preach at him.'"[31]

Tensions in Franco-American official relations in the northern departments tended to cluster around American treatment of property, such as "unauthorized requisitioning" of buildings and fuel, and (mis)behavior toward civilians.³² On a more popular level, the national gendarmerie report for March and April 1945 summed up the situation by reflecting that although the GIs had good relations with the civilians, the Americans did reprehensible things when drunk, mostly in the big cities such as Nancy and Lyon that served as rest and recreation centers.³³ But even in the large areas of France where no American had a chance to personally offend a French man or woman, the Americans' reputation began to suffer by early 1945. The gendarmerie attributed the decline in American popularity to two causes: the fact that certain products did not appear with the Americans and the "scandalous" way the Americans treated their German prisoners.³⁴ In brief, the French reproached the Americans for not being generous enough to the French while being too generous to the Germans. Such complaints found far less support in areas inhabited by Americans than in regions removed from the front where people knew about the Americans through the press rather than through personal contacts.

In the opinion of the French at the time, if not of later historians, the Americans were far too kind to the defeated Germans in the prisoner of war camps.³⁵ The CRR at Nancy, for instance, reported that, contrary to Eisenhower's nonfraternization orders, the American Military Police in the city had been organizing soccer games with their German charges and singing with them late into the night, "to the great scandal of the neighborhood." The scandal only increased as a consequence of this not being the first such complaint by the local residents about American "indulgence."³⁶

The soccer games, however, did not upset the French nearly as much as the café au lait and white bread said to be served to prisoners of war, referred to here as PGAs (*prisonniers de guerre de l'Axe*) to distinguish them from the French POWs in German captivity. Indeed, women from Château-Thierry (Aisne) protested outside the subprefecture against the "*régime de faveur*" given to German and Italian PGAs, particularly that the prisoners' meat ration was higher than their own.³⁷ Newspapers across the country carried detailed stories about the rations allegedly given to PGA in the American camps in what some administrators saw as a press and radio campaign "that does nothing less than demoralize the population."³⁸ Although it was a fact that the official rations in the PGA camps were higher than French civilian rations, the press reports and rumors greatly exaggerated the amounts of rare delicacies such as oranges and real coffee being given to the Germans.³⁹

Some editorialists scoffed at the necessity of feeding the defeated enemy so well. One CDL daily, *Le Cantal libre,* contrasted the supposed menu of the PGAs with that given to French prisoners in the notorious prison at Fresnes during the occupation—warm water and a morsel of bread—and suggested that half of the German rations be given to French children, who were used to "living on little." The article then went on to discount the "tactic of toast with jam," which persuaded Germans to surrender for American food, because "at the point where they are, sausages undoubtedly have sufficient power of seduction without its being necessary to add chocolate pudding."⁴⁰ Others interpreted such largesse as an added insult to the French people. For example, the front page of a newspaper from Romans carried a large cartoon of an evilly smiling American officer pointing at a somewhat surprised German soldier carrying a basket of food. "–Hello Fritz! good nourritioure? –Ja, Ja, et ch'est touchours une viktoire de pluch chur les chivils Franchais!!!" (–Hello Fritz! good food? –Ja, ja, and it's yet another victory over the French civilians!!!).⁴¹

These complaints expressed more than a jealous sense that it was unfair that, even after being defeated, the Germans were still eating better than the French. The generous treatment of PGAs seriously violated the hierarchy of justice of the après-libération. The French rationing system manifested that hierarchy by allowing double rations to repatriated deportees who represented the apex of moral and patriotic virtue. So to give *Germans,* the persecutors and torturers of those very deportees, more food than their victims turned justice on its head. As a correspondent from Rambervillers wrote in response to the rumors that POWs in Nancy were playing soccer with their guards and eating white bread and coffee, "When we think of our executed martyrs, our burned villages, our devastated cities, we would willingly send the aforesaid prisoners to play soccer on their minefields. Our American friends are truly too generous."⁴²

The status of the PGA, however, changed radically after the cessation of hostilities. In the late spring, "the population notice[d] with satisfaction that the rations given to the prisoners by the Americans ha[d] diminished in quality and quantity," although they did not stop protesting.⁴³ More important, the German surrender meant that the PGA were either sent home, kept in prisoner of war camps, or hired out as cheap labor for French reconstruction. Indeed, in the spring of 1945 a PGA working in agriculture cost his employer only seventy francs a day, less than a quarter of the average hourly wage for French men working in the provinces.

As an indication of the numbers involved, in October 1945 the region of Nancy employed 24,990 PGAs in the civilian economy and 1,705 for the military authorities while sheltering a further 17,477 in prisoner of war camps. At the same time, the region of Clermont-Ferrand employed 18,939 PGAs and housed 7,473 in camps.[44] PGAs worked in agriculture, forestry, mines, industry, public works, and the railways for the national government, the military authorities, private businesses, and local governments. In July and September 1945, Rambervillers, for instance, hired PGAs through the Water and Forestry Department to cut wood for the cost of assuring the men "maintenance, food, surveillance, and mustering," plus ten francs per day in wages.[45] The town of Saint-Flour similarly hired a unit of forty Austrian PGAs to work on maintaining the River Ander.

The presence of so many PGAs scattered in small groups throughout France created a controversy between those who saw them as representatives of the defeated Nazi regime and those who saw them as individual men. On the one hand, an editorial from Ugine (Savoie) entitled "Let us not Forget!" denounced individuals, especially "foreigners," for secretly giving food, cigarettes, and clothing to German PGAs laboring at the steelworks. "It is inadmissible that such disgusting things can happen in our locality that was so sorely tested by the Nazi hordes (executions, deportations, war damage [*sinistrés*]). Doesn't all this suffice to dictate each one's attitude?"[46] Further north in the Vosges, *La Liberté de l'Est* published a similar editorial, "Very Misplaced Generosity," after a young man in Remiremont gave a loaf of bread to some German prisoners. "What do the repatriates or the relatives of those who died of privation or torture in Germany or in France think about this gesture? The guilty party would do well to read the poster with the Prefect's instructions on the manner in which the French have the duty to treat German prisoners. The most debonair among them are often murderers of Frenchmen and destructive bandits."[47]

The prefect of Cantal also found it necessary to legislate the "proper" relations between French men and women and the PGA. In short, PGAs were to be treated as prisoners and forbidden to socialize with any women,

French or foreign.⁴⁸ Yet some French men and women continued to ignore the regulations and lectures about how to treat the PGAs, perhaps because they felt they owed a debt to these men and their kin for whatever kindness German strangers had shown to their own menfolk held captive as French POWs from 1940 to 1945. Their attitude scandalized others, such as Saint-Flour's police chief, who complained to the mayor in late 1945 that the town's detail of Austrian PGAs had no guard—a serious problem for a group thought to be prone to theft and escape.⁴⁹

Much more distressing to the police chief than the recent pilferage of vegetables and the possibility of escape, however, was the fact that these Austrian PGAs were socializing with the French citizens of Saint-Flour. They had been seen walking in the town at all hours of the night and drinking in bars. Still worse, certain of these defeated enemies had been received as guests in the homes of local people; the chief cited names, dates, and times for four such incidents. He ended his report by strongly urging that this situation be remedied quickly and energetically in order to avoid "violent criticism of the legal authorities by the population. In Saint-Flour, at least, one seems to have forgotten the treatment inflicted on our prisoners, the tortures undergone by our deportees, the majority of whom, alas, will not return, and, finally, the twenty-five *fusillés* of 14 June 1944 at [the Pont de] Soubizergues."⁵⁰ The memory of those patriotic sacrifices required that the survivors disdain the perpetrators.

While perceptions of physical danger lessened with the end of the war and the passage of time, economic fears grew steadily throughout the period to reach a crescendo a few years later. These economic anxieties grew out of the worsening shortages and the rising inflation that combined to create an increasing uneasiness about the short- and long-term future. The economic problems also discredited the government, which controlled prices and wages, ran the rationing system, and was in the process of nationalizing important sectors of the economy. Attempts to fix the blame for the economic troubles on scapegoats such as the "trusts" or the successors of Vichy's economic services did little to shift it from the national government, especially after the excuse of being at war ended.⁵¹ In the opinion of the people of Saint-Flour, Moûtiers, and Rambervillers, the new regime's economic policies represented severe mismanagement, if not outright failure.⁵²

No one, however, could have argued that the economy did not pose a considerable challenge to the new government. The occupation undermined the French economy by dividing the country into five zones, removing agricultural and industrial workers, and imposing the drain of "occupation costs."[53] The battle for liberation during the summer of 1944 further crippled it as the Germans stole a large portion of the rolling stock, the French themselves blew up roads, bridges, and power lines, and the contending armies destroyed homes, factories, and fields. The resulting destruction of the communications and transportation networks compounded all the other problems; factories, for instance, lay idle for lack of coal that lay heaped around mines for lack of transport. Indeed, the economy actually deteriorated after the liberation. So despite the popular assumption that liberation would magically reintroduce the economic bounty of prewar days, the French began the new era even worse off than they had been during the occupation. Years of deprivation undermined people's endurance and forced them to pay undue attention to otherwise trivial matters like buying a loaf of bread or replacing a button. The ongoing penury increasingly molded the public mood as it shifted from hope in the summer of 1944 to weary discouragement by Christmas of 1945.

Clothing symbolized the general poverty. By the liberation, the war had already affected the way the French dressed by limiting the amounts of fabric available for civilian clothes and of leather available for shoes. People hobbled along in wooden soles and patched outfits.[54] The shortages worsened at the end of the war because of the influx of repatriates, many of whom had only the worn-out prison clothes on their backs, and of refugees and sinistrés who had lost their belongings in the fighting. Demand therefore rose sharply above supply just as patience with shortages ended.[55]

The clothing shortage led to more than just a steep decline in the fabled French fashionableness; it generated crime and protests bordering on civil disobedience. Shortages naturally led to theft, such as that at the home of a recently deceased man in Rambervillers; although no money, gold, or silver was lost, the robbery was significant enough for notice in the departmental newspaper, because it involved "significant loot, notably sixteen pairs of underpants, a suit, four pairs of trousers, towels, and sheets, the lot valued at twenty-five thousand francs."[56] The shortage also created a new crime, the unauthorized wearing of military clothing, particularly pieces of American uniforms. The fall of 1945 saw an apparently ineffective stream of decrees from prefects regulating the use of military clothing. Indeed, in January 1946 special gendarmerie patrols in all garrison towns and major train stations in the Vosges cracked down on crime by questioning everyone wearing American, British, or French military clothing, especially men dressed in khaki.[57]

The fashion for military clothing may have represented a disciplinary challenge for the authorities, but it was a practical solution to a serious problem for civilians. Allied uniforms were, at the very least, rugged as well as being associated with power and victory. But as not everyone could secure a bomber jacket, civilians used other stratagems to obtain clothing. One tactic was the strike. In September 1945, for instance, two hundred quarry workers in Saint-Michel-de-Maurienne (Savoie) went on strike because they did not have any work shoes or clothes. The prefect sympathized with what he considered to be their perfectly reasonable complaint and negotiated on their behalf with the ministers of the interior and industrial production.[58]

Around the same time the cobblers and farriers of Savoie went on strike until they received more leather and nails with which to work. The departmental CGT and CFTC held a one-day general sympathy strike, closing all shops except those selling food, but the cobblers' customers were less understanding.[59] One man from Moûtiers complained to the editor: "I work in a factory and my shoes are in very bad shape. Am I supposed to go barefoot?"[60] This worker probably could not have turned to the black market, where, as early as February 1945, shoes were rumored to sell for three thousand to six thousand francs per pair.[61] Because of the strike, "the artisans [were] in turmoil, and the public [was] even more so." Putting his finger on the crux of the period, the prefect explained: "Neither the artisans nor the public want to believe that there are fewer materials to distribute today than there were during the German occupation and after the occupier's levies."[62]

Besides being poorly clothed, the French were also poorly sheltered.[63] And even families with adequate homes had trouble keeping them warm and lit because of the continent-wide fuel shortage. The winters of 1944–45 and 1945–46 were unusually bitter, creating a preoccupation with coal that translated into this humorous snippet: "Party game 1945. The mistress of the house: 'I propose a new game. Everyone leaves for an hour and whoever brings back the biggest piece of coal wins!'"[64] Yet the severe cold was hardly a laughing matter for an undernourished people dressed in threadbare clothing. Indeed, in November 1944 the people of Savoie became alarmed when they saw snow on the mountain tops but no coal or wood in their homes. The local shortage came about through a combination of problems that included disruptions in transportation and low production in the lumber camps, whose workers, mostly maquisards, had had other things to do during the summer of 1944. Local and departmental officials responded to public protests and demonstrations over the lack of fuel by negotiating deliveries from regional mines outside of the regular channels.[65]

Lack of heating fuel appeared on the lists of grievances of protesting housewives throughout the country and throughout the period, especially when it affected the schools. In early 1945, ministerial instructions required that children be spared from working in unheated rooms and that school hours be reduced because of the fuel shortage. In Lyon the schools doubled up classes in warmer rooms, served warm drinks, and kept classroom doors open.[66] Wartime shortages meant that children had neither the strength nor the energy to pay attention, nor the proper supplies or attire for school.[67]

The following winter saw little improvement, especially in the power supply. The dry weather of 1945 meant that the hydroelectric companies in both Cantal and Savoie had to ration electricity during the winter of 1945–46 by restricting the hours of service. In Saint-Flour power was provided only for twelve out of twenty-four hours, either between 1:00 P.M. and 1:00 A.M. or vice versa. As a result, the post office closed at the early nightfall of the French winter, all shops other than pharmacies and food purveyors closed at 6:00 P.M., entertainment establishments of any sort had to close between 5:30 and 9:00 P.M., and no shop windows or signs could be lit up.[68] Moûtiers endured similar restrictions and power cuts.[69]

In extending to transportation, the fuel shortage caused significant problems for industry and dashed hopes that the return of republican liberty would include the freedom to roam. Gasoline remained rationed after the liberation, leading to overcrowded public transportation—a particular inconvenience in Moûtiers.[70] It also led, inevitably, to abuses and the consequent complaints that certain people (generally identified as collaborators or officers) could go pleasure riding while doctors did not have the fuel that would allow them to attend the sick.[71]

But the shortages and tangles in the economy went far beyond such obvious problems as clothing and fuel to permeate every aspect of daily life. Soap and detergent, for instance, caused continual concern throughout the period. Even more frustrating, in some areas such an unremarkable yet necessary commodity as matches disappeared from the shops. The match shortage provided a regular topic for the letters to the editor column of Saint-Flour's *La Margeride*. The matter first came up in October 1944 through the letter of a reader who wished to retain her anonymity because "a woman should hardly draw special attention to herself," but who felt that "the subject is so interesting for all of us that every Sanflorain can acknowledge it as his own." Indeed, the author herself had only nine matches left, and her neighbor, who had run out, was already reduced to lighting her own fire from the author's. She suggested, discreetly, that the city should send someone with a trunk or two large suitcases to Aix, Marseilles, or Toulon to buy matches for the whole town, but did not discuss the ambiguities inherent in any such municipal foray into the parallel, if not solidly black, market.[72] The shortage then led to pleasantries, as someone suggested hiring the still burning *"Flamme de Pétain"* to tour the city each morning, earning a rebuke on behalf of the old and sick the next week.[73] The situation became so serious that two families fell to arguing over a box of borrowed matches, leading to a fist fight, a civil trial, and a fine of three hundred francs.[74] Matches did reappear in the shops later in the year but in such insufficient quantities that the departmental PCF demanded that the prefect ration them.[75]

The aggravations of shortage were compounded by an alarming rate of inflation that forced those on low or fixed incomes to restrict their consumption of basic necessities such as potatoes and fuel even more severely than the rationing system required.[76] After investigations into the family budget in December 1945, *La Résistance des Vosges* concluded that between 1939 and 1945 the cost of living had risen an average of 284 to 300 percent, as illustrated by Table 1. The article did not explain its figures—whether they represented official or black market prices, whether they were those of Epinal or an average of several towns, or whether they factored in dete-

Table 1.

	1936	1939	March 1945	Sept. 1945	Change 1936–March 1945 (%)	Change March 1945–Sept. 1945 (%)
Bread (kg)	2Fr10	3Fr05	4Fr90	7Fr40	142	53
Wine (liter)	1Fr06	3Fr33	10–	20Fr20	506	102
Meat (beef, kg)	8Fr40	12Fr65	56–	—	—	342
Butter (kg)	16Fr55	32Fr85	103–	169Fr70	422	65
Potatoes (kg)	0Fr40	1Fr30	3Fr20	5Fr10	292	72
Pasta (kg)	5Fr75	9Fr25	19Fr20	32Fr80	227	41.6
Sugar (kg)	3Fr45	6Fr20	15Fr10	20–	174	32.4
Eggs (dozen)	8Fr40	11Fr70	49Fr20	—	320	—
Electricity	1Fr50	2Fr20	3Fr06	5Fr33	138	74
Coal (sack)	62–	84–	—	—	35.6	—

rioration in quality. But exact or not, they represent the pressures people felt themselves to be under at the time.[77]

The government itself encountered difficulties quantifying the rising cost of living. The statisticians had trouble accommodating the localization of markets, the elusive nature of black market prices, and the common disregard for official price and wage scales. Nevertheless, the Institut national de la statistique et des études économiques (INSEE) has offered some figures, primarily for the national capital, which constituted an exception in that food prices were lower and wages higher there than in most of the rest of the country. Prices in provincial towns with over ten thousand inhabitants were higher than those in Paris by 15 percent in November 1944 and by 8 percent in November 1945. At the same time, wages were lower in the provinces: 321 francs per hour on average for men. Beginning in April 1945 the government began to revise the wage scales so that the greatest difference between Parisian and provincial wages dropped from 35 to 25 percent. Even in Paris, however, wages very obviously did not keep pace with prices, even official prices, so that salaries increased but purchasing power decreased. Indeed, despite wage increases, the 1945 purchasing power of a Parisian worker was only 55 or 56 compared to a 1938 base of 100.

The following figures for Paris, then, do not translate exactly to the provinces but help illustrate a general trend. The INSEE determined an index of (official) retail prices for twenty-nine food items in Paris with a base of 100 in 1938. The index was at 267 in April 1944, 317 in April 1945, 469 in November 1945, and 481 in April 1946. That meant a price increase of 1.6 percent between April 1944 and April 1945, an unnerving increase of 6.9 percent in the seven months from April to November 1945, and a rise of 0.5 percent over the winter of 1945–46. The Malignac Index, which figured in the cost of the official prices of rations that were actually delivered plus the black market cost of obtaining the necessary supplements for those rations, also operated on a base of 100 in 1938. According to it, the cost of living for a modest family in Paris was 590 in April 1945, 650 in November 1945, and 700 in April 1946. This index verifies the unsettling jump in the cost of living between April and November 1945, when, not coincidentally, most food protests took place.[78] The same trend can be seen from a different perspective by comparing the franc-dollar exchange rate; it was 49.63 in November 1944 and 119.1 a year later in December 1945.[79]

No matter how tenuous these attempts to quantify the daily economic pressures felt by the French in 1945, they are striking enough to confirm the administrative reports from across the country that citizens could not afford what they needed. As the months passed, concern over inflation began to overshadow the other major issues of the day. It also increasingly dictated the form and rhetoric of citizens' protests. On 25 May 1945, for example, the CGT and CFTC of Savoie called a symbolic general strike throughout the department from the hours of 10 A.M. to 3 P.M. *La Résistance savoyarde* reported regarding the day's events: "While remaining wholly attached to General de Gaulle's program, the mass of workers of Moûtiers and its region deliberately rebels against the rise in the cost of living, against those responsible for this state of affairs, against the government officials, no matter how highly placed, who, by their negligence, or that of their administrations, have led us on the fatal round of vicious dissimulation (*recel*) on which dance the increases in the minimum wage and the automatic increase in the cost of living."[80] A few months later, syndicates moved beyond symbolic strikes to more blatant expressions of their resentment against the government. Nor were the strikes limited to industrial workers, who were, in any case, being urged by the PCF to work longer hours in the "battle for reconstruction."[81] In mid-December 1945, civil servants went on strike across the country to protest their impoverishment by Vichy wage policy and the postliberation inflation. Ministerial instructions to the prefects not to receive the strikers' delegations did nothing to ameliorate growing hostility toward the government.[82]

In December 1945, the prefect of Savoie observed that the public "notes with anguish the rapid rise of prices and diminution of their purchasing power."[83] Indeed, the same prefect reported that "one frequently hears it said that if the authorities persist in this attitude and take no action to immediately hold down the rise in prices, the country will court catastrophe."[84] By this time, opinions expressed in public tended to center more on halting price increases than on raising wages because it was already evident that wages would not keep pace with prices. That Christmas even Santa winced at the legal, let alone black market, prices of toys and treats.[85] It was, claimed *L'Espoir du Cantal,* "Christmas for the Rich." Moûtiers' paper observed that "the first Christmas of peace was awaited with impatience. . . . And meanwhile this Christmas of peace has been for many a day as sad as the others. Why? Because everything was too expensive."[86] In less than a year the long-awaited peace had lost its luster, tarnished by privation, cold, and the anxiety of inflation.

Inflation and crime, however, were not the only disconcerting aspects of the après-libération. The Resistance's victory over Vichy caused a sudden shift in the social landscape. The change of regime was more than just a change of the palace guard; it was even more than the drastic change of personnel represented by the stereotypical maquisard mechanic turned liberation-era mayor. In 1944–45, public discourse constructed Vichy and the Resistance as polar opposites, as black and white, good and evil.[87] The Resistance's victory, then, inverted the official moral hierarchy. After the liberation, men and women whom Vichy had branded as "terrorists" were glorified by the new regime as patriotic martyrs. And the collaborators who had been Vichy's heroes became the most despised traitors and criminals. Only the status of black marketeers did not change when the hierarchy was inverted; both Vichy and the Resistance execrated them as the worst sort of traitors.

The new moral hierarchy sought legitimation in the premise that resistance was good and collaboration evil. Drawing on both Catholic and French patriotic traditions, it ranked resistants in an order that privileged suffering.[88] The Resistance's dead, usually referred to as "martyrs," occupied the pinnacle of moral authority and prestige. Below them sat the political deportees who had undergone the reputedly purifying suffering of the concentration camps.[89] Resistants who had neither died nor been deported for the cause occupied the third rung of moral elitism. The lower, darker rungs of the hierarchy housed various sorts of collaborators, with Vichy's Milice at the nadir. The new Resistance government endorsed both ends of this hierarchy with such policies as giving double rations to repatriated deportees and revoking the civil rights of collaborators.

In many regions the inversion of the moral hierarchy happened before the liberation as the "culture of the outlaw" slowly took root.[90] For the people of those regions, the liberation only meant that they could safely act out that hierarchy in public. But in other areas, people believed Vichy's equation of resistants with terrorists and bandits up until the summer of 1944. For them, the liberation required an immediate reversal of rhetoric and conviction. Publicly, nearly everyone made the sudden adjustment; those who did not risked arrest or worse as collaborators.

Those who had already weathered the sudden collapse of the Third Republic in 1940 and the rise and fall of Vichy could, of course, manage the readjustments of public sentiment demanded by the new Resistance regime. Society appears to have had more difficulty with the new government's reformulation of the national community. Vichy had tried to do this with its slavish mimicking of Nazi racial policy and ideology and participation in the Holocaust.[91] The provisional government reversed those xenophobic policies, most importantly by reintegrating Jews, although it did it so quietly that it may have escaped notice.[92] In the case of the Jews, the new regime returned to the republican tradition of equality, but it abandoned that and all other French traditions in its challenge to the prevailing gender order.

That challenge, however, came in the context of an international uncertainty about gender roles created by both world wars as industrial warfare undermined the assumptions of nineteenth-century gender ideology. The development of aerial bombardment, for example, blurred the constructed opposites of masculine/feminine to the extent that they rested on the distinctions of warrior/noncombatant. Women, too, were now targets and casualties of the enemy's weaponry. Indeed, in Vichy, where the Armistice had all but demobilized the French army, men and women shared the same military status.[93] In addition, the demands of total war created new opportunities for women, particularly in the workforce, that allowed them to disprove many of the old stereotypes about female incapacities. In response to these assaults on traditional gender roles, some argued that women deserved a full share of public life, while others wanted to reimpose order by reconfining women to the home.

Vichy represented the latter view, with its traditional program officially, if not effectively, designed to return women to the roles of housekeepers and mothers.[94] After the war, Vichy's ideal of feminine domesticity was reinforced from another perspective by those who equated peace and prosperity with domesticity for women.[95] At the liberation, however, de Gaulle and the Resistance championed women's rights, primarily by enfranchising women. Historians have since questioned whether or not the vote actually empowered French women, but the point was essentially moot in 1944–45.[96] What mattered then was that women had been brought into the community of full citizens and, perhaps, deserved a new status. The liberation began the negotiations over that new status.

During the après-libération, the government, the Resistance, and the Catholic Church welcomed women as voters and pointed to women's activities in the Resistance as proof that they deserved full civil status. Women's groups sketched a brave future for women as the moral leaders of postwar France; some of them even anticipated equal pay.[97] The local press also welcomed the full citizenship of women on the grounds of their contributions to the war effort. In its second issue, *La Résistance savoyarde* spoke very highly of the "often unknown, often heroic, always admirable role of the women of our country in the heart of the Resistance" and of the female vote as a means to the "'pure and strong' Republic."[98] A letter to the editor from Saint-Flour also rehearsed women's sufferings as housewives and resistants as evidence that women deserved to vote.[99]

The old habits and attitudes that had been reinforced by Vichy, however, died hard, the heroism of certain *résistantes* notwithstanding.[100] The freethinkers of Bourges, for instance, held on to the traditional view of women's intellectual abilities in their reported demand that the confessionals be locked before the municipal elections in April 1945 lest the priests dictate the female vote.[101] Nor did the new status implied by enfranchisement immediately overlap into less obviously political realms. The government continued to set women's wages below those of men, although it did decrease the difference from 20 to 10 percent.[102] The laws that bound women unequally to their husbands also continued to operate; the Tribunal correctionnel of Saint-Flour tried a woman for abandonment of her family in October 1944 and another for adultery in June 1945.[103]

Furthermore, the well-established habit of thinking of women as primarily sexual creatures influenced regulations promulgated in the northern areas of military operations. Like the authorities in other places to which the American army traveled during World War II, officials in Lorraine worried about the possible effects of the GIs on the local girls.[104] The prefect of the Vosges accordingly barred underage girls from any public place, especially cafés and cinemas, unless they were accompanied by their parents, in order to "prevent . . . any danger to the moral health of the Nation and to repress any attempt against public decency and morals."[105] There was no public challenge to his equation of the moral health of the nation with its girls' chastity. His initiative, it must be said, was greeted with widespread public approval, presumably among those who had already reached their majority and could still enter cafés.[106]

The gendarmerie also took steps to prevent what they saw as American attempts to "debauch French [female] youth," when, for instance, the GIs prevented French men or older women from accompanying French girls to their dances.[107] Admittedly, the American army at least partially deserved its reputation for being "overpaid, oversexed, and over here," and the French authorities could exercise little control over the males involved. But these attempts to protect French women indicate that at least the civil service continued to view them as somewhat irresponsible bearers of (sexually defined) honor.

Nevertheless, some women clearly appreciated the possibilities of their new status from the start and attempted to wield their influence as electors in the causes of most immediate concern to them. A group of housewives from Moûtiers, for example, submitted a letter to the editor asking for the speedy repair of one of the town's few public washhouses. When they had to repeat their request a month later, they underlined it in no uncertain terms. "In the meantime, it should not be forgotten that we the housewives will soon have the right to speak and that our voices will in the future count in the electoral balance!" As it turned out, the problem was not resolved for another year, at which point the paper announced: "Our housewives have gotten satisfaction. That is just because they are *électrices* [voters]."[108] Women also used their new status in disputes and complaints about food, a profoundly political subject during the après-libération.

In addition to these sudden changes in the social order, between August 1944 and May 1945 French men and women found themselves in the morally ambiguous and unprecedented situation of being no longer at war but not yet at peace. Of course, the country remained at war, as the people of the Vosges had good cause to know up to February 1945. But for all practical purposes the French experience of the Second World War had been the German occupation, and that ended when the Germans retreated. The liberation brought not peace but an odd limbolike state that was neither war nor peace and that provided neither justice nor plenty.

All these dilemmas of a shifting social landscape and moral ambiguity funneled into a nationwide controversy over dancing. Vichy had continued the ban on dancing instituted under the siege law of 11 November 1938 by the Third Republic.[109] At the liberation the general populace appears to have assumed that the liberties restored by Vichy's defeat included that of dancing and celebrated accordingly. As Jean-Pierre Azéma has remarked, "For those who had survived and those who were twenty years old, the dancing of the Liberation, dancing that had been forbidden by Vichy and that erupted spontaneously, was dancing unlike any other dancing had ever been."[110]

On 6 October 1944, however, the minister of the interior issued a circular in which he confirmed that public dances continued to be banned, because "the French must understand that the war is not finished, that many families are in mourning, and that three million [*sic*] Frenchmen are POWs or deportees in Germany."[111] Public dances could, however, be held with prefectural authorizations. As prefects generally only allowed benefit dances, the ban effectively gave charities a monopoly on a very lucrative form of entertainment rather than stifling it altogether. The minister reaffirmed the ban on 2 January 1945 and only lifted it on 30 April 1945, when the deportees and POWs had begun to return home and the end of the war was clearly imminent.

These decrees, however, led to considerable confusion because, first, many people did not understand that the ban allowed generous exceptions, and, second, even more people objected to the very possibility of those exceptions.[112] Although some repeated the traditional criticism of dancing as a sign of moral decadence, most objections to dancing during the après-libération centered around its inappropriateness in the particular circumstances of the time.[113] As the president of the Savoyard CDL expressed it in his proclamation announcing Savoie's liberation: "The war is not finished. It is not the time for demonstrations and rejoicing when soldiers fall in combat every day. When the time comes, we will honor our dead, we will fete our victory. Today, we make war, total war."[114] His confreres in Cantal similarly moved that dances be limited to charity events on Sunday afternoons, because "families everywhere mourn their dead, in the east the FFI still pursue the enemy, in Germany the prisoners still suffer in the camps, in a word, the war is not finished."[115]

Other opponents saw dancing as an affront to honorary justice and an insult to the dead or their survivors. A man from Angoulême particularly objected to dancing to the "Chant de la Libération," because, he explained, it was the hymn of partisans who had given their lives for their country, meaning that "you do not have the right to dirty that air by turning it into a tango."[116] And in April 1945 a woman from a village on the outskirts of Saint-Flour denounced the village's Centre d'entr'aide (CEA) for holding both a clandestine ball and a private feast at the expense of the POWs' fund. Her letter began by revealing that "this shameful ball [was held] a few meters from the place [Pont de Soubizergues] where twenty-five unfortunate victims paid with their lives for our liberty and at the moment when so many unhappy people suffer and die in the hell that is Germany."

The police investigation discovered goodwill and a certain naïveté on the part of the organizers, who had incorrectly assumed that the prefecture's failure to respond to their application to hold a dance implied consent. Nevertheless, the musician, who had also thought that permission had been granted, was given a severe dressing-down for playing at a ball when balls were forbidden and was made to donate his one thousand francs' fee to the POWs' fund. After concluding that the accusations of feasting at the expense of the fund were groundless, the investigators turned their scrutiny on the author of the denunciation. Because she had written several such letters in the past and was not well regarded in her community, they dismissed the inquiry into the CEA she had requested.[117]

Another series of complaints criticized the dances being held rather than the act of dancing. At least two newspaper readers in Cantal declared themselves scandalized by the presence of German PGAs at dances.[118] For his part, the rector of the Academy of Clermont-Ferrand forbade all dancing on university property because it would "diminish the prestige" of French fighting forces in the eyes of the Allies, as well as being an insult to the dead.[119] But most of the complaints expressed the sentiment that the dances, almost all of which benefited some charitable cause, were unbearably hypocritical both during and after the war. "A Mother" in Cantal begged other mothers to convince their children that dancing was not a "good work" owed to those who had spent five years behind barbed wire or who daily risked their lives at the front.[120] Anti-dansards also scoffed at the rationalization that dances were necessary to maintain the morale of the fighting troops.[121]

Whether or not those who attended the charity dances rationalized their pleasure by claiming to be sacrificing their energy and their shoes for a good cause, the organizers found themselves caught in a double bind. For instance, the AAS of Moûtiers organized a charity ball in April 1945 to benefit the families of resistants who had died or been deported. Their initiative aroused such a furor that they wrote an open letter to the prefect explaining themselves. The AAS, they said, had a duty to their comrades whose families could not survive on their meager daily pension of eleven francs. Not wishing that "prostitution become their last refuge," the AAS had organized a benefit dance as the only way to raise sufficient funds.[122] The town paper offered a solution by insisting that everyone had a duty to support the cause but recognized that some might find the paradox of enjoying themselves for the sake of others in misery offensive. For them it observed that one could support the families by buying a ticket without compromising one's principles by actually dancing.[123]

Dancing enthusiasts naturally found ways to circumvent any limitations on the numbers of dances. The creativity of local would-be dancers, for example, forced the prefect of Savoie to continually refine his regulations. After categorically affirming that all public dances were forbidden in October 1944, the prefect had to issue a ban on dancing schools in November. Therafter, dancing instruction could be given to no more than five couples at a time, on a weekday, and with the prefect's permission.[124] Despite these precautions, "violent and regrettable incidents" at dances forced the prefect to reissue the ban in the spring, although he did allow an exception for events from which all the proceeds would go to charity.[125] The legalization of public dances in late April did not end the prefect's troubles. In June he was obliged to expand the definition of a dance class still further as an event where no refreshments or orchestra were to be found and that observed the same hours as bars.[126]

The authorities had more reasons than moral standards to worry about dances: the refreshments offered at such events created opportunities for black marketeering, and the mixture of people all too frequently led to brawling triggered by accusations of collaboration. In fact, the CRR at Clermont-Ferrand suppressed all balls for any reason whatsoever in his region in March 1945 expressly because of unspecified "incidents between FFI and Police."[127] The illegality and volatility of such a popular form of entertainment meant even more work for the understaffed police, who nevertheless did try to enforce this law. Indeed, the prefect of Cantal issued a formal communiqué in which he recognized the importance of suppressing clandestine balls but deplored the number of anonymous denunciations about them, many without any foundation, that reached his office.[128] None of these obstacles—the censure of moralists or the surveillance of the police—stopped the dancing. In fact, by preventing dancers from traveling far from home, gas rationing and military curfews probably did more to stop dancing than all the pleas and all the regulations combined.

As might be expected, what Moûtiers' newspaper called *"la Balomanie"* got into full swing only after the dancing ban was lifted.[129] As was the case before the legalization of dancing, most public dances after it benefited a charity or celebrated a community occasion like the anniversary of a town's liberation.[130] The competition among balls for patrons and the high standards to which they were held by late 1945 may be judged by the arrangements for the Resistance-FFI Ball in Saint-Flour given to benefit the national monument to the maquis at Mont-Mouchet. The former maquisards organized a military jazz orchestra, a large buffet, and decorations of flags and parachutes but regretted not being able to obtain the machine guns, bazookas, and American rifles with which they had really wanted to decorate.[131] Wary of the opening provided by the dancing craze for financial abuse and disorderly behavior, the authorities continued to circumscribe the postwar "liberty of dance." By the fall, any charity event required prior prefectural authorization and control of the proceeds, all of which had to go to the charity.[132] Yet as long as the dances were being held for any of the broad range of war victims, prefects granted permission generously.

The dancing controversy aside, all the uncertainties and anxieties of life in the aftermath of war pooled together in the drama of the displaced persons. Millions of Europeans found themselves very far from their homes when the war ended. Some were refugees who had fled their hometowns, but not countries, to escape bombs or battles. Most, however, were displaced persons (DPs) whom the Nazis had removed from their home countries to serve in the German military, work in German industry, or suffer in German captivity.[133] France had its share of refugees, some of whom had fled their homes in the north in 1940 without being able to return for the next five years. Others, known as sinistrés, had been bombed out of their homes but generally stayed nearby. More important, the French could claim some two million displaced persons.

A small, generally overlooked, minority of these DPs were not French citizens but nationals of other Allied countries who ended up in France at the liberation. Some had evaded Vichy and German persecution during the occupation by joining the Resistance; others had worked for the Germans, either building or guarding the western defenses. After the liberation, they caught French attention as either welcomed liberators or unwelcomed troublemakers. The most troublesome of all were certainly the approximately fifty thousand Soviet citizens present in France courtesy of the Wehrmacht, the Todt Organization, or the Vlassov Army.[134] The regions of Limoges and Poitiers suffered the greatest ravages at the hands of Russian DPs; in Corrèze, Dordogne, Haute-Vienne, and Indre, Georgians and Tartars continued to act as they had while in German uniform. Although the CRR at Limoges could appreciate that much of the Russian misbehavior near the DP camp of La Courtine (Corrèze) stemmed from the inadequate provisioning of that camp, he could not tolerate that "they slip through the fields, demand bread without tickets [and] alcoholic drinks in the cafés, [and] harass women. The thefts of several thousand kilograms of potatoes, poultry, [and] livestock and the burglary of a hairdresser's have been reported."[135]

During the après-libération, however, the DPs who mattered to the majority of the French were the approximately two million French citizens caught in the Third Reich after the liberation and known collectively as the Absents. The exact numbers of Absents were unknown in 1945 and remain a matter of controversy today.[136] Approximately 950,000 of them were POWs who had spent the war in German camps or work details. As the darlings of Vichy propaganda, the POWs enjoyed a high public profile, but one that was slightly tainted with collaboration by association.[137]

A further 735,000 Absents, primarily men, were in Germany as laborers. "Working in Germany," however, could have very different meanings. Many of the workers were actually forced laborers who had been conscripted under Vichy's unpopular labor service, the Service du travail obligatoire (STO), and were known as *requis*. Approximately 200,000, including 42,654 women, however, had volunteered for employment in Germany, but even the category of volunteer presented certain ambiguities.[138] Some surely stepped forward out of a collaborationist desire to help the German war effort; others took German jobs for the promised high wages and benefits, reflecting an opportunism that indicates little about political commitments. Women who took German jobs to be near their POW husbands could argue that they had volunteered out of patriotism, as could all those who volunteered under Vichy's Relève program, through which it was popularly believed that a worker could trade him or herself for a POW. Although that was not actually the case, many workers went to Germany with the intention of sacrificing themselves so that a fellow Frenchman could come home.

Nevertheless, as early as 1941 German observers noted that voluntary laborers suffered the ostracism of their communities both before leaving and after returning from a limited contract or while on vacation.[139] The ostracism continued after the war. From the provisional government's point of view, voluntary laborers were not criminals: they had broken no laws by going to work in Germany; they were not collaborators, and they did not fall under the purge laws. On the other hand, neither did they qualify for any of the benefits meant to compensate French citizens who had been taken to the Third Reich against their will.[140] A significant number of ordinary citizens, however, did not share this objective view of the matter.

In addition, the concentration camps held 150,000 French men and women who came under the category of "deportees." Approximately half of these were Jews, or "racial deportees," although they were rarely designated as a separate category during the après-libération for several reasons. First, to have distinguished individuals by religion would have furthered Nazi concepts at the expense of the republican ideal of equality. Second, the government had a vested interest in portraying all the Absents as a unified group. Any specification such as distinguishing those arrested by Germans as resistants from those who were arrested by Frenchmen as Jews would weaken the claims of the Resistencialist myth. And third, although Jews made up half the deportees, they made up only 5 percent of repatriated deportees, an infinitesimal number within the much larger mass of POWs and laborers.[141] The other 75,000 deportees represented a constellation of resistants, hostages, political prisoners such as Freemasons or Communists, and even common criminals. One person, of course, could belong to several of these categories.

There was also an undetermined number of French citizens outside of France who would have counted as displaced persons but not as Absents because they had left the country as committed collaborators. Some had donned German uniform to fight Bolshevism on the Russian front; others had fled with their families in the German retreat during the liberation. The 300,000 Alsatian *Malgré-nous* who served in German uniform posed a more difficult case because of their presumed unwillingness to collaborate. In 1945, however, they, unlike the Miliciens in Germany, were generally unknown.

The burden of the Absents, however, was not spread equally throughout the country. The department of Cantal, for instance, claimed 7,500 POWs, 1,200 labor conscripts, and 350 political deportees. Many of these deportees were hostages taken in reprisal for Resistance fighting on Mont-Mouchet in June 1944 and thus had the slender advantage of a relatively short sojourn in Nazi captivity.[142] Savoie claimed 2,718 POWs, 1,800 labor conscripts, and 468 political deportees.[143] The Vosges, on the other hand, counted 19,000 POWs, 6,000 labor conscripts, 3,000 political deportees, and 4,000 civilian deportees who had been evacuated from the battle zone.[144] In Rambervillers, the mayor's office counted the town's Absents at 309.[145] The strikingly higher figures from the Vosges can be attributed to its location in the reserved zone during the occupation and in the war zone for five months during the liberation. Many of the labor conscripts as well as political and civilian depotees were arrested during the fighting and sent east to help the German, or discourage the French, war effort. In one example, a man from Rambervillers was working on a road crew elsewhere in the department in September 1944 when the Germans deported all the men in the village, including the road crew. He died in the concentration camp at Mauthausen in March 1945, although his fate did not become known until many months later.[146]

The Absents were essentially hostages held in extremely dangerous conditions by an enemy that gave neither information nor guarantees. In the case of the POWs and the workers, the French authorities usually at least knew where their citizens were. The POWs also had some measure of protection from the Red Cross and the Geneva Convention. The main concern for these groups lay in the possibility that they would perish in a bombing raid or Nazi reprisal before the Allied armies could reach them. The situation for the deportees was far more desperate. When they fell into the clutches of the Nazis or their collaborationist henchmen, they fell into a void; their families did not know where they were, or in what conditions they might be living, or even if they were still living. Some families did not even know whether or not a loved one had been deported, leading them to place requests for information in newspapers where the missing person had last been traced. In one ad published in May 1945, a Parisian couple asked for news of their twenty-two-year-old son who had joined the maquis in Cantal a year earlier.[147] Not even the GPRF's Ministry of Prisoners, Deportees, and Refugees could get enough information to compile an accurate list of deportees or to form an accurate understanding of the nature of the concentration camps.[148]

During the après-libération, the Absents and other war victims acted as a unifying source of concern and action for the French government and people. The war victims dominated public discourse and held a near monopoly on charity, which almost completely monopolized public entertainment. Families did their utmost to send packages to their Absents, although it became more and more difficult as the battle moved into Germany.[149] In order to ease "the anxiety of the families of our deportees," the Ministry of Prisoners, Deportees, and Refugees announced in January 1945 that the International Red Cross was delivering packages to French deportees regularly, even those whose families did not know where they were. Those families who did know their Absent's address could simply give it to the authorities so that packages would be sent at the government's expense.[150] Even so, the prefect of Cantal sent a letter to the minister in April 1945 asking that the government parachute food into the camps still in enemy territory, especially those north of Berlin, because, according to rumor, the Belgians, Serbs, English, and Americans had already been doing so for a month.[151]

Others also tried to help the war victims and to prepare a better future for the Absents. The people of France heard innumerable appeals to share their extra household goods and clothing with sinistrés and refugees, sometimes even from the mouths of children sent door to door to collect dishes and coats. The majority of appeals for war victims, however, asked for money. Fund-raisers spanned the full range from the national Week of the Absent, organized by the Ministry of Prisoners, Deportees, and Refugees under the patronage of Charles de Gaulle himself, to the spontaneous decisions of private individuals to pass the hat in a bar, to the collection of resistants' memories and photographs for a book about the liberation of Savoie to profit the "victims of the boches and the traitors."[152]

Charities offered raffles, dances, or theatrical performances such as the play staged to benefit the deportees of Rambervillers or the Troupe Zepp that amused the Moutiérains on behalf of the POWs and sinistrés.[153] Others evoked local traditions, as did the scout troop Vercingétorix of Saint-Flour when it revived the old Auvergnat custom of singing the "Chant de la Passion" and "Les Réveillés" in the surrounding villages during Lent.[154] The fund-raising even encroached on commercial entertainment. In November 1944, the CDL of Savoie raised the price of movie tickets throughout the department by two to five francs to benefit repatriated POWs.[155] Even sporting events might be affected. On 31 December 1944, for instance, the

Fédération française de football levied one to three francs on each seat at every amateur or professional game in the country. And Moûtiers' sporting association organized a "sports gala for the POWs" involving a football match, a parade, a ceremony at the Monuments aux Morts, and a raffle. The town's two cinemas respectfully delayed their show times until after the match.[156]

The frequency and configuration of charitable appeals naturally varied widely from place to place, reflecting local traditions of benevolence and local experiences of the war. For instance, Rambervillers, which had the highest number of war victims of the three towns, showed the greatest public activity on their behalf. Furthermore, although other communities treated the requis (forced laborers) as a peripheral afterthought, they were central to Rambervillers' efforts on behalf of the Absents and were always mentioned along with the POWs and deportees. The town even boasted a Centre local d'entr'aide des travailleurs en Allemagne, with the mayor as its president.[157] This concern for the requis undoubtedly stemmed from Rambervillers' former location in the reserved zone, where it had been extremely difficult to hide from the German press gang.

Indeed, the consequences of battle made the need for charitable generosity particularly pressing in the Vosges. Rambervillers itself housed many refugee families and a refugee center that appealed to the Rambûvetais in November 1944 to donate any extra clothing for the recent wave of refugees fleeing the front line as it moved east.[158] The CDL also appealed to all Resistance and charitable organizations to collect food, clothing, blankets, and cooking equipment to be sent to villages as soon as they were liberated.[159] With the fate of these same devastated communities in mind, the bishop of Saint-Dié requested a special collection for the sinistrés of the Vosges on Christmas Eve and the "adoption" of damaged villages by undamaged communities.[160] The Rambûvetais responded to these requests by donations, by "adopting" the sinistrés of Housseras and Saint-Benoît, and by creating a committee to coordinate "and group the generosity toward the unfortunates tried by bombardment, pillage, and evacuation."[161]

The depth of public response to the appeals on behalf of war victims may be seen in both the spontaneous contributions from unexpected popular sources and the receipts of official efforts.[162] Reports of weddings at the town hall repeatedly told of collections being taken for the POWs, deportees, sinistrés, or other local war victims. The hunters of Saint-Flour, for example, donated a total of 4,560 francs to the department's sinistrés; the *boules* players of Moûtiers collected 800 francs for the region's sinistrés on the occasion of their last tournament of the 1944 season.[163] The frequency with which the war victims were remembered at such unconnected events suggests that their plight struck a deep chord of sympathy or anxiety in the general public, or at least that such remembrance was fashionable.

Although a matter of some debate, the money was often channeled through the previously established national network of Centres d'entr'aide (CEA), which had branches of Maisons du prisonnier in every town. Usually run by local POWs repatriated before 1944, the CEA expanded their brief after the liberation to care for all Absents and their families. The local CEA applied the funds to particular projects such as paying the rent for a deportee's family or the *livrets du prisonnier*. Begun as a Vichy initiative but carried through after the liberation, the livrets were savings accounts established in the name of each POW, and later deportee, by his or her town. The money was meant as a token of esteem and a practical way to help the POWs with their transition to civilian life. They constituted quite possibly the single most common object of fund-raising, but even so, as one committee observed, the amounts would be small enough compared to the outrageous prices of the black market.[164]

Eventually, however, enthusiasm for the cause began to flag in the face of increasing anxieties about the economy. The CRR at Nancy remarked simply that "it is difficult to ceaselessly demand expressions of altruism from a region as sorely tried (*éprouvée*) as mine."[165] After the war ended, the authorities showed increasing suspicion of the endless charitable appeals. In late 1945, the prefect of Savoie took control of the receipts and expenditures of "self-proclaimed charity fetes and events" to forestall abuses.[166] Private citizens also began to object. A reader from a village near Saint-Flour submitted an article in which he bemoaned the constant collections for this and that which provoked a friend of his, a former POW, to say: "But it's like in Germany, you remember, one time Winter Help, another time . . . ."[167]

Given this widespread concern and investment in the plight of the Absents, it will come as little surprise that the crux of the après-libération was not, as might be expected, the defeat of Germany on 8 May 1945, but the Return of the Absents from captivity in the Third Reich. The Return is mostly forgotten today, but in the late spring of 1945 the return, or acknowledged nonreturn, of almost two million French men and women from Germany absorbed the country's emotions and energies. The first Absents came home in February 1945 to shock the official welcoming committee, who had not expected to see women so ill or haunted.[168] The majority, however, arrived during the Grand Return between 12 April and 15 May, when the U.S. Army flew twenty to twenty-five thousand French citizens from Germany to Paris every day. Others arrived throughout the year courtesy of the Allied militaries via trains, trucks, and ships, or through their own efforts.[169]

Returning French citizens were supposed to pass through the frontier at designated centers, where they would be examined for communicable diseases and vetted for collaborationist pasts. They would also receive various official forms such as ration cards and, in the case of POWs and deportees, new clothes and shoes. What anyone actually received at such a center, though, depended less on legal prescriptions than on local supplies and personalities.[170] Only 5 percent of Cantal's repatriates received their new suits at the frontier, shifting the burden to the department's already depleted stocks.[171] Repatriates, except those who had voluntarily put themselves at the service of the enemy, were also entitled to free medical care for nine months, a paid vacation for themselves and their spouses, their old jobs, access to small-business loans, and a welcome bonus of at least one thousand francs. Political deportees, legally defined as anyone deported (rather than conscripted) for any reason other than a criminal infraction, received a bonus of five thousand francs, later raised to eight thousand francs because so few actually returned. The government also recognized the special status of deportees and POWs by adding forty-eight POW and deportee delegates to the Consultative Assembly and creating special committees of deportees to review the decisions of the purge courts.[172]

Despite these arrangements, the government, particularly the Ministry of Prisoners, Deportees, and Refugees, impressed neither the public nor the repatriates with its management of the Return. The ministry appeared in the local press mostly as the object of criticism, if not of outright scandal. Many repatriation centers faltered under the weight of arrivals in May and June, but the problems at some could not be attributed to mere incompetence or overload. In fact, the centers at Longuyon and Dombasle-sur-Meurthe in the region of Nancy achieved national notoriety for their corruption. Nineteen members of the administration of the center at Dombasle eventually faced criminal charges for diverting center rations onto the black market.[173]

Yet at the same time that its own facilities were collapsing under the weight of its clientele, the ministry refused nongovernmental sources of aid. The people of Pontarlier, for example, created a repatriation center at their own expense and with the support of the mayor, subprefect, and Swiss authorities. But despite the overcrowding of other centers in the area, the ministry refused to allow a single deportee through Pontarlier, because, according to an inspector, it "came out of a private initiative with which the Ministry had nothing to do." The CRR of Dijon pleaded with the minister several times to make use of the center because "the population of Pontarlier has given itself heart and soul to this work," but to no avail.[174]

Official welcomes worked more smoothly on the local level where town CEAs and other organizations greeted repatriates at train stations with refreshments, shelter, and transportation to their homes. Saint-Flour's CEA, for example, ran a bureau at the train station staffed by former POWs and the wives and sisters of POWs and partially financed from municipal funds. During the week of 14–21 April, they assisted 139 POWs and forced laborers, 21 of whom they sheltered for the night and 46 of whom they delivered to their homes.[175] Those in Moûtiers and Rambervillers worked to arrange rides for local repatriates from the larger stations nearby.[176]

In April 1945 the news that the long-awaited Absents were moving along these pathways electrified the country. As the CRR at Lyon remarked, "Public opinion is entirely oriented toward the repatriation. Everything indicates it: conversations, newspapers, crowds at the stations, and anonymous letters."[177] The Return was *the* news of the day, despite the elections in late April and despite the end of the war in early May. Communities mobilized to watch for and welcome back their Absents, especially the deportees, martyrs at the apex of the living moral hierarchy. Moûtiers awaited 45 deported men; Saint-Flour 9 deportees, 5 of whom were women; and Rambervillers 155 deported sons and daughters.[178] Their homecomings were treated as public rather than private events.

The emotion that surrounded the Return, appearing almost like mass hysteria in more than one administrative report, partook at the same time of both joyous happiness and violent anger. Indeed, the two could be hard to distinguish. In one case that the CRR at Bordeaux felt "demonstrate[d] the state of excitability of the population," an announcer unwittingly identified a returning political deportee as a voluntary laborer. The crowd at the train station, knowing better, protested energetically and accused the organizing committee of being collaborators, which was tantamount at the time to putting their lives in danger from vigilantes.[179] The incident demonstrates both the public and upsetting nature of the Return. It also demonstrates how seriously the general public took the moral hierarchy and its consequent demands of honorary justice.

During the Grand Return crowds such as that in Bordeaux gathered at train stations throughout the country to greet repatriates. In Moûtiers, which had very restricted communications with the rest of the department, crowds gathered at the bus and train stations for the evening arrivals in hopes that a POW or deportee would appear. On one occasion the entire Scout troop came out to welcome a comrade who had been deported as a maquisard a year earlier.[180] Some towns also staged official welcomes like the elaborate receptions Saint-Flour gave to three of its women deportees, in particular Mme. Mallet and her seventeen-year-old daughter Madeleine.[181] The department's Catholic paper announced in February 1944 that the first news of Madeleine had arrived via a Red Cross postcard.[182] Then in May both the CDL's paper and Saint-Flour's own newspaper announced that the Mallets had arrived in Paris, only then to learn that the men of the family had all been killed the previous summer. After a week's rest, the women returned to Cantal. In Massiac the prefect's principal private secretary and a member of the Consultative Assembly greeted the women in the name of the government; in Coren they were met by the subprefect and mayor of Saint-Flour as well as the presiding magistrate and friends of the family. A crowd of neighbors waited for them outside their home.[183]

Those who could not gather at the train stations or participate in official welcomes could follow the progress of the Return through the media. Indeed, the local press of the late spring and early summer was full of news of the Return, owing not only to the overwhelming interest of its readers, but also to the express policy of the Allied supreme command to publicize the concentration camps.¹⁸⁴ No one came home without acknowledgment; if the returnee's town did not have its own paper, then the departmental press or radio announced the good news. Radio-Lorraine, for instance, presented not only the lists of repatriates but also requests for information about missing persons.

The press also spread the shocking news of the conditions and death rate in the Nazi concentration camps. *La Résistance savoyarde,* for example, periodically reminded its readers of who remained missing and informed them of the tragic stories of the deceased. So it was with great sadness that the paper reported that despite an earlier announcement of a young maquisard's imminent arrival, the seventeen-year-old would never return. Having been denounced on 21 June 1944 and tortured by the Gestapo, the young man survived imprisonment in Ravensbrück with the help of another young Moutiérain. He nevertheless died of exhaustion on 19 June 1945, weeks after his liberation.¹⁸⁵ Then in December 1945 the paper regretfully announced that the widow and child of a thirty-eight-year-old man who had been deported in May 1944 had just learned that he had succumbed to typhus almost a year earlier, in January 1945.¹⁸⁶ Such heartrending delays in notifying families were sadly common.

Along with local obituaries, newspapers such as *La Margeride* carried reports of the death camps of Auschwitz-Birkenau as early as December 1944, but not until the Return did papers publish the type of personal interview and memoir of concentration camps that would have engaged the emotions of a reader.¹⁸⁷ Reflecting on such accounts, *La Résistance savoyarde* commented: "There is something about it to make one shudder, to trouble our nights." And it concluded, "The Boches will never pay dearly enough for all Hitler's crimes!"¹⁸⁸

Those who doubted such press reports could find ample evidence of the horror of the Nazi camps all around them. Deportees, for instance, spoke publicly about their experiences in meetings that generally drew large audiences, such as the one held in July at the Maison du Peuple in Rambervillers.¹⁸⁹ Even more disturbingly than such testimony, photographic images of the camps circulated throughout France. The CRR at Rouen had American army films of the camps shown in the large towns of his region.¹⁹⁰ A similar film, called *German Atrocities,* toured the department of the Vosges. An editorial in the department's moderate daily insisted that it was every French citizen's duty to watch the film in order to ensure that such things would not be allowed to happen again. But after its first showing in Epinal, the theater management requested that "emotional" persons not attend that section of the program.[191] While the CRR at Poitiers recognized the utility of spreading the information about Nazi barbarity, he felt that the images provoked too much emotion, especially for the families of deportees who had not yet returned.[192]

Not all of the news, however, was quite accurate, because of what the CRR at Lyon called "a monstrous and silent information exchange that has spontaneously organized itself and which, from the Swiss frontier to the French interior, spreads very often contradictory news about the stalags and the oflags."[193] That same rumor mill provoked the Maison du Prisonnier et du Deporté of Cantal to formally deny two particularly troublesome rumors: that a ship full of POWs had sunk outside of Odessa and that an airplane carrying POWs and deportees had crashed. It begged individuals to refrain from adding to the "current worries" by spreading such false tales.[194]

The revelations about the Nazi camps, the sight of the horribly wasted and haunted survivors, and the dawning realization that the death rate among deportees would exceed 40 percent created a violent fury that boiled just below the surface of the entire period of the Grand Return.[195] Any gathering threatened to turn violent, and many of them did. On 24 May, for example, a national figure gave a two-hour talk about his experiences in the concentration camp at Buchenwald to a packed audience in Nancy. As chance would have it, a column of about a thousand German prisoners marched past the auditorium as the hall began to empty. Profoundly moved by what they had just heard, the French threw themselves on the Germans, beating several of them before the American guards could restore order by firing into the air.[196]

The most common catalyst for turning a crowd into a mob, however, was the presence of suspected voluntary laborers among the "worthy" repatriates such as POWs and deportees. Because they were the most available collaborators, voluntary laborers served as the scapegoats for all the suffering caused by more active collaborators. During the trek home, politically acceptable repatriates such as requis complained of being forced to associate with voluntary laborers in the welcome centers and trains.[197] Once they were home, the general public did not accept voluntary laborers any more willingly. A Vosgien paper summed up the local purge's position on them: "These people who went off voluntarily to offer their arms to Germany deserve sanctions. They were not French because they abandoned their *Patrie;* they were not worthy of being French because they helped the enemy martyr our brothers."[198] At the very least, voluntary labor in Germany was considered to indicate serious character flaws. *La Résistance savoyarde* explained the criminal behavior of an embezzler by citing his past as a voluntary laborer.[199] And *Le Réveil des Vosges* managed to blithely associate voluntary laborers with black marketeers, war profiteers, and foreigners in one short demand for their incarceration.[200] Such sentiments incited mob violence against voluntary laborers across the country.

Indeed, during the height of the Return, the gendarmerie reported that "each time a train arrives, it is not rare to see the population apply itself to those [male and female voluntary laborers] discovered among the POWs, deportees, and forced laborers. The police often have to intervene in order to prevent lynchings."[201] Most such attacks happened at train stations and often targeted women, possibly because, as women, they stood out in the overwhelmingly male flood of POWs and laborers.[202] Moreover, at a time when recent government propaganda had painted women's mission as that of tending the family home, a woman who voluntarily left that home to work for the enemy abandoned not only her country but her "true" nature and duties as a woman, thus displaying a doubly "unnatural" character.[203]

Such mobs occasionally made regrettable mistakes, as one did on 23 May in an incident at the train station in Epinal. The crowd turned on a woman thought to be a collaborator, threatened her all the way to the police station, and stole the clothing she had in a suitcase. As it turned out, the woman had come to the station to greet her husband, a POW for the past five years. Furthermore, she belonged to a Resistance family that included a brother who had been executed by the Germans. The prefect requested that, as the family had certainly suffered enough already, the public return her husband's clothing and that it reflect on the incident.[204] Finally out of patience with the mistreatment of defenseless and even pregnant women, the prefect threatened to close the station and its neighborhood to the public.²⁰⁵ Rambervillers, with its 114 honored forced laborers also witnessed demonstrations against voluntary laborers.²⁰⁶

The furious response to the voluntary laborers put provincial administrators in a difficult position. They were obliged to follow the national government's policy of not regarding voluntary laborers as criminals—no easy task when even the police refused to believe that voluntary laborers had not collaborated. In Savoie military security officers marked repatriation cards with a damning, and unauthorized, "voluntary laborer," and gendarmes arrested voluntary laborers on their own initiative.²⁰⁷ Yet following the national government's policy risked allowing these men and women to be murdered. Administrators therefore negotiated as best they could between the central government and the local community. At the recommendation of the CRR at Clermont-Ferrand, the prefect of Cantal sent official warnings to voluntary laborers suggesting that it would be advisable for them to absent themselves from the department.²⁰⁸ In Savoie and Isère, the prefects promulgated the Lyon CRR's decision to put all voluntary laborers under surveillance and set them to work in areas of forest remote from cities because "the majority of them were effectively stoned at their arrival."²⁰⁹

The violence generated by the Return, however, was not limited to the spontaneous expressions of crowds. Because the evidence of the camps and their survivors magnified the crime of collaboration by exposing the extreme consequences of nazism, the Return changed the timbre of the purge, providing it with more fuel in the form of new witnesses and defendants. Some of the new defendants were collaborators who had left France with the German army and then tried to slip back disguised as POWs or resistants. Military security attempted to screen out such individuals at the border, and the gendarmerie pursued them across the country. Indeed, the gendarmerie of Saint-Flour arrested a forty-one-year-old self-styled forced laborer working as a nurse at the town hospital on the grounds that he had really volunteered to go to Germany. The gendarmes took the matter in their own hands in this case because they "thought that he had things to answer for."²¹⁰

Other new defendants came from among previously unsuspected members of the community. As the CRR at Nancy remarked, "The deportees bring us interesting information about the precise reasons for their arrests (until now we were reduced to hypotheses), about those who denounced them, and about the prisoners who talked."[211] The authorities accordingly prepared new lists of suspects for the purge courts. Many deportees also sought action against those they accused of having sent them to the concentration camps. The gendarmerie reports for early summer 1945 list a number of incidents like the one in Billy-Montigny (Pas-de-Calais) in which fifty liberated prisoners and deportees "demonstrated to demand the arrest of two police commissioners and a police secretary."[212] In Rambervillers, repatriated deportees made a citizen's arrest of a former gendarme whom they blamed for their deportation.[213] The increased rate of vigilante violence in the summer and fall of 1945 suggests that other deportees or their friends did not rely on the courts to respond to the information revealed by the Return.

Violence, however, represented only one of the possible responses to the repatriates' homecoming. One could also respond with respect and care for the needs of those who represented the moral authority of patriotic suffering. The editor of Saint-Flour's paper described the transformative effects of patriotic suffering and its postwar implications in an editorial on the occasion of the return of a Sanfloraine from Ravensbrück. "The judgment that we want to carry to the end of our days, like a precious relic, will come from our comrades who [earned] the right to speak to the living during their tragic odyssey, verging on death at every moment. They [the deportees] do not condemn us. We will never be condemned. They encourage us; they support us; they bring us renewed affection. They are reborn hope for us. They retake their place at our sides. In the future we will find ourselves better, stronger, more confident. With them we will build the *lendemains qui chantent.*"[214]

The great prestige enjoyed by deportees in the summer of 1945 may also be seen in the twisted mirror of misplaced imitation. According to the Vosges' Catholic paper, "Some chattering socialites find it very spiritual to wear striped outfits in artificial silk. We would hope that these women who thus insult the glorious misery of our deportees follow this "fashion" to its end . . . to the end of the concentration camp, that is."[215] The editors and the socialites agreed on the honor due the deportees' sufferings, if not on the appropriate way to express it.

Accordingly, many people seem to have had a strong idea of how one should treat a returned deportee and to have been willing to enforce it. In Saint-Pierre-le-Moûtier (Nievre), for instance, two hundred people broke into an oil mill after someone there had refused to sell a repatriated political deportee a liter of oil.[216] And in Saint-Cloud (Jura) a "vast popular movement" was organized on behalf of a former mayor who had just been arrested for theft at the head of a band of young maquisards. Public opinion demanded that he be released so that he could welcome his wife when she returned from deportation. The prefect commented that "it is an easily explicable sentiment to which the judge conceded."[217] As a resistance leader the mayor might well have enjoyed wide popularity on his own behalf, but it was the unacceptable thought of his wife returning to an empty home that won him his release.

The public also showed its concern by continuing to support charities benefiting the Absents after their return.[218] One popular cause involved sending deportees on rural vacations where the fresh air and food might improve their health. In the Vosges the Communist Resistance network, the Front national, launched a campaign to give deportees a two-week vacation that enjoyed wide support from every part of the community. Arguing that "it is a duty; it is for France," the appeal asked everyone to donate money, time, or space. In Rambervillers the Class of '42 took up the cause with gusto, raising enough money so that all of the town's repatriated deportees could recuperate in the country.[219]

How deeply the popular imagination invested in stereotyped images of the moral hierarchy that turned deportees and POWs into paragons of virtue can be judged by the treatment of those repatriates who did not conform to them. In a few cases, their neighbors rejected repatriates who blatantly did not fulfill the stereotypes, despite the years or months of captivity that theoretically ennobled anyone. For example, a POW from Indre who came home with a German wife was greeted with such hostility that he had to quit the commune.[220] And in Rambervillers a schoolteacher came home from years as a POW, only to be derided in two different newspapers for not demonstrating enough hatred toward his former captors; the man had even had the nerve to compare "Young Germany" favorably to "Aged France."[221]

By August 1945, the pace and shock of the Return began to wane; if there were French men and women left in central Europe, they had fallen out of the official channels. The government announced in October that no more POWs remained in Poland or the Soviet Union, and at the end of the year it closed down the Ministry of Prisoners, Deportees, and Refugees. Communities accordingly began celebrating the collective return of their Absents with official receptions, religious services, and sports galas.[222] Indeed, banquets and dances to honor the return of POWs were so popular in Cantal that the departmental director of the provisioning service had to publish an announcement that he could not release any more food from the rationing system for them.[223]

Not everyone, however, gave up on the missing Absents. The CRR at Nancy, for instance, set up a missing persons bureau for his region that went as far as sending envoys into Germany to gather information.[224] As of August 1945, 11,756 Vosgiens had still not returned from Germany.[225] And, of course, the families of missing persons kept hoping. Some even traveled to Germany themselves, thereby provoking the prefect of Cantal to announce in December 1945 that he would not authorize any travel permits for the sake of searching for missing persons, searching for or visiting graves, visiting sick persons not on the point of death, or visiting fiancées, whose claims of pregnancy the prefect appeared to doubt as a matter of policy.[226]

Nor did the official end of the Return usher the repatriates off the political stage, where they remained because of the use to which the Gaullist mythmakers had put the deportees and, to a lesser extent, the POWs before their repatriation. In brief, at the liberation the Gaullist myth "nationalized" the Resistance by recasting the occupation as the struggle of the French people, led by the Resistance, against the foreign occupier and a mere handful of collaborators.[227] The Absents, who were undergoing a purifying suffering at the hands of the foreign enemy when de Gaulle first propagated the myth, provided its heroic model. This convenient but not wholly undeserved glorification of the Absents had several implications. First, the myth erased the distinctiveness and variety of the deportees by subsuming them all under the stereotyped image of the dedicated resistant. This served the Gaullist cause of national reconciliation by suppressing such divisive details as the fact that many deportees had been sent to their agony by *French* (not foreign) police on account of their race rather than their resistance, and that some of the Absents had gone to Germany voluntarily.[228] Whether this stereotyping served the repatriates themselves very well is debatable; it certainly did nothing to illuminate the specificity of the genocide endured by the Jews.[229]

Second, the myth unintentionally gave the Absents power over the national government's legitimacy. By making them the paragons of the Resistance and of French patriotism, the myth made them the ultimate authorities on who or what constituted Resistance. Furthermore, the myth glossed over the many divisions within the actual localized and fragmented resistance in favor of one unified Resistance, taken as Gaullist. So the repatriates, particularly the political deportees, enjoyed the unqualified and unusual position of being able to deny the Resistance qualifications, and therefore the legitimacy, of the Resistance government. Theoretically at least, the liberation-era moral hierarchy and the Gaullist myths of Resistance and unity allowed any of the 38,000 surviving political deportees to out-Resistance the First Resistant of France himself, Charles de Gaulle. None did so, but they represented a burning fuse that the government had laid within its own tower.

Any public dissension between the new regime and repatriated deportees therefore constituted a crisis, as the CRR at Dijon fully appreciated. On 14 July 1945, the first time the quintessential republican holiday was celebrated since the beginning of the war, the military authorities in Dijon refused to grant the city's deportees a place in the parade on the pretext that they did not know how to march. The deportees therefore held their own parade led by a banner that read: "Political deportees of the Côte-d'Or not allowed in the parade—Departed 1,800, Returned 200." As could be expected, the crowd showed much more enthusiasm for this rebel procession than for the punctiliously marching official parade. Alarmed by the political ramifications of separate parades, the CRR went to great lengths to heal the rift.[230]

It was, however, the economic situation that caused the most tension between the Resistance government and its most honored citizens. The repatriates' joy at their homecoming often turned into frustration when they encountered bureaucratic red tape and shortages of everything from clothes to food. In particular, the POWs experienced a shock at the state of the economy. They had left what they remembered as a prosperous nation in 1940 to return five years later to an impoverished country held to ransom by the black market. Because they had had no chance to become gradually accustomed to this change, the prices of 1945 struck them as utterly exorbitant. Furthermore, they had been told over the previous years, and were being told again in 1945, that the country owed them a debt and was grateful.[231] The laws about repatriation bonuses, the propaganda, and their own poverty gave them a sense of entitlement.

When the government did not deliver on its promises, the repatriates felt betrayed. Even more worrying for the government, others chose to feel disillusioned on the repatriates' behalf. As early as November 1944, before the Return had really begun, an editorial in *La Margeride* mocked the hullabaloo about how France loved and welcomed her POWs, when in reality all they were met with was a bloated bureaucracy that could give them nothing but a pack of cigarettes and an ill-fitting suit.[232] The dissatisfaction over that suit caused particular aggravation, even though the problem was absolute shortage rather than ill will. As a solution, the CRR at Poitiers suggested imposing a fine of a suit on every black marketeer and collaborator sentenced with national degradation, an idea that expressed the prevailing ideas of justice and the moral hierarchy in the provinces but that was not implemented by the national government.[233]

Unable or unwilling to believe in the shortages, repatriates made their discontent known through demonstrations, often with the encouragement of the PCF, which appreciated their symbolic weight.[234] Deportees in Ariège demanded larger rations in late 1945, but most protests came from POWs, who represented a considerably larger number of men.[235] Reports came in the summer of 1945 of POWs in Bayonne protesting the nonpayment of their welcome bonuses or nondelivery of their new suits, of crowds of POWs in Clermont-Ferrand searching clothing stores for hidden goods, of complaints by POWs in Limoges about the region's bread shortage, and of a committee of POWs in Loiret seizing bicycle tires at the factory. They paid for the tires with cash, but had no ration coupons, thus making their action theft. The police nevertheless decided to overlook the affair because the POWs had the support of the 1,800 factory workers.[236] In that bicycle factory at least, and undoubtedly in many other places as well, the threat inherent in the moral hierarchy and the Gaullist myths came true. The people took the repatriates' part against the government.

The physical, economic, and social insecurities of the après-libération combined with the goad of the Return to make what a Vosgien newspaper called "dangerous times," when people were attacked, even murdered, on the strength of whispered rumors identifying them as collaborators.[237] Tensions flared because over the course of the occupation and the liberation violence and illegality had become acceptable or at least omnipresent, because people were tired and hungry, and because they were disoriented in a shifting social landscape. Yet these same insecurities also created another possibility: that of renegotiating the social contract between the central government and the local community in order to create a brighter, stronger, purer future. The people of Saint-Flour, Moûtiers, and Rambervillers pursued those negotiations in the purge of collaborators, food protests, the construction of public memory, and elections. In all of them, as in the problems of crime, inflation, and displacement, they expected the new government to provide justice.

CHAPTER THREE

LEGAL JUSTICE AND THE

PURGE OF COLLABORATORS

At the liberation the French people and their new Resistance government agreed that the first order of business and first test of justice should be the purge of collaborators. Indeed, the Resistance had not only already drawn up and promulgated the legal framework of the postwar purge, but had already begun implementing it. The CFLN executed a former Vichy minister in Algiers in March 1944; resistants in the metropole summarily executed perhaps two thousand collaborators before the Normandy landings.[1] At the liberation itself, local resistants took the promises of punishment for collaborators that had been given in the clandestine press and over the BBC as both permission and command. Directly after chasing out the foreign enemy, they turned on the internal enemy in response to the pressures of public feeling and to expectations about the new government's intentions. The result was a tangle of mob violence and orderly policing.

However, despite the lurid accusations of a "savage" purge promoted through the postwar "black legend," violent purging was the exception rather than the rule at the liberation.[2] For the most part, local resistants arrested collaborators and began gathering evidence against them in anticipation of placing their cases in the hands of the central government, which they expected to provide justice against collaborators and other traitors through the state's legal mechanisms. It was only after provincials began to suspect that the government's idea of justice differed from their own that the purge split into two intertwined streams. In one, the national purge operated through the law courts and government ministries according to the dictates of Gaullist policy. In the other, the local purge followed the demands of justice constructed within the wholly local context of what had happened in a particular place during the war. Those involved in the local purge tried to enlist the courts of the national purge in their pursuit of justice, but when that effort failed they found other means, such as ostracism and vigilantism. Often called the "popular" or "extralegal" purge, the term "local purge" more accurately describes that part of the purge conducted by small towns because it indicates its parameters and its sources. Furthermore, it better suggests the essential conflict within the French purge, which was between the national and the local, not the legal and the extralegal.

During the first days of liberation, and to some extent throughout the *après-libération,* the French people and the Resistance government agreed on the reasons for having a purge, if not on the proper methods of doing it. On practical grounds, collaborators had seriously harmed the country and posed an ongoing threat to France as a potential fifth column. Indeed, it was clear that they had not all converted to republicanism or left the country at the liberation.[3] On a more abstract level, revenge and renovation also motivated the purge. Revenge would compensate for the torture inflicted by collaborators, for the terrifying years resistants had spent underground cut off from their families, and for all the humiliations of surrender and occupation. It would avenge the destruction of the nation.[4]

Although revenge as a motive has overshadowed renovation in the memory of the purge, during the après-libération resistants thought of the purge as a means to prepare for the future as much as a way to resolve the past. Indeed, resistants in Paris and in small towns all agreed that the purge was absolutely necessary for a better future.[5] In one case, a signed editorial in *Le Réveil des Vosges* argued that without a complete purge France would have only a *"drôle de paix"* (phony peace). Taking a more personal view of the nature of national renewal, *La Résistance savoyarde* feared that hopes for a better future could not be realized "if justice remains theoretical. How [can we] live without bitterness and without hatred in the vicinity of criminals and traitors, even if they are well locked up?"[6]

This common ground between the national and local purges can be seen in the matter of denunciation, which everyone harshly condemned at the liberation. Yet denunciation was an ambiguous crime that shows how quickly the moral and political sands shifted at the liberation. As Colin

Lucas has pointed out in the context of the French Revolution, the French language captures nuances in denunciation that English does not.[7] *Dénonciation* (denunciation) can be seen as a civic duty and a positive good whereas *délation* (informing) is a betrayal often accomplished under the cowardly cloak of anonymity.[8] Furthermore, the French legal system also recognizes a crime that might be translated as "malicious informing" (*dénonciation calomnieuse*). Thus the same act of bringing the authorities into the community, or a neighbor to the attention of the authorities, can be interpreted in different ways. The state can use the patriotic overtones of *dénonciation* to hunt down its political opponents; Vichy did so by exhorting its citizens to protect the *patrie* by reporting their neighbors who were communists, resistants, or BBC listeners. At the same time, and in every political context, denunciation can serve as a "weapon of the weak" through which otherwise powerless individuals such as women or the poor can avenge themselves on more powerful neighbors and relations.[9] Denunciations, of course, might also have such mundane motives as the offer of a reward or the chance to obtain property.[10] Indeed, wartime denunciations served the whole range of human greed and pettiness.[11]

Two cases reported in the local press illustrate how the weak could make use of denunciation during the occupation. In one, a woman from Cantal denounced the local subprefect and her husband, who had cheated on her, as "full-fledged communists." As an accusation of communism was tantamount to a ticket to the concentration camps under Vichy, it more than compensated for infidelity. The letter was intercepted, however, and at her postliberation trial both the husband and the subprefect requested clemency for the woman. She was sentenced to five years in prison and national degradation, a light enough penalty at a time when an informer could expect death.[12]

In the second case, a father in Chambéry reacted to his sixteen-year-old daughter's preference for German company by shaving half her head while the town was still occupied. The very next day the father was arrested, tortured, and deported to Mauthausen, where he perished. Arrested in turn after the liberation, the girl was confined to a convent until her majority by order of the Cour de Justice.[13] In addition to what these cases suggest about the effects of the occupation on family life, they both indicate the breadth of the purge's intentions. Notice that the attempt to inform mattered as much as its outcome; the Cantalienne's letter, after all, had never been delivered. In such situations, a case of denunciation engaged the purgers' desire for renovation rather than revenge. There was no need for revenge, but renovation demanded a sentence because it would be impossible to build a better future on the rot of the character weakness evidenced by informing.

It should also be noted that in the case of denunciation, not even the restricted definition of the purge courts considered collaboration to be a solely political or military stance. These were both *crimes passionnelles;* it is doubtful that either woman acted out of any concern for the Nazi cause. Yet both were convicted of collaboration, meaning that collaboration required no intellectual commitment whatsoever—only an act intended to harm a French citizen through the German or Vichy authorities. In other cases, of course, commitment alone would suffice to damn someone.

Interestingly, the practice of denunciation did not stop at the liberation, despite the very bad press it was then receiving. The new Resistance authorities demonstrated an ambiguous attitude toward the denunciations that arrived on their own desks. On the one hand, they firmly and categorically rejected any and all anonymous denunciations. For example, in Cantal both the CDL and the prefect condemned anonymous letters denouncing traffickers, clandestine balls, and the like as "a form of cowardice [that is] open to cloaking jealousy and personal hatreds, [and is] unworthy of the sense of honor that a true Frenchman should possess."[14] On the other hand, these same authorities openly welcomed accusations that were legibly signed and accompanied by an address.[15]

The postliberation denunciations directed to the Resistance authorities suggest several things. First, what mattered was the intended recipient of a denunciation and its motivation, not the act of informing. In 1945 alerting the republican prefect to a clandestine ball was a civic duty, at least so long as the signature was legible. But if the same person had addressed the same letter for the same reason to the Vichy prefect only a year earlier, it would have been treason, especially if the signature was legible. Second, it took more than a day or a liberation to change wartime habits such as violence, black marketeering, or informing on neighbors. Whether or not a purge could reverse such habits remained to be seen.

Notwithstanding their common aspirations, over the course of the après-libération the national and local purges gradually diverged in a four-stage process. In the first stage, at the liberation itself, the national and local purges were not yet estranged. The second stage, during the fall and winter of 1944–45, saw an increasing popular disillusionment with the slowness and mildness of the purge courts, which led to protests in the press and some violence. In the third stage, in early summer 1945, popular patience with the national purge ended abruptly because of the shocking stories brought home by returning victims of collaboration and a change in the central government's purge policy. This impatience often found expression in vigilantism. Nevertheless, in the fourth stage, at a time that depended wholly on local circumstances, the national government succeeded in taking control of the entire purge process.

The harmony of the national and local purges during the first stage flowed from a relative powerlessness on one side and false assumptions on the other. The national government simply did not have the authority or means to exercise strict control over the purge in the provinces in the days or weeks during which they were being liberated. The people who were in the towns and villages and exercising local authority, on the other hand, acted according to the promises of vengeance given by the Resistance in the clandestine press and radio and according to conceptions of betrayal that grew out of the local, not the national, context. It is hardly surprising that the speech makers and their audience had different notions of the ramifications of wartime promises.

Most commonly at the liberation, local purgers arrested local collaborators in order to send them before the special purge courts that had already been promulgated by the Resistance government in Algiers and that everyone knew would replace the courts-martial as soon as possible.[16] These new purge courts had a three-tier system; at the most exalted level, a Haute Cour de Justice tried such prominent men as Pétain and Laval. Despite reports in the local press, these trials stirred little comment in the provinces.[17] Prosecutors had a choice of sending more ordinary folk before either the Cours de Justice or the *chambres civiques*.[18] They could even send the same individual before both in order to compound a criminal sentence such as imprisonment with a civil sentence of "national degradation" (*dégradation nationale*) for the offense of "national unworthiness" (*indignité nationale*).[19]

The Cours de Justice were reduced versions of the French criminal Cours d'assises, employing only one judge and four lay jurors, who were drawn from lists of resistants that included women—an innovation for the time. These courts heard cases of felonies committed under the 1939 penal code, with a few modifications to prevent individuals such as informers from slipping through loopholes. Essentially, they tried criminal cases that included propagandizing in favor of the enemy, joining an enemy organization, committing acts harmful to the security of the French state, or the catch-all Article 75 that forbade consorting with the enemy with a view to favoring his endeavors. The Cours de Justice could employ the full range of penalties, including death.

The *chambres civiques*, however, had only one penalty: national degradation for five years to life. Although set up in the same manner as and under the aegis of the Cours de Justice, the *chambres civiques* tried "unworthy conduct" rather than criminal actions. Such "unworthy conduct" included activity that aided the enemy after 16 June 1940 or "any willful act of what might be termed 'lèse-liberté-égalité-fraternité,'" including belonging to a Vichy cabinet, belonging to a collaborationist organization, or writing or lecturing in favor of the enemy or of collaborationist, racist, or totalitarian doctrines.[20] A sentence of national degradation meant the loss of civic rights such as the franchise; prohibition from employment in influential positions in areas such as the civil service, banking, or journalism; exclusion from office in professional organizations; loss of rank in the armed forces; and prohibition from bearing or keeping arms. It might also include residential restrictions and confiscation of property.[21] Bourgeois individuals would naturally find such penalties far more onerous than poorer, less educated people who never had any hopes of running banks or commanding battalions. Likewise, men would have felt these restrictions more strongly than women, who had never before had a vote to lose. Indeed, national degradation symbolically degraded men to the second-class status French women had held before being enfranchised in October 1944. Public opinion generally suspected it of being no more than a derisory slap on the wrist.

After the liberation, resistants eagerly began compiling evidence and preparing testimony for use by these courts. Liberation committees in particular seem to have envisioned an active role for themselves in the purge trials as expert witnesses and references.[22] The courts, however, disappointed the public. The disgust with the courts that created the second stage of a growing estrangement between the national and local purges had three basic causes.[23] First, no courts, no matter how dedicated to the cause, could have made their way through the avalanche of cases very quickly. Furthermore, the cases could be notoriously complex because of the secret nature of Resistance activity, which occasionally hid behind seeming collaboration, and because some of the accused had played both sides of the fence and had Resistance deeds on their résumés to trump every accusation of collaboration.[24]

In addition, admissible evidence was often difficult to gather; the purge courts in the Vosges delayed their trials in part because police inspectors were being wounded while pursuing investigations in the eastern parts of the department that were still a battle zone.[25] The lack of staff and newness of the laws and even of the courts further delayed proceedings beyond the patience of many. During the après-libération, many people, such as the miners of Carmaux who threatened to strike if the purge were not completed by 30 December 1944, had wholly unrealistic expectations.[26]

Second, the reputation of the purge courts suffered from a general belief that the legal profession—from policemen, to lawyers, to judges—had compromised itself during the occupation.[27] It was far from certain that men who had enforced Vichy's harsh laws against listening to the BBC would act impartially in regard to their fellow collaborators. Indeed, the attitude of certain judges in Cantal not only caused popular protests but frustrated the prefect, who repeatedly requested their removal.[28] In September 1945 a Vosgien paper described the courts' activities as "a perfectly organized counterpurge" and "a flagrant sabotage of the purge."[29] Such suspicions became so widespread that according to the prefect of Cantal some individuals suspected that the government was using the legal purge as a political tool rather than an instrument of justice.[30]

The third cause of disillusionment lay in the courts' decisions, which appeared neither vigorous nor impartial. As the CRR at Nancy remarked, "The public who crowd into court show a very lively discontent in observing the indulgence of the verdicts rendered on traitors and collaborators, and remark that individuals prosecuted for minor trafficking in American foodstuffs are much more severely sentenced."[31] Protest over the courts' light sentences appeared in the press, in administrators' reports, and as a standard item in petitions of all sorts of local organizations. The newly elected municipal council of Rambervillers, for instance, included a complaint about the leniency of the purge in the message it sent to de Gaulle.[32] *La Résistance savoyarde* leveled a more sarcastic criticism of the national purge's idea of punishment by describing the "abominable tortures that surpass in horror anything that one could imagine" inflicted on the Parisian beau monde. For example, "M. Sacha Guitry has been obliged to perform a piece that is not one of his own. The refinement has been pushed as far as putting his name on the poster in smaller letters than those of the other performers."[33]

The public also complained that the courts punished the wrong people. For instance, Moûtiers' paper reported that a local man who had gone to Germany as a voluntary laborer received ten years of national degradation for "the crime of believing, in good faith, that his departure would mean the Return of a POW or prevent the deportation of a father of a family." At the same time, the court tried "two important personages of the collaborationist clique of Moûtiers" accused of having publicly, and in writing, supported Vichy's forced labor draft and the occupation. One had allegedly even gone so far as to report twelve Moutiérains who had placed flowers on the Monument aux Morts on 11 November 1942. Both men were acquitted, leading the editors to comment, "We will not add anything to these verdicts [that are] sufficiently eloquent except the bitter observation that was already made a while ago by a witness of the injustices of Justice: according to whether you are rich or poor, the court will make you white or black."[34]

The impression of a legal system that favored the rich grew over time as the courts gave lighter and lighter sentences for the same infractions. It was the wealthier defendants who benefited from this trend toward leniency because, as individuals who had more complicated cases owing to their positions of responsibility and who could afford to hire their own lawyers, they tended to appear in the courts at a later, more forbearing date. Instead, their underlings paid heavily for following orders. As Moûtiers' paper commented on a local case: "Once more the *lampiste* (underling) will take responsibility for the acts of the leaders (*meneurs*). After the recent acquittals of local leaders (*chefs*), one clearly feels the weakness of a justice of particularity and personality!"[35] Contrary to expectations, individuals who could be presumed to have a great deal of sympathy for collaborators seconded the criticisms of the legal purge. A Vosgien paper reported that "a woman whose son and daughter are detained at [the internment camp of] la Vierge, writes that, to be acquitted, it is necessary to be a doctor, priest or lawyer. We have also noticed this, and, for once, we unite our protest to hers; on this issue we agree."[36] That the courts satisfied neither the mothers of the accused nor the accusers suggests how thoroughly discredited they were.

By February 1946 a Vosgien paper did not have to explain its referent when calling the purge court "*l'atelier de blanchisserie*" (the whitewashing workshop).[37] The fear that "two-faced characters" would be able "by means of subterfuge to rehabilitate themselves in the eyes of the public" had appeared in the local press from the first days of liberation.[38] But the unequivocal identification of the legal purge as a mechanism for whitewashing shows its deep disrepute. Indeed, according to a longtime undercurrent of opinion, the legal purge was nothing but a charade. In remarking that Belgian resistants had released arrested collaborators as a protest, a Savoyard paper commented: "In France, it's much better. The swine (*salopards*) are not even arrested."[39]

Nevertheless, people in small towns continued to try to use the peaceful and legal means of the purge courts throughout the après-libération by submitting evidence, attending trials, sometimes quite vociferously, and voicing their protests.[40] When the purge courts in Epinal acquitted a local lawyer, for example, the CDL organized a protest march of six hundred resistants in what the CRR described as an example of the "popular outbursts of discontent" provoked by the national purge.[41] Others simply kept rearresting suspects until the authorities acceded to their demands to do something about them, whether or not the law provided for punishment. In July 1945 in Forges (Vosges), for instance, local men arrested a repatriated woman who was reputed to be a member of three collaborationist organizations, including the Milice. They took her straight to the court in Epinal, where she was released for lack of evidence because her dossier had disappeared (a distressingly common occurrence). Outraged, the CLL, which sent the communiqué to the newspaper, announced that "if this *collaboratrice* is now behind bars, it is thanks to the local committee of liberation of Forges which took charge of her arrest, without which she would still be walking about!"[42]

Before the German surrender in May 1945, CRRS and prefects could respond to such demands by placing the accused in administrative internment, which offered a deft compromise between the letter of the national purge and the spirit of the local purge.[43] Black marketeers and women accused of horizontal collaboration therefore often found themselves in what was essentially the protective custody of administrative internment. To their regret, provincial administrators lost the flexibility of administrative internment when the national government ordered the camps closed after the cessation of hostilities.

It was unfortunate that the decision to end administrative internment coincided with the Return, because it made the national purge less responsive to the demands of the local purge just as provincial opinion reached a peak of indignation and outrage over collaboration. As the prefect of Savoie remarked in explaining a riot, opinion was "particularly irritable since the Return of the deportees."[44] The combination of the emotional impact of the Grand Return and changes in national legal policies in April and May 1945 pushed most communities into the third stage of widespread opposition to, or outspoken disillusionment with, the national purge.[45]

All the complaints about the integrity of the purge courts did not themselves create the rift between the local and national purges. After all, the provincial purge courts had one foot in the local community in the form of the resistants on the juries. And, to a certain extent, the existence of the *chambres civiques* and the offense of "national unworthiness" provided a common ground for the local and national purges where both responded to a general sense that collaboration was a harmful attitude as well as a harmful activity. The real root of the alienation lay in the government's decision, for reasons of national policy, to overturn even the unsatisfactory work of the provincial purge courts with generous grants of clemency to convicted collaborators. The relevant policies reflected two concerns of the central government: standardization of the national judicial system and Gaullist mythmaking.

As could only be expected, the Ministry of Justice took a national perspective on the purge and attempted to impose some sort of standardization on the wildly differing sentences emerging from different regions.⁴⁶ As de Gaulle explained in his memoirs, this standardization was meant to preserve the impartiality of the legal system as much as possible.⁴⁷ What it meant in practice was that France carried out the mildest purge in western Europe.⁴⁸ Standardization reduced the purge to the lowest common denominator of those regions with the least aggressive purge courts, because equitable treatment required commuting sentences of every degree into lighter sentences or outright acquittals. That, in turn, meant angering local purgers and insulting communities in the regions with the most severe purges. The same concern with due process motivated the postwar directive to release as many suspects as possible, including those being held in administrative internment.

Furthermore, the national purge reflected de Gaulle's intention to use the Resistencialist myth to heal the country and get on with the future.⁴⁹ His insistence that all France had stood together in the Resistance gave him a vested interest in a purge that uncovered as few collaborators as possible. For if half of France were locked up as collaborators, how could all of France have been in the Resistance? His concern with national unity may also have motivated his decision to commute 73 percent of all death sentences as a means of reconciling the large segment of the population who had supported collaboration.⁵⁰ Although in the long term it proved to be an extraordinarily successful myth, in the short term the liberal pardon policy that supported it backfired on the new Resistance government.

The collaborators who benefited from de Gaulle's clemency had first been tried and sentenced with wide publicity by the purge courts in the departments where they had committed their gravest crimes. In contrast, "these measures of incomprehensible clemency" came from Paris in seemingly utter disregard of local feeling or provincial events.⁵¹ The coincidence of the first pardons with the Return exacerbated the sense of injustice. A petition passed by the CDL of Savoie on 2 June 1945 illustrates how provincial opinion conflated the Return and de Gaulle's pardons. It also illustrates how the local purge placed the demands of memory and honorary justice above those of due process or national policy. The petition listed five "scandalous remissions of sentences" in which three Miliciens condemned to prison were released, a fourth received a substantial reduction of his prison term, and an informer's sentence of transportation with hard labor was commuted to imprisonment. It then declared:

> Judging that in the current circumstances, at the hour when return among us our deported comrades, denounced or delivered by the Milice to the Gestapo, it is inadmissible that the guilty parties or their accomplices be set free.
>
> Remembering our FFI comrades fallen for the liberation of the territory and the deportees dead of torture in the camps in Germany, [the CDL] raises a solemn protest.
>
> [The CDL] stigmatizes (*flétrit*) the Magistrates who approved the pardons given to the condemned, and vehemently reproaches the Government for its clemency, *because at this time to pardon is to betray*.[52]

It is absolutely crucial to understanding the purge and the après-libération that because it was the national government that pardoned, it was the national government that betrayed not only the memory of the deportees and resistants but also their communities.

The consequences of the pardons and commutations for public order and the government's prestige alarmed provincial administrators.[53] The CRR at Clermont-Ferrand worried about the situation in Cantal, where not a single death sentence of the twenty-two already passed by the departmental Cour de Justice had been carried out. "These massive pardons," he explained, "satisfy no one, because the public would prefer that the sentences regularly passed in what was until now a relatively serene climate be carried out rather than to watch spectacular popular executions showing the Government's impotence to make the law respected and often striking individuals not eligible for capital punishment."[54] The prefect of Hérault also reported that "the pardons granted by the President to informers (*mouchards*) [who are] particularly hated in the department and condemned to death by the Cour de Justice, have produced an undeniably deplorable effect. The discontent of the public has turned into indignation."[55]

The general indignation over the national government's disregard for the decisions of its own provincial courts did not rely solely on the shock of the Return for its strength but continued throughout the après-libération. In December 1945 a signed article from Rambervillers expressed the "stupor and indignation" with which the town had received the news of the pardon of a man associated with the deportation of its football team. "Here is what you could call a challenge to our deportees, resistants, and all who have suffered at the hands of the Nazis' accomplices. It is necessary that it be known in high places that such a measure is not made to calm spirits that are already very excited." The article ended with an appeal to deportees and resistants that they "join in our protest and that it be understood, so that such things that dishonor the Republic are not repeated. Or then, that no one be astonished to see the people render justice themselves."[56] The article captured the essence of the conflict between the national and local purges remarkably well. It expressed both the desire for revenge and for a better, republican future that motivated the purge as well as articulating the local purge's demand for a fuller justice, in this case one that recognized the requirements of honorary justice. At the same time, it explained that the government was driving the people into taking justice into their own hands by its policies that not only insulted the resistants' sacrifices but also "dishonored" the republic for which they had made those sacrifices.

The example of how national and local purgers dealt with the Milice illustrates both how they operated in practice and how Gaullist policy alienated local purgers. The Milice have had a well-earned, profoundly black reputation; at the liberation both national and local purgers agreed on their criminal nature.[57] Yet to bring them to justice would be a long crusade: the first assassination of a Milicien took place within only three months of the unit's creation in 1943; the last trial of a Milicien, Paul Touvier, formerly a senior officer of the Savoyard Milice, took place fifty-one years later, in 1994. Some of the earliest cases in the purge courts were of Miliciens who were sentenced to death, often on the rather circumstantial evidence of information found in Milice offices and often in absentia because the defendants were in hiding or in Germany. The courts tried a second round of Milice cases in 1945 when more reliable information became known and the defendants were caught.

The press of the après-libération kept a close eye on the fate of Miliciens; it published membership lists as they were discovered and full reports of trials.[58] It is significant, however, that despite the evil reputation of the Milice, the label "Milicien" did not suffice in itself to secure a condemnation, even in Savoie. In several cases, local papers happily announced the exonerations of accused Miliciens. Around the same time as Savoyards were issuing vigorous protests against de Gaulle's decision to pardon some Miliciens, the spectators in the Cour de Justice applauded, and *La Résistance savoyarde* warmly approved, the court's decision to acquit a young man whose name had been found on the Milice's rolls but who had actually commanded a reconnaissance unit in the FFI.[59]

Cantal also had some complex cases in which a man had used the Milice as a cover for Resistance activities. For instance, the *chambre civique* of Cantal rehabilitated two brothers whose names had appeared on the Milice's rolls because they had aided the Resistance and Jews. As a doctor, one of them had delivered six hundred medical excuses to young men trying to avoid the labor draft.[60] Nonetheless, it often happened that when the courts failed to convict a Milicien of whose guilt the community was convinced, local purgers took justice into their own hands. Aware of the likelihood of violence, the CRR at Clermont-Ferrand decided to release Miliciens who had not been active, as he was required to do by the government, but to banish them from their home department "in order to avoid local incidents."[61]

Administrators' fears about public order were later fully justified when accused Miliciens became the targets of vigilante bomb attacks; indeed, their very presence could lead to rioting, brawling, or even murder. Such violence became almost predictable, as when, in October 1945, the police arrested ten Savoyard Miliciens in Marseille, including three men from Moûtiers or the immediate vicinity, and transported them back to Savoie to stand trial. "On their arrival in Chambéry, Monday at 7:59 P.M. the ten Miliciens were awaited by two to three hundred persons who hurled themselves on the carriage containing the Miliciens. The guard was overwhelmed, and there were bloody fights in the two compartments. All the Miliciens were wounded."[62] Whether the mob meant to punish the Miliciens themselves or to warn the authorities to do so hardly matters. No crowd would have gathered at the train station if the local purgers had been confident that the national purge would deliver justice as they understood it.

This was not the only riot over Miliciens in Savoie, nor the only bloodshed. As late as October 1946, more than two years after the Milice had fired their last shot in the department, the gendarmerie of Albertville answered a midnight call from the proprietor of a village bar. When they arrived, they discovered that "a certain effervescence reigned among the young people standing about in front of the bar." As the manager explained the situation, "an individual was recognized as having worn the insignia of the Milice. He was immediately violently attacked (*lynché*) by the gathering," but was rescued and locked in a side room "to remove him from public view." The gendarmes felt it best to take the man into custody.

The ringleader of the attackers stated that he had met the accused one day during the occupation in Grenoble wearing a Milice uniform and bragging of attending the Ecole des cadres at Uriage. He therefore felt that he should take the accused to the police. The thirty-five-year-old suspect admitted that he had worn the despised uniform but claimed that he had done so only to impress a girl and denied ever actually participating in any Milice activities whatsoever. Because his father had died in 1943, he had not joined the Resistance, but he had lent them his mule and joined the FFI in September 1944. He had been transferred to the regular First Army in November 1944 and been demobilized in February 1946. Taking their investigation to the man's home village, the gendarmes talked to two farmers who were amazed to learn that the accused, who they hinted was a little slow, was supposed to have been in the Milice. They confirmed that he had lent the Resistance his mule and had fought in the FFI and army. The gendarmes then called the public prosecutor, who referred them to the military authorities, before regretfully concluding that they had to release the man because he had not done anything warranting arrest.[63] Yet the crowd in the bar and the gendarmes must have felt otherwise. The gendarmes, after all, chose to arrest and investigate the man who was beaten senseless, not the aggressors. Perhaps they did not accept the man's FFI service as proof of his patriotism because it began so late, in September 1944, after much of the fighting in the department was over. The explosion of anger in the bar indicates both the strength of local feeling against the Milice in Savoie and the duration of and wide support for a local sense of justice.

The circumstances in which a community reached the fourth stage of abandoning the local purge in favor of the national purge varied by location. Because the war had spared them its worst tragedies, some communities had never been terribly alienated from the government's purge. Other local purges subsided because of a popular disgust with the consequences of violence, and yet others because of superior governmental force. In certain cases, individuals resorted to the authorities to stop local purges that they had begun to fear might turn against themselves.[64] By the time de Gaulle resigned in January 1946, the national purge had all but won its bid to stand as the official interpretation of collaboration and its penalties. But it had not managed to persuade the French people that it acted according to justice as well as the law.[65]

Why did people in small towns find the government's purge inadequate despite its 124,613 sentences and 768 executions?[66] Although national and local purgers agreed on the necessity of a purge, they parted ways over the fundamental questions of how to define and determine guilt. The national purge approached both these problems as judicial matters to be resolved through bureaucratic procedure and due process of law. The local purge took both a broader and a narrower perspective. It was broader because local purgers wanted the purge to respond to the demands of social and honorary justice in preference to the rules of juridical justice. It was narrower because while the national purge attempted to maintain a single standard throughout France and worried about the country's international reputation, the local purge rarely set its sights as far as the departmental border. The local purge demanded justice for what had happened here, in this town, to these people.

In particular, the local purge demanded honorary and social justice as well as legal justice; indeed, local purgers scarcely distinguished between the three. Champions of honorary justice who felt that honoring the Resistance martyrs and deportees necessitated avenging their sufferings wanted the purge to punish collaborators for the heroes' sake. In this sense, the purge became a debt owed to those who had paid, or were then in the concentration camps paying, such a high price for the liberation. The prefect of Cantal relayed one version of this debt view of the purge when he summarized the departmental press as saying: "Their [partisans of liberty] blood cries for vengeance . . . and the French traitors who took us to the edge of the abyss must pay."[67] Other proponents of the debt view presented the purge as something that had to be accomplished before the deportees returned from the concentration camps or that, at the very least, society owed to the bereaved families.[68]

The demands of the local purge came not just from resistance activists or bereaved relatives, but from entire communities. As the national gendarmerie report for late 1944 explained. "The mass of the French demand not only the rapid and pitiless punishment of those miserable creatures in the foreigner's pay, but also the 'purge' of those who, misled by a pernicious propaganda, supported the presence of the invader without reacting."[69] The CRR at Angers agreed: "It is not so much a repression of collaboration that they want as a repression of activities judged antinational."[70]

But what exactly constituted "antinational activity"? A Vosgien newspaper defined the Resistance's "worst enemies, the demi-traitors, *attentistes,* and opportunists without courage . . . [as] those who, without having committed enormous crimes, visited with sympathy the occupation troops, refused them nothing, serving them, if they were merchants, before Frenchmen, approved, without participating in it, Vichy's propaganda campaign, found nothing to say against the persecution of the Jews, [and] of freemasons, rejoiced in their hearts and saw nothing wrong in labeling the *réfractaires* of the maquis as terrorists."[71]

Although such accusations could intersect with the "unworthy behavior" considered by the *chambres civiques,* the proponents of the local purge wanted to go much further by defining collaboration as betrayal. This was not treason against the nation, which was covered under the legal purge, but betrayal of the community during a time of crisis. Betrayal for the sake of personal profit made the offense even more unpardonable. In this sense, the national purge punished crimes while the local purge punished transgressions. Certain people, such as Miliciens and informers, obviously fell under both the national and local definitions. Others, such as black marketeers, posed more ambiguous cases. The neighbors saw black marketeering as betrayal; the authorities saw it as infringement of the criminal code. Still other offenses completely escaped the government's net but fell squarely into the community's, such as, in particular, what was known as "horizontal collaboration," "intimate relations with the enemy," or, occasionally, "sentimental collaboration"—in other words, sleeping with the enemy.

Since the early days of the liberation, when Robert Capa and other journalists took their famous photographs of women having their heads shaved or being paraded through town naked and tarred with the swastika, horizontal collaboration has been inextricably linked to head shavings.⁷² Yet to understand what the concept of horizontal collaboration reveals about the local purge, it is first necessary to understand that women were also sent through the judicial mechanisms of the national purge, although in lesser numbers than men and occasionally for different reasons. For instance, a seventy-three-year-old woman was arrested in Cantal for being the mother of a Milice leader.⁷³ Another woman was arrested on various charges, but the one that seemed most telling at the time and appeared in the newspaper was "having been one of the [girl]friends of the sinister V——, Gestapo agent at Clermont-Ferrand."⁷⁴ Furthermore, local purgers also used head shaving to punish a variety of offenses, such as denunciation and voluntary labor in Germany.⁷⁵

At the liberation in 1944, shaving the heads of collaborationist women struck many French men and women as a natural and appropriate activity. In its first issue, the newspaper of the CDL of Savoie reported a "Just punishment—A certain number of women and girls who had trafficked in their charms with the late occupiers have been severely corrected by the Chambérien population. The arrest of these black sheep was followed by a radical shearing."⁷⁶ Indeed, the head shavings seemed so unproblematic that the police in Maurs (Cantal) could report that a notorious collaboratrice had her head shaved almost a year after the liberation in June 1945 but that no violence was committed against her.⁷⁷ That a head shaving could be understood as being nonviolent indicates how little personal autonomy women, and especially collaboratrices, exercised at the time and how pervasive violence had become.

Yet some did argue against head shaving. Catholic newspapers in different parts of France, for example, reprinted an article from September 1944 that updated the biblical story of the adulterous woman about to be stoned. In this version a woman in a newly liberated town is about to have her head shaved for sleeping with a German when, invited to cast the first stone, her persecutors slink off because all had somehow betrayed the community themselves: one was involved with the black market, another had cheated on her POW husband, and a third had tried to get a post with Vichy but failed.⁷⁸ More directly, the CLL of Albertville publicly disowned any acts of violence, particularly head shavings.⁷⁹

Why did the French turn to head shaving in the middle of the twentieth century? Why mark some people with a physical sign of humiliation and ostracism and send others into the modern state's criminal justice system? Alain Brossat suggests that the image of the male resistant shaving the head of a female who had chosen a German man over a French man was a reassertion of patriarchy after the occupation and all the humiliations it represented for French masculinity.[80] He further argues that the *tondues* (women whose heads were shaved) must be understood within the long tradition of the *fête populaire* and carnival that set the world right through rituals of inversion.[81] But Brossat only considers the first exhilarating days of liberation in the summer of 1944.

Among other things, the use of head shavings in 1944–45 reveals the state's weakness at the close of the Second World War and the divorce between the national and local purges. Because the state temporarily lost its monopoly on force, justice devolved back to the community. In some instances the communities chose to hand the power of punishment back to the state by arresting individuals and gathering evidence against them. In other instances, communities chose to exercise justice themselves with lynchings or head shavings in a manner more familiar to the eighteenth than the twentieth century. The ritual humiliation and violence of head shaving may well seem barbaric, but it would be well to keep in mind E. P. Thompson's words about a similar eighteenth-century ritual: "Rough music belongs to a mode of life in which some part of the law belongs still to the community and is theirs to enforce. . . . Because law belongs to people, and is not alienated, or delegated, it is not thereby made necessarily more 'nice' and tolerant, more cozy and folksy. It is only as nice and tolerant as the prejudices and norms of the folk allow."[82]

Indeed, head shaving belongs to neither France nor the liberation, but to a much older European-wide tradition going back to a time when justice inscribed the bodies of offenders with their transgression.[83] Tacitus thus reports that the German tribes shaved the heads of adulterous women.[84] In France, the early modern state punished and marked prostitutes by shaving their heads. As the state moved away from marking the body to other types of punishment such as incarceration, head shaving disappeared from the official roster of discipline. Yet it remained in the popular notion of justice. Whether because, unlike a prison, head shaving is readily available to almost anyone with the desire to punish or because it answers some more abstract need, it has continued to play a role in the repertoire of the "rough music" of community rituals of justice. In December 1769, for example, a London crowd seized a spy, cut off his hair, and attempted to cut off his ears before the Foot Guard rescued him.[85] Two centuries later in August 1997, three women in Delaware, Ohio, seized a convicted child molester and shaved his head as part of a more elaborate physical punishment for the crime they obviously did not consider sufficiently expiated by a prison sentence.[86]

Within this long history, there was a notable resurgence of head shaving in both popular and official punishment in the early twentieth century. After the First World War, Germans in the Rhineland shaved the heads of women who slept with French occupation troops.[87] Later Nazi law allowed for the public head shaving of German women as part of the punishment for having sexual relations with foreign men.[88] Across the continent during the Spanish Civil War, nationalists routinely shaved the heads of republican women of all ages, not for their personal conduct but for having allowed republican ideas into their families.[89] Then during the Second World War, the Polish and Greek Resistances dealt with some female collaborators by shaving their heads.[90] After the war, during the Allied occupation, German men shaved the heads of German women for fraternizing with Allied soldiers.[91] The importance of the head shavings has to do not only with the personal tragedy they entailed but also with what they reveal about the breakdown of the modern state and the mental habits of its citizens under the pressures of the Second World War.

Why did local purgers insist on the existence of the crime of horizontal collaboration and why did they often punish it with head shaving? In the first place, some of the *tondues* were censured for their love affairs both because they had had love affairs and because their lovers were German.[92] The contemporary gender order made women responsible for maintaining honor by denying sexual access to themselves to anybody but their husbands, thus exposing any woman engaged in an extramarital affair to community disapproval. During the occupation, public opinion and the government amply demonstrated this by carefully monitoring the social lives of POW wives and being ready to condemn these effectively abandoned women for the slightest lapse in a rigid code of moral conduct.[93] But to stray from that code with a German magnified the lapse, turning everyday adultery into collaboration of the mundanely immoral sort—horizontal collaboration. There were certainly more evil ways of collaborating, such as murdering and torturing, but none as accessible to the pedestrian imagination of the self-righteous. It was very easy to condemn a woman for fornication; in fact in 1944–45 the civil court in Saint-Flour heard at least one such case.[94] It was even easier to condemn a woman who compounded that sin with aiding and abetting the enemy.

Horizontal collaboration further offended public opinion by betraying the nation. Women, and control over them, were as much a symbolic battlefield in occupied France as in other places at other times. So the warlike metaphors for sex that are even stronger in French than in English helped to catapult the scandal of fornication into treason. It was as if each time a woman "surrendered" (in 1940 or after) to a German, she allowed herself (and France as epitomized in the female symbol of Marianne) to be "conquered" by the German army all over again.[95] Such metaphorical jumps would have been easy to make in occupied France while the collaborationists announced the country's happy future as the Third Reich's "bride." Once a woman's affair with a German became public knowledge, it was immediately susceptible to such symbolic links and exaggerations and therefore to becoming treason.

On a less abstract level, horizontal collaboration betrayed the community because it demonstrated a lack of solidarity on the part of the woman with her community in its time of trouble. She did not, for instance, wait for a suitable French man to come back from a POW camp or out of hiding, but instead chose a foreigner, which might in itself cause talk even if the foreigner were not also an enemy. Worse, in many cases the woman benefited materially from her rejection of the community. Her German lover might have taken her to restaurants and entertainments unavailable to her neighbors, or he might have given her gifts of scarce food and clothing. Anecdotal evidence suggests that the women who had their heads shaved were those who flaunted the benefits of their liaisons without sharing them, as well as those who used those liaisons to harm others.

The local purge therefore had a category of betrayal known as horizontal collaboration that was associated with women. It required a punishment involving shaming because it involved sexual misconduct, the treasonous aspects of which called for the extreme—but, in the end, temporary and not physically disabling—shaming of head shaving. In the first days of liberation when local purgers acted, as they thought, in the government's stead, they shamed women guilty of horizontal collaboration quite openly and with every confidence that they were acting appropriately. Why they also chose to shave the heads of other female collaborators such as informers, whose crime did not similarly necessitate shaming, cannot be determined from the available evidence. Perhaps they only shaved the heads of informers they thought had not done enough harm to merit legal proceedings or against whom they had no legal evidence. Perhaps they also meant to invoke the aspect of purification that head shaving has carried since biblical times. If so, head shaving would have been a ritual of reintegration into the community as well as of punishment for all the *tondues*, whatever their crimes. Or perhaps head shaving was so much a part of the formula of a "proper" liberation that, not having a horizontal collaborator in town (as many places in the south that had not been occupied by Germans necessarily would not), they shaved a vulnerable woman suspected of another type of collaboration just to do things right.

Although the national authorities refused to accept the local purge's category of horizontal collaboration, public opinion in the form of head shavings and citizen's arrests forced provincial administrators to bend the rules of the national purge enough to accommodate the local purge in order to protect the accused women.[96] The CRR at Clermont-Ferrand, for example, directed the region's prefects to channel women "reproached with having had relations with members of the occupation troops" into the *chambres civiques*.[97] Such a move would have both shielded the women from the harsher sentences of the Cours de Justice and protected them from head shavings and other signs of public displeasure by putting them out of harm's way in internment camps while they awaited their hearings. As a result, a woman servant in Cantal found herself sentenced to twenty years' national degradation for the noncrime of horizontal collaboration.[98]

However, appeasing local purgers and protecting the women with administrative internment only worked until the end of the war, when the internment camps were emptied. At that point, unfortunately during the inflammable period of the Return, women accused, and perhaps convicted, of horizontal collaboration and other betrayals went back to their communities. The continuing sense that horizontal collaboration deserved punishment can be seen in the alarmed reports in the local press that women who had had their heads shaved at the liberation had returned to public view, often on the arms of French soldiers. It can also be seen in the presence of such women among the victims of vigilantes.[99] The gap between the local purge's insistence on defining collaboration as a transgression, particularly as a betrayal of the community, and the national purge's equal insistence on prosecuting crimes explains why head shavings persisted into 1946, and why they evolved from public rituals into masked, vigilante attacks.[100]

That gap also explains the persistence of a local purge after the elaborate mechanisms of the national purge began to function and the central government reestablished its control. If determined local purgers failed to co-opt those mechanisms, they had two options left: ostracism and violence. Much of the local purge must have gone on as ostracism on the unrecorded level of snide remarks, averted eyes, and petty feuding. Such poisoned daily interactions left traces only when they resulted in tragedies such as the October 1945 case of a former resident of Moûtiers, then living in Chambéry, who injured his wife and killed himself and his teenage daughter. The report explained that the man "had become depressed since the liberation for fear of reprisals."[101] It is impossible to tell from the article, which goes on to praise the man's musical skill, whether he had reason to fear a vigilante attack or whether he had been driven mad by ostracism.

More obviously, at a time when most of the actively engaged segment of the population had recently been involved in armed struggle and the central government's authority was weak, frustration with the national purge and its courts led almost inevitably to violence. Indeed, in its forms and targets, some of that violence formed a continuum with the Resistance's clandestine struggle. As resistants had had to use violent punishment during the occupation because they had no access to state-controlled alternatives such as incarceration, so postliberation vigilantes used violence when they felt they had no access to other, more peaceful punishments. The times and places where resistants or vigilantes could impose fines were rare; they never could imprison anyone for any length of time.

The violence after the liberation, however, was not meant to overthrow the state but to influence its policies. In the first stage of the purge, before the split between the local and national purges, such violence did not act against the government's purge but in its stead, thereby reflecting the mistaken assumptions of local purgers about what the government intended to do. Very soon, however, such violence was intended either to influence or to replace the national purge. Violent incidents occasionally served to protect local purgers against government prosecution, but for the most part they targeted individuals who were released by the legal system but hardly forgiven by their communities.[102] In this way, local purgers inflicted the penalty that they felt the authorities should have imposed. In some particularly troubled places, such as Savoie in late 1945, local purgers were so utterly disillusioned with the national purge that they preempted its anticipated failure by attacking collaborators already in government custody.

Not all of France, however, shared Savoie's experiences or made similar demands. The development of the local purge and its negotiations with the national purge varied from town to town and village to village because it depended so heavily on local events and local personalities. Local discontent with the national purge also involved concurrent factors that varied by region, such as troubles in the local food supply and the return, or nonreturn, of local deportees. The stories of the purge in Saint-Flour, Rambervillers, and Moûtiers suggest the array of possibilities inherent in a constellation of local purges as well as the common features of head shavings, ostracism, vigilantism, and an attempted reliance on the national purge courts.

Having for the most part been spared the daily irritations of active collaboration and prizing order above all, purgers in Saint-Flour relied on ostracism and the courts more than on violence. The much more complicated local purge in Rambervillers, however, reflected the realities of having lived with the enemy for over four years. Purgers, for instance, emphasized the everyday economic collaboration of shopkeepers. In their turn, the Rambûvetais public demonstrated a subtle understanding of collaboration that refused to lump all types of it together. The Moûtiérains, on the other hand, lived in the midst of a notorious vigilantism, motivated by their insistence on vengeance for the depredations of the guerrilla war Savoie had just endured.

SAINT-FLOUR

In 1947 the subprefect of Saint-Flour summarized the purge there as "seeming to have occurred without excessive violence or marked injustice. The day of the Liberation, there were a number of arrests but not a single execution, and there were none of those [self-proclaimed] courts-martial that, in other departments, anticipated in a regrettable fashion the action of the Cours de Justice."[103] In 1944–45, however, relative calm excluded neither bomb attacks nor ostracism. Saint-Flour saw both, but its purge differed from the other towns' in its calm and its confidence in, or at least reliance on, the national purge.

On the morning after the final German withdrawal, 25 August 1944, a crowd gathered to watch the head shavings of four or five women in a common public ritual that left no mark on contemporary local records. It reappeared in 1983, however, when the gendarmerie blasted their way into a home in the upper town in order to evict the tenants. They found a fifty-eight-year-old woman, her forty-three-year-old brother, the decaying corpse of a long-dead brother, and mountains of garbage. At the liberation the woman, then a twenty-year-old telephone operator, had had her head shaved for denouncing a maquis, possibly unwittingly. Her parents, and after their deaths, her brothers, had devoted their lives to continuing the symbolic exclusion signified by the girl's *tonde* until it consumed them all.[104]

The head shaving itself and this particular tragedy remain shrouded in mystery, but it is possible that the ceremony took place under the quasi-official aegis of the town's Purge Commission, presumably composed of resistants and part of the CAL. The committee's laconic reports in the town paper indicate that it acted as a screening commission: it decided who would or would not be sent before the officially sanctioned court-martial in Aurillac or the anticipated Cour de Justice. The commission recommended an appropriate destination for each of the accused within the national purge; yet its reasoning indicated a certain independence from the national purge. In one case, the committee stated that "even though no crime or misdemeanor has been established against C——, the Commission considers that in a town where twenty-five hostages were executed, it is intolerable to see a supposed Frenchman fraternize with the boches or the Miliciens. It advises that the dossier be forwarded to the Prefect for long-term administrative internment." If the town had been spared the execution of twenty-five men at the Pont de Soubizergues, would such fraternization have been acceptable? Or would it merely have merited the lower-level punishment of shunning instead of legal action? In another case, "With a majority vote, the Commission advises that R——, being a notorious black marketeer against whom no act of treason seems to be established, should nonetheless be interned administratively. Individual of low morality and without a respectable means of existence."[105] Black marketeering and the additional disreputability of being "without a respectable means of existence" evidently overruled the acknowledged lack of treasonous activity.

These and similar reports suggest how dependent the local purge could be on the politics of community reputation and how one's prior reputation helped to shape the public interpretation of one's wartime activities. The black marketeer, for example, was doubly damned for being "without a respectable means of existence"—in other words, poor, landless, and not a "respectable" member of the community. Similarly, a woman condemned to death for denunciation was described as being a "loose woman, divorcée." Another alleged informer, only seventeen years old, was described as a "vicious kid" who had "an aplomb not often found in her sex and at her age, and she seemed haughty and disdainful."[106] The court had mercy on the girl, sentencing her to fifteen years' transportation with hard labor, but the journalist did not forgive her unladylike character. Although the reports do not explain whether the commission evoked flaws such as being divorced as a justification for a purge charge or an explanation of the accused's misdeeds, they reveal how thoroughly the local purge was based in the community with its well-established opinions about individuals and families and standards of respectability.

The crucial importance of reputation during the après-libération can be seen in the number of clarifications published in the local press throughout the country by or on behalf of individuals apparently suspected of collaboration. In some instances individuals announced that the courts had recently condemned someone with a similar name but that they themselves were free of suspicion.[107] In other cases people named in trial accounts issued the clarifications that, contrary to erroneous reports, they had acted as witnesses rather than as defendants.[108] There were even several instances in which the police or military authorities formally cleared the name of a woman or man, such as the maquisard who was "accused by public rumor" of having denounced a maquis unit. His captain wrote to "certify that the very serious inquiry made into this matter has completely cleared F——, who fulfilled all his duty in this affair and in whom all his FFI comrades can keep their full esteem."[109] Not everyone, however, could secure such an authoritative exoneration.

In another example of the politics of reputation at play in the local purge, four neighbors found themselves at the magistrate's court in Saint-Flour in February 1945. Three of the men were charged with having assaulted the fourth. "They declare that P—— spread the rumor that they were Miliciens and treated them as such on 24 September when they arrived at work. B—— admits punching him in the nose. And it bled, says he. C—— hit him twice, and he deserved it, he adds. H—— didn't do anything. He was released. The two accused who took it upon themselves to do justice will each pay a fine of five hundred francs and together will pay five hundred francs in damages to their victim the plaintiff."[110] The incident hints at the tremendous social stigma attached to being labeled a collaborator, and especially a Milicien, and at the ways in which the rhetoric of collaboration permeated social relationships, perhaps even reclothing old feuds in new insults.

Not everyone in Cantal, however, stopped at character assassination. The first vigilantism appeared in Saint-Flour the week of 11 November 1944, when someone cut the Saint-Flour–Aurillac telephone line and exploded bombs at the properties of a butcher, a *cafetier*, and a lawyer. The first report of the bombings in the departmental daily said that two of the targets had been acquitted by the court-martial; the second report made the correction that the targets had served as witnesses in the trial of the local Milice chief, presumably for the prosecution.[111] Given that vigilantes often attacked individuals acquitted or released by the courts, that misunderstanding may help to explain the motives for this particular attack. In a confidential report, the prefect stated that "it is a matter of public notoriety that the attacks . . . would have been provoked by extremist elements belonging to the Resistance." Indeed, the police had stopped their investigations for that reason. The prefect concluded that the bombs and the rumors about their origin were having "a deplorable influence on the morale of the population," the proof of which he felt to be the low subscription to the liberation loan at the market the following day.[112] If the prefect was right in connecting investment in the new regime's bonds with confidence in it, the low subscription confirms both the anxious atmosphere of the time and an early skepticism about the efficacy of the national purge.

The next bomb exploded in Saint-Flour on a March night at the home of a teacher. The gendarmes concluded from the minor damage (three cracked windows) that "it was a matter of a simple demonstration and that the author or authors of the misdemeanor did not want to harm [the target] but to impress him." The victim had belonged to the Pétainist veterans' organization, the Legion, and was known as a royalist and collaborator; indeed, he had encouraged his students to follow the *maréchal* and had punished them for drawing the Gaullist cross of Lorraine in their notebooks. He had also been the subject of a political investigation the previous September and been implicated in a sex scandal in January 1945.[113] Whether his Pétainism alone, without the sex scandal, would have provoked a bomb attack cannot be determined. Around the same time, the prefect reported unspecified "sabotages" in and around Saint-Flour that indicated a certain disgruntlement in town.[114] In July 1945, the last explosion in Saint-Flour ripped through *La Margeride*'s print shop. Given that the target was a leader in the Resistance establishment, it is hard to see this as a vigilante attack unless it expressed a very serious rift in the local resistance over the ration-ticket scandal then in progress. It might have been an accident, a personal squabble disguised as a vigilante attack, or even, as the report in the victim's newspaper sarcastically suggested, the work of the fifth column.[115]

Although distressing enough, in the context of the après-libération these attacks add up to negligible vigilantism and a quiet local purge. Interestingly, the department also experienced a quiet national purge. Only one person from the subprefecture received a death sentence, out of only twenty-three for the entire department, compared to ninety-three capital sentences in Savoie and fifty-eight in the Vosges.[116] Indeed, in his reports to Paris the prefect expressed considerable disgust with the delaying tactics and timidity of Cantal's Cour de Justice. Why did the leniency of the national purge in Cantal not provoke a more rigorous local purge as happened elsewhere?

The calmness of Saint-Flour's purge appears to have been due to popular disinterest and strong leadership. The case for popular disinterest comes from circumstantial evidence. First, except for the summer of 1944, collaboration did not cause a great deal of direct harm in Cantal. Indeed, the atrocities of the liberation were mostly the work of Germans, not of their collaborators. Furthermore, many of the victims were strangers. Only nine of the twenty-five *fusillés* of the Pont de Soubizergues, for example, were local men; the bereaved and angry relatives of the remaining sixteen would have been crying out for justice somewhere else. *La Margeride* published periodic reports on the attempt to try the responsible German officer as a war criminal, but that was not a matter for the purge. Collaboration, then, would not have seemed as damning to Cantaliens as to Savoyards, who had suffered considerable losses at the hands of Miliciens. This may explain why the CDL received what it considered to be a distressing number of testimonials on behalf of accused collaborators.[117] Second, evidence of a lingering sympathy for Vichy appeared in the postliberation presence of anti-Resistance groups in the Cantalien hills and in the October 1945 election of a high-ranking Vichy official to the Constituent Assembly. A populace that did not understand most forms of collaboration as betrayal would neither call for, nor give the necessary support to, an active local purge.

The second reason for a calm local purge was to be seen in every issue of the local press. Leaders from all factions of the community actively discouraged vigilantism or any other type of extralegal action. For example, on 11 November 1944, *La Margeride* published a signed editorial by a Resistance leader in response to the triple bombing a few nights before. Acknowledging that such gestures stemmed from a growing discontent with the legal purge, he nevertheless argued that "we are free; we are in the Light. And if, yesterday during the night of oppression, the realization of our revolutionary ideal depended on our arms, it should depend today only on our union and our will. It is at the heart of our legal organizations that, all unified and powerful, we must fight to create a new world, a just world, like [the one] dreamed of by our heroic dead (*grands morts*)." He maintained further that "the purge of loathsome traffickers and abject informers (*mouchards*) must be pursued by legal means if we do not want to lead our country to an abyss where its unity and grandeur will founder."[118]

La Margeride's editorial policy also helped to calm local purgers by creating confidence in the national purge. The paper printed exposés of collaborators, but it also devoted much more space to purge trials than the Savoyard or Vosgien press, thus creating the somewhat false impression of an active legal purge in the department. The almost weekly reports of purge trials in *La Margeride* exhibited the satisfying tendency of announcing severe punishments meted out to Miliciens or informers, but they generally omitted negative commentary on acquittals. The more embellished reports execrated the villainy of the defendants and praised the "mastery and impartiality" or the "habitual talent" of the lawyers and judges involved.[119] Moreover, the Abbé Lissorgues, the reactionary rival of Resistance leader and editor Amarger, agreed with Amarger on the necessity of trusting the purge to the authorities. *La Voix du Cantal*'s report of the November bombing called the authors "terrorists," as Vichy had called resistants who committed similar acts. It also presented a quotation from the national Catholic paper *Temps présent* that called vigilantism "banditry" and a failure of the authorities to stop "the arbitrary vigilantes (*justiciers*)" nothing but "pure Nazism."[120]

In marked contrast to their colleagues in the Vosges, but in greater conformity with the party line, even the Communists of Cantal joined in the official condemnation of extralegal justice. In April 1945, the regional bureau of the PCF defended itself from the public rumor that it had caused an explosion in the departmental capital by disowning any such "deplorable attack" that risked injuring innocents and by blaming the bombing on the "Aurillaçois fascists who have not disarmed," thus further contributing to the local fear of a counter-Resistance.[121] The Communist section of Saint-Flour followed suit by denouncing the two-week-old bombing of the teacher's house, although on practical rather than idealistic grounds. They explained that the bomb was wrong because it had hurt a bona fide resistant, the professor's landlord, whose property had been damaged. But they concluded: "We energetically object to such proceedings that now seem outdated, at the least, and only create suspicion, trouble, and discord at the very moment that we have such a great need to unite in order to finish the war advantageously."[122]

Whatever the reason—whether lack of motivation or lack of tolerance by otherwise squabbling community leaders—the purge had faded from the public forum by the late summer of 1945. The press protested against a handful of pardons, but overall, Saint-Flour skipped the third stage of violent reaction. The town easily entered the final stage of accepting the national purge because the rift between the local and national purges had never been great in a community that had few outstanding grievances against collaborators and little tolerance for violence.

RAMBERVILLERS

In contrast to circumstances in Saint-Flour, the occupation of Rambervillers had been intense, severe, and costly in deaths and deportations. The presence of a German garrison in Rambervillers also meant that much of the perceived collaboration there took an economic form, such as favoring a German clientele over French customers. In further contrast, after the liberation most of the Vosgien press demanded a harsh purge, sometimes calling for vigilantism outright rather than working to create confidence in the legal system. Nonetheless, although Rambervillers had its vigilantes, the very intensity of the German occupation there seems to have nuanced opinion about the purge by making everyone aware of the shades of gray inherent in most collaboration. If Saint-Flour showed the least tension between the national and local purges, Rambervillers showed the most tension within the local purge.

On 30 September 1944, events in Rambervillers followed what had already become the accepted pattern of liberation. After chasing out the Germans, resistants arrested local collaborators and shaved the heads of a few women. The diaries and reports from Rambervillers, however, suggest that this first official purge action was not the centerpiece of liberation that it has become in the stereotypical memory of that occurrence. Mme. Frachet, for example, did not mention the purge at all in her careful log of artillery exchanges.[123] In this civilian's mind, the real and present danger of the battle completely overshadowed the more abstract threat of collaboration. Another woman, Mme. Garner, did not mention any arrests in her diary until 3 October, when she noted them as an afterthought: "There are now new troops in Rambervillers, naturally there were sanctions almost immediately [after] the liberation of the town: imprisonment of collaborationists or [those] suspected of being so, and then the shaved heads of certain girls and women guilty of 'too tender' sentiments toward the occupiers."[124] Living on the outskirts of town and worried by the danger posed by the Germans who had retreated into her barn, Mme. Garner might not have heard about these arrests until days after they had happened. Her use of the term "naturally" suggests that such arrests were both self-explanatory and already formulaic.

The young Jean Vartier, in a passage that he surely would have included in his later disclaimer of his history's "juvenile lyricism," also described the purge. "At 1:00 P.M. (while the faubourg d'Epinal was not entirely liberated) the arrests began in town: a gathering of a first harvest, the most urgent, of traitors, of collaborators, and of those odious courtesans of the Teuton who would pay with their locks for all their servile indulgence toward yesterday's conquerors."[125] This vague passage in an otherwise precisely detailed contemporary account shows how the first gestures of the purge had already become a cliché even before the liberation had been completed. In contrast, the commander of the Rambervillers Maquis pared his report of all political or emotional commentary, or even adjectives, to observe: "As of 1:00 P.M. arrests were made by the Police."[126] It is significant that he felt no need to indicate whom the police arrested, thereby confirming the general expectation of a purge at the liberation.

It is hard to know from these accounts whether the people of Rambervillers had little interest in the first day's purge, felt that they had no part in the matter, accepted it as routine, or preferred out of uneasiness not to speak of it. In any case, the liberation-day crowds in Rambervillers were clustering about American tanks, not head shavings. It took a stranger with a professional, although not detached, interest in recounting the details of the day to give a full account. As a Gaullist officer attached to the FFI, Mario Faivre liberated their hometown with the Maquis of Rambervillers. Faivre described the purge:

> On the French side, this liberation was expected, prepared. As the number of those who did not behave as good patriots was minimal,

there was hardly any upheaval. I did not hear any political remarks. None of those who worked valiantly for the defeat of the occupier expressed the least personal ambition. . . .

From the balcony [of the Maquis headquarters] one saw the population stroll through a happy calm to breathe the air of regained liberty. A few American soldiers were there, to have a drink, make exchanges (cigarettes for butter, etc.).

Some maquisards told me that three "very loose" girls who had had intimate relations with the *feldgraus* were going to have their heads shaved. As I expressed surprise at this proceeding, L—— explained: "Neither [commanders] M——, nor P—— nor I occupy ourselves with this case, but to stop it would not be understood, especially by those who are in mourning because of the Boches." This formality took place in the most complete calm.

Two or three maquisards whose brother or father were killed or deported go to fetch the girl (who waits all ready at her home) and accompany her without a word to the hairdresser, who shaves her in his shop. They are then allowed to put on a head scarf and to cover their foreheads with a lock of hair. One after the other they return home discreetly and unescorted.[127]

The "odious courtesans of the Teuton" here become pitiable sacrifices to the bereavement of their community, and their humiliation a mere "formality," a ritual of liberation that required neither screaming crowds nor even public exposure of the stigma. Nor, significantly, did the officer think that the head shavings reflected the least "political remarks" or "personal ambition." This narrative reduced the stereotypically angry liberation-day purge to a calm, prepared exercise in honorary justice and symbolic retribution that exchanged a woman's hair for a man's life.[128]

After the first day, a good part of the local purge, or attempts at a local purge, unfolded in the Rambervillers columns of the departmental press. Indeed, a large portion of the news from Rambervillers involved exposés of individuals accused of collaboration or alerts over the nearly successful whitewashing maneuvers of said collaborators that became increasingly entangled in political infighting as the months passed.[129] Many of these exposés targeted economic collaborators who had made money from the

German occupation of the town. For example, a correspondent called for the purge of a shopkeeper who "made big deals with the occupiers, her prices being inaccessible to Frenchmen," by which it was implied that her crime had been to charge what the market could bear rather than possibly take a loss as a public service to her compatriots.[130] Indeed, she was open to charges of war profiteering, an equally unpopular activity that the government also prosecuted, although not with the same zeal as local resistants showed at the liberation.[131] The same correspondent later exposed the lack of cooperation on the part of local truck drivers and threatened: "We will demand an accounting from all those people whose attitude needs to be adjusted (*mentalité est à refaire*), and, if necessary, we will take action."[132] In one sentence the Rambûvetais revealed both the local purgers' concern with attitudes and feelings and the local purge's potential misuse as a bullying stick.

The same interpretation of collaboration as immoral economic activity appeared in an article calling for a boycott of collaborationist businesses as a "direct action [in which] the people render their justice themselves." It asked: "Wouldn't the bread of that fat Hitlerite baker seem bitter to you? Doesn't the wine of that pious trafficker whose sole and abiding worry was to amass millions by drowning the boches' gullets with the contents of his vast cellars while our deportees, deprived of potable water, agonized, overcome by typhus; this wine of treason, doesn't it burn your lips?"[133] Surely collaborators lost business to family, if not community-wide, boycotts for years after the liberation, but a principled refusal to patronize a certain shop requires no declaration and rarely leaves a trace in the historical record.

Overall, however, the local purge displayed a much greater interest in black marketeers than in shopkeepers. *La Margeride,* for instance, announced the arrest of a man long wanted for—note the order—"black market and relations with the Gestapo."[134] Many black marketeers fell under suspicion of collaboration because their customers had been German. More damning, in the popular mind black marketeering itself was tantamount to, if not even more heinous than, collaboration. Both the collaborator and the black marketeer, after all, betrayed their communities. If collaborators were associated with the Second World War, the black marketeers belonged to a much older tradition of betrayal, that of the *affa-*

meurs, the scoundrels who withhold food from their hungry, if not starving, neighbors for the sake of their own personal profit. It is hard to find a more thoroughly execrated villain in history or a better symbol of social injustice at a time of food shortages. Although they more properly belonged in the criminal courts, black marketeers often appeared in the purge courts because public opinion insisted that they belonged there. After provincial officials lost their power of ordering administrative internment, black marketeers frequently appeared on the lists of vigilante victims, thus testifying to the local purge's interest in social as well as legal justice.

In Rambervillers itself, public reaction to many of the exposés and calls for action found in the press suggests that the correspondents may have attempted to co-opt the purge into long-standing political antagonisms.[135] Attempts at manipulating the purge rhetoric, however, could go only as far as the community would allow. Blatant lies would simply be dismissed, or even actively countered, in a small town where people could judge for themselves the reputation of the accused against that of the accuser. This is not to say that mistakes and injustices did not happen, but rather that communities did not blindly second every call for purging or ostracism. In May 1945, for instance, one of the town's correspondents took his neighbors to task for creating the disappointing results of the legal purge because they lacked the "civic courage" to testify in court. He was particularly upset about the recent acquittal of a seamstress who had found no fewer than thirty people to give her "a certificate of good conduct and to affirm that the Boches did not visit her house assiduously."[136] Apparently at least thirty people did not believe that this woman's association with Germans deserved legal punishment. And, apparently, the correspondent did not consider that testifying on behalf of an accused collaborator showed as much "civic courage" as testifying against one—as unlikely as that seems in a period of mob and vigilante violence against collaborators. Such incidents cast doubt on whether or not the correspondents enjoyed their neighbors' complete confidence as the authentic voice of the Rambûvetais resistance or of the community. Rambervillers, then, offers an example of local purgers reined in by community opinion.

The apparent independence of the Rambûvetais readership did not, however, signify a lack of interest in the purge or even a lack of support for some local purgers. The first vigilante bombs in Rambervillers exploded simultaneously one March midnight in 1945 at a café, a lumberyard, an embroiderer's, a bakery, and a hardware store. Although the department daily called them "unexplained explosions," the CRR at Nancy blamed "*anciens résistants.*" He warned his superiors in Paris that although "the population remains calm . . . it is certain that the situation is in danger of getting worse if the repression of collaboration is not conducted with more energy."[137] The targets reflected the commercial nature of collaboration in this area where the Germans, but not their money, had been unpopular.

A second incident coincided with the Return and a wave of violent attacks on repatriated voluntary laborers throughout the department. On 31 May 1945 deportees and others established what different sources called a "revolutionary tribunal," a "people's tribunal," or a "head-shaving bureau" in a Rambûvetais café and shaved the heads of a dozen women accused of horizontal collaboration or voluntary labor. Somewhat belatedly, the gendarmerie intervened to arrest four of the young men who had organized the tribunal. That night bombs exploded at the homes of an "industrialist" who had been interned but then released, a hosier, and the same embroidery merchant who had been bombed in March.[138]

The bombings raised little comment, but the revolutionary tribunal caught the attention of the authorities. The prefect and the CRR at Nancy considered the women *tondues* as "scarcely interesting" but agreed to have three deportees who were involved in the incident arrested because, as the CRR explained, he "could not admit that even comrades who have suffered harshly may act this way."[139] The Rambûvetais were not the only ones to challenge the legitimacy of the legal purge through alternative tribunals. The prefect of Dordogne considered a spate of bombings in March to be the work of "certain of those revolutionary tribunals" that meant to intimidate "people considered to be compromised, such as lawyers who agree to defend [collaborators] in the Cours de Justice."[140] But the openness of the Rambûvetais revolutionary tribunal, its location in a café during the morning, made this counter-court a singularly public defiance of the government and assured the equally public response of the arrests.

Of course, by arresting the deportees the government ran the risk of making martyrs of men who enjoyed tremendous public sympathy at all levels, including from the CRR, just for being deportees. Furthermore, some people also admired their action. The town correspondent for the

Socialist paper cried: "Bravo to the courageous lads who have established that if Justice was dead in our department, the redressers of wrongs have returned from Germany firmly resolved to punish the traitors. Bravo to your guts, your dynamism, all the people are behind you!" Nevertheless, he suggested that efforts would be better directed at punishing the more culpable "*patrons,*" such as one of the merchants bombed in March.[141] That the arrested deportees did not become a cause célèbre suggests that the government dropped the charges.

In July 1945 more bombs exploded along the Mortagne. The CRR remarked that "public opinion generally comments favorably on these nocturnal expeditions," although that was soon to change.[142] Public opinion, it seems, supported the vigilantes only as long as their violence respected certain limits, such as breaking windows or shaving women's heads. But Vosgien vigilantes lost public support when someone murdered two families with young children in two villages east of Rambervillers. On 29 August 1945, the mailman discovered the bodies of a woman, her daughter, and her three-year-old grandson at their home in Saint-Stail. The women had been accused of collaboration by having "sympathized with German soldiers," but they had been recently released from custody for lack of evidence. Eighteen kilometers away, the same mailman discovered the bodies of a husband and wife and their two- and five-year-old children, all killed by machine-gun fire. The couple was under investigation for their activities during the occupation, but the case looked weak. One report concluded that because there had been "neither a break-in nor theft, [the killings] can only be a matter of a 'purge action' by bloodthirsty madmen."[143] The fact that the legal purge had failed to punish or even detain the murdered adults confirms the role of national purge policies in creating vigilantism.

In a signed article given unusual prominence, *La Liberté de l'Est* described and commented on the murders. "As far as we are concerned the individuals who have set themselves up as vigilantes (*justiciers*)—they are nothing but killers—do not belong to that magnificent phalanx of men who devoted themselves through patriotism and the holiest hatred to driving out the invader and to writing the most glorious pages in the drama of our liberation. They waged war against the Boches. We know that the blood of children has never sullied their hands!"[144] The Catholic paper added its plea: "Let us banish those who claim to serve justice themselves, going as far as killing innocent children."¹⁴⁵

These were not the first appeals for calm in the Vosgien press. Earlier appeals, however, had asked for moderation and careful thought; they had denounced the atmosphere of excesses rather than the manifestations of the local purge or the vigilantes.¹⁴⁶ But the murders of the young children at Saint-Stail and Hurbache so revolted public feeling that both papers disassociated vigilantism from resistance and, by extension, a justifiable local purge. By identifying vigilantes as simple murderers, the episode turned public sympathy away from them much more effectively than did any attempts to label them as "terrorists." From then on, the CRR could write that "for the most part the population [of the Vosges] disapproves of the attitude of those who want to pose as vigilantes (*justiciers*)."¹⁴⁷

The children's murders did not end interest in the purge in the Vosges, but they did restrain the tensions between the local and national purges there. Vigilantism was discredited, not because people felt they could trust the national purge, but because they preferred an inadequate legal system to the slaughter of children. So protests over pardons granted to locally notorious Miliciens at the end of the year filled the press but not the streets.¹⁴⁸ Rambervillers resigned itself to the national purge for lack of an acceptable option and out of weariness rather than confidence in its justice. Indeed, by the end of 1945 Vosgiens were too disillusioned by the mishandling of the food supply to expect any sort of justice from Paris.

MOÛTIERS

The circumstances of Moûtiers' occupation shaped collaboration—and so the local purge—differently from the way they did in Saint-Flour or Rambervillers. For instance, Moutiérains had collaborated with Italians in ways that were quite impossible in the other towns. Most important, the fratricidal conflict between the FFI and the Milice in Savoie in 1943–44 gave collaboration an all-too-bloody image. The Tarin Resistance lost seventy-four killed in action, sixty-four dead in deportation, sixty executed, and twenty-six civilian victims.¹⁴⁹ If Germans had pulled the trigger in some cases, collaborators had contributed to the catastrophe in all of them. Savoyards, then, were more personally invested in the purge than people from less ravaged parts of the country, and they present the clearest examples of the struggles between the local and national purges for the right to represent and define justice and memory. In Moûtiers itself the exceptional official organization of and community support for the local purge meant that the town carried out its purge very peacefully. In the department as a whole, however, that same belief in the local purge fueled a notoriously high level of vigilante violence against persons and property well into 1946.

Little is known about Moûtiers' first temporary liberation in early August 1944, and nothing at all about a possible purge at that time. Given how formally the Moutiérain resistants prosecuted the local purge in late August, however, they most likely judged that a purge would have been premature earlier that month, at a time when the battle was far from over, the enemy remained at large, and several dozen enemy POWs were in their custody. There is likewise no record of a ritual "first harvest" of the purge at the town's final liberation on 24 August.

Within two weeks of its definitive liberation, Moûtiers had an official purge apparatus in the form of the Milices patriotiques (MP), commanded by an FFI captain, and a Purge Commission, presided over by a professional policeman. The MP assisted the Purge Commission by accepting depositions and suggestions from the public and by pursuing collaborators.[150] These two organizations operated with all the trappings and conviction of government agencies; they acted as the law by arresting individuals, employing legal procedures, and gathering evidence. According to their own published reports, in the first two weeks of September 1944 the MP pursued sixty-two investigations in the region of Moûtiers and made fifty arrests, categorized as "intimate relations with the enemy, head shaving, eight; denunciations, six; consorting with the enemy, thirty-six; theft, one; requisitions, six; searches, twenty, and numerous police operations that permitted the seizure of many goods of every nature."[151] Once again, resistants acted on their remarkable assurance that women's personal relationships with enemy men were matters of public concern and that shaving women's heads to punish their choice of lovers was an acceptable, routine, and perhaps even necessary part of liberation police work. Although the report does not specify, head shaving probably replaced detention in those eight cases. How seriously the general public took the MP can be judged by the reaction of a man with an Italian surname in the nearby commune of Aigueblanche who attempted suicide "on the point of being arrested by the MP." He was taken to the hospital in Moûtiers but received little sympathy from the press in a report titled "A Traitor Renders Justice on Himself."[152]

During that same time, the Purge Commission imposed fines equaling 2,800,000 francs on a fabric merchant, a butcher, a grocer, a baker, a draper, and a restaurateur (not all in Moûtiers proper). It also suspended four gendarmes from the brigade in Moûtiers and one member of the brigade in Bozel.[153] From 8 September to 23 November 1944, the commission examined 117 cases, including 67 for consorting with the enemy, 12 involving civil servants, 2 regarding Miliciens, and 38 concerning black marketeering or war profiteering.[154] As it forwarded cases to the appropriate agencies, whether Military Security or the public prosecutor, the Purge Commission must have seen itself as an assistant to the national government, not as a rival tribunal or authority. Questionable sentencing, pardoning, and releasing of accused collaborators had not yet eroded local confidence in the national purge.

Any such confidence, however, did not imply obedience. When de Gaulle disbanded the Milices patriotiques at the end of October, the MP of Moûtiers transformed itself from a civil militia into a territorial military police, now called the Prévôté territoriale FFI de Moûtiers, and continued with its work until it faded from view at the new year, probably at the prefect's insistence.[155] And so in the five weeks after its official dissolution, the MP effected thirty-five operations categorized as:

> One case of counterintelligence leading to incarceration of the accused in the departmental prison in Chambéry; two cases of recovery of weapons; two verifications of foreigners; two transfers of foreigners concerning fourteen Italian nationals, sent to Military Security in Albertville; six cases of black marketeering leading to the seizure of nine kilograms of butter and seven kilograms of cheese sent to the provisioning service and seventy kilograms of nuts sent to the Hospital in Moûtiers; one case of illegal prices, concerning a big merchant in Moûtiers; eleven infractions of the regulations regarding hotels,

rooming houses, and bars; ten infractions of the traffic regulations; two cases of fraud concerning the weight of bread. All sent to the public prosecutor in Moûtiers for judgment.[156]

The arrest logs provide a good sketch of the possibilities for collaboration and malfeasance in Savoie. They also illuminate the extent of the local Resistance establishment's vision of its own authority and of the purge's purview. Some infractions, such as the traffic tickets, were simple matters of everyday policing, but most answered the local purge's broad definition of collaboration, which included economic betrayal of the community. Furthermore, the fact that the MP continued to act openly as a regular police force and to interact with the courts and Military Security even though they themselves enjoyed only a dubious legality in the eyes of the central government suggests how weak Paris's control remained in Savoie for months after the liberation.

As could be expected with any organization engaging in political and economic policing in a period like the après-libération, the MP and Purge Commission both came under criticism from within the community. Occasional defenses of these agencies in the press suggest that rumor, at least, had been attacking them. In particular, *La Résistance savoyarde* felt obliged to explain that "the Milices Patriotiques are charged with maintaining civil order, protecting the citizenry from theft, pillage, [and] personal vengeance, and acting, eventually, against the return of isolated Germans or other vindictive collaborationist elements. They have the power of arrest and search with a warrant delivered by the Purge Commission. They are charged with participating in the repression of the black market and enforcing [set] prices. The Milices Patriotiques are a civil force at the service of the entire nation." Similarly, the local Purge Commissions in Savoie, also planned by the clandestine Resistance, had the twofold mission of gathering evidence against collaborators for the purge courts and "satisfying the legitimate demands of public opinion regarding black market profits" by imposing fines on excessive profits. After vouching for the high character of members of such commissions, the article ended with the assurance that, "far from being an organ arbitrarily threatening the peace, liberty, or the very life of Frenchmen, the Purge Commissions on the contrary give them every guarantee."[157] These explanations and later events suggest that rumor had accused the Moutiérain MP and Purge Commission of skirting the edge of banditry and personal or political vendetta.

In marked contrast to such allusions, *La Résistance savoyarde* demonstrated its own appreciation when it bid farewell to the career police officer who headed Moûtiers' Purge Commission: "Thanks to his noble-heartedness and in spite of the ungrateful character of the task that he had to assume, he enjoyed much sympathy. It can, and it should, be said that he was one of the instruments, and not the least, of the maintenance of public peace in Moûtiers and in the Tarentaise" at the liberation.[158] This praise could not be completely mistaken because compared to the turmoil all around it in Savoie, and even compared to Saint-Flour and Rambervillers, Moûtiers was remarkably calm. There were only three—possibly four— vigilante incidents within the town.

The first bomb exploded on the night of 26 November 1944. The victim, claiming not to know why anyone would attack him, said that he had only one enemy in town, who had already turned him in to the Germans. Of course, bystanders to the investigation all claimed not to know anything, but they said enough to suggest to the gendarmes that the owner of the house was generally thought as a truck driver to be "at the bottom of the bread shortage in Moûtiers." Public opinion reproached him for having returned from the Midi without bringing flour in his truck.[159] That bomb was therefore not meant to punish past behavior that had escaped the courts' attention, as so many bombs were, but rather to influence current and future behavior. It marked the current betrayal of a man accused of having refused to put the interests of his community before his own. Whether or not he could have purchased flour in the Midi or secured the appropriate permits to transport it across regional and departmental lines did not matter. In the context of the time, when black marketeers were treated as collaborators and local purgers conceived of treason in terms of relationships in the Tarentaise rather than in France and Europe, there was no great distance between blaming someone for a bread shortage and branding him as a collaborator.

Indeed, only ten days earlier the town paper had published an editorial complaining that transportation could not be found for basic provisions such as flour but was never lacking to fetch profitable loads such as wine from as far away as Paris. The recent bread shortage in town, it argued, was the fault of egotistical truckers. The editorial ended ominously: "There was a maquis to chase out the occupiers, it could be that there will be one to wipe out the racketeers [*combinards*]!"[160] Such direct links between press and vigilante violence are rare. If no resistants actually set the November bomb, those on the editorial board share some of the responsibility for spreading the idea of equating truck drivers with collaborators and encouraging vigilante action.

The second incident happened on election day in May 1945 when the homes of two newly elected municipal councilors suffered significant damage from bombs.[161] One of the men, a wood merchant, had also been on the special delegation appointed by the CLL; the other, an insurance agent, had not. They both, like eleven other newly elected councilors, belonged to the non-Resistance slate. Clearly, someone did not feel that the victims deserved to be councilmen, but the exact reasoning has gone unrecorded. This incident, like the earlier one, appears to have had less to do with the purge of collaborators proper than with the tangential issues brought into a local purge that had aspirations of building a better future through a worthy community.

At this point, the associations that spoke for the groups assumed to be involved in vigilantism disclaimed the attacks. The usually silent Communist cell of Moûtiers met on 23 May and "raise[d] an energetic protest against the authors of the bomb attacks in town."[162] And the FFI veterans' association, the AAS, "ma[de] it known that it totally reproves these anarchistic demonstrations done by hotheads (*exaltés*) whoever they are."[163] This public disavowal of vigilantism on the part of both the Communists and the non-Communist Resistants surely contributed as much to keeping the midnight peace in Moûtiers as the work of the Purge Commission, whose commander, perhaps significantly, had left for Paris a month earlier.

There also seems to have been another attack around the same time, although it appeared as such in neither the press nor the detailed administrative records. It certainly caught the attention of Moûtiers, however, because on 2 June the AAS published a communiqué stating: "In the course of the explanations between M. B——and the Committee of the AS, it [has come out] that the insinuations spread by M. B——on the subject of the attack of which he was the object have no foundation."[164] The AAS would not have risked spreading slander unless the matter had already reached such currency in public discussion as to pose a serious enough threat to require the confrontation of the interview and the subsequent public retraction. If there were other vigilante incidents against civilians in Moûtiers, both the victims and the perpetrators kept them quiet.

Even if there were several others, the capital of the Tarentaise was a haven of calm in a department swirling with violence against persons as well as property. How could a centralized, twentieth-century state have so lost its monopoly on force that it faced the serious challenge to its legitimacy represented by vigilantes? The war, of course, provided the circumstances by, first, creating the tragedies that cried out for justice and, second, temporarily destroying the central government's lines of authority. In this sense, the liberation threw the relationship between state and people in France back to a form or level more familiar to the early modern period. Indeed, the temporary eclipse of the centralized state recreated what E. P. Thompson has described in another context as a "society in which justice is not wholly delegated or bureaucratized, but is enacted by and within the community."[165] The sudden return of justice to the local community explains the mid-twentieth-century appearance of early modern forms of punishment such as marking the body of the guilty or charivaris, both echoed in the head shavings. The challenge that this represented to the central government in turn explains the latter's zeal in suppressing vigilantes, more determinedly, it sometimes seemed, than in punishing collaborators.

Given French archival laws, little can be known about the vigilantes themselves.[166] Indeed, given the contemporary weakness of the police and popular support for the vigilantes, it is not clear how much was known about them at the time. Like the early resistance groups, vigilantes would have been local people responding to local events. Opinion, from the gendarmerie, through the administration, to the rumor on the street, tended to assume that the vigilantes were indeed former resistants. In fact, after a great deal of effort the prefect of Savoie concluded in July 1945 that the notoriously active vigilantes of his department were "former maquisards operating on the margin of official Resistance organizations in exceeding the orders of their leaders."[167] And although the "*maquis d'épuration*" were only a rumor in the Poitiers region in the summer of 1945, the existence of a "rebel FFI" of five to six hundred men who refused to disarm was a known fact in Haute-Savoie.[168] The occasional descriptions of men arrested for vigilantism do seem to support the theory of some tenuous connection between the resistance and the vigilantes. Vigilantes in Brittany, however, appear to have been resistance sympathizers rather than resistants.[169]

If some officials had actual physical evidence that at least some vigilantes were resistants, everyone else had the circumstantial evidence of method and motive. When vigilantes sabotaged a power line, threw a bomb in a business, or abducted and executed a collaborator, they used the same methods that the resistance had used. Of course, one hardly needed to be in the Resistance to do any of those things, as the necessary knowledge was a matter of everyday discussion and the country was littered with weaponry. Some incidents, though, did require the training and coordination of a maquis unit.[170]

"Authentic" vigilantes (rather than faux-maquis or those settling personal scores) and resistants also presumably shared similar motives.[171] Like resistants, vigilantes used violence to protect the community, if not from a foreign enemy then from what they perceived as an internal enemy. Furthermore, resistants seemed to have the most at stake in the purge as the continuation of their occupation-era struggles. Luca Alessandrini has determined that Italian vigilantes saw their violent postliberation actions as a way to establish the future as much as to settle scores.[172] There is good reason to expect that a more comprehensive study of French vigilantes would uncover the same motivation. Threatening articles and comments in the local press that might be taken to speak for or to the vigilantes presented them as the guardians of justice and, in a few instances, of the true republic. But most commonly, vigilantes figured as the guardians of the memory of the fallen martyrs of the Resistance that demanded the punishment of traitors, as men concerned with honorary as well as legal justice.

The assumption in official and public discussion of the vigilantes was that they were men. Was vigilantism truly an all-male realm? Given that women as well as men fought in the maquis, it is at least possible that some vigilantes were women. If so, they were quite safe from discovery because no one seems to have considered them as possible suspects. Women certainly played a part in creating the atmosphere in which the vigilantes operated, if only by refusing to talk to investigators. Nonetheless, the only public female voice in the discourse about vigilantism in this study came from the Savoyard UFF, which pointed out that bombing a shop inconvenienced more people than the shop owner because it also destroyed stocks of rationed goods and caused the shop's temporary or permanent closure.[173] What then were the women who regularly patronized that butcher or baker to do? They would have to find another shopkeeper willing to accept them as registered clients and probably wait at least a month for the next shipment of rationed goods. At least in contemporary opinion, then, women played a secondary role in vigilantism as victims, as bystanders, and, in their role as consumers, as secondary victims.

Whoever they were, the vigilantes used a variety of means. While some painted swastikas on the houses of accused collaborators, others, such as the Comité secret d'action immédiate of Clermont-Ferrand, sent threatening tracts inviting local authorities to "choose the work befitting a Frenchman or death."[174] Some vigilantes shaved the heads of women who had been released from government custody. Others took more definitive methods in the style of the four individuals who broke into a hospital in Thiers (Puy-de-Dôme) in order to shoot three political prisoners, two of whom they killed.[175]

The majority of vigilante attacks, however, involved homes or businesses in which bombs exploded during the night, injuring property rather than persons. During the height of the Return, the gendarmerie reported a national average of twelve bomb attacks per day, all against the property of persons suspected of collaboration or trafficking, and notably against suspects who were released from custody or who got lighter sentences in the purge courts than local opinion considered appropriate.[176] Because such bomb attacks responded directly to the national purge by challenging its right to acquit or release individuals, they increased with the numbers of persons released or pardoned by the national authorities.

In Savoie the authorities registered forty-eight attacks against property between 11 October 1944 and 11 January 1945, not an especially busy time, coming as it did before the major provocations of the Return and Gaullist clemency.[177] Not all such explosions, however, were the work of vigilantes; some incidents, such as the theft of thirty-eight thousand francs, constituted simple criminal attacks. Other incidents, such as the disarming of a constable or bombs that targeted resistants or Italians, remain unclassifiable without further information. The resistants might have been the victims of thieves, of other resistants, or of collaborators; indeed, in January

1945 the gendarmerie reported that a collaborator had murdered a Communist in Ugine (Savoie).[178] Some attacks, however, such as those against individuals who had been detained and then released by the purge courts, were clearly the work of vigilantes. And the vigilantes clearly thought that their purview included black marketeering and other unpatriotic economic activity, such as closing one's bakery. Savoie also witnessed sixty-seven summary executions after its liberation.[179] In December 1944 the Savoyard press carried reports of the abduction and subsequent murder of five men and the murder of one woman.[180] Vigilantism in Savoie therefore posed a continuing threat to the public peace and targeted a broad range of individuals: suspected collaborators, the relatives of those collaborators, black marketeers, bakers who ran out of flour, public authorities connected to the judicial system, and even, it seems, a few resistants.

Naturally, the government did not approve of these local usurpations of its monopoly on punishment, even if individual officials might be sympathetic to the vigilantes. But investigations into vigilante activities tended to suffer from a lack of police enthusiasm for the job and from what the gendarmerie called the "silence of the population, sometimes complicit, often terrorized."[181] The gendarmerie, however, was biased in the matter, and perhaps looking for an excuse for its own lack of success in stopping vigilantism. There were certainly cases in which the public not only supported vigilantes by silence, but very openly protested on behalf of local men who had been tried and sentenced for vigilantism. In an unusual but symbolically important event, trouble arose in early June in Dinan over the arrest of five young men, "honorably known" although perhaps "impulsive, partisans of direct action," who had been setting bombs at the businesses of "collabo merchants from Dinan."[182] Local Resistance leaders had lobbied for their release as far as the minister of justice himself but received no firm commitments.

Then "the release (*libération*) of D——, former commissioner-informer of the Gestapo, and the rumor that the prisoners would be transferred to Rennes that evening," galvanized the young men's supporters. A crowd of between five hundred (according to the gendarmerie) and four thousand (according to the local paper) gathered outside the prison, securing the men's release by the threat of invasion. It then carried the vigilantes in triumph through the streets to the Monument aux Morts to sing the "Marseillaise." The local paper commented: "Thus the population of Dinan will have in its annals the storming of a Bastille, because that event symbolically marks the fight and victory against a spirit of inertia that invites suspicion and that does not satisfy popular desires for cleanliness (*propreté*) and purification (*épuration*), for the advent of a Republic innocent of any compromise with a reactionary past under the enemy's heel."[183] It hardly boded well for the popularity or legitimacy of the Fourth Republic to have its prison labeled a Bastille. In this interpretation at least, these five bomb-throwing youths were neither criminals nor hooligans but heroes in the struggle against the looming tyranny of a government that compromised itself by treating the reactionary past too indulgently.

Not surprisingly, the representatives of the central government in Savoie and its region saw the suppression of vigilantism as a top priority and tried to convince the public to stop supporting vigilantism as well as to track down the vigilantes themselves. Having almost no confidence in the police, who were either afraid of the vigilantes or complicit with them, the prefect attempted persuasion through his own voice and those of other community leaders. In January 1945, "public rumor" and the increase in attacks moved several Resistance organizations to denounce vigilantism. The leadership of the FFI appealed "to all that remains of the good sense of the authors of these attacks to put an end once and for all to all these acts that terrorize the population because, voluntarily or involuntarily, they are making themselves accomplices of the fifth column. No one has the right to set himself up as a vigilante (*justicier*)."[184] The CDL issued a statement along the same lines and added that in order to finish the war the country needed union and discipline more than ever. And the PCF contributed "a still more energetic protest, declaring that it is a matter of veritable '*gangsterisme*' terrorizing the population."[185] The Communists' statement turned out to be more accurate than they had perhaps realized, because the bombing of a jewelry store in Aix-les-Bains and some other incidents that upset public opinion in January 1945 turned out to be the work of a band of bona fide faux-maquis rather than vigilantes.[186] The success of those thieves in masking their activities as expressions of popular justice underscores the atmosphere of confusion and fear in Savoie.

But the presence of thieves did not mean the absence of vigilantes. In March 1945 the prefect optimistically reported that he had put an end to the "machinations of the last groups who, under the pretext that certain of their members belonged or had belonged to the FFI, take reprehensible initiatives in the matter of the purge, of the repression of the black market, or of requisitions that I cannot tolerate." The last of the police operations involved captured two hundred kilograms of explosives, two machine guns, and a rifle, thus indicating how dangerous a threat vigilantes posed.[187] But the sharp decline in attacks in the early spring of 1945 proved to be only a lull before the Return, and a series of pardons provoked an upsurge of anger and subsequent vigilantism, summarized by the CDL's June declaration that "at this time to pardon is to betray."[188]

These goads were only aggravated by a widespread suspicion that the central government preferred collaborators to true patriots, as manifested in the case of a staff sergeant of the FFI who, in March 1945, was sentenced to five years' imprisonment for having participated in the 4 October 1944 summary execution of a man accused of consorting with the enemy. The day was important because it fell just after the liberation of the area and therefore past the date at which a summary execution was legally defined as an act of war rather than a crime. Because the victim was accused under Article 75 of the penal code, the proper procedure on 4 October would have been to turn him over to the courts.

The Savoyard community refused to see the execution as a criminal murder. For its part, the CLL of Moûtiers protested energetically:

> We show solidarity with these men who have fought for the liberation of the territory and have risked their lives in clandestinity and on the battlefield for the grandeur of France.
>
> The policy that aims by all means to eliminate (*faire disparaître*) the elements who are at the base of the recovery (*redressement*) of the country risks creating a rather serious malaise.
>
> We demand the immediate release (*libération*) of the patriots who are in prison in place of informers, Miliciens, [and] profiteers who are benefiting from an indulgence without measure while waiting to be decorated for all the evil that they have done to the country.

The wording of this petition suggests that in addition to proving the darkest suspicions about the national purge's idea of justice, the sergeant's case activated the local resistants' fears of being sidelined by the national Resistance.

So many individuals and groups, including the prefect, lobbied the minister of the interior on the sergeant's behalf that he was released in January 1946. An official delegation of resistants, municipal authorities, and girls bearing flowers welcomed the sergeant at the train station in Chambéry and escorted him to the reception held in his honor. *La Résistance savoyarde* commented on his return that "a flagrant injustice has finally ended with the Return of a true Resistant."[189] But the timing of the sergeant's release in the midst of weeks of intense vigilante activity in the department suggests that the authorities in Paris acted less from any sympathy with Savoyard opinion than from a desire to calm it by pardoning at least one Resistance hero to counterbalance the current flood of pardoned Miliciens.

It is interesting to note that no one in the community seems to have argued that the sergeant did not kill the collaborator, but everyone agreed that his imprisonment for that action was unjust. The response to the sergeant's case and the high departmental rate of vigilantism indicate both how thoroughly Savoie had entered "the culture of the outlaw" in 1944 and how completely the provisional government had failed to provide a secure enough environment for the Savoyards to leave that culture before 1946. They also underscore how arbitrary a politically or militarily defined date for the cessation of hostilities and therefore the transformation of "acts of war" into "crimes" must have seemed to the civilians living in a war zone, particularly a civil war zone such as Savoie.

At the height of the Return in May 1945, Savoie got a new prefect, Louis Martin, who, like his predecessor, was determined to put an end to vigilante attacks. Although pragmatically aware that vigilantism would only disappear "on the day when the last collaborator, or alleged collaborator, will have been removed from the department," he meant to reduce it sharply.[190] To that end, he demanded help from the government and from departmental Resistance leaders. From the central government, the prefect continually asked for police agents from outside the department and, more subtly, for a modification of Gaullist purge policy. He reminded his superiors in Paris that many of the attacks were "uncontestably attributable to an excessive indulgence of the [national] purge."[191] The prefect also begged the legal authorities not to allow notorious collaborators who had been released or pardoned to return to Savoie, where they were likely to be injured. He furthermore insisted that they warn him before releasing such individuals so that he could take steps to keep order.

From local Resistance leaders the prefect asked for a "sincere" disavowal of vigilantism, because the vigilantes would listen to them.[192] When he first took office in May 1945, he assured the CDL that he would "put all [his] energy . . . into punishing the traitors [and] pursuing speculators of all kinds."[193] Yet he did not achieve the desired response until after 23 July, when he organized a meeting with leaders of the departmental Resistance and workers' organizations, police chiefs, and the CRR at Lyon. The CRR "made everyone understand the duty that they had not only to disavow the illegal practices followed by certain misguided individuals, perhaps agitators, but to support the authorities in their search for the authors or accomplices of acts that undermine the good name of our country abroad and that harm the cause of Democracy." It is significant that the representative of the national purge brought in the question of international opinion, thereby forcing the local purgers to look beyond the purely local horizon within which they had been operating. He appears to have been more successful in doing so than the prefect of the Vosges, who constantly reminded his constituents of how bad their violence looked to their American allies and guests. In Savoie, the CDL and Communists responded by denouncing vigilantes as criminals. The prefect was cautiously pleased with the results: only two attacks between 28 July and 3 August compared to fifteen during the previous two weeks.[194]

But at this point the national authorities undermined the prefect's efforts with a series of pardons all but designed to provoke outrage in Savoie and to expose the fundamental conflicts between the local and national purges. The trouble began in September 1945 when a number of Savoyard Miliciens and collaborators were captured in other parts of the country, mostly the Midi. Although they had all been condemned in absentia, they were sent back to Chambéry to stand trial at the Cour de Justice. *La Résistance savoyarde* took the opportunity to rehearse the men's crimes, particularly when a prisoner was blamed for the death of a local resistant.[195] When the train carrying thirteen Miliciens and collaborators arrived in Chambéry on 1 October, a crowd of sixty people attacked it. Over the next couple of months, the press carried reports of more arrests and of the trials. *La Résistance savoyarde,* for example, covered the major trials and those concerning local men such as two members of the Milice and Waffen-SS "well-known in Moûtiers." One, a twenty-six-year-old mechanic, received a sentence of fifteen years' transportation with hard labor and national degradation for life; the other, a forty-three-year-old railway worker, received twenty years' transportation with hard labor and national degradation for life.[196]

In particular, the trial of a twenty-four-year-old mechanic named Capella drew a large crowd and police presence.[197] "In the course of the testimony, there were numerous incidents between the unhappy families of the victims and the accused. The audience was tumultuous, and the judge threatened to clear the hall several times." Capella was accused of being "the instigator of the horrible drama of Saint-Georges-d'Hurtières where eight FFI were killed, three farms burned, and the owners of the buildings deported to Germany." In March 1944 he had sought refuge with the maquis, only to return a few days later with German forces. As a Milicien and a Gestapo informer as well as the cause of the deaths and deportations of fellow Frenchmen, Capella represented the worst betrayal of collaboration. To the general satisfaction of the public, he was condemned to death by the Savoyard Cour de Justice.[198]

To the general scandal of the public, however, Capella was soon pardoned by the national government. The prefect reported that "Savoyard opinion in its entirety has been extremely affected" by the commutation of Capella's sentence from death to transportation with hard labor for life. The Capella pardon galvanized the latent hostility over the recent string of pardons granted to Savoyard Miliciens harshly condemned by the Savoyard Cour de Justice, and it came to encapsulate the clash between the local and national purges. In a crucial way, it also became the symbol of the national government's attack on Savoyard pride and memory. In this instance the divide between the local and national purges cannot be drawn along legal and extralegal lines, because the Savoyard Cour de Justice joined the Savoyard vigilantes in protesting Paris's decisions. It must be understood as a conflict between a province and the center over the meaning of justice and the construction of memory.

On 10 December 1945, the jurors of the Savoyard Cour de Justice went on strike because "they consider themselves to be outraged in their quality as Frenchmen and their dignity as citizens following the scandalous pardons from which all the convicted benefit, and consequently they will no longer sit as long as the unjust remissions of sentences are not reversed and the traitors not punished as the verdicts decided." The following Saturday the CDL and all the departmental Resistance organizations sponsored a public protest in Chambéry that drew four thousand participants.[199] On the dais stood the vice president of the CDL, the president of the Conseil général de la Savoie, the mayor of Chambéry, and the leaders of the military Resistance (both Communist and non-Communist), of movements of POWs, of deportees, and of families of fusillés, and of the trade unions. All the political parties also sent representatives, and the department's two deputies to the Constituent Assembly sent telegrams expressing their solidarity. After voting on a petition protesting Capella's pardon, the demonstrators marched to the prefecture to present it to the national government's representative. The CDL promised at least fifteen more meetings throughout the department in the following days.[200]

The depth of feeling evoked in the department by the clemency shown to Capella may be judged by a protest written by the returned deportees of the cantons of Aiguebelle-La Chambre.

> We who have miraculously come back from the death camps, in the name of our comrades [who] died in the most atrocious suffering, in the name of those who consented to the supreme sacrifice for the happiness of their *patrie,* we loudly demand the head of Capella. [We demand] that the generals and the spokesman of the heroic epoch know and understand that we want to avenge our dead! That shame and infamy cover the face of the ignoble Capella! That he be shot and that his hideous remains be thrown into the flames of a crematory oven.[201]

Their challenge of de Gaulle's, and by extension the Resistance government's, right to decide the fate of a traitor who had betrayed their comrades captures the root cause of the uproar to which they added their voice. This scandal was about honorary justice as much as legal justice.

Savoie was certainly in an uproar throughout December 1945 and well into January 1946. The government only fueled the flames by granting pardon after pardon after Capella's pardon, despite the prefect's explicit warnings. Indeed, anyone reading the local press would have realized that the government pursued a risky policy. In December, *La Résistance savoyarde* commented on the pardons granted to a Milicien and a Gestapo agent condemned to death by the Savoyard Cour de Justice: "These two new measures of clemency will be badly received by the Savoyard population, who have suffered so from the frightful Nazis and their stooges, the Miliciens."[202] In January the paper published a signed letter to the editor bemoaning "yet another one pardoned," the departmental commander (*chef*) of the Milice Francs-gardes. The Savoyard Cour de Justice had condemned this member of the Waffen-SS and recruiter for the Milice to death, but the national authorities commuted the sentence to ten years' transportation with hard labor. The letter ended: "We still remember all too well the slogans of London and Algiers: '*Miliciens, futurs fusillés*' to be able to understand the measure of clemency that has just benefited this bad Frenchman. And we do not understand [*comprenons mal*] the successive vexations inflicted on the Savoyards. *Still they simply demand that the work of justice be done.*"[203] There could be no clearer rejection of the government's version of justice, so provokingly symbolized by the pardons it granted to the men it had promised to execute less than two years before.

Even the police were astonished by the "abusive pardons," but at the news of Capella's pardon they prepared "to undergo the consequences of the violent discontent let loose among the population by the remission of the sentence of he who will particularly attract the public's hatred."[204] Indeed, two bombs immediately broke the vigilante cease-fire so laboriously constructed by the prefect. One targeted Capella's uncle and the other a man known as a sympathizer of Pétain. For the month after Christmas, *La Résistance savoyarde* reported ten bomb attacks in seven towns and hinted at others. The situation was particularly tense in Chambéry over New Year's, when bombs exploded at the sites of national authority, in particular the home of the president of the Cour d'appel and the prefecture. Armed units patrolled the streets at night.[205] Vigilantes also bombed the archiepiscopal palace, perhaps because they suspected that the hierarchy was harboring Miliciens such as Paul Touvier.

In late January 1946, the petitions, protests, and bombs finally elicited a response from the government in the form of a decision to try Capella again, but this time for crimes committed in Paris. This sop did little to mollify Savoyard opinion. *La Résistance savoyarde* announced the decision with great reserve, remarking that his "criminal acts committed in our department [have] been judged sufficiently serious to merit capital punishment. One knows that after his condemnation, Capella benefited from a decree of clemency granted by the President [de Gaulle]."[206] There is no suggestion whatsoever that the retrial would provide any sort of justice.

Nor did the measure restore confidence in the national purge among vigilantes, especially in Chambéry. At least three bombs exploded there in February 1946, one at the home of a man who trafficked in Swiss gold and two at the homes of condemned Miliciens. One home belonged to a family in which the son had been condemned to twenty years' transportation with hard labor and the mother and one of the daughters had been banished from Savoie for belonging to the Milice. The women had been pardoned, however, and had returned before the vigilante attack. Chambéry also witnessed two spectacular murders of naturalized Italians, identified by the killers as collaborators. Both were publicly gunned down while sitting with friends or family.[207]

In an unusual case that demonstrates how thoroughly such Savoyard vigilantes had divorced themselves from the national purge by late February 1946, five armed and masked men invaded the farm of a widow in a hamlet outside Moûtiers. They shaved the head of the woman and beat her nephew when he came to her defense. The town paper commented dryly: "One loses oneself in conjectures over the motives for these acts."[208] Indeed one does, but other attacks suggest that the widow may have been thought to be involved in the black market or to be an insufficiently punished collaborator.

The new wave of vigilante violence provoked by the pardons of Miliciens differed from earlier episodes in that, as the prefect remarked, they could no longer be considered to be the work of Resistance organizations, which had sincerely disavowed such violence.[209] Indeed, in January 1946 the Comité de l'AS du canton de Moûtiers issued un communiqué in defense of a comrade apparently reputed to be involved in a series of bombings in Chambéry. The committee asserted that the bombs "are the work of agents of the fifth column. Demands [that the authorities] discover the guilty parties, [and] condemn (*stigmatiser*) them as necessary to fully illuminate this affair."[210]

Whoever they were, the authors of the attacks were now thoroughly disowned by the Resistance establishment and branded as fifth columnists, if not outright collaborators. This was not as effective as the murder of the children in the Vosges, but it did represent an important step in disengaging the vigilantes from the support of the "culture of the outlaw." The change in the vigilantes' status can be seen in the way they staged their attacks in February 1946. They gunned a man down in a café. They broke into a woman's home to shave her head. Their identities are completely unknown, but they might have been the very same men who shaved the eight women in Moûtiers in September 1944 as a routine part of their police work. The difference in February 1946 was that they wore masks. Confident in their authority and the silence of their community, local purgers did not cover their faces in 1944–45. The late head shavers did not share that earlier confidence in the community's support, or perhaps in the government's powerlessness, even though they were confident in their authority to define justice and carry it out themselves. Finally, unlike Cantaliens, they had no confidence in the government's willingness to provide the justice they sought, nor had they resigned themselves to the injustice but safety of the government's law and order, as had the Vosgiens. The local purge in Savoie, then, did not reach the final stage of submission to the national purge until long after the transitional period of the après-libération had ended.

The purge of collaborators revealed popular aspirations for a multifaceted and subtle justice that responded to community grievances. It also revealed that the national government neither shared the local definition of justice nor had any intention of providing it. Indeed, from the provincial perspective, the Resistance government deliberately provoked local sensibilities by a policy of official leniency. As a result, the purge divided into a national and a local purge. The two never separated completely but merged in places, ran parallel in others, and clashed in yet others. On the surface the conflict between the national and local purges' visions of justice created the anxiety and tragedies of vigilantism. More profoundly, it undermined the new government's legitimacy by exposing it as unwilling and unable to provide justice as it was popularly understood.

CHAPTER FOUR

SOCIAL JUSTICE AND

THE PROVISIONING CRISIS

The Second World War did more than divide French society into collaborators and resistants; it reduced the country to penury. The latter effect had as serious consequences for the *après-libération* as the former. For if the purge raised the question of legal justice, the food supply broached the issue of social justice. Indeed, the black market linked the two, making the challenge to the government's legitimacy posed by questions of social justice as serious as any posed by issues of legal justice.

Although France escaped the famines that afflicted other parts of the continent during the war, food shortages there were bad enough to recreate conditions that mimicked those of the preindustrial, subsistence-oriented world.[1] Because the occupation drained agricultural productivity and divided the country into five zones and the liberation destroyed the transportation system, the provisioning economy of the après-libération looked more like that of 1738 than that of 1938 in terms of its vulnerability to the weather and the seasons, the prevalence of local economies over the national economy, and the conflict that developed between the state and the people over the moral imperatives of the economy. As commentators in 1944–45 identified food as "the primordial factor that determines the *mentalité* of the majority of the public," and provincial administrators at all levels remarked that "provisioning obsesses [people's] minds (*esprits*)," the French reentered a culture of scarcity.[2]

During the après-libération, the food supply varied so widely from place to place that the official rations decreed by the government indicated more about the delusions of the bureaucrats at the center than about the supplies available at the periphery. Indeed, the discrepancy between government decree and local availability and the common use of unofficial sources such as family food parcels or the black market make it impossible to determine exactly what people in a particular town or region had to eat. One can, however, generalize enough to say that if Saint-Flour usually received the full rations designated by Paris, the destruction of Savoie's rail links to the rest of the country and the burden of forty-six thousand extra military mouths in the department meant that Moûtiers suffered periodic local shortages, mostly of bread and dairy products.[3] Rambervillers, on the other hand, only rarely came close to receiving its official rations.[4] The end of active fighting in the department in February 1945 did not noticeably improve the food supply. The Vosges received no wine at all until March 1945 and no fresh vegetables until after June 1945, when departmental authorities gave up on the central government and went in search of produce using their own initiative and funding.[5] Indeed, the provisioning system improved so little that in September 1945, a full year after most of the department had been liberated, the CRR observed that in the Vosges "one tries above all to live."[6]

In recognition of economic realities, all levels of provincial administration from CRR through CLL to municipal council were involved in efforts both to improve their regions' status within the government's system and, despite government orders, to secure whatever could be seized for local use. Indeed, at the liberation the entire Resistance organization in Savoie acted so aggressively in dealing with the supply situation that the national provisioning service, the Ravitaillement général (RG), complained that self-styled "*Intendants généraux,*" such as the commander of the Tarin FFI, were usurping its authority.[7] More accurately, they were ignoring it altogether. Despite the existence of the national rationing system, for example, the CLL of Bourg-Saint-Maurice reestablished the free market in town in September 1944 because "France and the region have suffered enough."[8] A full year later, long after central authority should have been reestablished, the mayor of Ugine was arranging the town's provisioning by himself and in opposition to the RG's regulations.[9]

In a more orderly fashion, the municipal councils campaigned to have their communes reclassified into more advantageous ration categories.[10] In announcing the elevation of Moûtiers to the category of "special urban center," the town paper congratulated the municipal council on its work "to get justice for us."[11] In case of emergency, town councils also imposed local rationing, as Rambervillers was obliged to do for bread in December 1945, or organized volunteer milkmen, as Saint-Flour did when snow closed the roads to vehicles but not to cross-country skiis.[12] In addition, the councils and some of the CLLs issued various petitions and demands regarding provisioning—for example, that rations be delivered at the beginning of the month in Rambervillers or that the price of milk be reduced in Saint-Flour.[13]

These circumstances recreated the conditions of the traditional old regime social contract in which the people supported the state in exchange for state regulation of the food supply to ensure an equitable distribution in time of dearth. During both the eighteenth century and the après-libération, the state effectively guaranteed a basic social justice that the people conceptualized along the lines of the "moral economy of the crowd" discussed by E. P. Thompson and that expressed a traditional Christian ethic that no one should starve while others ate well.[14] The moral economy of the 1945 crowd, however, had added dimensions of rights and entitlement constructed since the French Revolution. In particular, local opinion insisted on the right to equality as well as social justice.

At the close of the Second World War, the French had two reasons to think of themselves as entitled to equality. First, the new Resistance government represented both a republic whose motto was, once again, "liberty, equality, and fraternity" and a regime that had fought the Nazis and Vichy on behalf of human and republican rights. Second, that government was running a rationing system that implicitly promised a certain type of equality. Rationing nationalizes the food supply in a time of crisis for the good of the community as defined by the controlling power. Faced with extreme conditions, the Soviet Union, for instance, used its wartime rationing system to ensure the survival of the nation by feeding those who were militarily important to the country at the cost of those who were not.[15] The Nazis, on the other hand, used rationing as a tool for their social engineering project in Poland, giving ethnic Germans acceptable rations of 2,613 calories per day, Poles a derisory 669 calories, and Jews an impossible 184 calories.[16] The French rationing system, in contrast, was constructed so that, in theory, everyone would share the burden of shortages equally and receive an equal portion of what was available. It promised neither victory nor racial superiority but equality, at least of hardship.

The rationing system that was enacted by the Third Republic in 1939 and continued by Vichy, the provisional government, and then the Fourth Republic until 1949, categorized the French by age and by location in city or countryside.[17] It assumed differences in the nutritional needs of infants, children, adolescents, adults, and the aged. Standard exceptions recognized that pregnant women needed more milk and that manual laborers needed more protein than other adults. In theory, at least, this system neutralized the role of money in the provisioning economy. One now needed ration tickets as well as money to buy food. No matter how rich, people would not be able to obtain more food than they were entitled to by their age. And all, no matter how poor, would receive their share because the government also controlled prices (and wages). Such equality would create the fraternity of social justice.

The French system, however, never lived up to its theory, in good part because no government ever controlled the food supply enough to enforce it. Indeed, Vichy failed so thoroughly that the system, or rather its failures in combination with the black market, created a situation in which, in the opinion of the gendarmerie, "the French are practically divided into two blocs, those who eat their fill and those who deploy all their ingenuity to procure the strict necessities."[18]

Politics also intervened to undermine the equality of the rationing system. During the après-libération, the Resistance government used the system to endorse its vision of society; certain categories of persons and certain events received special treatment. In the Vosges, for example, the families of children making their First Communion in 1945 could, with a note from their priest, have two liters of wine and six eggs to celebrate the occasion.[19] Such holiday largesse, whether it was to mark the POWs' return or Christmas, came from the provincial rather than the central provisioning authorities, but whether the extra egg came courtesy of a bureaucrat in Paris or in Epinal, these exceptions to the rules involved the government in endorsing a certain view of society, one in which, for instance, Catholic sacraments deserved public support. More blatantly, the double rations bestowed on repatriated deportees, albeit for sound medical reasons, firmly enthroned these martyrs of the Resistance at the top of the liberation-era moral hierarchy. The extra food confirmed their value to the nation and underscored the Resistance's superior rank. Although this system tended to promote a scramble to join those who qualified as exceptions rather than to result in open complaints, it nonetheless put the government's legitimacy at risk through the inherent tension between the equality promised to all and the moral hierarchy endorsed by the exceptions.

The tensions and resentments created by the rationing system's failures, however, did not fall along the usual social or geographic lines. During the occupation the coexistence of a rationing system and an inflationary black market effected what Dominque Veillon has described as "a quite spectacular change of *mentalités*." In short, it shifted the source of status from one's mode of employment to one's ration card category, thus making the bourgeois clerk suddenly jealous of the coal miner who received the extra food accorded to a heavy laborer.[20] Indeed, the rationing system and the black market together wreaked havoc on the staid prewar social hierarchy not only by rewarding physical labor more highly than desk labor but also by introducing many nouveaux riches in the persons of black market profiteers and peasants. Furthermore, they impoverished many a previously comfortable salaried family and reduced them to trading clothing or knickknacks for hams or lentils.

During the après-libération, people discussed their concerns about the food supply by using the terms "rich" and "poor" rather than the class labels whose meanings had been changed by the shortages. Many an editor and writer of letters to the editor echoed the outrage of a correspondent to *La Margeride* who denounced the day in which, "according to whether you are rich or poor, you eat good or mediocre bread."[21] It was hardly surprising that the rich would eat better than the poor; what made it so very infuriating in 1945 was that the rich were eating better than the poor in a republic that proclaimed equality in its motto and that had a rationing system. If the republic really stood for equality, and if the rationing system really worked, then everyone, whether rich or poor, would be eating the same.

In other places at other times in the twentieth century, mismanagement of the food supply has not only discredited the government but radicalized the populace, most notoriously in 1917 in Petrograd.[22] Things did not develop quite so far in France at the end of the Second World War, but the

French food shortages did begin a process of radicalization by provoking previously silent portions of the population such as women.[23] Indeed, the struggles of the daily economy of rations and prices dragged women into various forms of broadly defined political activity.[24] If much of their discontent found voice in demonstrations and petitions organized through such associations as housewives' committees and the UFF, much of it also found more informal outlets. Women often wrote letters to the editor in their role as "we mothers of families" and "we heads (*chefs*) of provisioning."[25] Others, expressing their displeasure about a late sugar ration identified themselves as "a group of housewives who do not have the money to buy it on the black market," and, in no uncertain terms, those protesting the poor quality of milk signed themselves "a group of [women] voters."[26] That last letter, submitted in January 1945, shows that even before women had actually voted, some at least had determined to wield their new-won political power.

Indeed, provincial administrators expressed alarm over the political ramifications of opinion about the food supply. From the midst of his particularly disadvantaged region, the CRR at Nancy constantly warned that "the discontent grows . . . , seriously antagonizes opinion, and risks having serious repercussions."[27] From a more national perspective, the gendarmerie warned in early 1945 that "until recently the provisioning problem was of an economic order; more and more it takes on a political aspect and could lead to popular reactions that might upset [public] order."[28] Some administrators detected even more ominous threats; the prefect of Isère concluded from the inability of union leaders to contain their constituents' protests over provisioning that "in a word, the working masses not only detach themselves from the Government, but appear ready to combat it openly."[29] Overall, the public objected most strongly to the central government's economic policies, the incompetencies of its provisioning service, the RG, and its failure to eliminate the black market.

To begin with the unpopular economic policies, the government's insistence on acting as if the economy had not fragmented caused increasing popular bitterness. The charade of publishing "national" rations at a time when they could not be honored in many parts of the country made the government look both incompetent and insensitive. In an all too common example from early 1945, the minister of provisioning issued a communiqué that expressed regret at having to reduce the meat ration to 200 grams and thereby rather upset consumers in the Lyon region who counted themselves lucky to get even 170 grams.[30]

People in small towns showed an extraordinary appreciation of their own situation within the spurious standard of the national ration and in relation to their neighbors' rations. In April 1945, for example, Moûtiers' town paper announced with some envy that eggs had gone on sale in Annecy, several mountains away in Haute-Savoie.[31] In June *La Margeride* announced that consumers in Aurillac and Arpajon (also in Cantal) would receive grape sugar although those in Saint-Flour would not, and pleaded: "Come on, Messieurs [of the RG, show] a little more justice."[32] According to the standards of the day, presenting grape sugar as a matter of justice was not considered at all hyperbolic. The rhetorical question posed in Moûtiers, "Do we not have a right to the same advantages as the other towns of Savoie," underscored the French understanding of their rations as a matter of right or entitlement as well as of justice.[33]

The disgruntled did not, however, limit their demands to regional comparisons. Protesters in Le Puy carried a sign reading: "Le Puy is in France, give it 500 grams of fats."[34] And an editorial summarized the sense of abandonment and betrayal felt by many hungry Vosgiens when it demanded: "Is there one France or several Frances? Why do the Lorrainers get less than the Comtois or the Campenois? Is this 1780 or 1945?" The lengthy article ended, ominously enough: "The trouble (*mal*) is profound: for great troubles, great remedies. We seek a new Robespierre." Given that the rest of the article dwelt on the "sabotage" riddling the rationing system, it seems that the author meant the Robespierre of the guillotine as well as of the General Maximum on prices.[35]

Public opinion, however, reacted more quickly to local differentials in some foodstuffs than in others. Consumers in the region of Nancy, for example, were particularly aggrieved over wine, that symbol of France and of the good life in France, that nectar of the gods and "killer of microbes."[36] Officially, every French adult had a right to two liters of wine per month. Naturally, even if delivered promptly and in good quality, this amount was generally regarded as unsatisfactory in a country with a prewar average consumption of just over one liter per adult per day.[37] Nonetheless, between the liberation of most of the Vosges in September 1944 and the

German surrender in May 1945, the department received only enough wine to distribute one liter to each consumer. Given the circumstances, the national government's announcement of a supplemental wine distribution to celebrate the victory achieved a certain irony.

Vosgiens were particularly upset to learn that the provisional government was able to find transportation to sell good French wine to the Belgians but not to send any to the Lorrainers.[38] Nor did it appease opinion that café owners were somehow able to obtain wine to sell at high prices (twelve francs the half glass) while the government could not organize the transportation to fulfill its promises of a measly two-liter ration.[39] Indeed, the "chronic dearth (*disette*) in wine" formed the subject of CLL pronouncements and of threats of strikes in the region's coal fields. Recognizing the "certain trouble" it was causing, the CRR at Nancy continually warned the central authorities about a situation that he blamed on the "negligence and ill will of the distribution services in Paris," sabotage by the same, and the inability of the government to organize the transportation system.[40] By November 1945, when Vosgiens had received only twenty-two liters out of the fifty-two to which they were entitled since the liberation, the wine drought had created a great deal of skepticism about the national government in the Vosges.

In a second instance of unpopular policy making, the government showed a devotion to the free market that, from the provincial perspective, was wholly unjustifiable and, at the very least, "a premature measure that will only create disappointment."[41] In short, the national authorities repeatedly tried to return only certain portions of the economy to the free market while keeping the controls on other sectors, despite the gulf between the available supplies and the high demand. Directive after directive issued from the pricing offices in Paris offended provincial common sense and upset provincial markets.

In April 1945, for example, the Ministry of the National Economy removed the controls from the markets in poultry and rabbits and decreed a free market in most fresh fruits and vegetables that had previously been controlled by set prices rather than rationing. Foreseeably, this immediately drained the relevant foodstuffs to the highest bidder, namely Paris, and raised prices asked in the provinces for the few remaining chickens and strawberries. The sudden appearance of fresh meat and produce undoubtedly pleased Parisian consumers a great deal, but their sudden disappearance had rather the opposite effect on provincial consumers, triggering a chain of food riots across the country.[42] As the CRR at Limoges put it, "The spirit of the majority opinion . . . forgets its recent joy of Victory to be justly scandalized over the free market prices (*libres cours*) of strawberries and lettuce."[43]

But perhaps the most important area in which provincial opinion blamed bad governmental policy for its sufferings was inflation. The complicated and debatable causes for the postwar inflation did not interest consumers nearly as much as their judgment that because the government was controlling both prices and wages it was responsible for both, and particularly for the way in which prices were bounding ahead of wages. As early as April 1945, the prefect of Savoie reported that a recent hike in the price of bread was seen as another proof of the government's bad financial policy.[44] People watched prices rise month after month with increasing horror. When a woman complained about shortages in June 1945, the editor of *La Margeride* responded by predicting that when the shops were full, no one but "millionaires" would be able to buy anything.[45] In a more likely prediction, a Vosgien paper complained that the black market in meat would soon disappear, not because the weekly rations would suffice, but because the consumers' purchasing power "will become nonexistent."[46]

By the end of the summer, inflation began to overshadow many other concerns, especially in places with severe supply difficulties such as the Vosges. Indeed, inflation became the context for much discontent in late 1945. Prices reached such high levels by January 1946 that the CRR at Nancy remarked that "the [lower-class] clientele limit their purchases."[47] In fact, those who were worst off could not afford to buy the rations that they understood to be theirs as a guaranteed minimum. The government had thus allowed its rationing system to turn from an exercise in democratic sharing into a preserve of the rich and a cruel mockery of the poor. And where was the justice in that?

Public opinion in the provinces had a second major provisioning grievance against the new Resistance government: the way in which it administered the food supply, which was, to say the least, inefficient. People did not complain about the absolute shortage of food so much as they did that the huge provisioning bureaucracy appeared to be aggravating the shortages through ineptitude or treason. Unfortunately for the GPRF, it inherited an unpopular and discredited RG.[48] Yet what could the Gaullists do? To have abandoned rationing at the liberation would have meant starving the less advantaged parts of the population, including civil servants and other sections of the bourgeoisie. The new government could, and did, replace top officials in the Ministry of Provisioning and its departmental offices with resistants, but it could not replace the RG's entire extensive staff. Nor did it streamline the byzantine legislation by which the RG operated.

Because Vichy had never fully controlled the food supply and had lost the public's confidence in the legal distribution system, the Resistance's RG faced an added challenge. As well as overcoming the problems created by shortages, communications and transportation breakdowns, and demographic uncertainties, it would have to convince both producers and consumers to deal exclusively on the legal market. For producers this meant delivering all their crops or livestock to the RG, and for consumers it meant buying only through the RG. The struggles between the RG and farmers belong to another study, but it should be noted that the producers enjoyed some sympathy in small market towns such as Saint-Flour, Moûtiers, and Rambervillers. On the basis of common sense alone the farmers won sympathy when the government paid three thousand francs for a three-hundred-kilogram cow that could fetch seventeen thousand to eighteen thousand francs on the illegal market.[49] Producers similarly showed some sympathy for their hungry neighbors in small market towns. During a nationwide meat shortage in the late summer of 1945, for example, the Vosgien farmers in the districts of Rambervillers, Charmes, and Bruyères unanimously donated their own meat rations "for the benefit of the [local] town."[50]

Producers and consumers also shared some complaints against the RG. The local press was full of tales of the woe caused to producers, consumers, and shopkeepers by the endless tickets and forms demanded by the RG's complicated directives.[51] Indeed, the tentacles of the provisioning bureaucracy and regulations so infiltrated French society that they created whole new realms of criminality.[52] Hunger drew some to crime as a way to find food. Conversely, the high prices other hungry people were willing to pay for food drew the attention of criminals to such formerly nonlucrative objects as cheese. Food crime fell into three main categories: fraud, theft, and black marketeering, which, of course, often included the first two. Yet, while theft and fraud were ordinary crimes applied to current circumstances, black marketeering skittered on the edge of treason and betrayal.

Many opportunities for fraud appeared for both merchants and consumers in the endlessly changing and endlessly complex regulations imposed by the RG on shopkeepers concerning every aspect of trade from quantities of sales to prices. As a producing department, Cantal offered a natural target for criminals interested in stealing valuable foodstuffs through trickery. In one case a twenty-five-year-old Parisian and two accomplices promoted themselves from unemployed manual laborers to "economic controllers" on a mission to find and "confiscate" illicit stocks. Although they won the goodwill of the mayor of Pierrefort, their spelling aroused the suspicions of his secretary. The Tribunal correctionnel in Saint-Flour sentenced the ringleader to a suspended year in prison.[53]

Less audaciously and much more commonly, ordinary people engaged in ration-card fraud. As with black marketeering, men and women had developed their ration-card scams under the occupation, when they could justify their misdemeanors as a blow struck against the enemy and its collaborators. One could acquire double or even triple ration cards by using false identities, falsely declaring that one had lost one's original cards, or keeping the cards of a family member who had left for some such reason as joining the FFI. One could also steal someone else's cards; in one case this provoked a certain Mme. C. to publish a warning to the known but unnamed person who had used her sugar card to either give her the sugar or face legal proceedings.[54]

At the liberation the CDL and authorities in Cantal intended to put a stop to food frauds. For its part, the CDL "urgently *demand*[ed] that members of the Order of Physicians strictly reserve certificates for dietary exemptions for the truly sick alone and unpityingly refuse them to others."[55] These would have been the same doctors, of course, that the Resistance had previously encouraged to issue a wide range of false certificates, especially to young men threatened with the labor draft. As for the provisioning authorities in Cantal, they demanded that everyone turn in all extra cards by 20 October 1944 or face the full penalty of the law. "The offending parties will kindly recall that every supplementary ration that is wrongfully received is a theft from the collectivity and distorts the normal provisioning of the population."[56] The effectiveness of such ethical arguments might be questioned, however, because in February 1945 *Le Réveil des Vosges* reported that bread cards were being stolen and sold for 150 francs in Epinal. Similarly, in July 1945 the CRR at Laon-Saint-Quentin reported that citizens were circulating false ration cards for bread and other staples as they had done during the war.[57]

The shortages and the exorbitant prices on the black market also drove people to theft for profit and for survival. The more spectacular thefts, such as the disappearance of 2,500 kilograms of sugar from the train station in Chambéry, were obviously motivated by profit; as was the theft of 110 liters of wine from a café in Rambervillers.[58] But many food thefts suggest more desperate causes. *La Résistance savoyarde,* for instance, reacted to a wave of pet abductions in December 1945 by warning its readers that eating cat meat was dangerous because it might be infected with diseases such as typhus. The paper did, however, recommend the meat of mules (many of which lost their footing on the mountain trails) as healthful and suggested preparing it in the same manner as beef, veal, or lamb.[59] One's vegetables, however, were more often in danger than one's pets through what the owners of gardens denounced as vandalism and marauding.[60]

The extent of such petty thefts and other food crimes during the après-libération may be gauged from the press reports of the Tribunal correctionnel. In its audience of 15 March 1945, for instance, the Sanflorain court sentenced a thirty-nine-year-old agricultural worker to three months' suspended imprisonment for stealing grain and eggs from his employer in order to pay for his laundry; a housewife to eight days in jail for picking her neighbor's carrots; a twenty-year-old, "of very bad repute," for neglecting to turn in his *mitraillette* when he left the maquis to fifteen days in prison; and a forty-five-year-old man from Hérault caught at the Saint-Flour station with an unacceptably large quantity of food to a five-thousand-franc fine.[61] Although petty theft and hooliganism are the common coin of such courts, the details of each of these cases were unmistakably shaped by the war.

For those who stayed within the bounds of legality, daily interaction with the RG and its red tape served as a constant source of aggravation and even, in the opinion of Resistance heroine Lucie Aubrac, humiliation.⁶² First of all, one had to be able to grasp the bureaucratic subtleties of the ration tickets that permitted access to the staples of life—meat, bread, dairy products, sugar, soap, clothing, fuel, and the like—as well as to the luxuries—wine, coffee, and chocolate (reserved for children). By the liberation, what remained unrationed, mostly fruits and vegetables, was still under government control in the form of maximum prices. The various ration coupons, points, and tickets had to be collected, kept track of, and matched to the announcements in the press and on the walls of the town hall as to when people of such and such an age had the right to buy this amount of that product.

The consumer could then repair to a shop to pay for the product in both money and ration coupons, if the item was available, and undoubtedly after standing in line for some time. Indeed, standing in line was such an integral part of daily life from 1940 to 1949 that Veillon has described the queue as a "new form of sociability" and a "barometer of public opinion." It influenced fashion, created a new profession, "*queutière*" (place holder), and acted as a civic forum.⁶³ The last function worried the gendarmerie, who reported during a period of food riots that "in the queues one hears reflections that are very severe toward the authorities as well as ill-concealed threats that are approved by all those who hear them."⁶⁴

But even with the appropriate ration coupons and limitless time, one could not necessarily buy anything at any store one pleased. The government's requirement that consumers register at particular shops for particular items such as bread or meat essentially indentured customers to their neighborhood shopkeepers. The shopkeepers themselves struggled under an avalanche of red tape but wielded tremendous power because they could exercise considerable discretion over the quality if not (legally) the quantity of a rationed item that they offered to each customer. Indeed, the CRR at Lyon remarked that "the grocer or the clerk at any distribution office . . . certainly has greater powers during the current impoverished times than the most respectable of subprefects."⁶⁵ Such power and its supposed access to wealth generated the type of bitter envy expressed in a cartoon called "The Parasites." Two bourgeois stand on a street watching a fat man with a cigar, nose in the air, cane in one hand and briefcase in the other, stroll by. Says one: "Eggs are fattening him up." "He eats a lot of them?" asks the other. "No, he sells them!"⁶⁶

The local press voiced the postliberation collapse of consumer patience with their indenture to shopkeepers by commiserating with "the unhappy clientele of 1945. . . . Ill humor is the only commodity that currently fills the shops and sells—pardon, is given—without the least ticket. The grocer resembles a bear, the butcher a big bad wolf, the greengrocer a tiger, and the tobacconist a wild cat. . . . The tiresome thing is that one is forced to run one's errands every day at the risk of being eaten. What is certain, indisputable, is that the attitude (*mentalité*) of the majority of merchants must change."[67] The frequency of vigilante bomb attacks on shopkeepers in Savoie may have contributed to changing those attitudes.

More commonly, articles about shopping warned consumers (and shopkeepers) against shady practices such as selling rationed goods behind the counter for excessive prices or imposing conditions on sales such as requiring that a customer buy expensive asparagus in addition to the more economical cauliflower.[68] Other articles complained that shopkeepers cheated their customers by falsifying the weight of bread or the quality of meat.[69] The Vosgien press in general expressed more spleen and threats against shopkeepers than the Cantalien or Savoyard press, perhaps because the shortages were so much more dire in the Vosges. Upon being asked to pay rather more than the posted price for peaches in Epinal, one journalist wrote: "The fine fool (*brave bougre*) of a customer has too great an impression of paying black market prices in the official market. Do we have price controllers, yes or no? If yes, where are they and what are they doing? We would like to know if they have decided to act. Or if the good yokels (*bon croquants*), tired of being taken for suckers (*poires*), should see justice done themselves?"[70]

Significantly, the article goes beyond castigating the offending shopkeeper to call the government to task for shirking its responsibilities. In it, the usually mundane act of purchasing a few peaches for dinner escapes its normally private, everyday boundaries to become a threat to the public peace and perhaps even the life of the shopkeeper, because the phrase "*faire justice eux-mêmes*" was often used as code for lynching collaborators. Yet even if that article were dismissed as absurdly inflammatory, the extent to which shopping for one's daily meal had become a public issue, even in better fed and calmer areas, could be seen in the prevalence of the topic in the local press and local politics.

But even with the friendliest merchants in the world, the average person could not rely solely on shops and the official economy to provide sufficient food. In March 1945 the prefect of Indre-et-Loire estimated that consumers obtained 50 percent of their necessary food on the legal market and 20 percent on the black market, thus leaving a 30 percent hunger gap that could not be filled in the country's current state of poverty.[71] Similarly, the gendarmerie had to admit for Poitou—although the observation would hold good for other areas as well—that, "the [provisioning] efforts [made] at the governmental level have not borne fruit, and it must be said that if on the whole the population lives, it is because of purchases made illegally (*hors-distribution*)."[72] In the Bouches-du-Rhône during the first trimester of 1945, extralegal purchases furnished on average 32 percent of daily caloric intake.[73]

"*Hors-distribution*" referred to goods obtained on the various levels of the parallel economy developed over the course of the occupation and spanning all the shades of legality and illegality. It ranged from individual barter arrangements, to packages of food sent from the countryside to friends and family in the city, to the gray market of unofficial and slightly higher-priced transactions among acquaintances, to the exorbitant commercial dealings of the black market.[74] The government itself essentially sanctioned the low-level private arrangements of individuals with laws that exempted black marketeering in family-sized quantities from prosecution and allowed for the shipment of family packages of certain dimensions throughout the country.[75] Such small efforts added up to a considerable total. The prefect of Côtes-du-Nord complained in May 1945 that the estimated 750 tons of butter and meat from the department sent by post to, or fetched by train from, Paris made a mockery of efforts to collect the department's quota.[76] The daily displacement of people and packages needed to attain this total must, at the very least, have put a considerable strain on the crippled transportation system and sapped the reconstruction workforce through absenteeism. Moreover, these laws eased the procurement predicament for the average person but muddied the line between legality and illegality.

Foraging expeditions and family packages formed an essential part of a family's "system D," named for the verb *se débrouiller,* or to make do.[77] One's system D involved every sort of clever repair and substitution and every alternative means of supply developed over the course of the occupation. By the liberation, then, housewives were already adept at what was called in Savoie's women's paper "Modern Gastronomy, or the art of making something with almost nothing." In this case it meant meat loaf with, if at all possible—although the author rather doubted it—nutmeg, a handful of bread crumbs, a bit of milk, and, most unlikely of all, an egg.[78] Many were also already accustomed to working with restricted power supplies that might allow a woman only an hour or two of gas or electricity a day in which to cook and to heat water for cleaning.

But if the liberation did not greatly alter the interaction of the citizenry and the government's provisioning services on the practical level of obtaining food, it altered it immensely on the rhetorical and reactive level. In the first place, it raised expectations by removing the Germans and installing the Resistance's republican regime. Vichy had actively fostered the association of the occupation with hunger and of peace with prosperity by blaming the shortages on the Germans, thus leading many to the incorrect conclusion that the food would reappear when the Germans disappeared.[79] Even those who had arrived at a more subtle analysis of the reasons for shortages expected the liberation to instantly resolve them. *La Résistance savoyarde,* for instance, remarked as early as November 1944 that "it is hard to explain how almost three months after the Germans' departure," the rich ate well at certain restaurants and dressed warmly while the great majority shivered with cold and hunger. The author had apparently expected the black market to leave in the German baggage train or crumble at the feet of the victorious Resistance.[80] From around the country, the gendarmerie often observed popular disappointment with a peace that did not include prosperity and even blamed some food protests on it.[81] That analysis, however, leaves out the crucial element that the peace that the people expected from the Resistance government was not only prosperous but just. It was the injustice within the continuing poverty that triggered protests.

Furthermore, the liberation opened the floodgates of complaint and protest by restoring civil liberties and elections.[82] The majority of complaints focused on the manifold shortcomings of the RG and, by extension, the rest of the government. Indeed, public opinion tended to blame the RG itself for the shortages for reasons ranging from conspiracy theories to plain ineptitude, and often a combination of both. The conspiracy theories grew from the fact that many of the staff of Vichy's RG continued in their places after the liberation, thereby seriously compromising the Resistance government's RG at a time when the purge courts were penalizing individuals for having served the Vichy regime. This suspicion of a fifth column harboring within the RG combined with the archetypal famine plots of the old regime that accused merchants or bureaucrats of withholding food out of incompetence or evil intent.[83] Groups such as the Comité d'unité d'action CGT et CFTC de Savoie et de Haute-Savoie accordingly demanded a purge of the RG management for the sake of increasing the food supply and insuring justice.[84]

Another widespread theory held that collaborators were profiting from the hunger and cold of the winter of 1944–45 by launching a whispering campaign in which "the commentaries made by the 'agents of the fifth column,' that is the enemies of the Republic, turn on the theme: 'we were better nourished during the occupation.'"[85] Disgruntled consumers, however, would hardly have needed provocateurs to bring the thought to mind, especially in places like Cantal, where it was true.[86] According to another theory, black marketeers were stirring up discontent over provisioning so that they could "incite the population against the Authorities," in order to obtain economic policies that would benefit themselves.[87] Black markets, however, are natural magnets for conspiracy theories; Vichy had tried to blame the French black market on the Jews.[88] Moreover, there hardly needed to be a conspiracy for the black market to threaten the government, as its very existence challenged it.

Those with vaguer forebodings simply ascribed all upsets in the provisioning system to sabotage, presumably by collaborationist traitors. Suspicions reached such a level that an editorialist in the Vosges demanded to know if the half loaf of bread seen in a garbage can in Epinal in December 1945 had been put there by "a madman or a provocateur."[89] The war's end in May 1945 made little difference to these variations on the famine plot dressed in the contemporary rhetoric of collaborators versus resistants. In both provisioning and the purge, the popular mind found the traitorous collaborators to be as dangerous to the community in December 1945 as in December 1944.

Without subscribing to any conspiracy theories, a section of opinion spanning from highly placed administrators to humble writers of letters to the editor blamed the shortages on the RG's ineptitude. It did, however, find such incompetence to be criminal if not treasonous. The CRR at Lyon, for one, felt certain that the people of his region's cities would be better fed if they "did not depend on bureaucrats who live on erroneous numbers."[90] Similarly, a "group of consumers" from Aigueblanche (Savoie) submitted a complaint about the misplaced zeal of RG inspectors who harassed individuals who took the initiative to provide food at reasonable prices rather than hunt down the "*affameurs*" causing the shortages.[91] In this case the consumers were using a rather elastic definition of the black market, but they made a good point—that the RG seemed to act without any grasp of the realities of daily life.

The complaints and suspicions against the RG found fertile soil in a constant stream of provisioning scandals involving the mishandling of food supplies and the quality of those supplies. These scandals were almost routinely interpreted as sabotage. Individuals and associations vigilantly reported transportation snafus to the local press and demanded action against the responsible parties. In the regions of this study, such scandals often involved potatoes allowed to rot, such as the thousands of tons of the spoiled tubers that had to be thrown into the river above Moûtiers at a time when the town's potato rations were in arrears.[92]

The death of livestock during shipment also upset the people in both the departments that raised the animals, such as Cantal, and in the departments that received them, such as Savoie. The public outrage over one case of five cows that arrived at Moûtiers' station already dead prompted the local editor to write: "we are counting . . . on the prefect's authority to see justice done; if not, the population might lose its temper because we know [towns] in the Tarentaise that have not touched a gram of meat for several months, during which time the persons responsible for provisioning us [have] let animals perish!!!"[93] Local representatives in Cantal spent equal energy browbeating the authorities to find the guilty parties, even tracing shipments of local livestock to their ill-fated ends.

The departmental authorities tried to defend themselves from these charges through the press. The very active director of the RG in Cantal, for instance, not only published detailed rebuttals to printed accusations of his service's bungling, but also provided a telephone number at which Cantaliens could verify the apparently rampant rumors about rotting butter, jam, and coffee (all declared false) and alert the RG to any stocks in danger of spoiling.[94] The prefect of the Vosges several times published detailed explanations of the causes of particular shortages and the record of his office's vain attempts to move the national government to work on the Vosgiens' behalf.[95]

Consumers also complained about the quality of the rations that they did receive. Milk soured before children could drink it; meat was indescribably tough. Not surprisingly, given the cultural symbolism of bread in France, the complaints waxed most lyrical over the daily loaf, which should have been as white as snow.[96] An editorial printed completely in boldface complained that the Vosgiens "have a right only to '*caca*' bread, stale and lumpy."[97] And correspondents in Cantal complained of bread "that is a black dough, gluey and sticky, and that has trouble forcing a route to the stomach," or that "is always [made of] rye and bran, compact, indigestible, almost as black and heavy as the basalt of [Saint-Flour] rebellious in the best stomachs."[98] Notably, such descriptions generally asserted that someone else, either richer or in a more favored locale, was at the same time enjoying the digestible white bread of happiness. An editorial from Romans even tied bread into patriotism with its demand that the police severely punish the "*mauvais Français*" who had allowed their children to throw away bread in the street. At a time of shortage the author considered the wastage to be a betrayal of the community.[99]

Consumers further complained about strange or unhealthy-looking foods.[100] The prefect of Indre, for instance, reported popular indignation over the fact that his region, where people cooked with butter, was exporting butter while filling its own fat rations with imported oil.[101] An alarm over sugar further underscored the importance of providing familiar food. During the summer of 1945 the RG distributed American brown sugar instead of the usual white sugar. As early as July, the CRR at Clermont-Ferrand reported the suspicions aroused by this sugar and remarked that it was not being given to "priority consumers" such as children and adolescents. In September, he reported that the American sugar had provoked several complaints.[102] By that time, however, the director of the departmental RG in Cantal had sent the prefect a formal note explaining that the sugar delivered for the September rations was "of bad quality, even dirty," and that housewives were crying sabotage. The prefect responded by explaining that it was American brown sugar and that a health professional had pronounced it safe and nutritious. The director then replied that he was himself only relaying public opinion, but a survey of grocers revealed that most had found things other than sugar in the sacks and had unhappy customers.[103]

Eighty tons of the same brown sugar caused similar troubles in the Vosges, where the authorities found it to be "absolutely unfit for consumption and even for commercial use."[104] The departmental daily took up the cause and warned all consumers to demand the white sugar to which they were entitled and to reject the various schemes by which shopkeepers were trying to dispose of their unwanted stocks.[105] Whether or not the suspect sugar was spoiled, it is hardly surprising that it would be rejected by French housewives, whose recipes do not use brown sugar as American cooking does, and who, by this time of rationed eggs and butter, would be using sugar mainly to sweeten ersatz coffee or to make fruit preserves, both of which call for white sugar in America as well as in France.

When it came to actual shortfalls in their rations, the long-suffering consumers of 1944–45 took to the streets in protest. The food protests of the après-libération followed two patterns: that of the early modern food riot and that of the late modern political demonstration.[106] From the incomplete evidence of this study, it appears that the more spontaneous reactions on the part of a community took the older form, while protests planned through official organizations, often connected to the Communist Party, took the newer form. Both attempted to force the government to honor its responsibility to provide sufficient and equal rations as required by social justice and promised by the rationing system.

In the eighteenth century food rioters employed a repertoire of actions that involved stopping the movement of scarce goods out of an area or forcing the sale of those goods at what the crowd considered a just price (rather than the market price). The riots occurred because the people's understanding of justice required the government to control the bread market after the government had renounced that control in favor of liberal capitalism and the creation of a national free market. They were meant to force the government to reverse its policies and honor the traditional social contract.[107] Although much altered, the situation was not wholly different in 1945. The populace again felt deeply that social justice required the government to control the food supply. Indeed, the government had accepted its responsibility by instituting a rationing system. Unlike the eighteenth-century government, the Resistance government did not eschew the controlled food economy, but it did fail to run the rationing system effectively. And it did experiment with opening a free national market in certain goods during a time of scarcity and official control of the rest of the market.

Intriguingly, this similar situation moved postliberation protesters to mimic the gestures of early modern food rioters and "consumer vigilantes."[108] The echoes between the eighteenth century and 1945 can be found in attempts to stop the movement of scarce goods (*entraves*), forced sales of such goods, and attacks on government agents. Seizures and sales of rationed goods occurred all over the country. In September 1945, a hundred people in Fougerolles (Haute-Saône) stopped a load of butter and forced an immediate distribution.[109] "Housewives" in Langeac (Allier) made a similar attempt at an "*entrave*," to use the CRR's term, of a load of meat.[110] In an interesting variation, *La Résistance savoyarde* printed an unusually nonlocal report that housewives in Aussy (Nord) confiscated black market goods and sold them at the town hall for the official prices. One of the black marketeers later lodged a complaint about being manhandled. "What do you think Justice did?" asked the paper. "It convicted, not the trafficker, but a housewife of Aussy to one month in prison." The paper made clear its admiration for the housewifely vigilantism and its contempt for the workings of official justice, particularly its mistreatment of honest folk with initiative.[111] The incident illustrates some important points. First, these women staged an eighteenth-century forced sale in all its particulars except that their "just price" was the government price rather than a remembered one. The difference between the original holders of the goods, black marketeers rather than merchants, hardly matters, as their contemporaries called both "*affameurs*." Second, in this incident as in so many in the purge, the popular understanding of justice sided against the government and in favor of those whom the government's justice defined as criminals but whose neighbors acclaimed as heroes.

These direct expressions of the popular will regarding food sometimes turned violent. In October 1945, for instance, housewives in an unspecified town in the region of Nancy armed themselves to protest an interrupted distribution of chocolate.[112] Earlier in the year 150 workers in the Orne descended on an abattoir to take back *"de vive force"* the 314 kilograms of meat that had been confiscated from their canteen.[113] More often, however, angry consumers attacked agents of the provisioning service. In Barbezieux (Charente), for example, a crowd of five hundred beat up two inspectors of the economic police and then attacked two passersby whom they took to be police.[114] And in Sens (Yonne) a crowd turned on a controller of the economic service while he was writing up illegal prices in the vegetable market.[115] Similar reports came from Montendre (Charente-Maritime) and Saint-Jean-de-Luz (Basse-Pyrénées).[116] All of these incidents occurred after the war ended, or, in other words, after the government had lost the excuse that the country was at war. Many also occurred during the traditional period of greatest hunger and anxiety—between the exhaustion of the old crop and the harvest of the new, the *soudure*—when the attackers preferred to pay high illegal prices than to see supplies disappear.

In yet another variation of après-libération protests, and in a striking echo of the October Days of 1789, two hundred women from the commune of Chaligny marched fourteen kilometers to protest their hunger in front of the prefecture in Nancy.[117] Although there is no indication that they took the king or his viceroy, the CRR, back home with them, the example illustrates how porous the distinction between early modern and late modern protests really is.[118] Most protests during the après-libération, however, did take forms more familiar to nineteenth- and twentieth-century industrial society than to earlier times. Provisioning issues, for instance, appeared in strike demands. Out of 256 strikes between 15 November 1944 and 15 August 1945, the gendarmerie registered 48 strikes motivated principally by provisioning concerns. It did not, however, indicate how many strikes included provisioning questions as subsidiary demands.[119] Over the course of 1945, strike demands shifted from the issue of larger rations to that of greater pay, thus reflecting the general displacement of economic anxiety from how to get food to how to pay the ever steeper inflationary prices for it.[120]

The great majority of food protests, however, took place as demonstrations. The typical protest of 1944–45 involved a gathering in front of the town hall, prefecture, or RG depot to demand more food more efficiently distributed; protests ranged from laying petitions before the prefect, to preventing the arrest of the town butcher, to pillaging a noodle factory.

Protesters might also process through town, carrying placards with sayings such as "Milk, sugar, butter, chocolate for our children," or "Purge the RG," and performing such patriotic gestures as singing the "Marseillaise."[121] Administrative reports most often referred to "women" or the obviously gendered term "housewives," although they occasionally spoke of "consumers." It is clear from the more detailed accounts that men joined in food protests, but women seem to have made up the majority of protesters.[122]

Between 15 October 1944 and 15 August 1945, the gendarmerie drew up an incomplete list of 231 demonstrations focusing on food issues. The largest recorded demonstration involved a hundred thousand people in Lyon on 11 March 1945. The greatest concentration of recorded protests fell between 15 March and 15 April 1945, although the list ends before the late summer wave of food protests and becomes less comprehensive over the course of the summer.[123] At the beginning of the period, food demonstrations tended to respond to local conditions, but increasingly over the course of 1945 food protests lost their local character and began to respond to what the prefect of Aisne called "exterior directives."[124]

The prefect's "exterior directives" undoubtedly meant direction by the Communist Party. During the après-libération, the PCF sought to safeguard industrial reconstruction by displacing worker grievances onto consumer terrain and channeling the expression of those grievances to times and places that would not threaten production.[125] While doing this, the Communists could claim to be champions of social justice and leaders in the demand for fair rations. It seems at least as likely, however, that they were struggling to co-opt a very deep popular discontent that was quickly developing quite independently of their efforts. The party often exercised its influence on the discontent over provisioning through the UFF; indeed, the only documented food protests in Moûtiers and Saint-Flour involved the towns' UFF chapters. Rambervillers appears not to have had any food protests despite its severe shortages; perhaps the people were satisfied with the local authorities' efforts on their behalf, or perhaps their protests escaped documentation.[126]

Founded at the liberation, Moûtiers' UFF and its interest in provisioning grew organically out of the local experience of occupation and sense of social justice. Indeed, the complicated symbolic commingling of hunger and oppression and of food and justice during the après-libération may be seen in the local UFF's description of the occupation as "the bread of bran and ersatz mixtures, the quart of skimmed milk that soured as soon as it was put by the fire, the parsimonious distributions of rutabagas, the weekly chop of sixty grams, all that under the haughty regard of the occupier, who, with his executioners in the Gestapo and [Vichy's] Milice, hunted down our husbands, our eldest sons, our brothers in order to martyr them or deport them to Germany."[127]

In December 1944, Moûtiers' UFF merged with the town's other Resistance-based women's group, the Comité d'action féminine of the MLN (AF-MLN), in order to act more efficiently on "the current very agonizing questions of provisioning [that interest] all women." The assembly sent a petition to the CLL and the prefect regarding "milk, butter, thread, yarn, infant cereals, and children's shoes, the almost nonexistent public transportation in Moûtiers, and the classification of Moûtiers as an urban center for provisioning and family allocations."[128] Moûtiers' union also showed considerable interest in supply questions.[129]

Moûtiers' only documented food protest took place on 7 April 1945 as an apparently unremarkable analogue to the UFF-sponsored protest in Chambéry on that same Saturday. Moûtiers' newspaper covered only the events in the departmental capital, which it treated sympathetically. The prefect explained both protests as an echo of demonstrations in Lyon and Grenoble and as the result of the natural hardships of April in Savoie. At this point in the traditional agricultural cycle into which the war had once again thrown the Alpine department, the winter vegetables had all run out before the summer ones had been harvested. This food gap had long ago created the ancient charity of the *Pain de Mai* in which the archbishop fed the people of Moûtiers from the gates of the archiepiscopal palace.[130] The town did, however, see protests for other supply problems such as a shortage of heating fuel, but for the most part the local resistance administration anticipated mass complaints with official petitions or action.

In contrast to Moûtiers, Saint-Flour did not have a UFF section until the late summer of 1945. The Sanflorain chapter emerged from a food protest organized by the deputy secretary of the town's Communist cell on 13 September 1945, a couple of weeks after similar protests elsewhere in the department and a suggestion from *La Margeride* that Sanflorain housewives follow suit.[131] The local PCF invited the women to the protest through the town crier and duly registered posters that summarized the major complaints against the Gaullist government: the shortages, the inequalities, and the government's failure to fulfill its responsibilities.

One hundred and fifty to two hundred women from among the "classes of workers, small businessmen, artisans, and civil servants" responded to the invitation and processed to the town hall singing the "Marseillaise" and carrying posters reading "We want potatoes, pasta, and butter" and "We want to be provisioned like Aurillac, Vic-sur-Cère, and Arpajon." Four (male) comrades led a delegation of ten to present a petition to the mayor asking for the same rations as Aurillac, the suppression of middlemen who were the "cause of the scarcity of foodstuffs," and a reduction in the price of butter and milk. The procession also visited the office of the Contrôle économique (CE), which was closed, and the subprefecture. The protesters then merged their cause with that of honorary justice through the patriotic gestures used in so many memorial ceremonies: a symbolic stop at the Monument aux Morts and another rendition of the "Marseillaise."[132]

Although the protest itself never troubled the public peace, it set off a flurry of reactions. In particular, some women established a "Union of Housewives of Saint-Flour," which changed into a recognized chapter of the UFF after a public meeting on the evening of 27 September.[133] That meeting of approximately one hundred persons (according to the police) began with a twenty-minute discussion of the local provisioning situation during which housewives complained about a vegetable shortage and the expense and poor quality of milk. They also remarked on the unfavorable comparison of Saint-Flour's supplies with those of other towns in Cantal. A militant Communist from Paris then took the floor to explain the provisioning situation in the capital and what the PCF was trying to do about it. He particularly blamed the obstructionist attitude of prefects for the country's shortages, and he ended with instructions on how to vote in the upcoming national elections and constitutional referendum.[134] The press reports all carried a seven-point petition submitted to the prefect by the committee of the UFF "in the name of more than five hundred [*sic*] participants (*auditrices*)."[135]

Both the departmental director of the RG and the subprefect responded to the meeting by denying that there was any vegetable shortage. The subprefect proved his point by commenting that two days after the meeting, "a great part of the vegetables remained unsold at 6:00 P.M." at the market and affirming that Saint-Flour had enough fruits and vegetables to "allow an almost normal provisioning of the population."[136] He did not, however, mention at what price the vegetables remained unsold. The committee of the UFF met again a few times, but aside from a somewhat acrimonious misunderstanding about a rumored distribution of children's galoshes, it had no other public impact.[137] Because it grew out of neither a local resistance group (although the department's UFF did) nor desperate local shortages (as housewives' committees turned UFFs did in other towns), it soon faded from view.

Although the economic situation of the après-libération that combined scarcity with a popular demand that the government provide social justice created certain echoes of the eighteenth century in the form of protests and the rhetoric surrounding the black market, in 1944–45 the people possessed a much more telling cudgel to use against the government than their ancestors' violence. The people—both men and women—could vote. Inevitably then, the subject of food slipped into the electoral politicking of the day, as may be seen in the "Potato Coup" in the Vosges, which represents a popular intrusion of the issue into politics and illustrates the congruence of the general anxiety over the price of food, misguided governmental policies, and electoral politics during the après-libération.

Because of the effects of the drawn-out battle for the liberation of the Vosges, the people there, many of whom were *sinistrés,* openly feared the onset of the winter of 1945–46 and worried about local stocks of food and fuel. As early as August, the CRR reported popular discontent over the fact that scheduled stocks of that winter staple, the potato, had not yet arrived.[138] The level of discontent made itself apparent in late September, when "the group 'Consumers and Co-op Members' of the Consultative Commission on Provisioning" published a most energetic open letter to the prefect and the director of the RG protesting the Ministry of Provisioning's *"politique de la pomme de la terre"* (potato policy). The group charged that the recent decision to raise the price of potatoes to 335 francs per 100 kilograms was "pure electioneering," and taken "under the influence of the potato-growing trusts." They demanded that the maximum price be set at 300 francs per 100 kilograms and that the police and authorities take "all necessary measures to assure each Vosgien his or her family stock, by force if necessary." The letter ended with the hope that "the measures tending to set workers against farmers be understood and combated by all. That potatoes be furnished to the consumers at the set prices. That the authorities [show] a more just understanding of the needs of a population starved for five years and whose patience is at an end. That the police forces watch over transactions and fight to the death against traffickers. That the population support the Group in its just demands against measures taken against good sense and only for partisan politics."[139]

Even by the inflamed rhetorical standards of the Vosges, that letter stood out for its vehemence. But it was only the opening salvo. Two weeks later, and only a week before the general elections, the ministry authorized a retail price increase from 4Fr90 per kilogram to 6Fr50 per kilogram, thereby provoking the usually moderate *La Liberté de l'Est* to scream: "A Kilo of Potatoes for 6Fr50. The price anarchy continues. The democratic potato that, up until now, has been somewhat spared by the price increases—everything is relative—is becoming a dish reserved for the tables of nabobs." In another article, the Center of Coordination of the Mouvements familiaux asked individuals and associations of families, workers, and farmers to send it letters and petitions to be collected for a protest "against a suggestion that, on the eve of gathering the family stock for winter, will weigh heavily on the budgets of the elderly, of small rentiers, of the middle and working classes, and of large families."[140] It was, indeed, the timing of the price changes that so upset the Vosgiens, who had the right to purchase a stock of a hundred kilograms per person from a producer or a retailer. The policy demanded that either individuals spend a large amount of cash at once or potentially lose a crucial food supply for the winter. The higher the price, and the larger the family, the more cash consumers would need to secure their potato rations.

The response to the proposed price increase filled most of the next day's paper. A remarkably long, signed editorial rehearsed the various reasons, focusing on the price of potatoes, why the current minister of provisioning "now appears to find himself in the middle of a crisis of electoral demagogy." The issue also carried a protest from the department's workers' and employees' unions addressed to the prefect, the director of the departmental RG, the press, and the relevant ministers. In addition, it published an announcement from the mayors of the canton of Remiremont, who had met with consumers' representatives (ex-POWs, deportees, family associations, restaurateurs) and determined to refuse the decree of 12 October by honoring the prices of the decree of 29 September. For its part, the prefecture felt obliged to explain that the ministerial decree had made 6Fr50 the maximum acceptable price for the entire nation, but that in the Vosges producers and merchants had the "duty to make potatoes available to consumers at reasonable prices," or, in other words, to recognize the demands of community solidarity and social justice.[141]

Three days later, *La Liberté de l'Est* proudly announced that the price of potatoes had been lowered to 4Fr50, forty centimes less than the late September price. It took part of the credit for this because the newspaper had alerted the minister of war, not coincidentally a departmental candidate in that week's election, who spoke to the minister of provisioning about the situation in the Vosges. This happy result meant that the Mouvements familiaux and the unions canceled the demonstration they had organized for the end of the week.[142] The prefect also took some of the credit for this resolution to the problem in an open letter to the mayor of Epinal in which he congratulated them both for their representations to government ministers on behalf of their constituencies. The Mouvements familiaux and the department's wholesalers also expressed their satisfaction.[143] The price repeal ended the commotion, although *La Liberté de l'Est* continued to keep an eye on all aspects of the potato market.[144]

It could not have escaped anyone's notice that the potato scandal took place in the last weeks leading up to an otherwise locally uninteresting general election. Certainly the department's Socialist newspaper ascribed the whole thing to political maneuvering that paid off handsomely, if vaguely, in election results for its authors. It then tried to make its own political profit by pointing out how the farmers had lost money on the deal.[145] But if the potato scandal was manufactured by politicians, it was a gift to Vosgien candidates from the national government, which issued the price directives before rather than after the elections. Those directives provoked no similar responses in either Savoie or Cantal, where the rural majority would more likely have appreciated the increase. In the Vosges, however, where it cut to the heart of survival anxieties, the official price increase united mayors, deportees, producers, wholesalers, parents, employees, workers, journalists, and the prefect against the central government. Local dynamics meant that with or without an election, a price increase on potatoes would have unified the community in protest. Whether the politicians would have responded quite so promptly or satisfactorily after the elections cannot be known.

The third and most damning charge leveled by the people of small towns against the national government was its failure to eliminate the black market.[146] Indeed, the black market posed a serious threat to the government's legitimacy in several ways. To begin with, by allowing food to be sold to the highest bidder on the black market rather than shared out through the RG, the government reneged on the promise of equality implicit in the rationing system. That same failure to control the black market also negated any claims the Resistance government might make to provide or guarantee social justice. Moreover, because black marketeers straddled the spheres of both legal and social justice, they underscored the government's failures in both. Finally, the black market offered the discontented citizen a way to escape from the official economy and to oppose the national government.

Without access to court records and other "delicate" documents, the actual dimensions of the black market remain vague. Even the wealth of terms for sketching out different levels of the nonofficial economy confirm the moral and definitional ambiguities surrounding it. Some farmers, for instance, considered themselves to be involved with the gray or parallel market rather than the black market because they made unauthorized sales to friends for prices between the official ones and the black market's. Indeed, the government all but encouraged individuals to deal in this vague alternative economy when it legalized family-scale trading outside of official channels. And if the government made it legal, how could it be black marketeering? It is clear, however, that both officials and private citizens in Rambervillers, Saint-Flour, and Moûtiers saw the world around them as saturated with black marketeering. In the opinion of the prefect of Cantal, and of many of his administrative colleagues, the black market "ha[d] practically become habitual (*passé dans les mœurs*)," and "it appear[ed] that the black market ha[d] become the regular market."[147]

Furthermore, the gendered rhetoric surrounding the black market suggests that it was understood as something serious and active to the point of criminal violence—in other words, men's work.¹⁴⁸ Women were surely involved in it, if only because women did most of the shopping and because farmers' wives traditionally handled the sale of eggs and dairy products and would have negotiated with buyers who came to the farmhouse door. Moreover, vigilantes attacked, and the courts prosecuted, women as well as men for black marketeering.¹⁴⁹ Yet public discourse almost always referred to the actors in the underground economy as men. Discussion of the legal exemption for family-scale black marketeering, for instance, considered the predicament of the father of the family, not the mother. The masculine gendering of the black market confirmed its importance and vitality in the same way as the slippage of women resistants out of the memory and discourse of the Resistance established its seriousness and importance.¹⁵⁰

One could obtain almost anything on the black market for a price, including items that could not be found on the official market at any price, such as the *mitraillettes* sold in Tarn by Polish miners for forty thousand francs.¹⁵¹ Throughout the country, black marketeers sold American army gasoline, clothing, and food. Indeed, in July 1945 the Sanflorain police caught a man from Marseille selling two thousand liters' worth of gasoline coupons at fifty-five francs per liter after obtaining them for less from American soldiers.¹⁵² The American authorities appealed to the civilian population for their assistance in capturing GIs engaged in illegal trading, but they were probably no more successful than in their constant reminders that civilians were not allowed to wear military clothing.

Most of the trading in American goods took place in towns such as Rambervillers that hosted American units and whose inhabitants must surely have been tempted by the long rows of crates full of rations stacked alongside roads with only one or two lackadaisical sentries to guard them; by the seemingly bottomless pipelines; and by the warm, tough uniforms. Indeed, anecdotal evidence suggests that many people relied on these resources. The Americans, however, sometimes protected their supplies quite actively, as four young men found out in December 1945 when they were surprised in the act of draining gasoline from the military pipeline outside of Rambervillers. The guards shot one of the Frenchmen; the court imprisoned the others for one to three months.¹⁵³

The disarray in the provisioning system, however, meant that the bulk of the black market dealt in food. Although there appears to have been an underground market in such essentials as meat and fats, especially butter, centered in Paris and the other major cities, the black market worked within local needs and possibilities. Accordingly, when not engaged in the "more important" traffic of accordions and typewriters, mountain-climbing marketeers in Savoie traded French salt and cigarette papers for Italian wine.[154] And Cantal's black market export economy specialized in cheese and meat; on one day in December 1944 alone, the police seized 450 kilograms of contraband pork in the Saint-Flour station.[155]

No matter what the product, the black market charged a high price for it. In September 1945, the RG in Cantal reported that the average prices on the clandestine market ran at: butter—300 francs per kilogram; eggs—80 to 100 francs per dozen; sugar—250 francs per kilogram; beef—150 francs per kilogram; and pork—250 francs live weight. By December these prices had dropped somewhat, by 20 to 100 francs, but not enough to discourage black marketeering.[156] Needless to say, the official retail prices were considerably lower. For example, in October 1945 the legal prices were: eggs—36 francs per dozen; regular sugar—21Fr60 per kilogram; and beef—46 to 85 francs per kilogram, depending on the quality.[157] Price differentials could be even higher elsewhere; in March 1945 in the region of Nancy a dozen eggs legally cost 28 francs but could command 80 to 100 francs on the black market.[158] Although legal prices were obviously lower, they applied only to official, unreliable stocks and carried quantity restrictions that black market goods did not.

Such prices and margins naturally attracted a criminal element—what both bureaucrats and editorialists called *gangsters* (always in English).[159] Although more spontaneous and friendly levels were more morally ambiguous, everyone could agree that the gangsters represented the blackest of an immoral black market. Indeed, the CGT-CFTC of the Haute-Tarentaise publicly offered to lynch "the confraternity of Gangsters of the Black Market . . . these kings of trafficking, these classified *affameurs* of the people, [who] never tire, dress well, drink well, eat even better, and smoke as they want and without tickets."[160]

Marketeers sometimes did attain the heights of the Chicagoland-Hollywood violence that contemporary French vocabulary evoked. In January 1945, for example, the RG of Cantal published a warning that "armed persons claiming to be soldiers" had been using their mitraillettes to forcibly "make off with" hundreds of kilos of vegetables from farmers and collectors in the Planèze. Victims of such intimidation were invited to take the gunmen's particulars and alert the police without delay.[161] And in October 1945 *La Liberté de l'Est* went beyond its usual local concerns to report on even more dramatic events in Marseille. It seems that six officers went to a nightclub called the Blue Parrot to celebrate the award of the Croix de la Libération and the promotion of one of their number but had a disagreement with the management over the bill of 110 francs for "a minuscule cake." When the officers left without paying, they were followed and fired upon by "a group of gangsters." The next night soldiers from their unit returned to the Blue Parrot to avenge the two injured officers; they threw grenades and fired their mitraillettes into the nightclub but, fortunately, did not hurt anyone.[162] The story may well be apocryphal, but if so, it only underlines the looming cultural presence of the black market during the après-libération.

Even without street battles, the black market had some well-organized professionals. The prefect of Loir-et-Cher, for instance, reported the following conclusions about black marketeers from his crackdown on motorized trafficking, which he carefully distinguished from family-scale trading. To begin with, the marketeers were skilled professionals who employed ingenious means to hide their goods under false bottoms and false labels. They also worked in well-organized bands in which, for instance, the leader would drive a truck to the department's borders and send out women or Algerians to collect foodstuffs from farms. Another band run by a departmental head of the SNCF used rail company labels to ship contraband to Paris. The prefect also remarked on the relatively large presence of "foreigners" among the traffickers, "50 percent if the Algerians are included." He did not, however, elaborate on the economic and legal circumstances that might have driven a foreigner into the illegal economy during the occupation. The prefect also bemoaned his powerlessness against what he called the "legal black market" of military officers and administrators who used it to fulfill their quartermaster responsibilities.[163]

The black market was not, however, the exclusive preserve of organized crime, as demonstrated by a sad incident in Saint-Flour. In December 1944 the gendarmerie arrested a widow for the illegal sale of fifty grams of tobacco for 140 francs. According to her own statement, the widow got eight kilograms of tobacco from a man in Clermont who, she believed, intended to charge her 2,300 francs per kilogram. She herself hoped to sell it at 2,800 francs per kilogram, or 2,500 francs if someone took an entire kilogram. She had entered into this agreement because: "I am a widow with two children to take care of and I do not have many resources. My friends knew my situation and, to help me earn a little money, arranged for me to get the tobacco." So far, she had sold only the fifty grams that had led to her arrest. The gendarmes did not detain her because she was a widow with two children and in bad health, but they did confiscate the tobacco.[164] The black market must have truly saturated daily life if a widow's friends thought it a good way to help her.

Most people would have engaged in the black market on either the supply or consumption side rather than as middlemen, although a number of city dwellers attempted to do away with the middlemen altogether by traveling to the farms themselves. Although the government tolerated such expeditions, the inhabitants of the regions they invaded often resented them and their effect on local prices. *La Résistance savoyarde,* for instance, happily reflected that after the departure of the summer vacationers who had made "the black market triumph," there would again be food available for the small pockets of the Savoyards.[165] Correspondents to *La Margeride* also noticed the unusual presence of city people in their countryside. One writer from Brezons sarcastically condemned the luxury cars that lured the young cheeses of Cantal to the shadow of the Eiffel Tower where, "forgetting their modest origins and above all their orderly life, they prostitute themselves for from 300 to 400 francs per kilogram!"[166]

Few of the extended personal shopping trips, however, could have reached the aplomb of a military chaplain who arrived in the meadow outside Saint-Flour on 22 September 1945 in a fighter plane. The chaplain and his RAF companion left two hours later with a large cheese.[167] The incident caused quite a stir, although it is not clear whether the gossips were more taken with the appearance of a fighter plane on their doorstep or the public flight of the cheese. At first *La Margeride* explained that the chaplain was a resistant who had worked with local resistants in the summer of 1943 before traveling to London.[168] But it later defended the local Resistance against the rumors of "a large traffic in foodstuffs" through sarcasm, remarking that next time the curé would visit "with a flying fortress, for the sole purpose of making off with twenty tons of Cantal [cheese]."[169]

The local press played the same role in the social debate about the grayer levels of black marketeering that it did in the debate about the lower levels of collaboration. Local papers carried both many more or less veiled accusations of food-related wrongdoing, such as not delivering one's full share of milk or overcharging American GIs for beer, and public denials of any involvement in such misdeeds.[170] For example, when the same Moutiérain truck driver whose house had been bombed for not delivering flour in 1944 was reported as having been arrested a year later for illegally transporting eighty-two kilograms of cheese and ten kilograms of butter, he made it clear that he had had "absolutely nothing to do with the misdemeanor."[171] But the many dimensions of local politics at play in the rhetoric and rumors surrounding the black market were made most clear by the Socialists of Saint-Flour in their response to the arrest of an Algerian for dealing in gasoline coupons. According to them, "Certain collaborators have taken this news and, in order to discredit the Resistance a little more, have immediately proclaimed: 'Young R—— is compromised in this affair.'" After categorically denying the rumor, the article ended: "For this time, we advise them [the rumormongers] to learn the definition of the word 'defamation.'"[172]

If the provisional government wished to establish its authority, fulfill its obligations to its citizens, and respect the Resistance dream of social justice, it had to seize control of the food supply and put an end to the black market and other food crime. In order to do so, however, it had to destroy something that it had helped to create. Throughout Europe during the war, the black market had acquired an air of patriotism and of protecting the people from the occupier's depredations.[173] Thus a leader of the Polish Resistance once remarked that the country's black marketeers, known more gently as smugglers, deserved a monument as saviors of a nation the Germans had tried to starve to death.[174] In France the Resistance had attacked Vichy by subverting its rationing system with a flood of false ration tickets and by encouraging patriots to sell their produce on the black market rather than deliver it to the Germans via Vichy.[175]

At the liberation, however, resistants performed a political pirouette and declared war on the black market. Aware of the incongruities of their sudden policy reversal, they tried to explain to their neighbors why they should suddenly give up the black market before the official market could be relied on to serve their needs. As an editorial in *La Résistance savoyarde* put it: "During the occupation, if the large-scale black market never had an excuse, the small-scale or parallel market found the double justification of individual necessity and patriotism. 'So long as the Boches won't get it' one could think. But, if I'm not mistaken, the occupiers have packed their bags. And so? . . . Couldn't we put a little clarity in all the black and recall merchants and consumers to the respect of an elementary solidarity?"[176]

Accordingly, the well-organized and active Resistance of the northern Alps turned on the black market as soon as the area was liberated. In September 1944, the CDLs of the eleven departments of the Lyon region jointly asserted their determination to end the black market and confiscate its illicit profits.[177] Even before the department was fully liberated, the CDL of Savoie issued a warning to the "traffickers of the black market . . . [who] continue to enrich themselves by speculating on the misery (*misère*) of the people" that the FFI had been ordered to "arrest, judge, and sentence individuals who continue this shameful traffic."[178] The prefect of Savoie seconded their determination by warning both producers and consumers against dealing on the black market because now that "the Boche is gone; the children of France are hungry: everything must be delivered to the Ravitaillement général."[179]

The CLL of the Haute-Tarentaise implemented that order by including repression of the black market and surveillance of prices in the standing orders of the Milices patriotiques. The Tarin MP fulfilled its duties as provisioning police not only by searching grocers' stocks and travelers' bags but also by publicly branding the guilty parties by listing their names in the paper under such headlines as *"Les Affameurs."*[180] They were, however, very careful to exclude fathers with small amounts of food, accepting that justice required that a man be allowed to feed his dependents by whatever means available.[181] This attitude contrasted sharply with the perceived governmental preference for punishing the underlings rather than the real black marketeers, in the same way that the purge courts punished the underlings rather than their superiors.[182] The exception for fathers illustrates both the subtlety of the local understanding of justice and the ambiguities of the black market.

Yet despite the "pitiless hunt for the traffickers of misery" announced in a radio speech by the CRR at Lyon, the liberation-era authorities did not manage to stifle the black market.[183] The very terms the bureaucrats used in their reports suggest how overwhelming they found the task; they wrote of their efforts to "curb the flight (*fuites*) of cheese," and counted the "escapes" (*évasions*) of cheeses, lentils, and meat—as if those cheeses, like collaborators, were busy fleeing the authorities in order to establish themselves as something else somewhere else. Indeed, the provincial administrators' efforts to eradicate the black market bore certain resemblances to their efforts to prosecute the purge. They encountered similar difficulties with the police and courts, and similar demands and expressions of disappointment from the public. Most strikingly, the rhetoric about the black market often echoed that of the purge when it came to accusations of treason within the gates.

As they did in the purge, the authorities asked the public to help them to end the black market by providing signed denunciations. Despite the danger of the misuse of denunciations, the CDL of Savoie welcomed information about both buyers and sellers, and the CDL of Cantal encouraged it by printing stories of the ways such (signed) information led to the recuperation of evading foodstuffs.[184] Yet given the economic situation, even a well-organized and ruthless police apparatus would have had difficulty quashing a working alternative economy in time of scarcity. During the war the NKVD, for example, could not eliminate the Soviet black market, despite shooting food criminals in the streets.[185] The French Provisional Government had neither a well-organized police force nor the will to gun down its citizens. Indeed, its efforts suffered because responsibility for surveillance and control of the food supply fell upon so many police agencies that they tripped over each other in some areas while neglecting others. Agents of the RG, CE, gendarmerie, and municipal police all had some authority over prices, ration cards, and the movement of food as well as the retail sale of it. During the first few months of the après-libération local Resistance organizations such as the Moutiérain MP also took an active role in the surveillance of the market and the hunt for *affameurs*.

In addition to the obvious problems caused by the size of the task and overlapping jurisdictions, all the French police in the provinces were understaffed.[186] The situation was so bad, the prefect of Cantal declared, that "no one hopes anymore that an end can be put to the black market."[187] Indeed, he blamed housewives' protests in Aurillac on the fact that all the CE agents had been mobilized, leaving merchants to oversee their own prices.[188] With somewhat less pessimism, the prefect of Savoie requested permission to provide the agents of the RG with manual laborer ration cards in order to encourage their zeal and give them a little more independence.[189] It would not have taken much imagination to suppose that a man chasing wrongdoing through the byways of France on the paltry provisions of a regular adult ration card might weaken before a bribe of a ham or loaf of bread.

Nor were such situations wholly imaginary. In a murky case in Moûtiers, a well-known Algerian black marketeer operating in the area and a gendarme came before the court over a case of stolen ration tickets and a disputed sum of fifty thousand francs. The gendarme claimed that the Algerian had offered it to him as a bribe; the Algerian claimed the gendarme had demanded it. Apparently not believing either of them, the court sentenced the gendarme to one year's suspended imprisonment and a fine of five thousand francs and the Algerian to six months in prison and a ten-thousand-francs fine. It also confiscated the fifty thousand francs.[190]

Yet if all these police forces were not able to put an end to the unofficial economy, they could at least create flurries of repressive activity that they publicized through the press. The CE of the Vosges, for example, alerted consumers to the fact that in June 1945 alone it had interfered with seventy-six transactions valued at 505,900 francs.[191] A similar report published in *La Margeride* and covering August 1944 to February 1945 ended with: "These figures eloquently demonstrate that if the Services charged with repressing the black market are not in a position to repress all infractions, at least the principal traffickers will all end up by being apprehended and punished as they deserve."[192] The more common reports of regular police dragnets in the Saint-Flour train station, however, undermined that confidence. The reports of the apprehension of a woman from Hérault carrying a suitcase with twenty kilograms of cheese in one hand and another suitcase with twenty-eight kilograms of meat in the other, or of two women from Marseille who had bought twenty kilograms of butter at 200 francs per kilogram, plus an unspecified amount of pasta and sugar, or of "lost" packages containing twenty-seven kilograms of lamb, eighty kilograms of cheese, and fifteen kilograms of butter, make for a stronger impression of a thriving black market than of a harsh police repression.[193]

If the police caught someone breaking one of the myriad food laws, the case could take several avenues. The prefect could order the temporary closure of a shop, a confiscation, a fine, or, while the war continued, the administrative internment of the accused. The prefect of Cantal regretted the loss of his power of administrative internment after May 1945, because it was "the only truly effective weapon against the black market."[194] The directors of the departmental CE and of the RG could also impose fines and confiscations. These penalties could be quite steep, as several café owners in Rambervillers discovered in March 1945 when the director of the CE of the Vosges confiscated 450 liters of wine from a woman café owner and fined another *cafetière* twenty thousand francs for overcharging for wine and a *cafetier* twelve thousand francs for selling eau-de-vie at illicit prices.[195] Finally, the case could go to the courts, which could impose fines, confiscations, and imprisonment, although the prefect of Cantal, for one, felt that "it would be illusory to count on the courts."[196] The prefect of Cantal, it might be noted, had a similarly low opinion of the departmental courts' activities regarding the purge.

Indeed, the reports of black marketeering trials in the local press portrayed a less than draconian legal repression. In April 1945, for instance, the Sanflorain court heard the case of a twenty-three-year-old local man who had bought butter for 150 francs per kilogram (already well above the legal price) and then resold it to Méridionaux for 400 francs per kilogram. Considering that in six months the young man had thus made a profit of 67,870 francs, the court-imposed fine of 15,000 francs probably did not incommode him overmuch, although the accompanying month in prison may have given him more pause. On the same day, however, the court took a more severe view of a thirty-year-old cleaning woman employed as a dishwasher who had fraudulently secured extra ration cards by claiming to have lost her own and those of her two children. The court sentenced her to eight days' imprisonment.[197] The marketeer's relatively light fine compared to the impoverished mother's heavy sentence undoubtedly added zest to the rumor then current that the big black marketeers had made such scandalous profits that they preferred to burn some of their bank notes rather than exchange them all for the new currency.[198]

Not surprisingly, given the economic realities of the time and the difficult arrangements individuals had to make in order to purchase food, the public was ambivalent about the authorities' offensive against the black market. Many families, after all, relied on it to make up for the shortfalls remaining after distribution of the official rations. Furthermore, public opinion about the black market changed over the course of the après-libération according to the level of public confidence in the Resistance government and anger at collaboration. The high point of condemnation of black marketeering came at the liberation itself, when many people seem to have expected an almost magical transformation of attitudes and conditions. Feeling peaked again in the late spring of 1945 when the Return enflamed passions against collaborators, including black marketeers, and when the end of hostilities seemed to promise a nostalgic "normality" that did not include the exorbitant prices of the black market. The consensus to condemn the black market, however, began to break down over the summer of 1945 as people lost confidence in the government's management of the food supply and commitment to social justice. At that point, the black market regained some of its wartime aura as a refuge against an unjust government. At the very least, it offered the only sure source of food to a population tired of being hungry.

Indeed, over the course of the après-libération, people began to support the black market openly, even by direct action. Reports came from across the country, from both the mountainous Jura and the coastal Charente-Maritime, of citizens attacking provisioning agents when they tried to arrest or fine local butchers, because, black marketeers or not, they were the only source of meat.[199] Moutiérains refrained from violence but were certainly upset in September 1945 when the prefect and gendarmerie closed a certain greengrocer's for three months. The event elicited an article in *La Résistance savoyarde* that praised the grocer himself as a sort of Ali Baba and his melons, tomatoes, and fish as jewels not to be found in Chambéry, Albertville, or the Midi. "Does he engage in the black market, this robust Catalan with the mischievous eyes? They say so, but, hands on heart, who has not done a little black marketeering. . . . Let's see, who raises his or her hand?" The article ended by predicting that the three-month closure would mean that the grocer "will return to us refreshed and jovial without having suffered from the provisioning crisis, and in Moûtiers they will fete his return.... What does *M. le Préfet* think of that?"[200] The newspaper had certainly changed its attitude since just a year earlier, when, in the enthusiasm of the liberation, it vilified black marketeering shopkeepers as *affameurs*.

The closure caused enough trouble in Moûtiers for the municipal council to take the unusual step of sending a petition to the prefect asking that the grocer's shop be reopened as soon as possible, because he was "the only merchant in Moûtiers capable of assuring a correct provisioning of the population. To delay his reopening any more could lead to low stocks of merchandise for the winter, to the detriment, it is well understood, of the population."[201] In short, the elected representatives of this small town asked the departmental representative of the central government to repeal the black marketeer's sentence, not because it was unjust or inappropriate according to the law or the guilt of the accused, but because, illegal or not, that grocery alone could assure the town's food supply. It would be difficult to find a clearer repudiation of the government's ability to regulate the economy or provide for the basic security of its citizens.

Yet the government's failure to control the black market had more serious consequences than supply difficulties. The moral aspects of black marketeering also made it a test of the new regime's commitment to honorary and legal justice. During the après-libération, black marketeers represented the worst sort of betrayal, that of the collaborator/*affameur* who combined the twentieth-century political betrayal of collaboration with the old regime social treason of the individual who betrays his or her community for private profit. An early letter to the editor in Savoie drew an unexpected conclusion to the equation of black marketeering with collaboration by putting it in the context of the plight of the sinistrés and war widows. "The heart falters and anger rumbles in us against those who, insensitively, continue to profit from such distress, to fill their dirty wallets with money extorted from a population starved by the war, thus allying themselves, by tacit agreement, with the Germans. They do not have a right to any pity; they do not have any excuse; no circumstances extenuate their faults. They must pay, return the fruits of their thefts. To punish them is to render homage to these sinistrées families, to avenge our Dead."[202]

A less indignant submission from a Cantalien correspondent to *La Margeride* threatened the "peasants who want to continue their filthy work in the black market" with the anger of the "mothers of Clermont and elsewhere."[203]

Many official and self-appointed representatives of the people followed these private initiatives in denouncing the black market. The Communist cell of Saint-Flour, for instance, officially urged the prefect to greater zeal in his pursuit of both collaborators and traffickers.[204] And the third item in the petition sent to the government by the newly elected municipal council in Rambervillers requested the immediate suppression of the black market.[205] Vigilantes seconded these demands with direct action against alleged black marketeers and cheating shopkeepers.

Finally, a reader in Savoie who signed himself *"le grincheux"* (the grouser) submitted a letter in which he took the government to task for wasting time on divisive superficialities such as the municipal elections when its primary goal should have been to root out the black market. At the end of the letter, the editor diplomatically but revealingly commented: "Our correspondent obviously says what many people think. But the remedies for our troubles are perhaps not as simple as he supposes."[206] Simplistic or not, the letter provides a rather trenchant expression of the fundamental misunderstanding between a government bent on the establishment of republican order and a populace insistent on justice.

In the end, the government's management of the food supply undermined its popular legitimacy. By failing to share out the available food supplies efficiently and equitably, the government reneged on its obligations in the twentieth-century version of the moral economy that it had endorsed with the rationing system. By failing to suppress the black market, it cast further doubts on its ability and commitment to provide social justice. Indeed, in terms of provisioning, the new Resistance regime scarcely seemed to be an improvement over Vichy.

The liberation of Rambervillers, 30 September 1944. Civilians greet the men of an American tank. (Courtesy of J.-C. Kempf)

Civilians cross the flooded Mortagne at the rue Carnot, Rambervillers, 8 November 1944. (U.S. Army Signal Corps, courtesy of J.-C. Kempf)

A U.S. Army truck drives down the flooded rue Carnot, Rambervillers, 8 November 1944. (U.S. Army Signal Corps, courtesy of J.-C. Kempf)

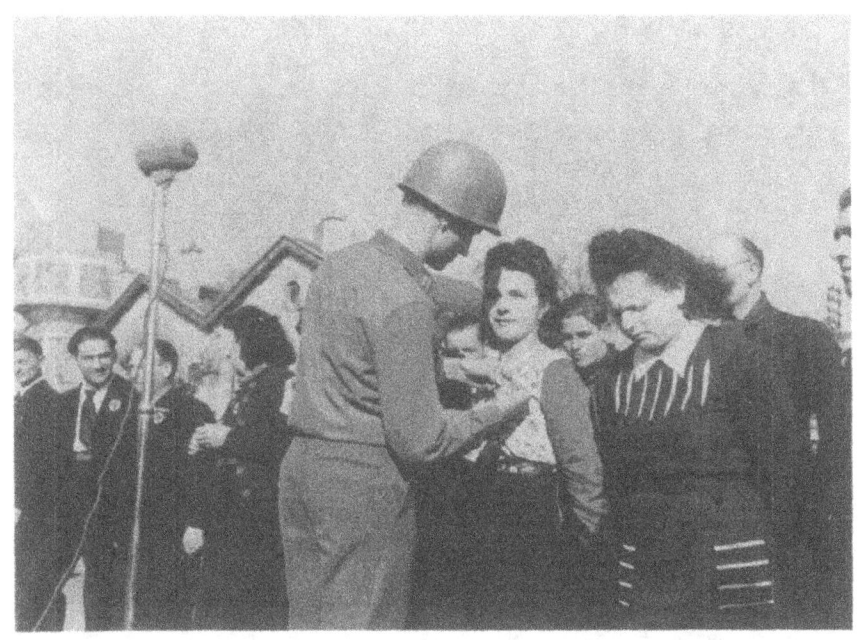

Captain R. Walter of the U.S. Ninth Evacuation Hospital recognizes the contributions of French civilians, Rambervillers, 28 February 1944. (U.S. Army Signal Corps, courtesy of J.-C. Kempf)

Rambervillers celebrates the victory—the Rambervillers Maquis on parade, Rambervillers, 8 May 1945. (Mme. Soyeur, courtesy of J.-C. Kempf)

Rambervillers celebrates the victory—a twenty-one-gun salute at the American artillery park just north of town. The man in the black hat is Mayor Bodson. The man in the striped uniform is M. Marcel Mathieu, recently repatriated from a German concentration camp. Rambervillers, 8 May 1945. (Mme. Soyeur, courtesy of J.-C. Kempf)

CHAPTER FIVE

HONORARY JUSTICE AND

THE CONSTRUCTION OF MEMORY

Alongside the legal justice that punishes malefactors and the social justice that feeds the hungry, there is an honorary justice that regulates the distribution of honor among the living and the dead of a community. During the *après-libération,* of course, questions of honorary justice revolved around the implementation of the Resistance's moral hierarchy, particularly the place of the Resistance's martyrs. A signed article printed in *La Résistance savoyarde* while the FFI were still establishing their hold on the Italian border summarized the meaning given to resistants' deaths and the demands that meaning placed on the survivors. "Maquisards and Terrorists become Heroes! These are our FFI liberators! Let us respectfully bow our heads before these tombs covered in glory that contain what our country counts as the most beautiful, the most generous. They died for the *lendemains qui chantent.* Their glorious sacrifices open a new path where we must enter boldly. It is the route of Duty for new victories, for a free France in a fraternal world."[1]

Resistants, however, did not all agree on the route that the bold new path should take. Some reacted to the execution of their comrades-in-arms by demanding that "an exemplary punishment be meted out to the informing traitors and authors of this tragedy."[2] Others, however, responded to similar events with the plea: "Let us speak less about the traitors, they will be judged and punished sooner or later because there exists an immanent Justice for them; let us speak much more about our heroes, our maquisards," because "if one wants the country to recover rapidly, it will not happen by wallowing in the mud, but by exalting the memory (*souvenir*) of those who have done everything so that France lives, independent, strong, and happy."³ Some heard the "ancestral voices" of fallen heroes call them to vengeance; others heard them demand future exemplary action.⁴

The debate over how to serve honorary justice permeated every aspect of après-libération social life. It played a large role in the contemporary controversy over dancing, and it motivated a certain "J. B." of Saint-Flour to write a letter to the editor lambasting the "Twerps" (*Foutriquets*) of France for daring to complain about shortages and red tape when martyrs like one of the town's resistants who had been tortured to death by the Gestapo had died and were continuing to die every day for France.⁵ It motivated both vigilantes and politicians. Primarily, however, the issue of honorary justice influenced the construction of an official, public memory of the war, occupation, and liberation in the form of ceremonies and in the commemorative politics that ran through all such occasions. The exact shape of après-libération commemorative politics varied by town, but the whole country shared a common ceremonial calendar.

After the first days of jubilation at the liberation, public ceremonies turned to the somber task of memorializing those who had died in the struggle. Public memorial services, however, honored only the *patriotic* dead: resistants, soldiers, hostages. Those who died from other causes such as disease, accident, or even bombing raids did not receive the same public honors. Certainly the thousands of collaborators who met often violent deaths during and after the liberation received only the most discreet of burials. Furthermore, memorial services overwhelmingly honored men, in part because they drew on the gestural and rhetorical tradition that conceptualized patriotism as the military endeavors of men and that had been most recently embodied in the cult of the male *poilus* of the First World War;⁶ and in part because men were usually the victims in most Resistance deaths that fit the military model of patriotic tradition and Gaullist myth, either because they died in battle or because the Germans generally executed men but deported women to a slower, more obscure end.

Yet women's sacrifices as resistants were not immediately forgotten on the local level.⁷ The Cantalien football league, for instance, inaugurated its postliberation season by honoring the memory of the wife of a member, a nurse killed at Mont-Mouchet, and Savoyard eulogies mentioned the women as well as the men killed in reprisals. There are, however, also indications that women's efforts could get overlooked. A Rambûvetaise wrote a scathing letter to the editor complaining that the name of a woman who had been shot while taking food to escaped "Hindu prisoners" hiding in a nearby wood had been forgotten in a departmental ceremony honoring the Resistance's dead. That oversight, she wrote, showed a sad lack of "Justice" and "Fraternity."[8] It might, however, have come from the independent and domestic nature of the woman's mission rather than from deliberate chauvinistic exclusion, but it does suggest that the national myth of a military Resistance that obscured the role of women had already begun to affect local memories, eclipsing *résistantes* as well as collaborators.[9]

At the liberation, the same patriotic traditions that privileged male activities provided a basic pattern for memorial services throughout France. The funerals of local heroes almost always included a religious service, a procession to the cemetery, and speeches by local dignitaries, all attended by government officials, resistants, local associations, and the public.[10] On many occasions, the speeches were given at the Monument aux Morts, thus firmly anchoring the Resistance's heroes in the cultural heart of the town and in the patriotic tradition epitomized by the poilus. Indeed, during the après-libération, what procession did not stop at the Monument aux Morts? The act of visiting the war memorial to lay a wreath, observe a minute of silence, or sing the "Marseillaise" carried such weight at the time that it completely escaped the control of mayor or schoolmaster.[11] There riotous crowds triumphantly bore the vigilantes they had rescued from prison. There housewives defiantly demanded better rations. There resistants respectfully stood as honor guards in memory of distant skirmishes. The Monument aux Morts was on the itinerary of every funeral and every procession, because, as the symbol of patriotic sacrifice, it sanctified anyone associated with it.

Funerals, however, were not always possible, leading to the additional memorialization of legend building. Towns buried their local heroes when they could, of course, but the nature of the war meant that not all of the dead could be buried at home. Soldiers died in POW camps or on the battlefield. Resistants died far from home in skirmishes, torture chambers, prisons, and concentration camps. The demands of clandestinity meant that they often died anonymously, their real names unknown even to their comrades. Their enemies threw their corpses into mass graves, or strangers gave them as decent a burial as they dared. Often those strangers showed great courage and compassion, treating them as members of their own honorary community and disregarding the threat of German reprisal.

Communities accordingly told the stories of all their martyrs as they became known. "In order to honor their memory (*mémoire*)," local papers printed obituaries for any man or woman who had died in the patriotic cause and had been born in town or had family there.[12] Under headings such as "Our glorious dead," "Dead on the field of honor," or "Dead for the Resistance," the obituaries rehearsed the terrible "price of our liberation," paid by often very young men, and occasionally women, tortured, executed, or killed in guerrilla actions.[13] Schools and civic associations also recounted the stories of heroes' and heroines' martyrdom.

In addition to honoring the dead by making their stories known, survivors also engaged in constructing more material memorials. Inevitably, people gave considerable thought to erecting a local monument for the Second World War as a counterpart to the Monument aux Morts of the First. But such a project posed innumerable difficulties, the very least of which were financial. Commemoratively speaking, the first war had been much neater than the second. On the whole, the war dead had all been men of military age who fought in the same uniform, united against the foreign enemy. Furthermore, they mostly died within a tightly described geographic area and within the army's bureaucratic structures. If they did not all die gloriously on the field of battle, they all died in similar enough circumstances to bear reduction into the eternally vigilant bronze *poilu* who now stands guard in so many town squares.

The French dead of 1939–45 exhibited no such commonalities. They included individuals of all ages and both genders who died scattered across Europe from a terrible array of causes. Most important, they had sometimes killed each other. Any general memorial raised a hornet's nest of questions. Should collaborators be included? Should civilians be included? If not, would the irregular fighters of the Resistance be included as soldiers? If so, would that include female liaison agents or only weapon-carrying men? What about hostages killed in reprisal for resistance activities? What about civilians killed by the Allies in bombing raids? What about forced or voluntary laborers, not to mention deported Jews, who died in Germany? Or the French men who died in German uniform on the

Russian front? The web of guilt and accusation woven by a war fought on so many levels and in so many ways defied any simple symbolic reduction.

Towns solved this dilemma by offering the simplest recognition of the war as a whole and focusing on particular individuals or groups. Indeed, most local monuments for the Second World War escape the complications by honoring individuals such as Dr. Mallet of Saint-Flour, specific groups such as the Resistance of the Tarentaise, or specific events such as a massacre or other atrocity. Certain parts of the country, such as the Vercors or the Margeride, are riddled with simple stones marking the places where FFIs fell in the summer of 1944 that were put up by friends of the deceased, local resistance groups, or municipal governments and financed through gifts from neighboring municipalities or public collections at banquets, movie theaters, or street corners.[14]

Rambervillers, for example, has a monument to the *francs-tireurs* of 1870 that stands just outside the cemetery, another monument to 1870 in the square outside the church, and a monument to the Great War that is a wall of names flanking the angel of victory on its main street. The town's crest bears its medals for heroism in the Franco-Prussian War, World War I, and World War II. But its monument to World War II is a plaque attached to the wall of names from 1914–18 that reads: "dead of the 1939–1945 war and civilian victims." Although some complained that a separate monument was needed as "a work of grateful acknowledgment and of justice," the plaque had the great virtue of taking no stand and of honoring whomever the beholder felt was qualified as a victim of that complicated war.[15]

Such a plaque also evaded the thorny problem of naming the killer. Few Second World War monuments repeated the frankness of a stele erected in Toussieux (Isère) in October 1945 that read: "Here, on the evening of 12 July 1944, twenty-eight French patriots were murdered in a cowardly manner by the Germans with the complicity of the Milice of Vichy."[16] The accusation against French collaborators as well as Germans is stunning in its directness and its rarity. It was even less possible during the après-libération to ascribe a death to the "friendly fire" of the Allied armies or air forces.

At the liberation, the easiest, quickest, and cheapest available monuments were place-names. Changing them also constituted a first order of business for newly liberated communes, because it symbolically reappropriated the town from occupation by Vichy, which had itself changed place-names to obliterate the Third Republic.[17] During its inaugural session on 14 September 1944, the special delegation of Saint-Flour therefore changed the names of three streets. Avenue Maréchal Pétain (previously Avenue Saint-Jacques) became avenue du Dr. Louis Mallet, "in memory (*mémoire*) of the Sanflorain doctor fallen under the Nazi bullets, as well as his two sons, and in grateful recognition of all his proven devotion to the town and region of Saint-Flour." The avenue de la Gare became the avenue des Martyrs, "in order to recall to posterity that the twenty-five *fusillés* of the Pont du Vernet [Soubizergues], taken hostage on 11 June 1944, took the last stage of their Calvary at dawn on 14 June 1944 by traveling this avenue that led to the place of their torment." And avenue de Bellevue became avenue de la République, because the town had no street of that name.[18] At the next meeting, the council unanimously voted to change the place Alfred Bert to place de la Liberté.[19] In March 1945, however, it indefinitely delayed responding to a PCF request that a street be named after a national labor leader killed by the Germans in 1942.[20]

In Moûtiers, the special delegation received a suggestion from the president of the CLL to rename the avenue Maréchal Pétain (formerly avenue de Salins) the avenue Jean Reymond. While acknowledging the great merit of Reymond, who died in combat, the mayor thought something like "Liberation," "Resistance," or "Liberty" would be more appropriate. The special delegation chose by a narrow majority of eight to six to call the road "avenue de la Libération 1944."[21] After a short delay necessitated by being on the front line, the special delegation of Rambervillers also changed some names. It renamed the place Maréchal Pétain in front of the cathedral the place du 30 September 1944, "in order to commemorate the Liberation of the Town," and changed the pont de l'Abbatoir to pont Jean Boura, "in memory (*souvenir*) of the brave Rambûvetais FFI, *mort pour la France*." It also named a street rue André Quinet, "in memory (*souvenir*) of a courageous FFI executed by the Germans while fulfilling his duty for the liberation of the *Pays*."[22]

The absence of the name de Gaulle, which might seem like an obvious replacement for Pétain, can be attributed to two causes. First, these municipalities apparently preferred abstractions such as Liberty or names or dates with local meaning to national names. Small towns did, after all, have reason to feel adrift from national leaders and events when the decisions were made. Furthermore, part of the purpose was to reclaim the town from the last, disastrous national government. It is probably not a coincidence that all three towns chose to cover over the name of Pétain with another name that signified the local rejection of Pétain and collaboration through either the person of a resistant or the liberation of the town. Second, de Gaulle himself did not want any public places or thoroughfares named after him, as he made clear through the Ministry of the Interior.[23]

The approaching victory began to lighten the tone of public occasions as the western Allies made their way into Germany. Public excitement grew with every step that marked the defeat of the Third Reich, from the liberation of Strasbourg in November 1944 to the fall of Berlin in May 1945.[24] Days before the Germans actually did surrender, the people of Epinal received warning that the fact would be announced by "a two-minute siren blow and the ringing of the bells." They were then asked to "decorate their homes, as a sign of joy, and to take flowers to the various Monuments aux Morts, as a sign of gratitude."[25] Throughout the region of Nancy, however, French civilians and Allied troops started celebrating the victory days before the official announcement.[26]

In Rambervillers itself, French and Americans celebrated together on 8 May. First, four hundred guests attended a reception held by the local Resistance network, the CDLR, that featured patriotic toasts; the French, American, British, and Russian national anthems; and a minute of silence for "all the FFI fallen in the struggle against the Germanic oppressor." The need to take their places in the afternoon parade, however, cut short the hurrahs. At 4 P.M. the bells and sirens sounded, and the procession formed. The municipal band led, first, the American and French officers, then the mayor and his deputies, the American and local flags, veterans of both wars, workers' associations, American troops followed by artillery pieces on which rode Rambûvetais deportees recently returned from Buchenwald and wearing their striped concentration camp uniforms, the municipal council, the local FFI led by a color guard of two FFIs on leave and two women, the nurse Mlle. Charlotte and the "courageous liaison agent Marie-Thérèse," and then the schoolchildren, firemen, and the workers of a local factory holding little flags. This comprehensive cortege moved from the Monument aux Morts, to the Monument to 1870, to the American artillery park on the outskirts of town, and back to the heart of town, the place 30 September 1944, at each stop laying wreaths, hearing speeches, singing the "Marseillaise" and Allied anthems, or giving a twenty-one-gun salute (twice).²⁷ The Rambûvetais most likely spent the evening dancing, the "liberty of the dance" having been restored some days earlier for just this eventuality.

The festivities went on in the department for quite some time. Epinal celebrated the victory with as much gusto on the ninth as on the eighth. In the morning the archbishop said a Te Deum at the basilica in honor of "those who have fallen for the liberation of the civilized world," during which the organ played the "Marseillaise," an unusual choice for sacred music but one pregnant with political significance given that republican and Catholic symbolism had been estranged before the war.²⁸ On the eleventh, the municipality organized religious services at the Protestant temple and Catholic basilica in honor of the town's civilian victims of the (Allied) bombing raids of 11 and 23 May 1944 and of the fighting on 19 June 1940 and 23–24 September 1944, and to commemorate all other citizens "fallen victim to German barbarism, whether in Epinal or in the concentration camps in Germany."²⁹ More informally, the nights were filled with open-air balls and the days with groups of young people marching through the streets carrying flags. "One even attended a picturesque burial of Hitler."³⁰

The people of the war-ravaged Vosges were not the only ones to bury Hitler in a mocking parody of the funerals they gave their own heroes; the people of the small and relatively sheltered Cantalien village La Chapelle-Laurent celebrated the news of peace in the same way. A procession of men, women, and children escorted a wagon decorated with a cross and bearing a shrouded effigy of the "monster" from the town square to the station and back. There the schoolchildren laid bouquets of lilacs at the Monument aux Morts and sang the "Hymne aux morts pour la patrie." After a minute of silence, the crowd sang the "Marseillaise," and then "the Hitler of the day knew the horrors of the pyre" while the people danced in circles around the flames.³¹

The episode conflates a very old carnivalesque tradition of ritually disposing of one's powerful enemy and the much newer tradition of marking significant events at the First World War Monument aux Morts. The townspeople showed no awareness of any contradiction between the old and the new symbolism and gestures. They probably found it wholly fitting to consign Hitler to hell in a heretic's fire in the symbolic presence of the men who had not survived the living hell of the trenches created by the German invasion of 1914. Indeed, both the dignified minute of silence and the dancing rings around the bonfire honored the patriotic dead.

As befitted the many solemn memorials Saint-Flour had already staged since its liberation, the town celebrated the victory with more gravity than its neighboring village. After de Gaulle's radio announcement of the German capitulation during the afternoon of 8 May, flags flew up across town, and crowds poured into the streets to follow the municipal band in a torchlight procession. But "the ninth was consecrated to memory (*souvenir*)," because, in the words of *La Margeride*, "our fellow citizens know not how to forget, in the most exalting hours, what price has been paid for regained Liberty and Victory." The day began at the Monument aux Morts, where representatives of all local associations and the widows of two local resistants attended a ceremony that included speeches on the martyrs' sacrifices given by the mayor and the subprefect. After a Te Deum at the cathedral, the assembly processed to the home of the late Dr. Mallet to hear a speech given by Amarger, in his capacity as secretary of the CDL. The day ended with a pilgrimage led by an honor guard to the site of the execution of the twenty-five fusillés two kilometers outside of town.[32]

Despite the dancing and ringing of bells, shadows cast by the anxieties of the Return, the food shortages, and suspicions that the joy of the victory was not unanimous lay over all these celebrations.[33] Because they had not given their workers the afternoon of 8 May off, for example, a correspondent from Rambervillers denounced two factory owners as "war profiteers."[34] And the same Cantalien correspondent who found the mock burning of Hitler "charming" decried the attitude of the mayor for hiding himself in a "cagoulard café" rather than mixing with the people. Even worse, in his opinion, a woman responded to the cheer "Vive la Résistance!" with an acerbic, "Ah! It's beautiful, the Resistance!"[35] In the context of the après-libération, such reprimands represent the best documented evidence of dissension within communities over the official memories and interpretations enshrined in public ceremonies.

During the summer of 1945, the emphasis of commemorative activities shifted from mourning deaths and celebrating victories to serving a martyrology according to the requirements of honorary justice. In general, that martyrology responded to the pull of the Gaullist myth in terms of its exaltation of those who suffered and died on behalf of the Resistance. During the night of 18 July 1945, for example, the department of Savoie held a vigil in honor of the war dead. In Moûtiers the POWs, deportees, and resistants organized an honor guard for the specially illuminated Monument aux Morts in the conviction that "our friends will not be dead as long as we—simply, piously—honor them like this."[36]

Although communities throughout France observed the same ceremonial calendar and employed the same ritual traditions, the rhetorical subtleties of ceremonies and monuments differed from town to town. The variations grew in part from location; all ceremonies in Rambervillers, for example, had a more martial air than the same occasions in Saint-Flour or Moûtiers, simply because of the presence of so many regular French and American troops in the Vosges. More important, however, the variations occurred because the ceremonies embodied a contested memory and therefore engaged the full play of commemorative politics.[37]

The end of a messy war and the advent of a new regime meant that liberation-era commemorative politics would stretch beyond domestic politicking to the construction of a new postwar identity for France based on the country's wartime record. There was, after all, some cause for confusion. Were the French collaborators, as suggested by Vichy? Or were they resistants, as epitomized by de Gaulle? Were they the losers of 1940 or the victors of 1944–45? Were they trustworthy allies of the postwar West like the British or defeated enemies like the Hungarians? Charles de Gaulle offered a clear answer in the Resistencialist myth: the French were trustworthy partners in victory who had stood united together in their heroic, and primarily military, struggle against the foreign oppressor.

This official memory had a number of ramifications. By recasting the complex struggles of wartime France as a straightforward conflict between the Gaullist military Resistance and the Germans, the myth reduced the many French resistances into one overarching Resistance and the enemy into the Germans and a handful of misguided collaborators. Furthermore, it "nationalized" the memory of the war by replacing the fragmented, localized experiences of occupation and liberation with a single "French" experience that resembled the myth more than any particular reality.[38] The myth was meant to unite the French, win them an honorable place in the postwar world, and serve in the domestic politics of legitimating a new elite and reimagining a new identity. Indeed, it represented the national government's bid for both; it would make the Resistance the new elite in Paris and the provinces and reimagine France's identity as the (mythical) Resistance.

Yet if the myth's drastic simplification of the war and liberation neatly disposed of some delicate matters among the Allies, it created its own problems at home. On the one hand, it served the interests of the majority of *attentistes* by casting a retrospective mantle of resistance over them. Indeed, the collaborators' agenda in attending memorial functions did not involve honoring the dead so much as making an honorable place for themselves among the living, leading to continual alarums and complaints that collaborators were whitewashing themselves by using the patriotic symbols and gestures to which resistants felt themselves exclusively entitled.[39] It also benefited some communities by giving their actual, relatively dull experiences a more heroic air; such towns and individuals did not complain overmuch about the myth's inaccuracies.

On the other hand, the myth also served the interests of resistants, who certainly agreed that their dead comrades should be given the greatest honors as patriotic martyrs.[40] Resistants might even benefit from a process of glory, rather than guilt, by association. Yet towns and individuals who had fought heroically against the occupation and Vichy protested bitterly against the myth's dilution of their sacrifices and triumphs. The question at the heart of après-libération commemorative politics, then, asked not whether the French would accept the Resistencialist myth, but to what degree they would accept it. The French were willing to remember themselves as Resistants, but would they also remember themselves as collaborators and *attentistes*?

Accordingly, the Gaullist myth and its proposed identity of a nation of Resistants acted as the touchstone of all local commemorative politics during the après-libération. Some towns, such as Saint-Flour, not only welcomed the myth but worked hard to conform to its image. Other towns fought hard to protect their own memories from the myth's hegemony. Rambervillers objected to having its long tradition of opposition to invasion subsumed into the national Resistance. Moûtiers would not accept a national memory that forgot the collaborators who had harmed the Tarentaise. The range of commemorative politics within communities and between small towns and the national government can best be appreciated by studying the ceremonial rhetoric and activity of each of the towns.

SAINT-FLOUR

Throughout the après-libération, Saint-Flour and its hinterland formed a coherent and tightly interwoven commemorative region that put the same rhetorical intensity into ceremony and memory that other regions, such as the Tarentaise, put into the purge. The fighting in the Margeride in June 1944 and, more important, the reprisals of executions and deportations taken by the Germans for that fighting, left Resistance dead scattered throughout the region. After the liberation the smaller towns of the area commemorated those deaths openly and grandly. Some of the deceased even received multiple honors in their hometowns and in the places where they died, both of which claimed the right to recognize "their" martyrs.[41] These outlying ceremonies followed the same pattern as those in Saint-Flour and often commanded the presence of departmental officials of both the government and the Resistance as well as mayors from neighboring communes. The reports of the ceremonies hardly mentioned the cause of death, let alone the killers, but dwelled instead on the devotion to duty and beautiful sacrifices of the deceased.[42] Indeed, the memory of the liberation in Saint-Flour and its arrondissement turned on the axis of "redemptive martyrdom."[43]

In Saint-Flour itself, Resistance leader and town editor René Amarger and the other memory makers personified by the Remembrance Committee aligned the town's memory of the war and postwar identity with the Gaullist myth through the construction of memorial cults based on two episodes connected to Mont-Mouchet: the execution of the Twenty-five Martyrs at the Pont de Soubizergues and the sufferings of the Mallet family. The death of sixteen-year-old Pierre Mallet at the Pont de Soubizergues linked the two. They further betrayed their eagerness to belong to that myth in two articles that complained that Paris did not seem to realize or know about Cantal's martyrdom and the "sacred rights of our five hundred *sinistrés*, of our one hundred *fusillés*, and of all our dead."[44]

On 10 June 1944, the same day as the more famous atrocity at Oradour-sur-Glane, German and collaborationist forces attacked the FFI redoubt on Mont-Mouchet and began repressive police action in the towns and villages of eastern Cantal.[45] Two days later, maquisards killed the SS captain in charge of the repression, seven other Germans, and two Miliciens (not Cantaliens) in Murat. In revenge, the Germans selected twenty-five men from among the fifty-three men, women, and adolescents being held hostage or prisoner in Saint-Flour's Hotel Terminus. The list included Jews, resistants, police inspectors from Clermont-Ferrand, hotel keepers, an escaped French POW, and hostages such as the young Pierre Mallet. They ranged in age from seventeen to sixty; seven were under twenty-five. At dawn on 14 June, the Germans drove the twenty-five men two kilometers out of town to the Pont de Soubizergues, lined them up, and shot them in the back. The remaining twenty-eight prisoners, including Pierre's mother and twin sister, Madeleine, were taken to Clermont-Ferrand and deported.[46]

The Germans did not allow any public burial of the twenty-five executed men at the time, but the Sanflorains quickly made up for the lack of a proper funeral after their liberation ten weeks later. According to *La Margeride*, which devoted most of its first issue to complete reports of this and two similar ceremonies in the arrondissement, on 27 August ten thousand people, including Allied servicemen who had fought with the maquis, gathered in Saint-Flour in a show of "the spontaneous élan of a whole population united in a fraternal gesture of grateful recognition and of patriotism." The cortege began with the municipal band and three companies of FFI, followed by the civil, military, and religious authorities, the fire brigade, the railway workers, and other groups such as the Sanflorain Sporting Union and the schoolchildren. It wound through town to meet the families of the nine Sanflorain men among the Twenty-five Martyrs at their mass grave by the bridge.

After the gestures of a military funeral, including the song, "Ils sont tombés sous la mitraille" (They have been felled by the machine gun), the bishop of Saint-Flour took the microphone. He pleaded with the assembled that they rise above hate to solidarity, fraternity, and charity and led them in prayer. The temporary subprefect then proceeded to contradict the bishop's message by drawing parallels between the events of 14 June 1944 and "the same savagery" he remembered seeing in 1914 in his hometown in Lorraine. He spoke threateningly about the Milice and Waffen-SS responsible for the atrocities in the region and, in an unusual manner for Cantal, promised the shades of the Twenty-five: "We will avenge you." Next, as secretary of the CDL, Amarger spoke at length about the sacrifices of the Resistance's martyrs, drawing the moral that "by faithfully serving their memory (*mémoire*) we will earn the right to still be among the living." He ended, not coincidentally, by recalling the sacrifice of Pierre Mallet.[47]

The town took its duty to remember the Twenty-five Martyrs very seriously indeed. At the liberation, the municipal council renamed the road leading to the execution site the avenue des Martyrs. A month later, on 24 October 1944, Saint-Flour ceremoniously exhumed the mass grave to bury the men properly. The coffins were taken into the heart of town to rest overnight in the cathedral or, in the case of the Jewish victims, in the town hall. The next morning the Bishop of Saint-Flour and the Grand Rabbi "eloquently glorified the sacrifice of our dear departed, and implored all the living to be worthy of them and their rich teaching by working for Justice and Liberty." The town's various irregular military detachments and civilian and military authorities then led a long cortege to the cemetery for the burials. Amarger's signed emotional report in *La Margeride* drew "a lesson of sublime humility and of union" from the occasion.[48]

Other Sanflorains shared the editor's sense of duty toward the Twenty-five, demonstrating it in subsidiary ceremonies held by groups such as the local PCF section and the municipal band.[49] In early October, for instance, the tribunal of Saint-Flour officially opened its new year in the form of an homage to one of the Twenty-five Martyrs, the judge Henri Rassemusse. The judge's widow and daughter joined the town's authorities and family friends as guests at the ceremony, which involved two eulogies to the "volunteer martyr" of the Pont de Soubizergues.[50] The court's decision to so honor their martyr, it must be said, may not have been wholly disinterested at a time when the judiciary was widely believed to have compromised itself with Vichy. Indeed, attempts by collaborators to whitewash themselves by associating themselves with Resistance martyrs must have worried the family. The notice announcing the judge's burial in Molompize on 27 October ended: "*Collaborators are requested to abstain from attending these different ceremonies, notably at Molompize.*"[51]

By the time of the first anniversary of the execution, Saint-Flour had an official Remembrance Committee to orchestrate the ceremonies. In order to assure that they "take place with the respect (*recueillement*) and perfect order due to such a commemoration," the committee started issuing instructions to the populace in May. The announcements covered the details of timing, the roster for the guard of honor, the hours during which homes and businesses should close their shutters as a sign of mourning, and the ordering of flowers. They tended to focus, however, on the proper bearing of pious respect that was desired of participants and observers.[52]

The anniversary commemoration began at 6:00 A.M. when the judge's widow lit a memorial flame near the twenty-five temporary steles erected at the execution site. A religious service for all the fusillés of the arrondissement followed. At noon all businesses and shutters closed. During the day individuals could take flowers to the execution site until 5:30 P.M., when the town's authorities, societies, and schools gathered in the place de la Liberté for the procession down the avenue des Martyrs to the site for a ceremony featuring the usual patriotic hymns, two minutes of silence (twice), a speech by the mayor, and the relighting of the memorial flame by Mme. Mallet, mother of the youngest victim and herself a deportee.

The mayor's speech touched on the brutality of the German executioners but dwelled on the beauty of the victims' sacrifice and the community's duty to honor their memory and live up to their idealism. The Remembrance Committee then took over the honor guard until the flame was extinguished at 8:00 P.M. Following its custom, *La Margeride* devoted most of its front page to a report of the "grandiose and moving anniversary at the Pont de Soubizergues," an editorial entitled "Do Not Forget Us," and photographs of eight of the victims, that of Pierre Mallet being somewhat larger and more prominent than the others.[53]

After this, "our dear fusillés" and "our martyrs of the Pont du Soubizergues," most of whom were strangers, lapsed into the role of a standard reference in ceremonial rhetoric, although the town did continue to mark the anniversary of the atrocity.[54] Their invocation served to demonstrate Saint-Flour's suffering in the cause of the Resistance and the liberation, thus establishing the town's credentials as part of the France of the Gaullist myth. In Saint-Flour's Resistencialist myth, the martyrs simply elided the town's four years of a relatively easy occupation in a burst of violence and horror. They also elided collaboration through a rhetorical sleight of hand. In the first days of liberation they were referred to alternatively as the "Twenty-five Fusillés" or the "Twenty-five Martyrs." Martyrs quickly won out definitively. "Fusillés" evokes concrete images specific to the fighting between resistants and collaborators during the Second World War. It conjures images of blindfolded resistants or hostages forced to their knees by Miliciens holding rifles cocked against their temples. "Martyrs," however, is comfortingly vague about the actual circumstances of the exemplary death. Eaten by lions or tortured by Nazis, "martyrs" suggests moral redemption, not civil war, and wraps a cloak of virtue around those who serve their cult.

Today the martyrs are remembered in a memorial park at the site of their execution. By the side of the small country road, at the entrance to the enclosure, stands the deliberately jagged base of an obelisk, vaguely recalling a broken sword. The side facing the road is decorated with a raised stone cross of Lorraine and, inscribed in gold, the words: "On 14 June 1944 at the base of this slope, twenty-five patriots were executed by the Germans." The other side is similarly decorated with the words: "To our martyrs." The visitor walks through the adjacent gate in the wooden fence lined with roses and down a little slope to stand before a graveled area from which rise twenty-five black stone pillars reminiscent of execution posts. The name and age of the victim are written in gold on each of the pillars, except for the four that read: "An unknown." In early November 1997 there were flowers in front of four of the columns.

The second memorial cult constructed after the liberation honored the Mallet family. Dr. Louis Mallet had been a well-known physician in the region before the war. During the war he played a leading role in the local resistance, and, as a consequence, he and his older son Etienne joined the maquis in the Margeride for the mobilization after D-Day, only to be shot on 24 June with three unknown patriots in a potato field near Chaudes-Aigues. With the three Mallet men dead and the two women taken away without any word whatsoever until February 1945, the family would have been erased if not for the memorial impulse that swept the region after its liberation and the repeated efforts of Dr. Mallet's friend and resistance colleague, René Amarger, to keep their memory alive. Indeed, he did more than keep their memory alive; by the time the women miraculously returned from Ravensbrück in May 1945, he had turned the family into the symbol of the virtues and sacrifices of the Resistance and of the sufferings of Cantal. During the après-libération, the cult of the Mallets far exceeded that of the martyrs of the Pont de Soubizergues.

Even under normal circumstances, Dr. Mallet's death would have drawn attention because of his activities as a physician, friend of the peasant, and *conseiller général*. So Amarger's efforts on behalf of the family's memory met with wide sympathy. As one of its first official actions, for instance, the special delegation renamed the avenue Maréchal Pétain the avenue Dr. Louis Mallet. The agricultural office also worked to memorialize the loss of its "dear and highly venerated founder-president."[55] Beyond the doctor's professional contacts, the Mallets also had both family and friends in the area, one of whom may have been "their comrade, J. B.," who submitted a poem, "To Pierre and Etienne Mallet," to the town paper in October 1944.[56]

Events for the family were broken into three parts for commemorative purposes: the doctor and Etienne who died together, Pierre who died among the Twenty-five Martyrs of 14 June, and the women deported together to Ravensbrück, for whom it would have been reasonable to fear the worst. Pierre, or Pierrot as *La Margeride* usually called him, was not only honored but singled out in August and October 1944 at the ceremonies for the victims of the Pont de Soubizergues. The first memorial service for the doctor and Etienne took place at the initiative of the local resistance on 17 August, after the liberation of Chaudes-Aigues. Maquis units from throughout the region sent delegations to attend a requiem and a ceremony at the Monument aux Morts, where an important Resistance official eulogized Dr. Mallet as a man so devoted to his country that he gave it his own life and those of his sons, and as a symbol of the Resistance's glory.

The three unidentified maquisards killed at the same time were then buried in the town cemetery and the Mallets removed to a family tomb in Faverolles. *La Margeride* carried a full report of the ceremony in its first issue, preceded by a long obituary by Amarger forecasting the role that the family would play in the community's postwar reimagining. "The martyrdom of the Mallet family," he wrote, "is an immense sorrow for us all. This martyrdom also creates a pressing duty for all of us. Let us never forget that, more than a fine family, they were and will remain a symbol and that they impose upon us the pious homage of gratitude and of fidelity to the ideal." The memory of the doctor would "guide us to the future, to the light, to liberty, and to fraternity."[57] He therefore became a primary example of the demands of honorary justice.

After the exhumation of the bodies of the twenty-five fusillés in October 1944, an honor guard of Pierre's schoolmates accompanied representatives of the Resistance and the authorities as they escorted his remains to the family tomb to rest beside his father and brother.[58] The idea to celebrate 24 June 1945 as a "Day of Remembrance" in honor of Dr. Mallet and his sons came from several sources among the local resistance and the peasantry. It first appeared in the press in a letter to the editor suggesting that because the doctor had done so much for the peasantry, they should do something for him by holding a pilgrimage to, and a religious service at, the site of his execution.[59] In February the general assembly of the local bureau of the agricultural credit union of Saint-Flour voted unanimously to have a requiem said at the Sanflorain cathedral on 24 June and to commission a plaque in the doctor's memory.[60]

The 1945 Day of Remembrance became a two-day pilgrimage, beginning in Faverolles on 23 June with services at the church and cemetery. On the twenty-fourth, deputations from communes and Resistance organizations throughout the area joined the authorities and Mme. and Madeleine Mallet, returned from deportation to find their menfolk dead, for a memorial Mass and a secular ceremony at the site of Louis and Etienne's deaths.[61] The final ceremony came on 8 July when the three Mallets were buried together in the nearby commune of Neuvéglise with the attendance of representatives from throughout the region of Saint-Flour and of the highest levels of the departmental administration and Resistance, including the prefect. After a religious service, the ceremony at the cemetery featured three speakers to represent Dr. Mallet's roles as physician, friend of the peasantry, and resistant. Having always been a leader in the Resistance, he was now firmly enthroned as the department's chief martyr.[62]

But ceremonies alone, no matter how lavish or frequent, did not satisfy the Sanflorains and their neighbors; they also wanted to honor the doctor and his sons in a more lasting, material manner. The Remembrance Committee created in September 1944 thus took charge of erecting monuments to the Mallets and to the Twenty-five Martyrs. Between September 1944 and March 1945, some news of their "Œuvre du souvenir et de la Reconnaissance" (Work of Remembrance and of Gratitude) appeared in the town paper on an almost weekly basis. The committee took several approaches to raising funds: soliciting direct contributions from municipal councils in the arrondissement and Resistance organizations, sending collectors from door to door, organizing entertainments, and contacting Cantaliens in Paris. It also received spontaneous help from local associations. The departmental football league, for instance, urged its members to devise all sorts of extra fund-raisers, although, being illegal, dances were expressly forbidden. The Sanflorain team accordingly opened its postliberation season with a raffle and a benefit match against Riom-ès-Montagnes. Before the mayor started the play, the stadium observed a minute of silence for the arrondissement's fusillés.[63]

Yet despite such generous gestures as the gift of ten thousand francs from the war-damaged village of Fridefont (population 241), the committee expressed a frustrated disappointment in the response to its appeals. A signed letter to the editor from Ruines suggested one reason for the sluggish response. The author felt that a medical clinic would make a much more fitting monument to Dr. Mallet than a statue and assured the committee that more money could be more easily raised for such a cause.[64] The committee replied to the objections implicit in the low response by formally assuring the public that the monies were destined for the two monuments. More often, they employed guilt and shame. Many of the reports in the paper made jabs comparing the immense sacrifice made by Dr. Mallet to the beggarly pittance begrudged to his memorial by his beneficiaries. To reinforce the message, the committee also posted lists in the press and at the town hall of who had, or had not, given what.[65]

The committee faded from view during the summer of 1945, however, until a letter from Paris demanding to know what had become of the "Work of Remembrance" jogged the committee into completing the monument that now sits at the foot of the park at the entrance to the upper city.[66] Its two taller outer columns of black blocks list the names of the 125 victims of German reprisals from Saint-Flour, Clavières, Ruines, and Murat. The left-hand panel of the triptych reads: "To Doctor Mallet, To his Sons," and the right-hand panel: "To the fusillés of the arrondissement of Saint-Flour." The shorter central panel of white stone is a bas-relief with the two Mallet boys standing in the background. Their father stands between and in front of them, his right foot resting on a rock so that he can support a maquisard who has collapsed over his knee in the classic suffering pose of the Pietà. The pedestal bears the date "1944" and the inscription: "To the heroes of the Liberation." The only military accoutrements of the four figures are their army boots. As an image of proud victimization rather than aggressive victory, it accords well with the local interpretation of the war constructed during the après-libération.

The agricultural office and local credit union also bear a more modest monument to Dr. Mallet. It is made of a stone plaque with three bronze bas-relief insets of the doctor and his sons, a carved emblem combining a sheaf of wheat, a sickle, oak leaves, and the cross of Lorraine, and an inscription recognizing the doctor's work for the poor and the peasants and his and his sons' deaths at the hands of the Germans, and signed: "His friends, the peasants." The General Assembly approved the plan for the plaque in April 1945 and had it up by the end of June.[67] Presumably with less general consent, the agricultural office also made a bid to turn itself into a living memorial in its early 1945 subscription drive. An announcement urging peasants to pay their twenty-five francs' dues exhorted: "Everyone knows that from beyond the tomb, the life of a martyr, fallen for the cause of liberty, calls them to duty. Not to ensure the survival of the organizations created by our lamented friend, Dr. Mallet, is no doubt the same as to allow his memory to be tarnished."[68] It would not be surprising if such heavy-handed, moralistic browbeating did more to mar than to serve the memory of the generous and patriotic doctor.

The Sanflorains further honored the memory of Dr. Mallet through the old tradition of honoring his widow. Having been deported before any of the Mallet men were killed, Mme. Mallet was neither physically present in Saint-Flour until May 1945 nor aware that she was a widow. But she was very much symbolically present. Bereaved wife and mother, herself undergoing the reputedly purifying hell of deportation, the name of Mme. Mallet came to stand for all the tragedy, sorrow, and grandeur of the occupation and the Resistance's victory. As a deportee, Madame received significant honors in her own right, but as the widow of Dr. Mallet, they were heaped upon her.

While still in captivity, Mme. Mallet and her daughter were, of course, remembered in the many religious services held for the doctor and the two boys. But she was also given a political role in town. Like other Absents, Mme. Mallet was named to the special delegation of the municipal council at the liberation. In April 1945 her name was placed on the slate of Resistance candidates for the municipal elections, most probably without her knowledge, and received the highest number of votes. In May, the town officially celebrated her return from Ravensbrück. Mme. Mallet then took up a ceremonial role, lighting the flame at the first anniversary of the Pont de Soubizergues at which her son was honored among the victims. In June 1945, she was named to the honorary council for the departmental UFF at its first congress. In September, she ran for her husband's seat on the Conseil général, thereby provoking a stifled controversy about alleged exploitation of her name. Having won that election, she was elected to a vice-presidency of the Conseil.[69]

The construction of the cult of the Mallet family and the uses made of Mme. Mallet's name before and after her return illustrate the merger of memory and politics. If the public use of memory always holds some trace of politics, in après-libération Saint-Flour it was saturated with them. Commemorative politics there had two interrelated goals: to establish the town's Resistance credentials and to establish the authority and legitimacy of the new Resistance government, both national and local. De Gaulle's Resistencialist myth served those goals admirably. Fashioning the town's postwar identity along the lines of the national identity reimagined by de Gaulle boosted the claims of resistants to authority on a local level by analogy with the general's own claims. A series called "Mémoires d'un résistant" in La Margeride helped draw that analogy by publicizing the previously secret exploits of the local resistance in glowing terms. The proximity of Mont-Mouchet also helped to align the official memory of Saint-Flour's war with the Gaullist myth, because the fighting there and its horrendous aftermath gave the region most of its martyrs. After the liberation, the siting of a national monument at Mont-Mouchet further underscored Saint-Flour's links to the Resistance's military struggle.

Indeed, in the first memorial held at Mont-Mouchet on 20 May 1945, Saint-Flour staked its claim to be a national *"ville martyre."* After the monument's cornerstone was laid on top of Mont-Mouchet, the ceremony and its ten thousand participants turned into a pilgrimage along what the regional military commander called the area's "Way of the Cross." The procession first stopped to honor the village of Clavières, destroyed in June 1944, before moving on to Ruines to honor the twenty-seven hostages executed there. The pious journey ended in Saint-Flour, stopping first at the Pont de Soubizergues, where the CRR laid a wreath in honor of the Twenty-five Martyrs. The crowd then climbed the hill to Dr. Mallet's house in the old town. No less a personage than de Gaulle's own representative laid a wreath there to honor the doctor, indicating both the doctor's own merits and the clout of those sponsoring his cult.[70]

Finally, the mayor spoke in front of the Monument aux Morts. He thanked "the official personalities for having been kind enough to associate themselves with our sorrows, and sharing with the Sanflorains the permanent cult of our dead: those of the Great War, those of the War of 1939–1940, those of the Maquis, the martyrs of the Resistance, the good doctor and his children, the commander André Delorme, fallen close to his home, [and] the courageous and good Etienne Mallet." This Etienne Mallet, who should not be confused with Dr. Mallet's son of the same name, was arrested by the Gestapo and tortured to death in May 1944. The town's sporting association dedicated the day to his memory and created a boules tournament in his honor, thereby giving the day honoring the "heroes of the Resistance fallen for Liberty" its closing ceremony in which the CRR awarded the boules trophy in the presence of Etienne Mallet's widow, the prefect, and other important personages.[71]

An official visit by de Gaulle and the sultan of Morocco on 1 July 1945 further underscored the alignment of Saint-Flour's memory and identity with the Gaullist myth. Although the general only stopped in Saint-Flour for fifteen minutes, local organizers maximized that quarter of an hour to illustrate the town's Resistance identity. De Gaulle presented Dr. Mallet's posthumous Croix de la légion d'honneur to Mme. Mallet and was introduced to the families of the town's dead, executed, and deported heroes. The organizers regretted that the First Resistant could not take the time to tour the sites of Saint-Flour's martyrdom, but nonetheless interpreted his visit as "an eloquent homage to our miseries, to our sufferings, to our losses," and as a mark of "the gratitude of the country for so many of our sacrifices made in the cause of Liberty."[72]

As further testimony to the affiliation between Saint-Flour and the national (military) Resistance, it was Mme. Mallet who unveiled the national, "monument to the glory of the French maquisards" at Mont-Mouchet during its inauguration in June 1946.[73] The fact that of the three towns of this study only Saint-Flour collected money for the national Resistance monuments at Mont-Valérien and Mont-Mouchet cannot be ascribed solely to the region's easier financial circumstances or to its emotional involvement with the latter site. The area supported those national monuments because it supported the Gaullist myth that shaped them.[74]

These commemorative politics were undoubtedly successful in binding Saint-Flour into the national history and myth of the Resistance. During the summer of 1945, the Sanflorains and their neighbors observed the anniversaries of skirmishes, executions, and atrocities with great pomp and rhetorical flourish. Whether they were anonymous maquisards who died as strangers or local men, all who died by German hands during the liberation were treated as "those who have piously died for the *Patrie*."[75] The many religious and patriotic ceremonies filling June and July were designed to demonstrate that "their names were synonyms for patriotism, honor, and loyalty," and to pay "the ransom of the living to those who have died for them" by tending the graves of the Resistance's martyrs and their memories.[76] They were also meant to encourage the unity of the living through such examples as the two Sanflorains who were "symbols of unity in sacrifice, one Catholic, the other a freethinker. For all of us who mourn them, two friends whose memory (*souvenir*) will never burn out in our hearts."[77]

But it is not as clear that the ceremonies and rhetoric had the same success in legitimating the members of the local resistance as postwar leaders. Willing to participate in a "cult of memory" (*souvenir*) that painted them as the martyred victims of German savagery, the Sanflorains showed themselves less inclined to remember or celebrate the Resistance as active, and surviving, heroes. Most noticeably, this town of a hundred memorial ceremonies neglected to mark the first anniversary of its liberation, a rather glaring omission in 1945 and in the region. Amarger noted the occasion with a signed editorial in which he lamented that the living had not fulfilled the promises of the dead but suggested that amends could be made in the upcoming elections.[78] One other, embittered, commentator suggested that the Sanflorains had forgotten their liberation because they considered it unimportant.[79] That is possible, although it is more likely that the Sanflorains remembered the liberation and what preceded it all too well to risk a public opening for recriminations with any ceremony. Had the local resistance had the public support their rhetoric implied, or had they fashioned their image less as victims and martyrs, they would surely have arranged to commemorate their victory as efficiently as they had arranged to commemorate their losses.

RAMBERVILLERS

The Rambûvetais also constructed their postwar identity around the heroism of local resistants, but they were proud of them as the latest manifestation of a long tradition more than as members of the Resistance per se. In 1944–45, the makers of official memory integrated the latest martial calamity into the town's long history of standing firm against invaders, particularly German invaders. Just a week after its liberation, a correspondent submitted a signed article to the departmental daily placing Rambervillers' liberation by the FFI in its chronicle of invasion. After surveying the historical highlights culminating in 1870, the article ended with: "And yet this example of valor [of 1944] is not exceptional in our region where so many different invaders, from the Huns and Vandals to the Cossacks and Germans (*Germains*), have followed one another without ever being able to tame the potential for resistance of a people [who are] courageous and energetic to the highest degree."[80]

A year later another signed article honoring the anniversary of Rambervillers' liberation drew direct parallels between the fighting of the *francs-tireurs* of 1870 and of the FFI in 1944. "It seems, from a distance of seventy-four years, that it [was] a renewal of the same combat, that of a town always jealous of its liberties, ready for any sacrifice to defend them. It was definitely the same blood that animated the national guardsmen . . . in 1870 and, in 1944, our valiant FFI."[81] The obvious analogy, however, was only superficial. The *francs-tireurs* of 1870 fought out of patriotism and the need to defend their homes. Their later counterparts shared these motives, but also fought, at least officially, for the ideals of a Resistance dedicated to crushing Nazi ideology in order to create a more just future. To gloss over that crucial difference glorified the Rambûvetais but slighted the national, and by extension the local, Resistance.

Rambervillers did not hold as many public memorial ceremonies as Saint-Flour, in part because of the continuing warfare in the region and in part because Vosgiens seem to have been content to let maquisards lie where they had died and been buried.[82] The correspondents from Rambervillers, however, minced no words in naming the killers in the town's few public memorials; for example, they explained the death of a twenty-five-year-old maquisard wounded and then killed in cold blood by a German patrol as an instance of "the eternal Teutonic barbarism."[83] Unlike either Saint-Flour or Moûtiers, however, Rambervillers celebrated the anniversary of its liberation with great pomp. The celebrations on 30 September 1945 followed the pattern of military ceremony that was already well established in the town and was all but necessitated by the presence of American and French troops.

The official celebrations actually began on Saturday evening, 29 September, with a torchlight parade of the municipal band and a large crowd. The town awoke the next morning to a 7 A.M. reveille, early enough for everyone to attend the Mass said by a former maquis chaplain in memory of all those (both civilian and military) who died during the liberation. At nine the sirens sounded to signal the hour of the FFI attack a year earlier and the current gathering for the parade. The assembled dignitaries included the mayor and municipal council, the prefect and other departmental civil and military officials, and an American major who had taken part in the town's liberation. The procession's first ceremony presented the flags of the town and of the maquis to the local Resistance in the person of a maquisard who had lost an arm during the liberation.

A cortege representing the entire community then wound its way through the streets, which were decorated with flags and triumphal arches (the work of the CDLR), to the monuments to 1914–18 and 1870 and to the graves of four maquisards, all Rambûvetais except one who became an honorary Rambûvetais by dying there. The ceremony at each memorial stop followed the standard pattern of appropriate military music, a minute of silence, the deposition of a wreath, and a few words. At each of the maquisards' graves, a municipal councilor read out the man's name and the story of his death. The procession then traveled via the Monument aux Morts to the place du 30 September 1944, the rue André Quinet, and the pont Jean Boura to inaugurate the new Liberation names with ribbon cutting and further speeches. After the parade the authorities, resistants, widows and orphans, and organizers gathered for a lunch during which speeches were given by the prefect, the maquisard honored by receiving the flags, a member of the CDL, and the mayor. Meanwhile the general public could amuse itself at football matches or a retrospective of the life of the maquis. At 5 P.M. the garrison band gave a concert, which was followed by fireworks and a public ball at the Maison du Peuple.

The day's rhetoric tended to stress the ongoing need for the type of unity experienced a year earlier among the heroic FFI, a common trope suggesting how much resistants throughout the country worried about the lack of such unity in 1945. The mayor's speech at the place du 30 September 1944 acknowledged the seventeen civilians killed there on 3 October 1944 by German artillery and the "numerous [persons] without arms, without uniforms, men, women, girls who accomplished often perilous missions and rendered appreciable services" for the liberation. But he dwelled on the maquisards who actually liberated the town. "Their great merit," he said somewhat remarkably for the praise of soldiers, "was to detach themselves from all authorities under whom they had been up until then, in order to undertake, alone and at their own risk, the deliverance of our Town." This deliverance, he made clear, was from both German plans to burn the town and deport the townspeople on 3 October 1944 and from American bombardment. The point of the anniversary celebration and the change of street names, the mayor explained, was to commit the glorious events of the town's liberation to memory and so publicly honor those who had delivered the people. The press reports followed the mayor's lead in reducing the Americans to, at best, the status of bystanders, and linking the maquisards not with the rest of the French Resistance but with the Rambûvetais volunteers of 1870.[84]

In Rambervillers, then, the official memory of the liberation had an ambiguous relation to the Gaullist nationalized memory of a Resistant France. On the one hand, it seconded the Gaullist point that the French had themselves thrown the Germans out of the country, with little mention of Allied troops or collaborators to muddy the story. On the other hand, the constant linkage of the maquis of 1944 with the *francs-tireurs* of 1870 subtly rejected the national Resistance, and possibly the claims of its new government. In this interpretation the maquisards were patriots of their *petit pays,* defending Rambervillers as their forefathers always had. Any further goals, any wider conflicts were eclipsed. Even the preferential use of the term "maquis" or, secondarily, "FFI" instead of "resistants" buttressed the localized interpretation.

This official memory of the liberation did a certain violence to the fact of collaboration and gave rather short shrift to the American troops who had until quite recently had such a large presence in Rambervillers. The question of the Americans' exact role in the town's liberation remains a matter of contention to this day, one's position on the matter having more to do with one's family history than the cold, hard facts. During the après-libération, when Resistance legitimated authority, it was obviously in the interest of the resistants to diminish the Americans' contribution and in the interest of those wishing to diminish the resistants' postwar claims to augment the Americans' role.

The debate about the Americans' role in liberating Rambervillers, however, cannot be easily cast in terms of resistants versus antiresistants. The mayor, after all, was an acknowledged resistant and undoubtedly meant to exalt the local, if not the national, resistance. Indeed, it cannot even be considered as a purely local matter, because since September 1944 departmental politics had insisted as a matter of pride on dubbing Rambervillers as the only town in the Vosges liberated by the FFI. Nonetheless, an odd controversy over the town's patron saint suggests that there may indeed have been an anti-resistance faction that attempted to use the debate over who liberated Rambervillers to discredit both the Americans and the maquis. Some of the town's correspondents certainly acted as if they believed in such a cabal.

The town's patron saint, a fourth-century virgin martyr from not far away in the Vosges foothills, first appeared in the après-libération press in a small notice in the department's Catholic newspaper announcing "a Mass of thanksgiving and gratitude to Saint Libaire, patroness of the town, for her protection during the liberation," to be held on her feast day of 8 October. The notice appeared in the same issue as a long report on Rambervillers' commemoration of its liberation on 30 September—the only one, it is significant to note, to mention the Americans, although it still gave all the glory to the FFI.[85] The idea of giving thanks to a heavenly patron was hardly out of place in the Vosges. After all, the departmental capital held a "pious pilgrimage to the Virgin" on 22 September 1945 as part of the *fête de la libération* organized by the municipality and local resistance.[86]

But if the pilgrimage in Epinal symbolized the end of Vichy-era civil tensions, as suggested by Brossat, the Rambûvetaise day of thanksgiving demonstrated that the liberation had provided only a temporary or incomplete resolution to the long conflict between Catholics and anticlericals.[87] The day of prayer in thanksgiving to Saint Libaire fulfilled a vow made a year earlier and involved a Mass and the appointment of a parishioner in whose home the saint's statue would be hosted over the following year.[88] This might strike some as ridiculously old-fashioned or even superstitious, but hardly offensive or inexplicable, considering that the town was under artillery fire on the previous saint's day.

Certain Rambûvetais resistants, however, interpreted the homage to Saint Libaire for her protection during the liberation not as an acknowledgment of their divine support but as a challenge to their claims to have saved the town. Their suspicions undoubtedly rested on the sense of at least one correspondent that the collaborator/resistant fault lines in the community had fallen along the long-standing Third Republic divide between Catholics and anticlericals.[89] Such suspicions found support in the fact that the plans for the accompanying "project for the restoration of the Chapel of the Calvary in gratitude for the protection accorded our town by Saint Libaire" were prominently displayed in the same shop front that had previously held a large portrait of Marshall Pétain and then, at the liberation, an equally imposing picture of de Gaulle.[90]

Resistants defended themselves in print from the perceived attack on their honor and memory with sarcasm and logic. One article warned:

> But watch out for a row in Paradise. The patrons of Brû and Jean-ménil are going to be jealous; they won't get anything. After all, it is their fault, they had certainly gone off for a walk with Deodat, patron of Saint-Dié; that's why their protégées suffered such serious damage, or were they collaborators? Maybe we should demand that there be a

little purging in Paradise, and we are sure that Dame Justice will be respected.

And you, maquisards and resistants, be quiet. Do not talk our ears off anymore with your so-called deliverance of the town, you are impostors, and respect her who, with her grand saber, chased away the Boches: Saint Libaire.[91]

Another article in a paper with a more general circulation warned the town's Pétainists against plotting to discredit the FFI through the reconstruction of the chapel. "Know, messieurs, that your efforts are destined to certain failure because all the Rambûvetais have understood that without our maquisards Rambervillers would have undergone the same fate as Jeanménil, and the Boches, in particular, were in a position to realize that they found themselves not before a Saint, but in front of hearty fellows determined to voluntarily sacrifice themselves so that Rambervillers would live." The article ended by asking to whom the Rambûvetais should build a monument in gratitude for their deliverance, although it was obvious that the author meant the maquis.[92]

The monument "to the maquisards of the group of Rambervillers who died (*morts*) for the liberation of the *patrie*," is a simple granite stone, polished on one side to bear the names of the twenty fallen maquisards (four of whom are buried nearby), and the legend, "Remember that they died for your (*ta*) liberty," inscribed in gold.[93] In June 1950 it served as the site of a brief remembrance ceremony during the elaborate festivities for the award of the Croix de Guerre 1939–1945 to Rambervillers, Jeanménil, Brû, and Anglemont. Except for the absence of the American army, these ceremonies followed the pattern established in 1944–45, with the ringing of bells and a torchlight parade on the eve, a Mass in the morning, a procession stopping at the town's monuments, a banquet, fireworks, and a public ball.

The maquisards of Rambervillers have not been forgotten; indeed the town still had a Comité de la Libération in 1997. But the shape of their memory might not be quite what the correspondents of 1945 wanted. The rhetoric of the après-libération subsumed the maquisards into the glorious local history of ardent patriots and lovers of liberty, thus disengaging them from the Resistance of 1940–45. Rambervillers' official memory of the war as constructed during the après-libération, then, makes a deft compromise. It bursts with well-deserved local pride and accedes to the Gaullist myth of a resistant nation throwing out the oppressor. But it also neatly sidesteps the claims for future influence made by that same myth and rejects any claims Paris might make for having saved the nation by placing Rambervillers' liberation in the town's long history of invasion.[94] The lesson to be learned from this memory has nothing to do with the Resistance; it is that the Rambûvetais have always resisted foreign oppression and will do so again in the next war.

MOÛTIERS

Like the other towns, Moûtiers honored its dead and exalted their patriotism. But where Saint-Flour's cult of memory dwelled on martyrdom, on willing sacrifice, if not victimization, Moûtiers' remembered an active heroism cut down by barbarism. It was not so much that the Savoyards painted themselves as victims as that they portrayed themselves as the ultimately victorious prey of a savage and evil enemy, both German *and* French. They remembered themselves as resistants, with all the best moral echoes of the term, and they had the scars to prove it, lending a furious undertone to the articulated memory and casting them into open conflict with the national government.

Indeed, the reports of funerals in and around Moûtiers left no room for doubt as to who killed the deceased. As one report put it: "For every coffin, or almost every one, we know who is to blame: a Milicien already executed or in hiding. The ceremony over, one evokes memories, one recalls the cursed names. The tempest having subsided, one counts the victims, the heroes. One draws up the doleful balance sheet."[95] The report of a ceremony to mark the second anniversary of the death of a resistant blamed "the Vichyssois police."[96] The obituary for a twenty-one-year-old explained that he had been "betrayed by a Milicien and delivered to the Gestapo."[97] Another announced the funeral of a man shot three months earlier by the "German hordes."[98] Two reports further explained that the execution of men who were not FFIs happened because "the Nazis . . . [were] . . . drunk on French blood," and "the boches were drunk on blood.

They needed victims."⁹⁹ In *La Résistance savoyarde,* the deaths of French men and women at the hands of the Germans or their collaborators were always "murder" and almost always "cowardly." The mysticism of the cult of the patriotic martyr so prevalent in Cantal was replaced in Savoie by a hard-edged anger at the consequences of the collaborators' betrayal, especially the Miliciens'.

That edge of fury so plain in the memorial rhetoric and the actions of vigilantes may explain a singular decree issued by the prefect of Savoie in late 1944 forbidding the sale or circulation of photographs of fusillés.¹⁰⁰ The decree does not specify whether the ban extended to pictures of the fusillés before they were shot or was restricted to the rather gruesome photographs taken after the executions. Nor does it specify the prefect's motives. He may have found the idea of profiting from the deaths of fellow resistants to be morally repugnant and insulting to their memories. But the additional ban on distributing such photographs free of charge suggests that as guarantor of law and order in Savoie, the prefect may have seen the photographs as a threat to public order.

Catholic tradition allows for remembering the dead with a small Mass card that has the deceased's name and dates—but usually these are passed out only among family and friends. The distribution of the photographs must have gone far beyond those restricted circles to attract the prefect's attention. And they were being sold rather than handed out at funerals. Furthermore, why circulate the photographs of fusillés, especially if they were the bloody ones taken after execution? Why do this except to create a vengeful memorial cult? It is easy to imagine a vigilante orator pointing to these photographs, evoking the barbarity of Germans and collaborators and the claims of dead comrades, and inciting his men to violence. It is easy enough to imagine a woman condoning the vigilantism because of what the collaborators did to the poor mangled body in the photograph. The prefectural decree, then, suggests a wholly unauthorized "popular" cult of memory.¹⁰¹ Unfortunately, aside from the telling, but circumstantial, evidence of the decree and the rampant vigilantism, such a popular martyrological cult has left no traces in the documents. There is, however, ample documentation of official commemorations.

Overall, while giving due honor to the dead, Moutiérain ceremonies focused on the resistance's victory rather than its losses. Yet one event in the town's liberation overshadowed its celebration. When they evacuated what was essentially a guerrilla war zone at the end of August 1944, the Germans took twenty-one Moutiérains, as well as smaller numbers of men from other communities along their path, as hostages or human shields for their escape. The Germans selected those particular twenty-one men because they were FFIs, or relatives of resistants, or simply in the wrong place at the wrong time. Most were in their twenties, although four were younger than that. One, the Abbé Muyard, was offered the chance to stay in Moûtiers but refused to leave his parishioners. Three of the men actually lived in the outlying commune of Pomblière-Saint-Marcel but were always considered Moutiérains. The archbishop and mayor extracted a promise from the Germans that the men would be treated as POWs but could do nothing else for them.

That was the last the Moutiérains heard of these twenty-one local men and boys for eleven months, but they clung to the hope of the German promise to treat them as POWs. As soon as the department was essentially liberated, the press published the names of the Moutiérain hostages, and, as happened elsewhere, the local resistance named one of the deportees, the Abbé Muyard, to the special delegation, with another priest acting as his proxy until his return.[102] The continuing awareness of and anxiety for the hostages found expression in their remembrance at Masses said for special occasions and at charitable events. The Sporting Association of Moûtiers, for instance, held a benefit football match in early November 1944 for the families of the hostages.[103] After November 1944, however, specific mention of the twenty-one disappeared from the press, undoubtedly as a consequence of an order by the regional military censors absolutely forbidding the use of the names of surviving family in press accounts of Resistance funerals. Because members of such families, particularly of fusillés, had often been deported, the censors feared bringing their names to the attention of the Germans.[104]

The excitement of the Grand Return of the POWs and deportees in April and May 1945 brought the twenty-one hostages back to the forefront of public concern in Moûtiers, where crowds gathered every evening to meet the train. The prevalence of talk about the hostages may be judged from an article in *La Résistance savoyarde* in early June entitled "Beware of Tall Tales

Construction of Memory   221

(*bobards*)." In particular, the article officially disclaimed three rumors, all having to do with the hostages. Apparently, according to the gossip that had troubled the town enough to provoke a denial in the newspaper, the twenty-one "Moutiérain friends" had either (1) "undergone dreadful tortures," (2) been executed on Mont-Cenis, or (3) been "discovered in a mass grave at [the pass of] Petit-Saint-Bernard" and "the families had [even] been called to identify the bodies." The article went on to explain the terrible effects such rumors must have on the men's families and to expose the self-serving motives of the rumormongers. It ended by warning the "*bobardiers*" of severe official punishment.[105] With some satisfaction, the paper was able to further undermine the rumors by reporting that the Ministry of Prisoners, Deportees, and Refugees had informed one of the families that it had found traces of their hostage at a concentration camp near Weimar, thereby suggesting that the other twenty would soon be located.[106]

The longed-for news, however, did not come. At the end of the month the neighborhood of Saint-Pierre decided not to revive its annual July festival, because "they consider that it would be inappropriate to organize public festivities while our twenty-one Moutiérain hostages of August 1944 as well as a few political deportees have not yet given a sign of life."[107] As the flow of repatriates slowed over the next few weeks, Moûtiers' anxiety grew. Then, on 21 July 1945, a delegation of departmental and local civil, military, religious, and medical officials, the press, and family members traveled to the Italian border to investigate two shallow, unmarked mass graves a dozen kilometers past the frontier and the pass of Petit-Saint-Bernard at a place called Terra Nera. They discovered the bodies of twenty-seven men, all of whom were easily identifiable as hostages from Moûtiers, Bourg-Saint-Maurice, and Séez because their papers and personal effects were still in their pockets. Italian shepherds reported that on the night of 25 August 1944 a German convoy had stopped, taken the men out of trucks, and mown them down with machine-gun fire. The evidence supported their claims. The graves contained the gifts pressed upon the men when they were taken from Moûtiers: a bottle of wine, a jar of jam, a packet of tobacco. The abbé's rosary and breviary remained in his pocket, indicating that the massacre came without any warning to the victims.

Moûtiers reeled under the news. The town had, in the words of its newspaper, "learned with a profound sorrow of the discovery" that their hostages "have been murdered in a cowardly manner by the hideous, barbaric Boches." Struck with sorrow, the town was also struck with an anger that raged through the article and two signed editorials about the atrocity. The anger hinged on the fact that "the Boches, like the true barbarians that they are, did not keep their word." They had promised to treat the hostages as POWs, but "it is necessary to believe that these savages do not know the meaning of the word humanity because at the end of August they gunned down our [men] at the side of the road." One of the editorialists deeply regretted the honorable way in which the Tarin FFI, and particularly two of the hostages, had treated the German soldiers whom they had temporarily captured in early August 1944. Had they shot them all, one might not have escaped to bring the German army back into Moûtiers. Another writer called for the punishment of the two Wehrmacht officers in charge: "No pity for these savages without honor. Our dead demand vengeance. It will be necessary to find these war criminals and their accomplices, to give them an exemplary punishment. That way we will avenge our twenty-seven dead."[108]

The Saturday after the terrible discovery, Moûtiers and the Haute-Tarentaise buried their murdered hostages with the greatest honors. Monseigneur Terrier, who had been Moûtiers' archbishop during the occupation, traveled from Bayonne to officiate at the religious service, which was held under the trees in the place des Victoires to accommodate the crowd. By turns, the current archbishop, the Protestant pastor, the mayor, the commander of the Tarin FFI, the president of the CDL, and the prefect spoke; they eulogized the men, castigated the perpetrators, and offered the government's condolences.

The cortege to the cemetery could not have been larger or more comprehensive. It was led by a band and the schoolchildren of Moûtiers and surrounding communes followed by the religious, civil, and military leaders of the Tarentaise and Savoie. Then came the twenty-one coffins, covered with flags and flowers and followed by every possible civic association and the public. The procession traversed the town, marking its landscape with the sorrow and the memory, further inscribing the twenty-one hostages in Moûtiers' identity. The men were then buried together in the cemetery, leaving a lesson for their survivors: "Let us weep and guard inside ourselves the living image of those who collapsed under the fire of German cowardice with the most noble sentiment in their hearts: Frenchmen in a Free France."[109]

La Résistance savoyarde printed the full text of the speech given by Commandant Lungo, as leader of the Tarin FFI and president of the CLL. As one of the men who had received the German promise to treat resistants captured in the region as POWs, he focused on the perfidious trail of executions they had left in their wake instead. He made it clear that these were not members of the SS or Gestapo, but Wehrmacht officers, ordinary Germans. His speech differed from other discussions of the atrocity when he extended the blame beyond the Germans to their collaborators. "It will be necessary to take those Frenchmen who wished for the victory of Germany to the mass graves; they will need to be able to contemplate the infamy committed by the bandits of whom they made themselves the accomplices. If those people had a conscience, they would not (despite the cross of Lorraine that they sport or that they are ready to sport) feel very proud of themselves today."[110] Savoyards did not forget the fact of collaboration as quickly as some.

The shock of the atrocity reverberated through Moûtiers, affecting more than the official level of the resistance. The elected (non-Resistance) municipal council recognized the public nature of the loss by bearing the costs of the funeral and establishing savings accounts for the thirteen children orphaned by the atrocity.[111] It also canceled the celebration of the first anniversary of the town's liberation, considering it to be inappropriate during a period of mourning. Indeed, the mourning was more than an official gesture. The owner of a dance hall closed what could only have been a booming business for a month "in memory (*mémoire*) of the fusillés of Moûtiers." The owner does not appear to have been directly related to any of the twenty-one hostages, although she may have been the widow and daughter of two men executed in June 1944, explaining her choice to close in memory of the "fusillés" rather than the more commonly used term "hostages."[112] The town band also postponed its summer concerts "owing to the great loss (*deuil*) that has so tried our town."[113]

Not surprisingly, the town also decided to erect a monument to the twenty-one hostages. A committee, whose honorary president was the archbishop and whose active president was the mayor, began work in September, but it apparently ran up against similar efforts by resistance groups. A meeting in the town hall at the end of October amalgamated all efforts into a single committee charged with building a monument to the twenty-one hostages in the cemetery and another in honor of all the war dead of the Tarentaise, to be placed in a public area. This committee raised money through direct collection door to door, entertainments such as a grand concert gala, and benefit nights at the cinema. In July 1946 the municipal council contributed twenty thousand francs.[114]

Certain individuals, however, preferred a more active form of mourning, proposing to avenge the hostages by killing twenty-one German prisoners of war working in and around Moûtiers. Alarmed by the talk of such vengeance in the Tarin capital, the prefect reinforced the gendarmerie there. Vigilantes nonetheless managed to wound one of the Germans.[115] As the prefect had arranged for a meeting of the departmental Resistance with the CRR at Lyon in order to quell the department's vigilantism during the very week that the mass graves at Terra Nera were discovered, it must have crossed his mind to be thankful that this atrocity, at least, was wholly the work of Germans, without any direct help from collaborators. A responsible collaborator, and possibly his or her family, would have been in even greater peril than a prisoner of war. The dangerous emotions aroused by the discovery of the murders of the twenty-one Moutiérains were stoked in the fall with each new discovery of an atrocity, such as the November identification of the charred remains of four hostages from Saint-Michel-de-Maurienne.[116] These delayed demonstrations of the realities of Nazi rule did little to help the prefect stop the vigilantes.

So Moûtiers, like Saint-Flour, did not celebrate the first anniversary of its liberation, although for very different reasons. Respect for the recently discovered atrocity led the local resistance to change its celebratory plans to two more modest commemorative ceremonies at the Monument aux Morts and at the hostages' graves.[117] Circumstances forced what would have been a public elaboration of the memory of the liberation as a victory of the local resistance in its guise of FFI and community supporters into a ritual of death and sorrow. Certainly the planned ceremony would have acknowledged and honored the Resistance dead, but it would undoubtedly have done so in the manner of the FFI Day in October 1944, in which the fallen were included as a glorious part of the victorious troops, rather than receiving the full emphasis, as happened in Saint-Flour.

Despite the lack of public celebration, an editorial in *La Résistance savoyarde* reminded its readers of the meaning of the liberation. Reciting the battles and atrocities of the summer of 1944, particularly those in Savoie, the article recognized the Allies' role in freeing France from the Nazi yoke, but stressed how slight a role they had played in Savoie. There the resistants liberated their *patrie* from not only the foreign enemy but also the French "Milice and their friends" and other traitors. Now, a year later, the war was over. "But the sorrow, the losses (*deuils*) will remain in the hearts of all those who have lost one of their own in the task of redemption." The editorial ended with the expression of a fear often heard from local purgers, who pleaded that the anniversary of the liberation not become an empty formula like Armistice Day, because "France can hope for beautiful tomorrows if her children do not forget this great lesson."[118]

The local FFI veterans' organization (AAS) took what steps it could to ensure that the Resistance and its lessons would be remembered. It gave Moûtiers another chance to celebrate the local FFI and its achievements in October by marking the anniversary of the dissolution of the Tarin battalion. Not as elaborate as the FFI Day in 1944, the 1945 ceremonies nonetheless included all the standard commemorative gestures. The parade, of course, marched to the Monument aux Morts for the deposition of a wreath, the delivery of a speech, and the singing of the "Marseillaise." After that a former POW priest, who preached on the need for charity and love of one's neighbor, celebrated a Mass for the FFIs' fallen comrades in place of the battalion's own chaplain, now on occupation duty in Germany. The day finished with a banquet and a dance.[119]

The local Resistance also constructed a striking monument in the center of town on the square de la Liberté. First suggested in July 1945, the committee responsible for it later merged its efforts with those to memorialize the twenty-one hostages.[120] It changed into a committee for the monument to the 224 dead of the Tarin Resistance in 1947 and fulfilled its mission in 1952. As they had at the liberation, the municipality and the local Resistance worked together on this project, with the town providing and preparing the land on which the statue stands.[121] The inauguration ceremony drew departmental and local civil and military leaders, the archbishop, an English major who parachuted into the nearby valley of Beaufortin during the war, and a delegation from the Czech embassy, as well

226   The Expectation of Justice

as resistants of all ranks. It followed the pattern of Resistance ceremonies held during the après-libération: a Mass at the cathedral, ceremonies at the Monument aux Morts and memorial to the twenty-one hostages, now referred to as fusillés, the inauguration ceremony itself, speeches by the local Resistance commander, the mayor, and the prefect, and a banquet. The 1952 newspaper report drew parallels between the dead of 1914–18 and of 1939–45 and emphasized the unity of those who died in battle with those who perished in the concentration camps in a manner uncommon during the après-libération, although otherwise it laid the same emphasis on the sacrifices and accomplishments of the Resistance.[122]

The statue of the Resistance of the Tarentaise understandably drew the attention of the president of the Fourth Republic while it was on display at the Salon of French Artists in the Grand Palais in Paris. It is an unsettling conflation of France in the female person of Marianne with the fighting men of the Tarin Resistance. The figure stands with one foot advanced, arms outstretched overhead in the moment of release after breaking the chains still wrapped around its wrists, a fearsome expression surrounding its mouth, which is opened in a call. It wears a billowing, ankle-length slitted skirt, rolled at the waist, and nothing else. The hair is short but could be thought (mistakenly) to be pulled back in a bun. The hands and musculature are most definitely those of a man, but the breasts belong to a woman. The legend carved in relief on three sides of the white Savoyard marble pedestal reads: "AS FTPF—The Resistance of the Tarentaise in the Service of France—Its Sacrifices: 74 dead, 64 dead in deportation, 60 fusillés, 26 civilian victims."

The statue of the Resistance of the Tarentaise captures the postwar identity imagined by the valley and its capital, Moûtiers, in the months just after the liberation. The statue's slurred gender points to France in the image of Marianne, underscoring the region's French patriotism, as did the anti-Italian sentiment rampant in the area during the après-libération. At the same time, the fiercely masculine musculature and stance point to the local Resistance's understanding of its achievements as the work of strength and determination. The simple marble words on the pedestal conjure the deep roots of the Resistance in the community. It is a high death toll, and one that ignores the lesser costs of lives crippled, communities rent, and homes and fields destroyed.

This conception of the local resistance as a patriotic, community-wide military endeavor would seem to converge with the Gaullist myth of a resistant France, except that the Savoyards were less prone to instant amnesia than the Gaullists. If, for the sake of national unity, the Gaullists could conveniently forget that many of the Resistance's mortal sacrifices were caused directly and indirectly by French collaborators, the Savoyards of the après-libération, still grieving, still discovering their griefs as late as November 1945, would not forget it for the sake of justice. The Gaullists' nationalized memory and the Savoyards' local memory diverged not over what the Resistance had been or done, but over who the enemy had been. The Savoyards took the Gaullist half-memory, which portrayed the enemy as almost wholly German, as an insult to themselves and to their dead.

The insult reached the point of injury when de Gaulle began pardoning convicted Miliciens. At the same time that women were going from door to door in Moûtiers to collect money for the monument to the twenty-one hostages, at the same time that the charred remains of four hostages from Saint-Michel-de-Maurienne were found a year and a half after they had been murdered, de Gaulle pardoned not one but several Miliciens who were not only convicted of serving the enemy but personally known to many a Savoyard to have raged through their *pays*, torturing, murdering, and burning.

The Capella affair exploded so spectacularly in December 1945 because it offended the Savoyards' sense of honorary justice as well as legal justice. It was the offense to memory rather than law that moved the surviving deportees of Aiguebelle-La Chambre to protest the pardon, "in the name of our comrades dead in the most atrocious suffering [in the concentration camps], in the name of those who consented to the supreme sacrifice for the happiness of their *patrie*."[123] In similar circumstances, the CDL had earlier protested the pardoning of Miliciens on the grounds that "at this time, to pardon is to betray."[124] To the Savoyards, both Gaullist judicial policy and Gaullist memorial policy betrayed their own experiences of the war and occupation and the memory of those experiences that they felt they must maintain in order to honor those who had died in the Resistance's cause.

The demons of memory that have haunted France since the war openly raged through the country during the après-libération.[125] De Gaulle tried to exorcise them with the national myth of a united France standing together in the Resistance. It offered a tempting, and flattering, solution that found an easy reception in some quarters. But it was not true, and in 1944–45 all too many people were still reeling from the effects of the truth of collaboration to tolerate half-truths. It would take time for them to submit to the forgetfulness required by the national myth; until then they tried to assert their own memories through countermemorials and vigilantism. For those who rejected it, the Gaullist myth served as further proof of the Resistance government's inability to provide justice, even the elementary honorary justice of remembering the true nature of a patriotic death.

CHAPTER SIX

POPULAR JUSTICE OR

REPUBLICAN LEGITIMACY?

At the end of the Second World War, the logic of the times and Gaullist policy demanded that concerns about legal, social, and honorary justice be translated into republican politics, which meant electoral politics.[1] The French had not gone to the polls for almost a decade, during which time they had witnessed the fall of the Third Republic and the creation and collapse of the Etat français. The new Fourth Republic therefore needed to hold elections in order to establish its republican or democratic legitimacy in the eyes of its own citizens and of its western allies. So 1945 saw a wearisome train of ballots: in April the municipal elections, in September the cantonal elections for the departmental Conseils généraux, and in October general elections for the Constituent Assembly and a referendum on constitutional issues.

For the provisional government, the many elections of 1945 provided a means to establish republican legitimacy and order. That order, it turned out, meant a return to the type of party politics more familiar to the Third Republic than to resistance dreams of the "pure and strong France." The left and center parties that had joined the Gaullists in exile resumed open operations in the metropole with the liberation; as officially acknowledged members of the Resistance, these parties won places on many local liberation committees regardless of their actual activity in an area during the occupation. They were joined during the *après-libération* by a few new parties, such as the short-lived attempts to create a "Resistance party" or the Catholic Mouvement républicain populaire (MRP). With each election in 1945, the parties gained firmer control of political life. Indeed, as it

230   The Expectation of Justice

turned out on the national level, the elections of 1945 represented a confirmation of the political parties, especially those of the Left, rather than of the Resistance.²

Provincial voters, however, approached the elections, as so much else during the après-libération, as a matter of justice. For them, the elections represented not so much an encouraging return to order as a disheartening return to the discredited prewar politics. Indeed, the voters in small towns such as Moûtiers, Rambervillers, and Saint-Flour showed enthusiasm or interest only in those elections, or aspects of elections, that bore on questions of honorary or social justice—an emphasis that undermined the national government's attempts to legitimate itself through the polls. The earliest elections evoked issues of honorary justice as the country endeavored to identify those worthy of postwar leadership. But as the parties became more influential and the entire country shifted its focus to economic matters over the summer of 1945, the primary concern of the provincial electorate shifted to social justice.

The first, municipal, elections brought up honorary justice not only in the question of who should rule but also of who should choose the rulers. No one publicly disputed the female vote, but the timing of the municipal elections in most of the country on 29 April and 13 May 1945, during the Grand Return and the victory celebrations, inevitably meant that the paragons of honor, the Absents, would be on everyone's mind. It also meant that many of them would not be able to participate, a fact that many found troubling. Indeed, as late as March, administrators reported a general disbelief that the poll would proceed as scheduled before the completion of the Return.³ "The dominant opinion considers that having lived provisionally for five years, France can permit herself to live [that way] another two or three months in order to allow to take part in the electoral consultation all her sons, for whom events foretell an imminent return."⁴ Once it became clear that the government really did intend to hold the elections without the Absents, some resistance groups and communities protested. The UFF of the Tarentaise, for instance, declared that women "regret that the elections will not be postponed until the return of millions of prisoners and deportees still under the German yoke, because all women agree that one cannot know how to elaborate the new regime in France without the participation of those Frenchmen who have suffered the most." It nevertheless recommended that women vote in these "imposed" elections.[5] And the people of Capelle Biron (Lot-et-Garonne) simply neglected to appear at the polls because they did not want to vote until the village's men returned from deportation.[6] In general, however, the elections proceeded calmly on the appointed dates.[7]

Communities had ways other than violence to subvert the national government's timing and to demonstrate the honor in which they held the Absents. Some towns, for example, treated the elections as wholly provisional and extracted promises from candidates that they would resign in order to force a valid election as soon as all the POWs and deportees had returned. This was so common in Cantal that in the fall of 1945 the harried prefect had to publish his determination to refuse all such resignations.[8] Other towns registered their disapproval by electing POWs and deportees who had not yet returned. Given the circumstances and the facts then being revealed about life in the Third Reich, it would have been more rational to assume that Absents would never return rather than to elect them to office. It would certainly have been impossible to ask the Absents in question whether or not they wanted to be on the municipal council. Nor would it have been possible for the electors to determine the absent candidates' views, although the rhetoric of the time assumed that all POWs and deportees, qua Nazi prisoners, shared the highest aims of the Resistance, a more reasonable assumption for a political deportee than for a POW removed from France almost before the Resistance existed. For those who put forward the names of Absents, the moral purification of suffering counted as sufficient qualification for leadership.

The practice of running Absents as candidates was so common, and people felt so strongly about it, that two armed men stole and burned the ballots in Chamonix (Haute-Savoie) precisely because not a single POW or deportee had figured among the candidates.[9] The election of Absents and their next of kin, of course, did not stem exclusively from a desire to shame the government. It also manifested a genuine desire to honor these heroes and thank them for the sufferings they had endured for the common good. The more cynical might also detect the maneuverings of politicians eager to capitalize on the tremendous prestige of and sympathy for

POWs and deportees. Indeed, a father from a village outside Saint-Flour publicly complained about the unauthorized use of his POW son's name and withdrew it from what he called a "Vichyssois" list.[10]

As an alternative, a close relative of an Absent sometimes ran in the quality of mother, father, or wife of a deportee. Indeed, the association with patriotic suffering could play a crucial role in these elections; the CRR at Clermont-Ferrand reflected that female candidacies did not prosper unless the woman could be seen as a suffering substitute for a deportee or *fusillé*.[11] The same fact might be explained slightly differently by observing that a woman became a martyr in her own right once a family member was killed or deported.[12] In that case the successful female candidates embodied not substitute martyrs, but martyrs in a different key. Indeed, they could be seen as double martyrs, with the authority of the deported husband shadowing and reinforcing that of the martyred wife. In either case, these women won election by virtue of their high status in the moral hierarchy as patriotic martyrs. Of course, in some voters' minds patriotic qualifications may have substituted for administrative experience, which few French women would have had the opportunity to develop before 1944.

A second controversy in the municipal elections, which set communities against themselves rather than against the national government, involved the subsidiary point as to who, other than the indisputably worthy Absents, qualified for the honor of election. Resistants argued that they themselves did qua resistants. At least publicly, local resistants took victory in the municipal elections for granted as both their due and the electorate's wartime duty. Patriotism, they sometimes argued, demanded that the French show the world their unanimity by electing the Resistance lists.[13] Much more often, resistants simply stated that "the sacrifice of a man who has risked everything except his honor to safeguard the interests of the *patrie*" entitled that man to a place of leadership, influence, and honor on the municipal council.[14] The bitterness with which resistants complained about the ingratitude of electors who rejected a resistant candidate revealed how invested they were in this moral paradigm.[15]

At the suggestion of national Resistance organizations, local resistants put together "common republican lists" with specified numbers of representatives of all the political parties, unions, and regional networks associated with the Resistance.[16] These single lists claimed to represent everyone (except collaborators), but many people balked at the idea of single lists running unopposed, no matter who chose them. The prefect of Savoie reported complaints that such lists reduced the elections to a formality.[17] In Cantal the virulent Abbé Lissorgues went further. Calling it "fascism, and of the worst [sort]," he recommended that everyone vote but vote "*en blanc*" by crossing out every name on the ballot.[18] As it happened, the abbé provoked few blank ballots, but neither did the common lists sail through the elections. In many places they faced opposing slates, inevitably branded as Vichyite.

In addition, not everyone agreed that justice and the future required that a municipal council have more than a few, perhaps token, heroes. In many places Resistance credentials did not count as much to voters as the individual's personality, and many required only that a candidate had shown an attitude of "great coldness" to the occupier.[19] As the prefect of Ain put it: "While giving all due respect to the merits of Resistants, it [the great part of the population] has difficulty admitting that only the title of active resistant can confer the qualities necessary to direct public affairs, and thinks that one should not leave out of communal and departmental assemblies the citizens with experience in the administration of communes and the department and who have not shown themselves unworthy from the national point of view."[20] If resistants looked for heroism in their municipal leaders, many of their neighbors looked for administrative competence. The two did not always coincide.

The municipal elections in Saint-Flour, Rambervillers, and Moûtiers played out these controversies over honorary justice in sometimes surprising ways. In the eyes of the CRR and the prefect, the elections in Cantal passed in calm and order, causing no great political upset but shifting the department's political portrait slightly to the left because the Resistance's use of a common list allowed the election of councilors one would not expect to have been elected under their left-wing party labels. Thus the traditionally moderate municipal council of Saint-Flour gained two Communists and three Socialists.[21] On the pages of the local press, however, the municipal elections appeared altogether less calm. There were, for instance, the Abbé Lissorgues' characterizations of the Resistance common lists as fascist and the challenges of opposition or "Vichyite" lists, presumably pitting a commune's traditional councilors who had served under

Vichy against the newcomers appointed to the special delegation at the liberation by the regional Resistance. Indeed, the campaigns in and around Saint-Flour could reach high levels of invective.

On the night of 24–25 April, for example, someone posted typed tracts in the village of Ruines that read: "P—— Hardware store owner in Ruines, former collaborator of Pétain. Nouveau riche with the money of the Resistance. Twenty-six fusillés on your (*ta*) conscience [you] coward and traitor to France. You will pay your debt." The tract mobilized the worst suspicions about the resistance in its attack on a man who was both the head of the Resistance in the canton and a candidate in the approaching elections. It played on fears of whitewashing by accusing P—— of being a collaborator masquerading as a resistant. Ignoring the first charge, it then evoked the widespread rumor of misappropriation of funds by resistants. And, worst of all, it accused a resistant of having essentially killed the town's martyrs, who would soon be recognized during the ceremonies at Mont-Mouchet. In a certain sense, the resistance had indeed killed those twenty-six men, because its actions provoked the reprisals that included their executions, but that was not a publicly acceptable line of argument during the après-libération. The people of Ruines generally disapproved of the tracts, and the gendarmerie investigated. They traced the typewriter back to Aurillac and to two men from Ruines who confessed before coming to trial.[22]

The rhetoric elsewhere in the arrondissement did not require the attentions of the gendarmerie, but the emotional tone of it may be judged from the postelection remarks of the correspondent from La Chapelle-Laurent. "The counter-Resistance enjoyed a striking success. . . . It was clear that the question was this: if you vote for the list of the Resistance, you are against the boches; if you vote against [it], you are for the boches and against de Gaulle. The voters opted for the boches. People who speak of Dr. Mallet with tremors in their voices and tears . . . (of a crocodile?) in their eyes, did not hesitate to drop in the urn the names of notorious collaborators, thus sullying the memory (*mémoire*) of the martyrs of the front of the Interior."[23] Among other things, this quotation demonstrates the attempt to extend the cult of Resistance martyrs so prevalent in the region beyond ceremony into political office.

Things did not reach quite such a pitch in Saint-Flour itself, although the CRR, for one, did not expect the common list to win.[24] Indeed, the documented campaign focused on such perennial issues as reducing water rates and luring new factories to town.[25] Unusually, however, the common list eschewed traditional political categories with only a vague assurance that "the particular [politics] of each of us are more or less tilted to the left, but we are all convinced democrats, partisans of the most perfect order in a broad and tolerant Republic, respectful of all liberties and of all religious beliefs." This adhesion to "perfect order" confirms Saint-Flour's support for the Gaullist program that was also evident in the town's calm local purge and in its commemorative politics.

More significant, not one of the twenty-three candidates identified his or her party affiliation; instead they gave either a profession or a quality that placed them in the patriotic pantheon. For example, the list included a *"grand mutilé* of the 1914–18 war"; an *"ancien combattant* 1914–18" currently fighting with the Allies in Germany; a POW; an "ex-POW"; two repatriated POWs; a "father of a deportee"; a "mother of a martyr and of a deportee in Germany," and a "deportee in Germany." This last was Mme. Mallet, who was also the mother of a deportee and two executed sons, the widow of a Resistance hero, and herself the great symbol of the martyrdom of Cantal and its Resistance. She was also, incidentally, still in a concentration camp.

Because all but eight on the list had been appointed to the special delegation at the liberation, everyone in Saint-Flour would have known that this slate represented the Resistance.[26] In case anyone did not, *La Margeride* made the point elsewhere, calling it "the list that claims to be of those who have fought, who have suffered, and who have fallen so that Liberty [and] the Republic be reborn, so that France regain its grandeur and prosperity." In other words, this list, and especially the nine indisputable patriotic martyrs from both world wars, incarnated the moral hierarchy that honorary justice required lead the nation. They could also, of course, be trusted to lead that nation in the right direction as they had already proven their determination to do so.

The proponents of the opposing slate, the Republican Democratic List, did not have the opportunity to express their views in *La Margeride* but may have been able to use posters despite the paper shortage. An article in the election issue suggested that some of the rival candidates might be acceptable if they supported a "union with sincere republicans, animated by an ideal of progress and of social justice." But most of the slate, it argued, were members of the Vichyite municipal council and, as such, had been "vomited out by the republican population of our town." The article waxed eloquent in listing their crimes under Vichy, even suggesting that they had denounced certain resistants to the collaborationist authorities. Another article in the same issue dredged up an old, unfulfilled campaign promise from 1929 to expose the prewar council's administrative failures. Finally, it interspersed the candidate lists from the neighboring communes with edifying quotations such as: "TO VOTE FOR THE REPUBLICAN LISTS, born of the Liberation . . . is to vote for LIBERTY—TO VOTE FOR THE VICHYSSOIS AND REACTIONARY LISTS . . . is to vote for Slavery."[27]

The first ballot elected thirteen members of the common list, including six of the nine self-proclaimed patriotic candidates and two "Vichyites." Mme. Mallet led the list with a total of 2,443 out of 2,552 votes for both Saint-Flour *ville* and *faubourg*. The second highest vote winner, the mayor of the special delegation, received only 1,786 votes.[28] The second ballot, then, pitted the nine remaining members of the common list against the rest of the Republican Democratic List. Seven of the eight councilors elected on the second ballot came from the common list, including three of the four previously unchosen "patriotic" candidates, all of them former POWs.

Of the three women on the common list, two ran in their role as Resistance martyrs: Mme. Mallet and the widow Raparie, whose son had been executed and daughter deported. They were both elected, but the third woman, the principal of the girls' school, was not, confirming the CRR's observation that women stood a better chance of being elected if they were associated with a patriotic hero or martyr. Of the two women on the Republican Democratic List, only one was elected. This gave the new municipal council twenty-one members from the Resistance list and two from the rival list, including one of the three women elected. It is of interest that the widow Raparie had publicly joined the Communist Party in January.[29] She was, however, probably elected as the mother of a martyr and a deportee rather than as a Communist, so that one of the PCF's two new seats on the municipal council would count more as an honorary than a political victory.

The victorious candidates of the common list thanked their constituents for their votes and congratulated them on their "love of Liberty and [their] great desire for a policy of social progress."[30] For its part, *La Margeride* pronounced itself most gratified by the "Republican victory," particularly the almost unanimous vote for Mme. Mallet, which showed "the affectionate sympathy, the profound gratitude that rises from all hearts toward her and her tragic family. Grandiose homage rendered to the memory (*mémoire*) of Louis Mallet and his children." It should be noted, however, that one could support the widow Mallet out of respect for her husband's prewar work among the peasantry without supporting the Resistance at all. The paper also condescendingly commented that the fact that the women had voted proved "that they have evolved politically."[31] However, it particularly disapproved of whoever had replaced Mme. Mallet's name with that of a man who had shaken the hand of the Milice chief in June 1944. And it bitterly bemoaned the ingratitude evident in the failure of Saint-Flour to elect the former "leader of the irregular force of Saint-Flour and the railway sabotage group," who was also a "*blessé* (wounded) of the Resistance."[32]

The people of Saint-Flour clearly chose the Resistance council over the old council and for the most part endorsed the Resistance's claims that patriotic suffering entitled one to leadership. Yet the election was neither unanimous nor completely transparent, and there were small signs of disaffection, such as the crossing out of Mme. Mallet's name. A minor scandal in August suggests that the political disaffection did not diminish with time. After the municipal elections in May, the republicans celebrated according to tradition by planting liberty trees. When two of the trees disappeared a few months later, "some believed that it was an attack by our adversaries, but upon reflection they considered that our reactionaries (*réacs*) were much more apt to spread calumnies than carry off such sabotages." To the reporter's disgust, it turned out that the trees had been cut for a public works project, "as if our forests were completely devastated."[33]

As in Cantal, the municipal elections in Savoie represented a slide to the left and opened a number of municipal councils to Communists.[34] Events in Moûtiers, however, differed in several ways from those in Saint-Flour: the campaign waged in the press was much calmer, candidates ran as members of political parties, and, surprisingly, the local Resistance did not do as well. The Moutiérain resistants, however, seem to have approached the elections with a great deal more confidence than their Sanflorain colleagues, apparently worrying only that the women would not vote properly and that certain persons complained that the common list was not democratic.

Articles about the upcoming election in *La Résistance savoyarde* focused on women's role as grieving guardians of memory. The *électrices,* one article signed by a woman argued, "will not betray the memory (*mémoire*) of their heroic dead (*grands morts*), they will not let down the living heroes who are still fighting, they will not abandon those POWs and deportees who return panting from the Nazi prison camps, . . . they will vote on Sunday for the ideal that nourished the revolt of captive France and that will preside tomorrow over the recovery of liberated France; they will vote for the list of the Resistance." The crux of the article and the election lay in the claim that honoring the memory of the war's victims required electing their heirs, "the living heroes," and that the single list represented those heirs. Another "appeal to women" recalled the sufferings of women in 1914–18 and 1940–45 and promised that a vote for the Resistance meant the end of slavery, war, and the tears of mothers whose sons fall on the field of battle.[35]

Following the CDL's guidelines, the Moutiérain common list included members of all parties and associations acknowledged by the CDL as belonging to the Resistance. It had four members of the left Catholic party, the Jeune République; two members each of the Radical-Socialist Party, the SFIO, the PCF, the CGT, and the CFTC; three each of the Resistance networks the MLN and the FN; and one from the Mouvement prisonnier. Of the twenty-one, four were women. In contrast to the Sanflorain practice, the candidates identified themselves by party affiliation and, for the most part, profession. Only one, the wife of a deportee, listed herself by patriotic category. Nonetheless, nine of the candidates would have been known as resistants because of their service on the CLL of the Haute-Tarentaise or the appointed special delegation. This again contrasts with events in Saint-Flour, where almost the entire special delegation appeared on the Resistance list. The significant difference between the appointed special delegation and the Resistance slate in Moûtiers may have been the result of trying to reshuffle the local resistance to include specific parties and organizations as decreed by the departmental and national Resistance.[36]

It might also have caused Moutiérains to think that this Resistance list did not really represent the resistance that they knew and for which their martyrs had suffered.

Despite an ominous hint about "clandestine lists" in the region, this slate does not appear to have had any opposition. The returns from the first ballot accordingly came as quite a shock.[37] Of the twenty-one candidates, only seven, including one woman, received enough votes to be elected. Of these, only two had been on the CLL or special delegation, thereby suggesting a certain dissatisfaction with those two bodies. The votes went to all four members of the Jeune République, two of the CFTC, one of the Radical-Socialist Party, and the representative of the Mouvement prisonnier. This breakdown indicates that there was more support for Catholic ideas (CFTC and Jeune République) and less support for the Marxist Left (PCF, FN, SFIO). Indeed, the low profile of the local Communist cell and comments in the press assuring the readers that the PCF belonged to the Resistance point to a certain strain of anti-Communism in the Alpine town. In that case, the construction of Resistance lists according to a formula of political parties rather than patriotic categories may not have served the local Resistance well, because it cast the choice in terms of prewar electoral stances that voters did not necessarily associate with resistance. A person could, after all, want to vote for the Resistance but refuse to support the Communist Party regardless of the wartime record of the Communist candidate.

The analyst for *La Résistance savoyarde* chose to blame the Resistance's defeat on the women, saying that "Those who counted the ballots must ask themselves if the Moutiérain vote represented the moral health of the population. If so, we are very sick. I know well that the hard years that we have just lived through have been able to throw confusion into [people's] minds, to sow rancor and hate. Nazism is not yet completely extinguished among us." He then explained that the Resistance list represented all opinions, for was it not true that in the Resistance priest and Communist fought side by side? Invoking the memory of the Resistance's martyrs, the author reminded the women of their duty to take the election seriously and vote for the Resistance list on the second ballot.[38]

With only the evidence in the Resistance's own newspaper, the causes of the rebuff remain opaque, although that evidence does offer two possible explanations. In the first place, the paper's insistence that the single list was democratic because it represented all the parties suggests that people had objected that the list was *not* democratic. The nonelection of the single list may then have represented a vote for the principle of multiparty elections more than it did a vote against the Resistance. In the second place, the heavy emphasis on the debt owed to the memory of the fallen indicates a dispute over the nature of that debt. The high level of vigilantism there proves that the Savoyards heard the "ancestral voices" of patriotic martyrs. But if they heard those voices ordering them to attack the martyrs' enemies, the collaborators, they did not, apparently, hear them say to elect the martyrs' self-proclaimed heirs, the Resistance list. This may be because the Moutiérains did not think that the single list actually spoke for the "ancestral voices." Just weeks after the liberation, after all, the soldier-priest who celebrated Mass for Moûtiers' FFI Day had warned the Tarins against "opportunists" who were using the name of resistants for their own ends.

During the week before the second ballot, Moûtiers' politicians regrouped and offered a second "independent" slate of candidates, who called themselves the URD, possibly for a Union républicaine (or, with less likelihood, *résistante*) et démocratique (Republican and Democratic Union). Of the twelve men and one woman on it, three of the men had also been on the special delegation and so were officially resistants, if not part of the Resistance list. This time, the list gave no political affiliations. They were all elected, along with a Radical-Socialist from the Resistance list who had been a member of both the CLL and the special delegation. The new mayor and his two deputies came from the "independent list," but all three had been on the Resistance special delegation and therefore may have been compromise candidates. This gave Moûtiers a municipal council of eight from the Resistance list and thirteen from its rival URD. However, candidates who served on the CLL or special delegation, added to those who ran on the Resistance slate, make for a total of eleven officially acknowledged resistants on the twenty-one-member municipal council.

The successful candidates from the Resistance list published a thank-you with a promise to carry out the program of the CNR Charter. The victorious independent candidates did not; perhaps *La Résistance savoyarde* did not welcome their submissions. Indeed, after the second ballot the newspaper all but ignored the elections except to give the relevant statistics.

Not everyone, however, was willing to pass over this affront to the official Resistance in silence. Bombs exploded at the homes of two of the newly elected councilors, both members of the URD list, one of whom had served on the CLL and special delegation but had not figured on the single list.[39] The dynamics of the local purge suggest that, unfortunately for unknown reasons, someone wanted either to brand these men as unworthy (by treating them like collaborators) or, perhaps, to warn them against something. The Moutiérain elections, then, represent a popular rebuff of the Resistance establishment as constructed by CDL guidelines. Given other events in town, however, they cannot be seen as a complete rejection of what the people considered to be their local resistance.

The elections in Rambervillers resembled those in Saint-Flour more than those in Moûtiers in their ratification of the local Resistance establishment. The belated liberation of the eastern part of the department of the Vosges postponed the municipal elections there until 5 May and 20 May, making them compete for people's attention with the victory celebrations and the uproar over the Return. These distractions and the severe shortage of paper made for what administrators considered a very "calm" election campaign. "Calm," of course, might have simply meant "disinterested," because the abstention rate reached 34 percent on the second ballot.[40]

Differing only in the strength of their rhetoric, the different branches of the Vosgien press all gave the electorate the same advice: do not vote for collaborators. The department's Catholic paper offered a sharp contrast to the Abbé Lissorgues' *Voix du Cantal* by joining the consensus and using moderate language. It counseled that "the defeatists (*capitulards*), the cowards, the friends of the occupier should be pitilessly crossed off the lists; they are unworthy to represent the French." Instead it recommended that voters give serious consideration to youths, repatriates, and former councilors who had retained their honor.[41] The press did not, however, carry any local campaign platforms, presumably because of the area's severe paper shortage and communications disruptions.

The documents, then, reveal only the results of the election in Rambervillers, leaving the actual campaign obscure.[42] On the first ballot nineteen members of the List of the Union of the Resistance won seats. These nineteen included the outgoing mayor, who had been elected in 1936 and appointed to the special delegation at the liberation. Indeed, there were five men elected in 1936, appointed to the special delegation in 1944, and reelected on the first ballot in 1945, thereby giving Rambervillers an impressive administrative continuity for the time. Including these men, eighteen members of the special delegation won election under the Resistance list. Eleven of them also served on the quiet but assuredly resistant CLL. In addition, three also served on the FFI Veterans' Committee, a fact that clearly associated them with the town's military resistance.

This left four empty seats, all of which were won on the second ballot by members of a list representing the MRP.[43] These men figured on none of the committees representing the Resistance establishment or on the list of FFI liberators, although they may have been involved in the resistance in a less publicly acknowledged manner. Their association with the new MRP certainly suggests a sympathy with Catholic thought and may have made them the choice of a right wing without any truly rightist alternative. Their election provoked outraged tirades from the correspondent to the department's Socialist newspaper. Dropping dark hints about anti-Semitism in the campaign, the fifth column, and cagoulards, the correspondent blamed the indifference of the workers who had abstained for allowing "fanatics of a Pétainism that one had wanted to believe dying" onto the municipal council. It boded ill, because "thus the spirit of the resistance dies by the abandonment, by the culpable indifference of its members. The fascists raise their heads and reintroduce themselves everywhere." Furthermore, in an echo of fears about the national purge, "at the pace at which things are going, in a few months the resistants will have become the undesirables and the cagoulards and collaborators will take over the direction of affairs."[44] The reference to cagoulards, of course, betrayed the correspondent's own attachment to Third Republic politics.

Yet with an overwhelming majority on the municipal council of nineteen official resistants to four members of a party that in any case professed allegiance to Resistance ideals, this election can hardly be seen as a defeat of the Resistance per se, although it might have been a defeat for the parties on the left who chose to see themselves as the Resistance. It was certainly not a victory for feminism; women scarcely even figure in the documents except for observations that the women fulfilled their duty by voting—apparently a matter of some doubt for administrators throughout the country. The one woman on the appointed council, who was also on the CLL, was not elected; in fact, unlike either Saint-Flour or Moûtiers, Rambervillers did not elect a single woman to municipal office in 1945.

Why did women have such a slight presence in Rambûvetais politics? The apparent absence of a politically oriented women's organization, whether sponsored by the Catholic Church or the Communist Party, might help to explain it, but is in itself puzzling. The women of Rambervillers certainly had as much interest as the women of Moûtiers in the "social" questions of provisioning and the welfare of the troops that contemporary women's groups championed. Perhaps Vosgien women were too harried by having to search for food and clothing to have the time or energy for electoral politicking. Or was the atmosphere in the Vosges too militarized—sharply dividing women into refugees and men into soldiers—to allow women to break into politics there at the very close of the Second World War?

The CRR at Nancy confessed to being unable to make any definite political analysis of the Vosgien results unless it was to say that the voters appeared to have shifted slightly to the left. The two-thirds of the electorate who had voted in the region as a whole had "given an overwhelming victory to the spirit of the Resistance more than they had voted for partisan reasons."[45] In other words, the voters saw the election as a ratification of honorary justice and the ideals of a just society rather than as the contest between parties that the Gaullist idea of republican order required.

The questions of honorary justice that motivated complaints about the timing of the municipal elections and arguments over the lists of candidates did not play as important a role in later elections, except in the nationally notorious October 1945 legislative elections in Cantal. That campaign mobilized all the polemical weapons available to the Abbé Lissorgues and his rivals in the departmental Resistance establishment in support of lists representing the SFIO, the PCF, the Radical-Socialists, and the Action Paysanne et Sociale (Peasant and Social Action), referred to by its opposition as "the Reaction." The prefect, however, called it "moderate," despite his personal disapproval of its leader's Vichyite past.[46] The press bulged with reports of political meetings and polemics using the same rhetorical categories of resistance and collaboration that suffused the municipal elections and commemorations in the department. Indeed, the prominent presence of a former high-ranking Vichy bureaucrat made a discussion of occupation-era attitudes inevitable.

However, the vehemence of the campaign launched against Camille Laurens, former adjunct national syndic of the Corporation paysanne and holder of the Vichy honor "the Francisque," shocked the public. It also cost the CDL's daily a fine of three thousand francs and ten thousand francs' damages to Laurens for slander, even though the documents it reprinted to demonstrate Laurens's past were undeniably authentic.[47] In its part of the general press attack, *La Margeride* emphasized Laurens's activities in the Vichy government, with an occasional feint at unmasking him as a rich exploiter rather than the honest representative of the little peasant he claimed to be.[48] The agitation over the Laurens candidacy, however, spread beyond the press.

For example, the day before the election the bureau of the Amicale des Anciens de la Résistance et du maquis du canton de Saint-Mamet (Cantal) published an eloquent protest in which it said "that it is immoral that sieur Camille Laurens, adjunct national syndic of the Corporation Paysanne, appointed by Pétain and active collaborator, propagator of Vichy's policies that he always approved and supported in all the Corporation's meetings, can today, one year after the liberation, run as a candidate in a Republic that he fought against in 1940 and 1944." They urged all peasants to vote against Laurens, reproved the authorities for allowing him to run, and reminded everyone that at the liberation Laurens had been put under house arrest.[49]

The public was even more scandalized by the crisis of honorary justice created by the fact that this high-ranking collaborator had a running mate who was the president of the departmental Association of Political Deportees. The former maquis of Saint-Mamet considered the slate to be "an insult to the memory of those who fell for the Resistance at the hands of Vichy." For its part, *La Margeride* was at a loss to explain this "union of victim and executioner."[50] And a Socialist candidate publicly expressed his sadness to see the name of the deportee associated with that of Laurens.[51] This alliance of the deportee and the Vichy functionary provoked such distaste because they occupied diametrically opposed positions on the moral hierarchy. The deportee symbolized the highest levels of Resistance devotion, suffering, and morality, while the collaborator stood for evil. To see them together really did insult the memory of the Resistance martyrs. But it also challenged the prevailing rhetoric and its worldview: if they were both what they symbolized, then their association would, indeed, have been inconceivable. Yet the deportee willingly joined his name to the collaborator's. So one or the other was not as good or as evil as he was supposed to be in the moral universe sponsored by the Resistance.

Despite his rather damning past, Laurens had the formidable support of the Abbé Lissorgues and the vote of a good many Cantaliens, although not the majority. Indeed, the Action Paysanne won 30,182 mostly rural votes against the Socialists' 28,610, the Communists' 16,530, and the Radicals' 12,832 votes. Saint-Flour, *ville* and *faubourg*, cast its majority for the Socialist candidate but also gave a sizable vote to Laurens.[52] In the runoff, Cantal elected both a Communist and a former Vichy functionary to the Constituent Assembly.[53] The Vichyite's election did not surprise the CRR, but he called the concurrent election of a Communist "absolutely unpredictable," especially as it unseated the long-term Third Republic Radical deputy in what had traditionally been a bastion of Radical-Socialist strength.[54] Indeed, in the last prewar elections of 1936, less than 5 percent of voters in Cantal registered as PCF.[55] The prefect similarly expressed surprise that the department had divided into the two extremes, but was the more surprised by the unprecedented success of the Communists. He attributed it in part to a desire of some voters to block the Vichyite candidacy rather than to support communism, in which case the Communist becomes the Resistance's man, making it a contest between the Resistance and Vichy.[56] The election returns suggest, at the very least, that thirty thousand Cantaliens did not consider collaboration per se to be the automatic cause for national excommunication that the prevailing Resistance rhetoric painted it to be. Indeed, in an address to the Conseil général, the prefect referred to the Peasant and Social Action's success as the "specter of the fifth column" haunting the young republic and proof of persisting admiration for Pétain and his system in the department.[57]

Yet the people's mandate alone did not suffice for a seat in the Constituent Assembly. The departmental press gleefully followed the assembly's hemming and hawing over whether or not to validate Laurens's election. The relevant committee first decided to wait until the regional *chambre civique* in Riom heard Laurens's case, even though, according to *La Mar-*

géride's man in Paris, their own dossier on him contained a statement of noneligibility by the Ministry of Agriculture, invitations from prominent Nazis, and a declaration in which Laurens "made a gift of his person to the Maréchal and swore fidelity to Vichy."

Finally, because Laurens had already been sentenced to *indignité professionnelle,* the assembly voted 253 to 187 to hear his case without waiting for the purge court. Laurens defended himself by saying that he had helped many young men to escape the forced labor draft. But amid cries that holders of the Francisque were not qualified to sit in the assembly, that body determined to invalidate his election by a vote of 252 to 4, with 184 abstentions. The president of the Association of Political Deportees then took the Vichy official's place as deputy for Cantal, thus restoring the moral order of the Resistance universe.[58]

The Abbé Lissorgues responded to the invalidation by declaring that "Camille Laurens has become, through the hateful attitude of his adversaries, the symbol of peasant liberties." These liberties, he assured his readers, were under threat by a government akin to those of Hitler, Stalin, and Franco that was all but a communist tyranny; it had rejected its most patriotic sons, such as members of Vichy's veterans' organization, the Legion, in favor of traitors such as the Communists of 1939–41. Yet the abbé need not have gone to the trouble represented by this skillful mangling of facts and plays on anxieties. As so many vigilantes feared, the national purge had a very short memory. Laurens served as minister of agriculture for the Resistance's Fourth Republic from 1951 to 1953, less than a decade after his similar service for the collaborationist Etat français.

But the Laurens affair was the exception in drawing interest to the fall elections. According to administrators and the press, the cantonal elections for the departmental Conseils généraux in September were most notable for their dullness. *La Résistance savoyarde* had to admit that even "the candidates have not done anything to impassion this electoral consultation," in many cantons not even calling a single meeting or making any allusion to the political problems of the day. "It was above all a question of roads and highways. . . ."[59]

Except for the unexpected alliance of collaborator and deportee in Cantal, the legislative elections in October provided scarcely more drama. The election of deputies to the Constituent Assembly accompanied a referendum asking the French people two constitutional questions. The first question, essentially requesting permission to abandon the Third Republic and its constitution, received an overwhelming 96 percent of the vote. Because the second question dealt with the relative powers of the Constituent Assembly and the president, it was taken as a test of strength between de Gaulle and the PCF and received considerable attention from the political parties. De Gaulle's choice won 12.3 million votes, the PCF's 6.2 million votes.[60]

The politically engaged campaigned for the second referendum question according to their party's directives; indeed, what ostensibly began as a protest meeting over food shortages in Saint-Flour in late September ended with an explanation of the PCF's position on the referendum.[61] But how little the referendum excited the voters may be seen in a pun, printed in *Le Réveil des Vosges,* that played on the realities of physical and political reconstruction: "The point of view of the *sinistré:* For the next Constituent, are you in favor of one or two Chambers? For me, one chamber and a kitchen."[62] As the election itself drew closer, administrators agreed on the almost total indifference of the electorate in regard to political questions, as compared to the interest aroused by the more pressing economic issues of shortages and inflation, such as the price of potatoes.[63]

Why such disinterest in the steps necessary to reestablish a republic that everyone with a voice during the après-libération wanted? In part, the general lack of enthusiasm about the elections can be traced to an increasing alienation between the central government and the provincial populace that the prefect of Indre attributed to "this impression of 'nothing changed' that, for just cause, irritates the population and makes it say, not without reason, that the Liberation has disappointed the hopes that had been placed in it and in a Government that the victorious insurrection had installed in Paris."[64] Similarly, the prefect of Haute-Savoie detected a profound malaise among the people during the summer of 1945 because of their impression "that the government administers more than it governs."[65] Furthermore, as the gendarmerie put it, "the people sense that the administrative machine is functioning badly."[66] The most common accusation on this point in both the local press and in administrative reports charged the government with having a bloated bureaucracy filled with Vichy administrators of dubious loyalty and/or competence. Indeed, *La*

Résistance savoyarde called the bureaucracy and its excessive red tape "a significant delaying factor in the recovery of France."[67] Everyone who had ever tried to negotiate the maze of ration tickets and coupons needed to buy the ingredients for a meal must have been at least somewhat sympathetic to such arguments.

For the most part, de Gaulle avoided the discredit falling upon his government and its administration. As the gendarmerie remarked, perhaps sanguinely, in March 1945, "For everyone, he incarnates hope."[68] Observations of even mild disaffection with the general appeared only slowly in reports from the provinces. It was not until July that the gendarmerie noticed any open criticism of de Gaulle, even then ascribing it to party maneuverings for the legislative elections and concluding confidently that the populace remained well disposed to him.[69] If the CRR at Clermont-Ferrand had already hesitatingly reported "a certain coldness" toward the general that excluded any outright attacks in April 1945, the CRR at Nancy did not note any criticism of the general at all until January 1946.[70] By that time, however, de Gaulle had resigned without any great surge of popular outcry, despite the widespread satisfaction at his election to the presidency of the Fourth Republic just three months earlier.[71]

Another reason for the disinterest in the general election lay in the worsening economic situation, which overshadowed most other concerns, including those as remote as the politicking of an unsatisfactory government in Paris. As the prefect of Savoie phrased it, "To tell the truth, the masses remain indifferent to these questions [of electoral politics], and unfortunately at the present time everything seems to return to a question of the stomach."[72] *La Résistance savoyarde* provided an interesting response to the problem of voter indifference in its quest to explain a high abstention rate for the cantonal elections, which it attributed to the women. The paper suggested that the lack of female candidates — only one in the whole department — might have played a role, but it placed most of the blame on the poor political education of the women, who did not understand their duty.[73]

The paper did, however, send a reporter to actually ask women why they had not voted in the September cantonal elections. He began in the market in the departmental capital and then took the train high up into the mountains through Moûtiers to the frontier town of Bourg-Saint-Maurice, interviewing seven women along the way. Four women were offended at the assumption that they had not performed their duty, and one even cried calumny. Three of these women gave the names of the men for whom they voted; one had voted as her party recommended, and another as her husband had suggested. The fourth said she had not voted because none of the candidates pleased her. Two other women expressed disillusionment with electoral politics. A greengrocer said: "Why didn't I vote! If you think that with my four children I can waste my time on such trivialities!" And a worker replied: "I did not vote because I know very well that whatever the result is, I won't pay any less dearly for my rent or my meat or my potatoes!" Only one woman, surprised (as the reporter told it) in the act of fixing her makeup, gave the sort of frivolous answer he presumably expected: she said that she did not want anything to do with those sorts of people (politicians).

The reporter concluded that he still did not know why women had not voted but that their political education obviously needed attention.[74] Yet his survey did give him an answer. First of all, the majority of his sample claimed to have participated in the election. True, one of them did not vote, but she abstained as a conscious rejection of the candidates, which is itself a political action. Second, two of the women clearly rejected electoral politics as having nothing worthwhile to offer them. That makes three women who voted, three women who abstained as a rejection of electoral politics and the proffered politicians, and one woman who may indeed have benefited from some "political education." If this is taken with other indications of the political consciousness of local women, such as the activities of the AF-MLN/UFF or the use of the label "*électrices*" in letters to the editor and petitions, it paints a picture of women not as apolitical but as political in a different way.

If the women lagged behind the men in voting, as *La Résistance savoyarde* claimed, they did so because electoral politics did not interest them. What interested them was the more fundamental politics of social and honorary justice that lowered the price of potatoes and gave positions of responsibility to individuals with moral authority. That interest in social justice, furthermore, appears to have been generalized throughout the department, because, despite the mild warnings against the left issued by the Catholic paper, the new Conseil général of Savoie had seven Socialists and five Communists.[75]

The national government acknowledged the increasing obsession with "questions of the stomach" among voters through two potentially popular provisioning decisions announced during the legislative campaign. In the first, the government made a bid for female loyalties by announcing that as of 1946 women, as well as men, would have a right to a ration of tobacco. But the news was not welcomed in the provinces as the government presumably had hoped. The UFF's newspaper in Cantal accepted the general premises of the offer but complained that the men would receive a distribution before the women did. "*Electrices* we are, but we still have to make up for lost time in order to benefit from the same consideration given to the *électeur*."[76]

Others rejected the tobacco ration as an acknowledgment of female equality and instead turned it into an occasion for complaint about national economic policy. *La Résistance savoyarde* editorialized that the government would have been better advised to do away with the tobacco ration altogether rather than increasing the opportunities for black marketeering.[77] Women readers of the same paper wrote in to say that as nonsmokers they would prefer something else, such as chocolate—an idea that appealed to the editor on the grounds that it would increase the men's share of the tobacco.[78]

More significantly, an unspecified but clearly pronatalist "women's group" in the Vosges circulated a petition that was also published in the departmental daily. The petition commented at length on the tobacco ration, saying that "to want to follow the lead of America by giving the women of France the right to vote and cigarettes is nice (*beau*), but why not also Americanize provisioning, that would be still better. Duty [requires] giving French women nourishment and clothing." It therefore rejected the offer of cigarettes and demanded food and clothing so that the women of France could fulfill their own duty of repopulating the country.[79] If the widely supported petition exposed the depths of economic anxiety in this war-torn department, it also demonstrated the miscomprehension between the central government and many of its provincial citizens at the end of 1945.

Much more significantly, in August 1945 the national government announced the suppression of the bread ration in October, just in time for the general elections and the referendum that pitted de Gaulle against the PCF.[80] To do so constituted an utter reversal of provisioning policy. Until then, the official bulletins of the departments of the Vosges, Cantal, and Savoie groaned with ordinances regarding the use of flour and the manufacture and sale of bread. The shape, weight, content, and age of legal breadstuffs were all carefully defined, and the price and quantity of bread sales strictly limited. Pastries and other frivolous uses of flour were all forbidden, with occasional exceptions made for certain, usually plain, pastries that indicated either the approach of a holiday or an enviable level of local wealth. Police made searches for illegal pastries and fresh bread in the back rooms and under the counters of shops.

To suddenly abandon this intense surveillance of all aspects of the bread market and let people buy as much as they wanted constituted a tremendous symbolic gamble for the government. French governments have traditionally paid, and still pay today, considerable attention to the bread supply, because of its almost sacred meaning in French culture. Indeed, until the nineteenth century the popular legitimacy of a regime rested in large part on its efforts to safeguard and fairly distribute the bread supply.[81] The shortages of the war and occupation revived these symbolic meanings to the extent that many of the complaints about the quality of bread and the cheating ways of bakers found in the local press during the après-libération echoed complaints common in the eighteenth century.[82] In the immediate postwar world, it would not have been hard to understand how, in the words of Steven Kaplan, "to eighteenth-century Parisians the presence of bad bread in the markets or shops was an intolerable affront and menace. It signified either an act of social crime or a mark of social breakdown, two different levels of crisis."[83]

Not even the Vosgiens of 1945 were as dependent on bread for their very survival as eighteenth-century Parisians, but they and their compatriots were still susceptible to the symbolism of bread and the sense of crisis caused by any failure in its distribution. If the "liberty of bread" worked as it was supposed to—that is, miraculously flooding the country with fresh loaves—the government would win a tremendous victory by solving a symbolic crisis. But if those loaves failed to appear, the government would expose its inability to run the economy or deliver the expected benefits of peace. Worse yet, the coincidence of the elections and the new policy meant that the government would stand accused of toying with the people's basic security for its own ends.

Provincial administrators, who had kept a constant eye on the fluctuations of flour stocks over the last year, did not wholeheartedly support the government's experiment.[84] The gendarmerie, however, reported that the announcement of the "liberty of bread" was widely welcomed, although a few of the more realistic voices did suggest that it might be better to keep the cards but increase the ration lest unscrupulous sorts waste the bread or feed it to their animals.[85] The CRR at Nancy added: "The population fears that the promise of the suppression of the bread card is only an electoral mirage."[86] Indeed, the Lorrainers had little reason to think that the end of the bread ration could be anything but a mirage; they had endured a particularly difficult late summer *soudure* during which the authorities had had to request emergency relief supplies from the Americans and the prefect of the Vosges had had to order an addition (or adulteration) of 20 percent starch to the bread.[87] At least one town in the department ran completely out of bread in September.[88]

In October, the central government postponed giving bread its freedom until November. The move undoubtedly seemed reasonable to the Moutiérains, whose bakeries closed for lack of flour several times in late October.[89] The longed-for day of unrestricted bread dawned in November with some dark clouds on the horizon. To begin with, bread turned out to have a narrower definition than expected. As an editorialist writing from Chambéry reminded readers, everything other than the most basic forms of baked flour was still difficult to obtain.[90] This was especially true for pastries, which were effectively rationed either by the simple expedient of withholding ingredients or by decree. Indeed, the end of the bread ration only increased the flow of byzantine prefectural decrees restricting the use of flour. Other than limiting the legal size, shape, and age of loaves, the most common bread-related pronouncements of November and December 1945 involved the consumption of bread and, particularly, the species of the consumer. The law stated in no uncertain terms that bread was to be eaten by human beings and human beings only. In fact, it allowed for rather steep penalties for feeding grain, flour, or bread to one's livestock or other animals: imprisonment from two months to five years and fines of twenty to ten thousand francs. The authorities claimed to know how much bread each family should really need and warned against "overconsumption."[91] The ominous talk about "overconsumption"—that is, eating more bread than the bureaucrats had planned for—alerted the people that the authorities expected them to replace government rationing with self-rationing. Such threats, however, had little effect when opposed to the simple economics that made it cheaper for a peasant to buy bread for his pigs than to buy feed.[92]

As time and administrative decrees revealed that the removal of the bread ration meant neither a selection of bread nor complete liberty in quantity of bread, "the population was riled up (*s'émeut*)," especially when the local bread supply failed.[93] Not surprisingly, the prefect of the Vosges encountered particular troubles keeping bread in the bakeries. The fact that the department had not had truly adequate stocks of flour since before its liberation was only aggravated by an "overconsumption" of eight thousand quintals of flour above administrative forecasts for the month of November.[94] Despite measures that severely limited the available types of bread and a ban on Christmas treats, the flour supply failed. On 15 December 1945, Rambervillers became the first town in the department to impose a municipal ration of three hundred grams of bread per person per day, less than the lapsed national ration.[95] The insults to the town's honor that this measure apparently provoked drew a heated defense from one of the town's correspondents. The author, who signed his name, began by saying that if people had wasted bread in Rambervillers, others had certainly also wasted it elsewhere. "We are not ogres and it will be difficult to make us swallow [the claim] that the Rambûvetais population has, all by itself, gobbled up the provision of flour allotted to our department." More to the point, however, he argued that the fault lay with the authorities rather than with the consumers; the suppression of the bread ration had been a mistake. The author called on the department's deputies to work so that "we be treated, not as pariahs, but as true Frenchmen, like the others!"[96] Within the week, municipal rationing had spread throughout the department.

On 1 January 1946, the central government reinstated the national bread ration, but not before worsening the situation by formally denying that it would do so. Thus the new Resistance government displayed a reprehensible lack of dedication to the principles of social justice and an inability to implement them. Furthermore, because the regime had apparently cynically manipulated the *bread* supply, it failed the traditional French test of popular legitimacy.

Disastrously, the failure of the experiment of taking bread off rationing gave what the CRR at Nancy called a "fatal character" to the central government's reputation.[97] Not only was the public upset at the mismanagement of their daily staple, but it also felt betrayed. The CGT of the Vosges, for example, issued a statement in which it maintained that the bread card meant the black market, which meant the slavery of the workers. It warned that "the sheep [workers] are still calm and harmonious, but beware if they are changed into wolves!"[98]

The prefect of the Vosges issued several communiqués to calm the public. One explained in great detail why France had run short of flour despite the government's best efforts, and blamed both domestic "overconsumption" and ice on the Saint-Lawrence Seaway, which delayed grain imports from North America.[99] He followed that explanation a few weeks later with another detailed account as to why the government in Paris, rather than his own office, was responsible for the Vosgiens not getting their January fat ration.[100] Another communiqué entitled "The alarmists (*paniquards*)" berated these individuals who had bought as much bread as possible on the days before the resumption of rationing, thus leaving their neighbors with nothing. "These bad Frenchmen have failed in the essential duty of social solidarity and in the most elementary discipline without which any recovery is impossible."[101] An editorial on the front page of *Le Travailleur vosgien* addressed the same panic buying, calling it "the obliteration of the moral sense and a profound contempt for others," but partially excusing the transgressors as being "pursued by the obsessive fear of famine."[102]

Others met the news with the type of violent criticism summarized in a letter to the editor written by a former POW from Trieux (Meurthe-et-Moselle).

> We POWs consider that the unrestricted sale of bread was an electoral maneuver [and] that the reestablishment of the [bread] card is

due to the sabotage of the [Vichyite] *comités d'organisation*. The POWs judge as criminal the attitude of the authorities who have allowed the most scandalous abuses during two months of unrestricted sale. . . . [And they] think that certain Frenchmen balk at their duty and sabotage the life of the nation. They blame this state of things on the relevant Ministry and condemn its attitude.

Let us work, yes, but before that, let us clean house; let us throw out all those who profit from the situation, who lounge about in armchairs before the levers of command and who refuse to use them because "their" moment has not yet come. But our moment, people of France, has perhaps arrived.[103]

Rancor over the suppression and hasty resumption of the bread ration, however, was not confined to the unusually sorely tried Lorrainers. *La Margeride* reported the rumor of the return of the bread card with exaggeration and sarcasm. "It's already going better, let's roll up our stomachs," commented the paper, playing on the government's reconstruction slogan, "It's already going better, let's roll up our sleeves!"[104] The same reference occurred to those at *La Résistance savoyarde*. An article entitled "New Year's Gift" made the observation: "Decidedly, they are giving us the runaround: Monday the bread card is suppressed; Tuesday it is reestablished; Wednesday bread is back on unrestricted sale; Thursday they take registrations; Friday sheets of bread coupons are distributed. All that makes the consumer think twice before believing what is announced. And I'm rolling up my sleeves!"[105] The whole episode quickly became a byword for the national government's incompetence and untrustworthiness. *La Démocratie savoyarde* used the bread ration fiasco as its prime example in an editorial on government bumbling.[106] And the Moutiérain paper published a denial of the persistent rumor "that the bread card had only been reestablished in order to furnish the occasion of suppressing it a month before the next elections" in such a way as to make it clear that the editors, for their part, fully believed it.[107]

In terms of reestablishing the republic in France, the elections of 1945 may be counted as victories for the Resistance regime. But they trace an ultimately far more significant failure, the return to politics as usual despite the desire of the populace for something else, something vague but more moral, more just. The first elections in April for the municipal councils had an air of that vague something else. The election of Absents signified the moral dimensions of a campaign fought on the moral ideals of the Resistance, which were also espoused by the resistants' electoral opponents. Neither of the later elections had the unusual qualities of the first. In a mere four months the country had been remarkably disillusioned: the parties had seized control of politics, and inflation overshadowed almost everything else. Afraid of the future, the French found little comfort in the elections and only further anxiety in the national government's manipulation of them.

A successful withdrawal of the bread ration would certainly have represented a popularity coup for the national government. But as provincial administrators foresaw, it failed from the simple fact that the country was still too poor to support a free market in bread. Furthermore, that failure was handled so sloppily that the blame fell not on the proposed scapegoats of the "overconsuming" citizenry or the weather, but on the government itself. Worse yet, the government came out of the fiasco as a cynical manipulator of the people's security. The new Resistance government, supposedly dedicated to the renovation of France and the ideals of liberty and justice, could not have made a worse faux pas. If for centuries the test of a good government in France had been the wise management of the bread supply to ensure that all the people, both rich and poor, received a sufficient share in times of economic trouble, the Provisional Government failed it through its own bravado.

By New Year's of 1946, delays and shortages in the rationing system and the prominence of the black market had already impugned the government's credentials as a guarantor of social justice. Moreover, the contemporary uproar in Savoie over de Gaulle's pardons of locally notorious Miliciens underscored the government's failure to establish itself as a font of legal justice and cast further doubts on its commitment to honorary justice. The failure to preserve legal justice by pardoning a Milicien reinforced the failure to guarantee social justice seen in the contemporaneous bread card experiment. The government itself built the bridges between these areas of disillusionment and republican politics in the bread card debacle and the offer (bribe?) of a tobacco ration to the recently enfranchised women.

The elections of 1945, then, represented both a victory and a failure for the national government. In terms of its own agenda of establishing republican order, the elections were a solid success. Yet in terms of the more elusive necessity of rooting the new regime in popular legitimacy, they were a profound failure. The disinterest in the fall elections and the reaction to the experiment with the bread card demonstrated that the people would tolerate their new government, but they would not look to it for justice.

CONCLUSION

Given the government's machinations in regard to bread rationing, the rising cost of living, and the Gaullist policy of pardoning locally notorious collaborators, the French did not greet New Year's, 1946, with great optimism. In fact, the recorders of public opinion showed a remarkable consensus in reporting a prevailing mood of discouragement and disillusionment. The CRR at Nancy wrote: "The year 1946 has gotten off to a bad start. The situation is even considered critical by public opinion in the political domain as much as in the psychological, social, and economic domains. The Government is criticized. The supply of hopes begins to be exhausted; the discontent is general."[1]

In almost identical language, the editors of the Savoyard CDL's newspaper proclaimed, in special type: "General discontent. The year 1946 begins badly. The discontent reaches all social milieux. Are we being too demanding? . . . We have understood that we must wait and limit our desires. But the general impression has been that our governors did not have and still do not have the elements of our renaissance in hand."[2] These and the majority of other assessments of the new year placed the greatest blame for the discontent on the economic situation, particularly the recent reimposition of the bread card. *La Résistance savoyarde* neatly summarized the provincial perspective in a short weather report turned political commentary. "Gray skies overhead. There is the returned bread card, the shrunken franc, taxes, the electricity shortage, shoes that are deformed or without soles because the cobbler has no leather. Let's go anyway! Let's roll up our sleeves!!!"[3] As in earlier commentaries on the vagaries of the bread card, the last phrase mocked the government's reconstruction slogan. Issues like the purge of collaborators and the government's *"politique de la grandeur"* also appeared as secondary sources for the nation's troubles.[4]

Even those who remembered that 1945 had brought the defeat of Nazism and the end of the most horrendous of wars could muster only a grim optimism for the near future. As he offered a New Year's greeting to resistants and men of goodwill, the prefect of the Vosges admitted that the peace and liberty gained over the past twelve months were an "austere" peace and an "austere" liberty and surveyed the calamitous situation of most of Europe. He encouraged his readers to look back at their recent accomplishments to find "the strength and the reasons to face the [next] stage, 1946, that should bring us closer to the final goal, to that goal for which so many of ours have suffered and died, the grandeur and the independence of France in justice and in the union of all the French. The road that remains is long. It demands of us a great many efforts and still more sacrifices, but the prize is worth the trouble, and we owe it to ourselves as to the memory of our dead to take pride in it."[5]

The government's manipulation of the bread card certainly laid the foundation for the discontent of early 1946, and it may have struck the final blow to the confidence of some citizens, but it created neither the general discontent nor the disillusionment. Both had been growing steadily since the liberation; indeed, some of it appeared almost simultaneously with the liberation. The Conseil départemental des Milices patriotiques of Savoie, for example, expressed such instant disillusionment in October 1944, when it described itself as "an assembly of all the French who are discouraged to see that between yesterday and today not much has changed. . . . Why? . . . because the *affameurs* continue their frightful commerce, because the police have not been purged, because the functionaries, who, yesterday, were in the pay of the Vichy government and who, today, are still in the pay of traitors to the French Nation, have not been purged."[6] The Milice patriotique no longer existed at the end of 1945, but its members would assuredly have been less than pleased by the Capella Affair or the bread card fiasco.

The disillusionment was rooted in popular aspirations for and expectations of justice at the liberation. Naively or not, many people thought that a Resistance government would bring about the clandestine struggle's dream of a "pure and strong France," and that it would reform and govern society according to the dictates of legal, social, and honorary justice. So they expected collaborators to be punished, food to be shared out equally, and the patriots, both living and dead, to be honored. To a certain extent, the Gaullist government recognized and engaged the call for justice coming from the small towns of France. It did prosecute (some) collaborators through special purge courts; it did maintain an (inefficient) rationing system; it did (mostly) honor the moral hierarchy through memorials. Yet the government gave more importance to two considerations that limited, even crippled, its provision of justice: its role as a national government and its legitimacy as a republican regime.

The policies that the provisional government followed in pursuit of national considerations often ran afoul of local understanding and local realities at a time when, in the wake of the Second World War, the local mattered a great deal. The publication of so-called "national" rations in regions that had no hope of attaining such largesse was a public relations mistake. But other policies that propagated the Resistencialist myth struck irreparable blows to the regime's reputation. In the case of granting clemency to Miliciens, the national authorities could easily have taken the advice of provincial administrators and acknowledged the depth and importance of local griefs and angers with such slight policy modifications as delaying the announcement of certain remissions of sentences or forbidding released suspects from returning to the scenes of their alleged crimes. Instead the government ignored local sensibilities, followed a national policy, and exposed its disregard for legal and honorary justice as it was understood by its citizenry.

A similar misunderstanding marred the government's quest for republican legitimacy. Both the government and the people wanted postwar France to be a republic. But the government failed to understand that during the *après-libération* the trappings of republican legitimacy took a secondary place to the implementation of justice for the people in small towns such as Saint-Flour, Moûtiers, and Rambervillers. By arresting local resistance heroes for dubious activities just after the liberation, for example, the national government pursued the form of republican legitimacy to the point of sacrificing the local understanding of justice to the cause of law and order. More damaging, the government insisted on holding elections without the Absents, thus making a charade of the democratic process in the minds of those who had believed the Resistance propaganda that the deportees and POWs were France's most valued sons and daughters.

Until October 1945, the government could have made a not particularly convincing argument that its various affronts to the local conception of justice offended only resistants, who were a minority. As a democratic government, the argument would run, the new regime had to consider the needs and desires of the majority. The stunning faux pas of the bread card fiasco, however, affected everyone and set the question of the government's dedication to justice on a plane where it could not conceivably be dismissed as purely a concern of the resistants or a minority. In effect, when it toyed with the people's daily bread, the new government voluntarily put itself in the dock of the traditional French trial of a regime's legitimacy: its careful husbandry of the bread supply.[7] And in this realm, in the management of the food supply and the provision of social justice, the government failed the popular test even more spectacularly than it failed in the realms of legal and honorary justice.

Ironically, then, just as the Resistance government achieved the final steps of republican legitimacy by electing and seating a constituent assembly, it definitively failed the requirements of popular legitimacy. Why, then, did the French tolerate the Fourth Republic as long as they did, even if that was for only twelve years? The answer undoubtedly involves three considerations. First, governmental gestures and time dulled the demands of justice. The new government disappointed but did not utterly betray Resistance ideals. After all, if de Gaulle pardoned many collaborators, he also signed 768 death warrants. Furthermore, beginning in 1945 the deteriorating economic situation funneled attention into the realm of social justice, where, again, the government took some important steps. The postwar nationalizations and changes in welfare provisions that were called for in the CNR Charter, for instance, did move France closer to the ideal of social justice than it had been before the war. Moreover, for many people the end of rationing in 1949 removed the daily aggravation and reminder of the question of social justice. So the new regime met the demands of justice halfway, and circumstances made the other half fade.

Second, an unknown proportion of the French did not share in the public consensus of the après-libération. Because the French neither discredited Vichy nor rooted out collaborators in the 1940s, those with collaborationist sympathies could simply lie low until the passions of the liberation burned out or the public was distracted by economic troubles. Indeed, the Resistencialist myth all but denied that the French had done anything wrong during the war, making it very easy for collaborationists to challenge the après-libération definition of legal and honorary justice within a few short years. Consequently, the last people with sentences of national degradation were granted amnesty in 1953, and the last collaborator was released from prison in 1964.[8] The hopes and aspirations of the après-libération fell as thoroughly under the smothering cloud of the Resistencialist myth's forgetfulness as did the facts of the occupation.

Third, the international situation encouraged the French to resign themselves to the Fourth Republic. At the end of the Second World War, after all, very few people would have welcomed the additional disorder of a revolution or civil war, especially as many people in France feared that any open opposition to the Resistance government could lead to a Communist takeover. The dynamics of the early Cold War, when widespread pessimism predicted an imminent third world war and a grim future for France as an atomic battlefield or a Soviet zone of occupation, also counseled resignation.[9]

Indeed, in many ways France and Europe did not make the transition from war to peace in 1945 so much as they moved from an open, mechanized war into a muted, ideological war that suppressed some of the demands of justice created by the original war without either resolving or destroying them.[10] Now that the Cold War, too, has ended, the injustices of the Second World War are resurfacing in the muted postwar phase of the 1990s. Thus in 1997, fifty-three years after the defeat of the Vichy regime, France was obsessed by the trial of Maurice Papon for crimes committed during the Second World War, and the French hierarchy and police both admitted and formally apologized for their corporate collaboration of a lifetime ago. Other examples of the public remembering the Second World War in the 1990s could be found across Europe, especially in Eastern Europe, where Communist regimes diligently stifled memories of injustices and hatreds.[11] Cold War ideologies ensured that the Second World War continued after the cease-fire of May 1945 in the memories and motivations of an unknown number of Europeans. The lesson of the après-libération and of the close of the Cold War, then, is that a modern war does not end until the peace brings justice as well as an end to the fighting.

NOTES

INTRODUCTION

1 For a primarily political survey of the period from the national and Parisian perspective, see André Kaspi et al., *La Libération de la France, juin 1944–janvier 1946* (Paris: Perrin, 1995).
2 Hoffmann goes further to say that at the liberation "each man, each family, each village or town tended to become a little sovereign island again" (Hoffmann, *Decline or Renewal? France since the 1930s* [New York: Viking, 1974], 56).
3 Maurice Larkin, *France since the Popular Front: Government and People, 1936–1986* (Oxford: Clarendon Press, 1988), 117, and Frances M. B. Lynch, *France and the International Economy: From Vichy to the Treaty of Rome* (London: Routledge, 1997), 7–8.
4 See Kaspi for the political demands faced by the Gaullists, especially the American insistence on early elections (50–60).
5 Henry Rousso, *The Vichy Syndrome: History and Memory in France since 1944*, trans. Arthur Goldhammer (Cambridge, Mass.: Harvard University Press, 1991), 15–18.
6 The major works in the expanding field of Vichy France include Philippe Burrin, *La France à l'heure allemande, 1940–1944* (Paris: Editions du Seuil, 1995); H. R. Kedward, *In Search of the Maquis: Rural Resistance in Southern France, 1942–1944* (Oxford: Clarendon, 1993); H. R. Kedward, *Resistance in Vichy France* (Oxford: Oxford University Press, 1978); Pierre Laborie, *L'Opinion française sous Vichy* (Paris: Editions du Seuil, 1990); Robert O. Paxton, *Vichy France: Old Guard and New Order, 1940–1944* (New York: Columbia University Press, 1972); and John Sweets, *Choices in Vichy France: The French under Nazi Occupation* (Oxford: Oxford University Press, 1986).
7 Pieter Lagrou, "Victims of Genocide and National Memory: Belgium, France and the Netherlands, 1945–1965," *Past and Present* 154 (1997): 194–97.

8 At the end of the war, of course, many people (other than French collaborators) welcomed such instant amnesia. See Jeffrey Herf, *Divided Memory: The Nazi Past in the Two Germanys* (Cambridge, Mass.: Harvard University Press, 1997), 203.

9 For the relationship between legitimation and justice in the ancien régime, see the literature on eighteenth-century food riots begun by E. P. Thompson, "The Moral Economy of the English Crowd in the Eighteenth Century," *Past and Present* 50 (1971): 76–136, and in large part cited in chapter 4. For that relationship during and immediately after the world wars, see Richard Bessel, *Germany after the First World War* (Oxford: Clarendon, 1993), 41; H. R. Kedward, "The Maquis and the Culture of the Outlaw (with Particular Reference to the Cévennes)," in *Vichy France and the Resistance: Culture and Ideology*, ed. H. R. Kedward and R. Austin (London: Croom Helm, 1985), 244; and Robert G. Moeller, "War Stories: The Search for a Usable Past in the Federal Republic of Germany," *American Historical Review* 101, no. 4 (1996): 1020.

10 An English text of the charter appears in Peter Novick, *The Resistance versus Vichy: The Purge of Collaborators in Liberated France* (New York: Columbia University Press, 1968), 198–201. For a discussion of the charter, see Claire Andrieu, *Le Programme commun de la Résistance, des idées dans la guerre* (Paris: Editions de l'Erudit, 1984); René Hostache, *Le Conseil national de la Résistance: Les Institutions de la clandestinité* (Paris: Presses Universitaires de France, 1958); and Andrew Shennan, *Rethinking France: Plans for Renewal, 1940–1946* (Oxford: Clarendon, 1989).

11 See, for example, Archives nationales de France [unless otherwise noted, all archival materials are from the AN] F1a 4024, Rapports et correspondance du CRR à Nancy I, October 1944–June 1945, 1–15 October 1944; *Le Démocrate de l'Est*, 1 October 1944; *La Margeride*, 18 November 1944; *La Résistance savoyarde*, 21 December 1944; and the petition from the municipal council of Rambervillers to Charles de Gaulle printed in *La Résistance des Vosges*, 17 June 1945.

12 For the violent political role that the voices of the dead can play in a culture attuned to them, see Conor Cruise O'Brien, *Ancestral Voices: Religion and Nationalism in Ireland* (Chicago: University of Chicago Press, 1994).

CHAPTER 1   THREE TOWNS, THREE LIBERATIONS

1 The most famous such images, of course, were taken by photojournalists such as Robert Capa. For an analysis of these gestures and the posturing they generated, see Alain Brossat, *Libération, fête folle: 6 juin 44–8 mai 45* (Paris: Editions Autrement, April 1994), 119–25.

2 It does, however, give the highlight of what appears to have become the "proper" way to be liberated: head shaving. Lottman suggests that the idea for head shaving may have spread through a report of one on the BBC on 20 August 1944

(Herbert Lottman, *The People's Anger: Justice and Revenge in Post-Liberation France* [London: Hutchinson, 1986], 68).

3   Although the bulk of the country was liberated between June and September 1944, some parts of the northeast were not liberated until February 1945. Paris was liberated from 19 to 25 August 1944. A handful of "Atlantic pockets" were not liberated until the Germans who had retreated there surrendered in May 1945.

4   See, for example, Tzvetan Todorov, *A French Tragedy: Scenes of Civil War, Summer 1944*, trans. Mary Byrd Kelly (Hanover, N.H.: University Press of New England, 1996).

5   For a narrative of the challenges facing the Gaullists, see Kaspi.

6   For a summary of the process, see Charles-Louis Foulon, "Prise et exercice du pouvoir en province à la libération," in *La Libération de la France: Actes du colloque international tenu à Paris du 28 au 31 octobre 1974* (Paris: Editions du CNRS, 1976), 501–49. For the history of the CRRs, see Charles-Louis Foulon, *Le Pouvoir en province à la libération* (Paris: Presses de la Fondation nationale des sciences politiques, 1975). Although the CRRs mostly took power at the liberation of an area, there were a few cases in which they began their administration before Vichy or the Germans had left, for example, in Mauriac (Cantal). See Eugène Martres, "La 'République de Mauriac' (mai–août 1944)," *Revue d'histoire de la deuxième guerre mondiale* 99 (1975): 73–90.

7   For concerns over self-fashioning, see *La Margeride*, 20 December 1944, 21 July 1945, 6 October 1945, and 18 October 1945; *La Démocratie savoyarde*, 2 December 1944 and 23 June 1945; F1a 4028, Service central des Commissaires de la République, Bulletins sur la situation dans les régions et départements, juin 1945–décembre 1945, no. 76, 26 April 1945, Prefect Orne, and F1a 4024, 1–15 February 1945.

8   The 1946 census placed 25 percent of the population in communes of up to five thousand and 31 percent in communes ranging between five and ten thousand. See Institut national de la statistique et des études économiques, *Mouvement économique en France de 1944 à 1957* (Paris: Imprimerie nationale; Presses universitaires de France, 1958), 31, and *Dictionnaire des communes* (Nancy: Editions Berger-Levrault, 1949).

9   For maps comparing such factors as population density and industrial activity by department, see François Goguel, *Géographie des élections françaises de 1870 à 1951* (Paris: Armand Colin, 1951). For levels of religious practice by department, see Fernand Boulard, *Premiers itinéraires en sociologie religieuse* (Paris: Editions ouvrières, économie et humanisme, 1954).

10 I have used the population data from the 1946 census as the closest available approximation to 1944–45 figures. The demographic upheaval of the war makes the 1946 numbers only estimates for the prior years.

11 According to Martres, on 1 June 1944 there were 2,400 men in Cantal in the FFI, making a ratio of one resistant to every sixty inhabitants over eighteen years old (Martres, *Le Cantal de 1939 à 1945: Les troupes allemandes à travers le Massif Central* [Cournon d'Auvergne: Editions de Borée, 1993], 187–88, 168, 199–200).

12 One indication of the backing for Vichy, at least in the early years, comes from an announcement published in 1942 by the Vichy prefect. He had received so many anonymous denunciations that thereafter the authors of such letters would themselves become objects of investigation (Martres, *Cantal*, 37, 199–200).

13 Martres, *Cantal*, 350–492. For a brief discussion of Mont-Mouchet in English, see Sweets, *Choices*, 222–24.

14 Near Saint-Flour, the Germans also executed twenty-seven in Ruines and burned Clavières to the ground. (F2 4366, Rapports généraux sur le département, 1946 [occupation et libération], Cantal, 1947.) Also see Martres, *Cantal*, 504–10.

15 Archives départementales du Cantal [hereafter AC] 1 W 72, Situation du département, rapports de la préfecture, RG et gendarmerie, gendarmerie, daily reports.

16 Martres, *Cantal*, 510, 617–25, 659.

17 Martres, *Cantal*, 643.

18 *La Margeride*, 16 September 1944.

19 There was also one man who stood for another, apparently unrelated, man who was a political prisoner (*La Margeride*, 4 October 1944).

20 *La Margeride*, 16 September 1944, and *Le Cantal libre*, 13 September 1944.

21 Conseil municipal [hereafter CM] Saint-Flour, 4 October 1944.

22 *La Margeride*, 29 November 1944. The elected council inherited many of the same problems, including complaints about inadequate sewers and very large rats in the municipal abattoir (*La Margeride*, 29 August 1945 and 8 September 1945; FIC III 1211, 16 August 1945 and 16 November 1945, and *Le Cantal ouvrier et paysan*, 29 December 1945).

23 AC R.8.293, CLLs, letter from CDL to President CLL Saint-Flour, 16 January 1945, and *La Margeride*, 10 January 1945.

24 *La Margeride*, 27 December 1944, 17 January 1945, 14 February 1945, 21 March 1945, and 7 April 1945, and AC R.8.293.

25 The minister of information, for one, suspected that the feuding in Saint-Flour stemmed from long-standing rivalries. See AC 1 W 328, *Presse*, Ministre de l'Information à M. le Directeur régional de Clermont-Ferrand, 9 March 1945.

26 For the liberation-era press, see Kaspi, 323–34.

27 Martres, *Cantal*, 670–71, and AC 1 W 328, Ministre de l'Information à M. le Directeur régional de Clermont-Ferrand, 9 March 1945.

28 FIC III 1211, 16 August 1945.

29 *Le Cantal ouvrier et paysan*, 26 May 1945, and *La Margeride*, 8 September 1945 and 15 September 1945. The abbé's activities, however, led him into court on charges

of both defamation and collaboration. See Fic III 1211, 16 November 1945; *La Margeride*, 27 October 1945, 26 November 1945, and 8 December 1945; *L'Espoir du Cantal*, 24 November 1945; *La Voix du Cantal*, 8 September 1945; and Martres, *Cantal*, 671–72.

30 AC I W 358, Occupation, crimes de guerre, prisonniers (regarding anti-Resistance meetings in a Sanflorain garage); Martres, *Cantal*, 652–53 (regarding arrests of spies and saboteurs); and *La Margeride*, 4 October 1944.

31 Only 5,800 of these were accepted for active service (Burrin, 441).

32 Fic III 1226, Rapports de préfets, Savoie, octobre 1944, décembre 1944, et février-décembre 1945, 16 March 1945; also see *La Résistance savoyarde*, 1 March 1945.

33 For an example of the sympathy of many resistants with communist ideas, see the speech against capitalism given by the president of the Savoyard CDL (not, himself, a Communist) in *La Résistance savoyarde*, 26 November 1944.

34 It was followed distantly by the SFIO. See, for example, F1a 4024, 1–15 June 1945; Fic III 1211, Rapports de préfets, Cantal, janvier–novembre 1945, 16 November 1945; Fic III 1226, 24 October 1944; and F1a 4021, Rapports et correspondance du CRR à Clermont-Ferrand, octobre 1944–janvier 1946.

35 The CRR at Nancy remarked on the regional PCF's success at organizing the discontent among *sinistrés* behind its banner (F1a 4025, Rapports et correspondance du CRR à Nancy II, juillet 1945–janvier 1946, 1–15 September 1945). See chapter 4.

36 See, for example, *La Résistance savoyarde*, 7 December 1944, or *La Voix du Cantal*, 13 October 1945 and 24 November 1945.

37 *La Margeride*, 6 January 1945.

38 Buton names Saint-Flour as one of the twenty-eight towns with a Communist *"insurrection limitée"* at the liberation (Philippe Buton, *Les Lendemains qui déchantent: Le Parti communiste français à la Libération* [Paris: Presses de la Fondation nationale des sciences politiques, 1993], 104).

39 See *La Margeride*, 16 September 1944, 21 October 1944, 13 December 1944, and 16 May 1945, and *Le Cantal ouvrier et paysan*, 23 September 1944.

40 *La Voix du Cantal*, 29 September 1945.

41 F1a 4021, 15–31 October 1945.

42 *L'Aurore du Cantal*, 4 August 1945.

43 *Le Cantal libre*, 20 July 1945; see also AC R 5.491, Secours national, rapports mensuels, 1944–49.

44 *Le Cantal ouvrier et paysan*, 28 July 1945 and 4 August 1945; *La Margeride*, 26 July 1945, 1 August 1945, and 4 August 1945; and *La Voix du Cantal*, 22 September 1945 and 20 October 1945.

45 Fic III 1211, 16 August 1945.

46 Yves Brêche, "Moûtiers: Le grand destin d'une petite cité alpine," *L'Histoire en Savoie* 59 (1980): 1–32; François M. Hudry, *Histoire des communes savoyardes*, vol. 4,

Albertville et son arrondissement (Roanne le Coteau: Editions Horvath, 1982), 348–65.

47 For an overview, see André Palluel-Guillard, *La Savoie de la Révolution à nos jours, XIXe–XXe siècle* (Rennes: Ouest-France, 1986), 479–525.

48 For the Savoyards' refusal to think of themselves as defeated by the Italians, see *La Résistance savoyarde*, 23 June 1945.

49 Louis Chabert, *Les Grandes Alpes industrielles de Savoie: Évolution économique et humaine* (Alban Leysse: Imprimerie Gaillard, 1978), 377. For prewar xenophobia, including the 1931 murder of Italians in Savoie, see Eugen Weber, *The Hollow Years: France in the 1930s* (New York: Norton, 1994), 89–92.

50 F1C 1226, 16 November 1945, and F1a 4022, 15 February–15 March 1945. The prefect of Haute-Savoie was particularly concerned that the draft would allow Italians to take the jobs of young Frenchmen (F1a 4028, no 39, 10 February 1945, Prefect Haute-Savoie).

51 *La Résistance savoyarde*, 26 January 1945.

52 The authorities inflicted only the minimum punishment on Italian workers without the proper papers and allowed them to stay (Archives départementales de la Savoie [hereafter AS] 11 M III 109, Gendarmerie, 1941–46, infractions à la police des étrangers 1945–46; and *La Résistance savoyarde*, 1 February 1945).

53 *La Résistance savoyarde*, 8 February 1945, 8 March 1945, 24 March 1945, and 22 April 1945; see also 10 November 1945.

54 *La Résistance savoyarde*, 12 January 1946, and F1a 4022, 15 February–15 March 1945.

55 For the story of the Savoyard Resistance, see Charles Rickard, *La Savoie dans la Résistance: Haute-Savoie—Savoie* (Rennes: Ouest-France, 1986).

56 F2 4395, Rapports généraux sur le département, 1946 [occupation et libération], sous-préfecture d'Albertville, 1946, and Robert Dodin, *Les Vosges de 1939 à 1945* (Epinal: Editions du Sapin d'Or, 1990), 174.

57 F2 4395, sous-préfecture d'Albertville, 1946.

58 Palluel-Guillard argues that the Savoies were engaged in a civil war from 1942 (498).

59 *La Résistance savoyarde*, 12 October 1944, 1 March 1945, 8 March 1945, and 9 June 1945.

60 Palluel-Guillard, 522.

61 *La Résistance savoyarde*, 21 September 1944.

62 *La Résistance savoyarde*, 21 December 1944 and 16 June 1945.

63 AS Rav 466, Plan de détresse de RG, 20 June 1944, and *La Résistance savoyarde*, 21 September 1944.

64 *La Résistance savoyarde*, 15 March 1945.

65 F1C III 1226, 22 December 1944 and 16 March 1945, and *La Résistance savoyarde*, 18 January 1945.

66 For medical care, for example. Moûtiers' civil statistics register the deaths of twenty-eight men from "firearms" or "war wounds" in 1944. Eight were German soldiers; many died at the hospital (AS 99 X 7, Etat civil, causes de décès, 1944).
67 See *La Résistance savoyarde*, 9 September 1944, 24 March 1945, 21 October 1945, and 15 December 1945.
68 Despite the hierarchy's disapproval of priests bearing weapons, the abbé was a *chef de section* in the Bataillon de Basse-Tarentaise. The author would like to thank Abbé Hudry for giving her a copy of the sermon that he delivered on the occasion that he remembered in 1991 as the *"fête de libération."*
69 *La Résistance savoyarde*, 5 October 1944, and *La Savoie française*, 30 September 1944 and 7 October 1944.
70 They collected in every commune in the Haute-Tarentaise. *La Résistance savoyarde*, 21 December 1944, 28 December 1944, and 18 January 1945; *La Vie nouvelle*, 24 December 1944; and *La Sasson*, 4 April 1945 and 27 June 1945. See also *La Résistance savoyarde*, 7 April 1945.
71 FIC III 1226, 24 October 1944.
72 *Les Quatre vallées d'Albertville*, 2 September 1944.
73 FIC III 1226, 16 March 1945; see also 16 August 1945.
74 *Les Allobroges*, 28 September 1944.
75 *La Résistance savoyarde*, 9 September 1944.
76 See *La Résistance savoyarde*, 9 September 1944, 14 September 1944, 19 October 1944, 2 November 1944, 8 February 1945, and 14 July 1945, and AS Rav 467, Notes de service, 14 September 1944.
77 *La Résistance savoyarde*, 28 April 1945.
78 *La Résistance savoyarde*, 9 September 1944 and 5 October 1944. Lungo presided again when both the prefect and subprefect visited Moûtiers in February (*La Résistance savoyarde*, 16 February 1945). The CLL also organized a conference of the mayors of the canton of Moûtiers in January 1945 (*La Résistance savoyarde*, 26 January 1945).
79 *La Résistance savoyarde*, 24 March 1945.
80 *La Résistance savoyarde*, 21 September 1944, 23 November 1944, and 14 December 1944.
81 FIa 4022, Rapports et correspondance du CRR à Lyon, septembre 1944–decembre 1945, 16–31 January 1945, and 1–15 February 1945.
82 FIC III 1226, 16 March 1945. The CFTC-CGT represented workers from the region's chemical and metallurgical factories, transportation services, construction industry, food services, public health services, communications services, and railroad. It vehemently protested the unsatisfactory supply situation in the Tarentaise and supported strikes by the cobblers and civil servants (*La Résistance savoyarde*, 21 December 1944, 11 January 1945, 1 February 1945, and 31 March 1945, and *La*

Vie nouvelle, 21 January 1945). Administrators remarked on the influence of the Church among peasants and workers as well as among the bourgeoisie (F1a 4022, 1–15 February 1945).

83 The occupation-era archbishop transferred to Bayonne for reasons other than reputation and was also credited with protecting the town (*La Résistance savoyarde*, 18 January 1945 and 11 January 1945, and *La Vie nouvelle*, 28 January 1945). In contrast, *La Margeride* all but ignored the Sanflorain bishopric except to cast occasional aspersions on its activities.

84 *La Résistance savoyarde*, 5 October 1944.

85 F1c III 1226, 16 March 1945, and *La Résistance savoyarde*, 26 October 1944 and 1 March 1945, and *La Savoie française*, 27 October 1944.

86 *La Résistance savoyarde*, 19 October 1944, 30 November 1944, 14 December 1944, 28 December 1944, and 1 March 1945, and F1a 4022, 15 March–15 April 1945. On a departmental level, however, the UFF played the greater role in providing welfare assistance and promoting women's rights and political education (*La Sasson*, 1945). See reports of UFF groups in towns near Moûtiers in *La Résistance savoyarde*, 7 December 1944 and 22 April 1945.

87 *La Savoie française*, 25 August 1945.

88 For debates over the conduct of military operations, see *La Résistance savoyarde*, 9 September 1944, 19 October 1944, 21 December 1944, 24 March 1945, and 31 March 1945.

89 *La Résistance savoyarde*, 21 December 1944; see also 26 November 1944 and 28 December 1945.

90 For the formal retraction of unspecified slanderous remarks by a barkeeper, see *La Résistance savoyarde*, 2 February 1946.

91 For the history of the occupation of the Vosges, see Dodin.

92 Jean Vartier, "Rambervillers: Son occupation—sa libération" (typescript, 1945). In a letter to the town's mayor thirty years later, M. Vartier vouched for the solid research of his history of the town from 1939 to 1944, but found his style "very outdated in its juvenile lyricism" (he was seventeen at the time). The author would like to thank Mayor Chevrier for a copy of this document, which can also be found in 72 AJ 206, Fonds du Comité d'histoire de la deuxième guerre mondiale, Vosges.

93 It read: "TOULON, 1918, V, VICTOIRE." Vartier.

94 Jean Mueth, "Rapport de Mr. Mueth" (typescript, n.d. [October 1944?]), official diary of the founder and commander of the Rambervillers Maquis with the reports of three other officers attached. The official honor roll of Rambûvetais FFI who participated in the liberation of the town names 107 men and 6 women. This may give a lower number of partisans than the commander's report because it only includes Rambûvetais. Given the demographic chaos of the time and the use of the maquis as hideouts, it is unlikely that any unit would have been composed exclusively of men and women from one town. At least one Parisian fought in

Rambervillers' maquis; he was probably joined by "strangers" from other Vosgien towns and maybe even some eastern European deserters from German service. Alternatively, some of the Rambervillers maquis may have been engaged in missions elsewhere.

95 The author thanks M. Jean-Claude Kempf of Rambervillers for sharing documents that make up this account of September and October 1944 in Rambervillers. They come from contemporary reports written by the following witnesses: Mme. Auger, "La Libération, août–octobre 1944" (typescript, 1 December 1944), a diary kept for her granddaughter by a woman living on a large property with a sawmill on the outskirts of town; Mario Faivre, "Notes à propos de l'année 1944" (typescript n.d. [1945?]), the report of an officer of the BCRA/OSS on his activities during the liberation; Mme. Frachet, "Compte rendu sur les événements de la libération à Rambervillers par une habitante" (typescript, [1944?]), diary of military events affecting civilians; Mueth, "Rapport"; and Vartier "Rambervillers."

96 F2 4403, Rapports généraux sur le département, 1946 [occupation et libération], Vosges, 28 February 1947.

97 Mueth, "Rapport."

98 See CM Rambervillers, 10 December 1944; *Le Démocrate de l'Est,* 23 November 1944 and 4 January 1944.

99 See CM Rambervillers, 21 December 1946.

100 National Archives and Records Administration, record group 407, entry 427, WWII Operations Reports, 7th Army [hereafter NARA 407] 345-INF(157)-0, and 107-5, G-5 Reports, November 1944.

101 The author's name does not figure on the official list of the town's FFI liberators (*La Résistance des Vosges,* December 1944; see also January 1945).

102 According to the French reports, there were seventeen to twenty deaths; according to the official American report, fifteen civilians were killed (NARA 407, 345-INF[157]-0.3).

103 Auger, "Libération."

104 For the infantry's justly proud view of their own achievement, see *Beachhead News,* 10 December 1944.

105 Frachet, "Compte rendu," 31 October 1944.

106 Hoover Institution Archives, F. Sammis Jr. collection, m46031-10.AV.

107 Auger, "Libération."

108 The council decided that the prefecture should pay the Entr'aide's debt of 5,250 francs for meals (CM Rambervillers, 10 December 1944, and NARA 407, 107-5, G-5 reports, November 1945).

109 *Le Démocrate de l'Est,* 7 December 1944.

110 *Le Démocrate de l'Est,* 19 October 1944. The peace did not bring light back to the town; over the winter of 1945–46, poverty and power shortages effectively recreated the blackout. See *Bulletin officiel du département des Vosges,* decrees of

6 November and 12 November 1945, regarding the hours of shops and places of entertainment.

111 F1a 4029, Service central des Commissaires de la République, bulletins sur la situation dans les régions et départements, juin 1945–décembre 1945, no. 13, 18 August 1945, Prefect Vosges.

112 F2 4403, Vosges, 28 February 1947.

113 The full text, dated 11 November 1948, reads: "Commune whose population had to submit to the rigors of an inflexible occupier who deported 155 of its inhabitants without shaking its patriotism. In 1944 was almost entirely liberated by the French Forces of the Interior. 51 dead, 47 wounded, 10 hostages."

114 As of November 1944, Vosgiens could send form postcards approved by the U.S. Third Army (F1a 4024, September 1944–May 1945).

115 In October the FFI and the U.S. Army reached an agreement whereby passes could be issued by the mayor for travel within the canton or by the prefect for travel within the department. Rambûvetais could apply for a pass at the town hall from 10:00 A.M. to noon six days a week (NARA 407, 107-5, G-5 reports, 12 October 1944); *Le Démocrate de l'Est*, 31 October 1944, 7 November 1944, 28 November 1944, 30 November 1944, and 12 December 1944. These restrictions eased as the battle moved into Germany (*Bulletin officiel du département des Vosges*, 9 February 1945).

116 The study included bread, meat, butter, cheese, sugar, potatoes, skimmed milk, and preserves. Supplies of butter, cheese, and preserves fell seriously short, but the bread supply had improved by 75 percent. The author estimated that nonrationed fruits and vegetables, in very short supply, would add only one hundred calories per day to the average diet (NARA 407, 107-5, G-5 reports, November 1944). The CRR, however, reckoned that the average adult in the Vosges received only 727 calories per day from rationed food in November (F1a 4024, 1–25 November 1944).

117 The trucks were driven by FFIs. The power shortages also meant that many communes could not operate their threshing machines (Archives départementales des Vosges [hereafter AV] 54 W 214, Collecte des céréales: approvisionnement en pain 1943–1944, letter from Major W. Batt, G-5, to French authorities, October 1944, and NARA 407, 107-5, G-5 reports, 25 September–4 October 1944, and November 1944).

118 They cleared 108,000 land mines, 118,800 artillery shells, 175,000 grenades, almost 13,000 bazookas, and more than 2,700 bombs (Dodin, 146).

119 F1a 4024, 15–30 March 1945.

120 *La Liberté de l'Est*, 18 March 1945 and 31 March 1945.

121 Paul Légé, "Souvenirs de 1944" (typescript, n.d.). M. Légé was eleven years old at the time. The author would like to thank M. Jean-Claude Kempf for sharing this document with her.

122 Danièle Voldman, *Attention mines, 1944–1947* (Paris: Editions France-Empire, 1985), 93–104 and passim.
123 *La Croix de Lorraine*, 20 May 1945.
124 F1a 4029, no. 126, 1 August 1945, Prefect Creuse.
125 See CM Rambervillers, 30 September 1944.
126 See CM Rambervillers, 27 October 1944, and *Le Démocrate de l'Est*, 1–2 November 1944. The general sent his thanks via his principal private secretary (CM Rambervillers, 6 January 1945).
127 Vartier, "Rambervillers."
128 See CM Rambervillers, 23 March 1946, 29 September 1946, 5 October 1946, and 21 December 1946.
129 The author would like to thank Deputy Mayor Fevotte for sending her the relevant documents from the municipal archives.
130 See NARA 407, 107–13; 345-INF(157)-0 to 0.3; 3100-0.3; ARBN-191-3.2; ENGP-32-0.1 to 0.36.0; SVCO-20-0 (47209).
131 Germaine Kempf, private letter to the author, 28 February 1993.
132 See NARA 407, MDEH-9-0.1, Nurses' History, July 1942–June 1945, and MDEH-9-0.1 (17615), Monthly History of the 9th Evacuation Hospital, October 1944–March 1945.
133 *Le Démocrate de l'Est*, 19–20 November 1944. In March 1945, four thousand Vosgiens held similar well-paying jobs with the American army (F1a 4024, 1–15 March 1945).
134 Légé, "Souvenirs," and *Bulletin officiel du département des Vosges*, 10 November 1944.
135 *Le Démocrate de l'Est*, 3 November 1944, and *La Libérte de l'Est*, 7 November 1945.
136 See AV 54 W 40, Ravitaillement, réquisitions 1940–45, cantonnement de soldats américains 1944, demandes.
137 For example, *La Résistance des Vosges*, February 1945, and F1a 4024, 1–15 November 1944.
138 See NARA 407, 107-5, G-5 reports, 25 September–23 November 1944.
139 *Le Démocrate de l'Est*, 13 January 1945.
140 *Le Démocrate de l'Est*, 21–22 January 1945, and *Le Liberté de l'Est*, 9 August 1945.
141 *Le Démocrate de l'Est*, 4 January 1945.
142 *La Liberté de l'Est*, 6 July 1945.
143 Faivre, "Notes."
144 Légé, "Souvenirs"; it happened in his home.
145 There were certainly a number of more or less serious crimes committed by American troops in the region, to the continual dismay of the CRR at Nancy, whose city served as an American R&R center (F1a 4024 passim). From 15 August 1944 to 31 January 1945, the criminal investigations unit of the U.S. Army Provost Marshal investigated 117 felonies but proved the GIs innocent in only 31 cases (NARA 407, 107–28, 7th Army Provost Marshal Section Reports).

146 Auger, "Compte rendu," 1 October 1944 and 3 October 1944.
147 Liliane Vouaux, "Rambervillers, Septembre 1944" (manuscript, n.d.) and personal interview with the author, 1992.
148 Légé, "Souvenirs."
149 *Le Réveil des Vosges*, 3 June 1945.
150 *La Liberté de l'Est*, 21 July 1945.
151 For a discussion of these tensions, see *Le Travailleur vosgien*, 29 July 1945.
152 *La Liberté de l'Est*, 9 August 1945.
153 F1a 4024, 15–30 March 1945, and Dodin, 119.
154 *Le Démocrate de l'Est*, 28 November 1944, 7 December 1944, and 28 December 1944, and *La Résistance des Vosges*, December 1944.
155 *La Liberté de l'Est*, 24 August 1945, and *La Résistance des Vosges*, February 1945, July 1945, and September 1945.
156 The author of the first charge remained unconvinced by the membership's arguments (*Le Travailleur vosgien*, 5 August 1945 and 5 October 1945).
157 For the variety of Catholic responses to the occupation, see W. D. Halls, *Politics, Society and Christianity in Vichy France* (Oxford: Berg, 1995).
158 He estimated, for example, that in the spring of 1945 the department had forty thousand members in the Ligue féminine d'action catholique but only two thousand adherents in the reputedly Communist UFF (F1a 4024, 1–15 February 1945 and 1–15 March 1945).
159 The pilgrimage took place on 22 September 1945 (*La Liberté de l'Est*, 30 September–1 October 1945).
160 *La Croix de Lorraine*, 9 December 1945.
161 See, for one example among many, Norman Lewis, *Naples '44* (New York: Pantheon, 1978). See chapter 5 below for the controversy over Saint Libaire's role in the liberation.
162 See CM Rambervillers, 29 September 1945. Predictably, the public school teachers responded by creating an "*amicale laïque*" with the support of the Socialist Party to defend the rights of the public school and its students (*Le Travailleur vosgien*, 8 February 1946). Because Vichy had subsidized Catholic schools, the effort to continue the subventions in the Fourth Republic reopened the well-worn Third Republic battle between clericals and anticlericals over the schools, mostly through a "popular referendum on the family's freedom of education." See F1c III 1211, 16 April 1945, F1c III 1226, 16 April 1945, and 72 AJ 384, 15 March–15 April 1945.

CHAPTER 2   LIVING IN THE AFTERMATH OF WAR

1. For a statistical breakdown of regular criminal trials, see Bruno Aubusson de Cavarlay et al., "La Justice pénale en France, Résultats statistiques (1934–1954)," *Cahiers de l'IHTP* 23 (1993).
2. *La Résistance savoyarde*, 3 November 1945; see also *La Liberté de l'Est*, 22–23 July 1945.
3. *La Margeride*, 2 June 1945.
4. See *La Margeride*, 3 March 1945 and 1 August 1945; *Le Démocrate de l'Est*, 10 October 1944; *La Croix de Lorraine*, 19 November 1944; F1a 4022, 16–31 January 1945; *La Résistance savoyarde*, 1 February 1945; and *La Savoie française*, 14 July 1945. For vigilantes who were also criminals, see F1a 4021, 1–15 February 1945.
5. For the opposite case of the ceremonial reinstatement of a police agent who had been fired by Vichy, see *La Margeride*, 7 April 1945.
6. F1a 4028, Service central des Commissaires de la République, 1945–1947, Bulletins sur la situation dans les régions et départements, novembre 1944–juin 1945, no. 26, 27 February 1945, CRR Orléans. This problem only multiplied everywhere after the Return of the surviving deportees (F1a 4025, 1–15 July 1945).
7. F1c III 1211, 16 March 1945.
8. F1a 4021, 15–31 October 1944 and 1–15 February 1945.
9. F1a 4021, 15 November 1944.
10. See, for instance, Marc Bloch, "Réflexions d'un historien sur les fausses nouvelles de la guerre," *Revue de synthèse historique* 33, nos. 97–99 (1921): 2–35, and Ute Daniel, *The War from Within: German Working-Class Women in the First World War*, trans. Margaret Ries (Oxford: Berg, 1997), 241–50.
11. Roger Absalom, *A Strange Alliance: Aspects of Escape and Survival in Italy, 1943–1945* (Florence: Leo S. Olschki, 1991), 19.
12. *La Résistance savoyarde*, 28 September 1944.
13. Buton argues that the PCF followed a policy of actively encouraging fears of a fifth column, Buton, 168–69.
14. Gendarmes also took preventive measures such as arresting twenty-two *volksdeutsche* in Lille, with, they claimed, full public support (72 AJ 384, Fonds du Comité d'histoire de la deuxième guerre mondiale, Ministère de la Guerre, Direction de la Gendarmerie, 15 December 1944–15 January 1945 and 15 January–15 February 1945). Internment of civilian German citizens was standard practice (F1a 4029, no. 144, 6 September 1945, Prefect Haute-Savoie; F1a 4025, 1–15 October 1945 and 1–15 February 1946).
15. F1a 4028, no. 33, 27 January 1945, Prefect Saône-et-Loire, and F1a 4024, 15–31 December 1944.
16. See 72 AJ 384, 15 September–15 October 1944.

17 F1a 4028, no. 49, 6 March 1945, CRR Clermont-Ferrand, and F1a 4029, no. 129, 7 August 1945, Prefect Loire.
18 See AC 1 W 358, letter dated 15 November 1944. See the map of enemy agents in the Massif Central from September 1944 to January 1945 in Martres, *Cantal*, 653.
19 *La Margeride*, 11 November 1944; see also F1a 4028, no. 18, 23 December 1944, CRR Rennes.
20 F1c III 1226, 17 May 1945. Also see AC 1 W 359, Propagande, terrorisme, collaboration, 18 October 1945.
21 *La Résistance savoyarde*, 15 September 1945.
22 *La Liberté de l'Est*, 12 June 1945.
23 For a discussion of the semiotics of the maquis in the summer of 1944, see Brossat, *Libération*.
24 F1a 4021, 6 October 1944, 1–15 November 1944, and 1–15 February 1945; F1c III 1211, 16 February 1945; F1a 4022, 13 September 1944; F1a 4028, 28–36, January 1945; and F1c III 1226, 22 December 1944.
25 *La Margaride*, 3 January 1945–31 March 1945, and *La Voix du Cantal*, 17 February 1945.
26 See 72 AJ 186, Savoie, A.18.1, reports by Angelini, May 1949, Lestien, May 1945, and Pochard, November 1970.
27 *Le Cantal libre*, 1–2 November 1944.
28 F1c III 1211, 16 February 1945.
29 See *La Résistance savoyarde*, 15 September 1945, and *Le Travailleur vosgien*, 30 November 1945.
30 Dominique Veillon, *Vivre et survivre en France 1939–1947* (Paris: Payot, 1995), 307. See also Jean-Pierre Husson, "Le Retentissement de la victoire dans la Marne," in *8 Mai 1945: La Victoire en Europe: Actes du colloque international de Reims, 1985*, ed. Maurice Vaïsse (Lyon: La Manufacture, 1985), 371–79, and Kaspi, 469–75.
31 72 AJ 384, 15 January–15 February 1945.
32 See, for example, F1c III 1226, 16 March 1945; F1a 4024, 1–15 January 1945; and F1a 4028, no. 11, 7 December 1944, CRR Laon.
33 See 72 AJ 384, 15 March–15 April 1945.
34 See 72 AJ 384, 15 November–15 December 1945.
35 See 72 AJ 384, 15 January–15 February 1945. For the controversy about American treatment of German POWs, see James Bacque, *Other Losses: An Investigation into the Mass Deaths of German Prisoners at the Hands of the French and Americans after World War II* (Toronto: Stoddart, 1989), and the rebuttals in Günter Bischof and Stephen E. Ambrose, eds. *Eisenhower and the German POWs: Facts against Falsehood* (Baton Rouge: Louisiana State University Press, 1992).
36 F1a 4024, 15–31 May, 1945. See also F1a 4028, no. 26, 11 January 1945, CRR Dijon.

37 Forty women protested on 3 May and one hundred on 4 May (72 AJ 384, 15 April–15 May 1945).
38 *Le Cantal libre,* 10 March 1945.
39 The press in the Lyon region made similar complaints about GIs and FFIs having butter on their toast (F1a 4022, 20 April 1945, and *Le Volontaire des Alpes,* 21 October 1944).
40 *Le Cantal libre,* 15 February 1945.
41 *La Paix,* 9 June 1945. See also *La Résistance savoyarde,* 24 March 1945; *Le Réveil des Vosges,* 20 May 1945; and *La Margeride,* 21 February 1945.
42 *La Résistance des Vosges,* December 1944.
43 See 72 AJ 384, 15 May–15 June 1945.
44 F1a 4021, 15–31 October 1945, and F1a 4025, 15–31 October 1945. The CRRs reported the PGA tallies every month.
45 See CM Rambervillers, 29 September 1945 and 5 October 1946.
46 This happened only weeks after Moutiérains threatened to murder twenty-one of these same PGA in revenge for a war crime discussed in chapter 6 below (*La Résistance savoyarde,* 1 September 1945).
47 *La Liberté de l'Est,* 13 September 1945.
48 *La Margeride,* 15 December 1945, and *Recueil des actes administratifs du département du Cantal,* 1 October 1945 (for a more restricted list of prohibitions).
49 The PGA had indeed been caught stealing (*La Résistance savoyarde,* 21 October 1945). They had also escaped (*La Margeride,* 30 May 1945 and 14 July 1945).
50 See AC 1 W 286, PGA, incidents.
51 Everyone, from reactionary priests to Communists, berated the rather vague "trusts" during this time. For examples, see *La Margeride,* 13 January 1945 and 10 February 1945.
52 For how those policies led to the "stillbirth" of the Fourth Republic, see Steven Philip Kramer, "La crise économique de la libération," *Revue d'histoire de la deuxième guerre mondiale* 111 (1978): 25–44.
53 See, for example, Jean-Pierre Azéma, *From Munich to the Liberation, 1938–1944,* trans. Janet Lloyd (Cambridge: Cambridge University Press, 1984), 190.
54 See Dominique Veillon, "Une Politique d'adaptation spécifique: Les ersatz," *Cahiers de l'IHTP* 32–33 (1996): 59–78, and *Vivre.*
55 F1a 4024, 1–15 June 1945.
56 *La Liberté de l'Est,* 7 November 1945.
57 *La Liberté de l'Est,* 26–27 January 1946.
58 F1c III 1226, 16 September 1945, and letter from Minister of Interior to Prefect of Savoie, 2 November 1945.
59 *La Résistance savoyarde,* 4 August 1945, and F1c III 1226, 16 August 1945.
60 *La Résistance savoyarde,* 21 July 1945.

Notes to Chapter Two

61 *La Résistance savoyarde*, 8 February 1945.
62 FIC III 1226, letter from Prefect of Savoie to Minister of Interior, 11 August 1945. In a similar move, hairdressers, both owners and employees, went on strike in September to protest an 18 percent tax levied by the national government on their services (*La Résistance savoyarde*, 22 September 1945).
63 For the housing crisis, see Danièle Voldman, "Le Logement: Crise, pénurie ou restrictions?" *Cahiers de l'IHTP* 32-33 (1996): 377-88, and Marie-Françoise Sanier-Dehu, "Le Logement: L'Exemple de la ville de Saint-Denis," *Cahiers de l'IHTP* 32-33 (1996): 389-94. For public health at the liberation, see Robert Menchérini, "Conséquences sanitaires et sociales dans les Bouches-du-Rhône," *Cahiers de l'IHTP* 32-33 (1996): 419-32.
64 *Le Travailleur vosgien*, 7 December 1945.
65 *La Résistance savoyarde*, 9 November 1944, 23 November 1944, 30 November 1944, and 28 December 1944.
66 FIa 4022, 1-15 February 1945.
67 For what the bombings and shortages meant for higher education, see Claude Singer, *L'Université libérée, l'université épurée (1943-1947)* (Paris: Les Belles Lettres, 1997), 78-116.
68 *La Margeride*, 24 October 1945, 24 November 1945, 1 December 1945, and 8 December 1945.
69 *La Résistance savoyarde*, 19 January 1946.
70 See *La Résistance savoyarde*, 24 August 1945, 29 September 1945, and 6 October 1945.
71 *La Résistance savoyarde*, 28 December 1945. See also AC R 8.293, CLL Saint-Flour, 21 December 1944 and 11 January 1945, and response from health department.
72 *La Margeride*, 4 October 1944.
73 *La Margeride*, 18 November 1944 and 29 November 1944.
74 *La Voix du Cantal*, 23 December 1944. See also *La Margeride*, 16 June 1945, 10 February 1945, and 17 March 1945.
75 *Le Cantal ouvrier et paysan*, 15 December 1945 and 29 December 1945.
76 FIC III 1211, 16 November 1945; FIa 4025, 15-30 November 1945 and 1-15 December 1945; FIa 4021, January 1946; and FIC III 1226, 16 December 1945.
77 *La Résistance des Vosges*, December 1945. For very similar conclusions from the peasant's point of view, see *La Margeride*, 7 April 1945.
78 See INSEE, *Mouvement économique en France de 1944 à 1957*, 106-20.
79 Lynch, 89.
80 *La Résistance savoyarde*, 2 June 1945.
81 Buton, 195-96.
82 FIC III 1226, 16 December 1945, and *Le Cantal libre*, 13 December 1945. The civil servants had already made their discontent known earlier in the year (FIa 4022, 15 May-15 June 1945). For coverage of the strike, see *L'Année politique, 1944-1945*:

Revue chronologique des principaux faits politiques, économiques et sociaux de la France, de la Libération de Paris au 31 Décembre 1945 (Paris: Editions du grand siècle, 1946), 373–80.
83 F1c III 1226, 16 December 1945.
84 F1c III 1226, 16 September 1945.
85 The CRR at Lyon remarked that the legal prices of toys stunned people (F1a 4022, 15 November–15 December 1945).
86 *L'Espoir du Cantal,* 22 December 1945. See also *La Résistance savoyarde,* 28 December 1945.
87 Scholars have since traced some remarkable continuities between the two. See Shennan, *Rethinking France,* and H. R. Kedward, "Patriots and Patriotism in Vichy France," *Transactions of the Royal Historical Society,* 5th ser., 32 (1982): 175–92.
88 The après-libération moral hierarchy continued in the "hierarchy of suffering" used by postwar veterans' and victims' associations (Rousso, *Vichy Syndrome,* 24). For the application of a wartime moral hierarchy in a different setting, see Herf, 80–95.
89 For deportation as a mythical concept, see Lagrou, 203–4. For the application of the concept of redemption through suffering to fighters of twentieth-century wars, see Sarah Fishman, *We Will Wait: Wives of French Prisoners of War, 1940–1945* (New Haven: Yale University Press, 1991), 56, and George Mosse, *Fallen Soldiers: Reshaping the Memory of the World Wars* (Oxford: Oxford University Press, 1990), 39.
90 Kedward, "Culture of the Outlaw," 232–51.
91 See Michael R. Marrus and Robert Paxton, *Vichy France and the Jews* (New York: Basic Books, 1981), Donna Ryan, *The Holocaust and the Jews of Marseille: The Enforcement of Anti-Semitic Policies in Vichy France* (Urbana: University of Illinois Press, 1996), and Susan Zuccotti, *The Holocaust, the French, and the Jews* (New York: Basic Books, 1993).
92 See Lagrou and Marie-Anne Matard-Bonucci and Edouard Lynch, eds., *La Libération des camps et le Retour des déportés* (Brussels: Editions complexe, 1995), 87–115, 233.
93 Danièle Voldman, "Les bombardements aériens: Une Mise à mort du "guerrier"? (1914–1945)," in *De la Violence et des femmes,* ed. Cécile Dauphin (Paris: Albin Michel, 1997), 154, 152. See also Yannick Ripa, "Armes d'hommes contre femmes désarmées: De la dimension sexuée de la violence dans la guerre civile espagnole," in *De la Violence et des femmes,* ed. Cécile Dauphin (Paris: Albin Michel, 1997), 131–45.
94 For women's status, see Claire Duchen, *Women's Rights and Women's Lives in France 1944-1968* (London: Routledge, 1994), and Fishman, *Wives,* 1–21, 168–72. For the gender controversy, see Marie-France Brive, "L'Image des femmes à la

Libération," in *La Libération dans le Midi de la France,* ed. Rolande Trempé (Toulouse: Eché Editions, 1986), 389–402; Cheryl A. Koos, "Gender, Anti-individualism, and Nationalism: The Alliance Nationale and the Pronatalist Backlash against the *Femme moderne, 1933–1940*," *French Historical Studies* 19, no. 3 (1996): 699–724; Francine Muel-Dreyfus, *Vichy et, l'éternel féminin: Contribution à une sociologie politique de l'ordre des corps* (Paris: Editions du Seuil, 1996); Miranda Pollard, "Women and the National Revolution," in *Vichy France and the Resistance: Culture and Ideology,* ed. H. R. Kedward and Roger Austin (Totowa, N.J.: Barnes and Noble Books, 1985), 36–47; and Mary Louise Roberts, *Civilization without Sexes: Reconstructing Gender in Postwar France, 1917-1927* (Chicago: University of Chicago Press, 1994).

95 See, for example, Fishman, *Wives,* 167; Elizabeth Heineman, "The Hour of the Woman: Memories of Germany's 'Crisis Years' and West German National Identity," *American Historical Review* 101, no. 2 (1996): 354–95; and Maria Höhn, "Frau im Haus und Girl im *Spiegel:* Discourse on Women in the Interregnum Period of 1945–1949 and the Question of German Identity," *Central European History* 26, no. 1 (1993): 57–90.

96 Hanna Diamond, "Gaining the Vote: A Liberating Experience?" *Modern and Contemporary France,* n.s. 3, no. 2 (1995): 129–48; Claire Duchen, "Une Femme nouvelle pour une France nouvelle?" *Clio* 1 (1995): 151–64; and William Guéraiche, "Les Femmes politiques de 1944 à 1947: Quelle libération?" *Clio* 1 (1995): 165–86.

97 See the reports of local women's meetings in *La Résistance savoyarde,* 15 March 1945; *La Vie nouvelle,* 29 October 1945; and *La Liberté de l'Est,* 14 March 1945.

98 *La Résistance savoyarde,* 14 September 1944.

99 *Le Cantal ouvrier et paysan,* 28 April 1945.

100 Just before the liberation of Savoie, a mayor declined to recommend a woman for a committee position because he did not think she was doing enough for her POW husband (AS 9 M II 76, Correspondance, affaires particulières du Cabinet du Préfet, enquêtes divers, 1944–1949). See also Pollard, 36–47.

101 They also wanted the pubs closed to protect the male vote (*La Croix de Lorraine,* 29 April 1945).

102 See INSEE, *Mouvement économique 1944 à 1957,* 107–8.

103 *La Margeride,* 18 October 1944 and 4 July 1945.

104 For a fascinating discussion of the "sexualization" of Australian women by the American army, see Marilyn Lake, "Female Desires: The Meaning of World War II," in *Feminism and History,* ed. Joan Wallach Scott (Oxford: Oxford University Press, 1996), 429–49.

105 *Le Démocrate de l'Est,* 21 February 1945.

106 The prefect of Meurthe-et-Moselle also banned girls from movie theaters (F1a 4024, 15–28 February 1945).

107 See 72 AJ 384, 15 January 1945–15 February 1945.
108 *La Résistance savoyarde*, 21 September 1944, 12 October 1944, 9 June 1945, and 14 October 1945.
109 Veillon, *Vivre*, 228. Forbidding dancing as inappropriate during a time of national crisis was neither a new nor a particularly French idea. See Adrian Gregory, *The Silence of Memory: Armistice Day, 1919–1946* (Oxford: Berg, 1994), 61–77; Michael H. Kater, "Forbidden Fruit? Jazz in the Third Reich," *American Historical Review* 94, no. 1 (1989): 29; Gary D. Stark, "All Quiet on the Home Front: Popular Entertainments, Censorship, and Civilian Morale in Germany, 1914–1918," in *Authority, Identity, and the Social History of the Great War*, ed. Frans Coetzee and Marilyn Shevin-Coetzee (Providence, R.I.: Berghahn, 1995), 62; and Veillon, *Vivre*, 311–16.
110 Azéma, *From Munich to the Liberation*, 197.
111 Text in *Bulletin officiel du département des Vosges*, 31 October 1944.
112 For complaints that a prefect had authorized such exceptions, see AC R.8.293, CLL Saint-Flour, 25 January 1945, and AC 1 W 409, Réunions publiques et privés, letter of 26 January 1945.
113 For dancing as debauchery, see *La Margeride*, 7 October 1944; *La Démocratie savoyarde*, 3 November 1945; and Weber, 196.
114 *Les Quatre Vallées d'Albertville*, 2 September 1944.
115 *La Margeride*, 28 October 1944. For similar sentiments expressed in letters to the editor, see *La Résistance savoyarde*, 19 October 1944 and 11 January 1945.
116 *La Libération en armes*, 31 March 1945.
117 The dance was held on 15 April 1945, the denunciation was dated 22 April 1945, and the first report was dated 26 April 1945 (AC 1 W 409). For similar sentiments, see *La Femme d'Auvergne*, 21 October 1944.
118 *La Femme d'Auvergne*, 10 March 1945, and *La Margeride*, 30 June 1945.
119 *La Margeride*, 31 January 1945.
120 *La Margeride*, 24 March 1945. See also *La Vie nouvelle*, 25 February 1945.
121 *La Résistance savoyarde*, 8 February 1945. See also *La Résistance des Vosges*, December 1944 and August 1945.
122 *La Résistance savoyarde*, 15 April 1945.
123 *La Résistance savoyarde*, 24 March 1945.
124 *La Savoie française*, 8 November 1944.
125 *Recueil des actes administratifs. Préfecture de la Savoie*, 1 February 1945 and 8 February 1945.
126 *Recueil des actes administratifs. Préfecture de la Savoie*, 30 June 1945.
127 F1a 4021, 1–15 March 1945. For similar cases of student high spirits ending in tangles with the police, see Singer, 66–73.
128 *La Margeride*, 10 January 1945.
129 *La Résistance savoyarde*, 3 November 1945.

130 *La Résistance savoyarde,* 19 May 1945, and *Le Cantal libre,* 26 July 1945.
131 *La Margeride,* 8 December 1945.
132 *Recueil des actes administratifs. Préfecture de la Savoie,* 18 October 1945, and *La Savoie française,* 3 November 1945.
133 For the population movements created by the war, see Michael R. Marrus, *The Unwanted: European Refugees in the Twentieth Century* (Oxford: Oxford University Press, 1985).
134 Annette Wieviorka, *Déportation et génocide: Entre la mémoire et l'oubli* (Paris: Plon, 1992), 106. Official displeasure was not reserved exclusively for Russians; the CRR at Nancy complained that the Poles stationed near Toul were misusing the weapons that the Americans had given them to guard German POWs (F1a 4025, 15–30 October 1945). The CRRs at Rennes and Rouen issued similar complaints (F1a 4029, no. 103, 22 June 1945, CRR Rennes, and no. 157, 25 September 1945, CRR Rouen).
135 F1a 4028, no. 37, 6 February 1945, CRR Limoges; no. 45, 24 February 1945, Prefect Deux-Sèvres; no. 48, 3 March 1945, CRR Limoges; and no. 67, 11 April 1945, CRR Limoges. See also 72 AJ 384, 15 October–15 November 1944; 15 November–15 December 1944, and 15 December 1944–15 January 1945; F1a 4028, no. 29, 18 January 1945, CRR Clermont-Ferrand, and F1a 4021, 15–30 August 1945.
136 I am using the numbers in Matard-Bonucci, 19. See Wieviorka, 423–31, for a discussion of the controversy over the figures. Rioux gives the figures as 1,200,000 POWs, 700,000 laborers, and 200,000 deportees (75,000 Jews, 41,000 resistants, 22,000 "other" political prisoners such as Freemasons, and 50,000 common criminals (Jean-Pierre Rioux, *The Fourth Republic 1944–1958,* trans. Godfrey Rogers [Cambridge: Cambridge University Press, 1987], 13–14). Larkin cites the figures of 44,000 French women drafted to work in Germany and a total of 3.3 percent of the French population working in Germany (Larkin, 102).
137 Sarah Fishman, "Grand Delusions: The Unintended Consequences of Vichy France's Prisoner of War Propaganda," *Journal of Contemporary History* 26 (1991): 229–54.
138 Burrin, 289–90.
139 Burrin, 292.
140 Burrin, 288–93.
141 Wieviorka 25–30, 47–48, 67.
142 F1a 4021, 15–30 August 1945. Research has since reduced the number of deportees from Cantal to 324, made up of 78 resistants (including 9 women), 127 hostages, 105 "racial deportees" (including 13 women), 12 deported for political motives, and 2 common criminals. Of these, 102 returned (72 AJ 106, Eugène Martres, "Le Cantal de 1940 à 1944, Déportation, Internement" [typescript, n.d.]).
143 F1a 4022, 18 February 1945, and F2 4395 (1947).
144 F2 4403, 28 February 1947.

145 170 POWs, 114 *requis*, 11 political prisoners, and 14 deportees *"outre-Rhin"* according to undated lists compiled by the town hall and the Service social de l'armée. The author would like to thank Deputy Mayor Fevotte for making these lists available to her.
146 *La Résistance des Vosges,* November 1945.
147 *La Margeride,* 5 May 1945.
148 For the history and organization of the Ministry of PDR, see François Cochet, *Les Exclus de la victoire: Histoire des prisonniers de guerre, déportés et STO (1945-1985)* (Paris: Editions SPM et Kronos, 1992), 89–150, and Wieviorka, 31–67.
149 See *La Margeride,* 9 December 1944 and 20 January 1945. For the sacrifices these packages entailed for the families of POWs, see Fishman, *Wives,* 59.
150 *La Margeride,* 10 January 1945.
151 FIC III 1211, 16 April 1945.
152 *La Résistance savoyarde,* 22 February 1945.
153 *La Liberté de l'Est,* 19 December 1945, and *La Résistance savoyarde,* 14 December 1944.
154 *La Margeride,* 21 March 1945.
155 *La Résistance savoyarde,* 16 November 1944 and 23 November 1944.
156 *La Résistance savoyarde,* 5 May 1945.
157 *Le Démocrate de l'Est,* 30 January 1945.
158 *Le Démocrate de l'Est,* 19–20 November 1944.
159 *Le Démocrate de l'Est,* 17 October 1944.
160 *La Croix de Lorraine,* 17 December 1944.
161 *Le Démocrate de l'Est,* 30 January 1944.
162 For the accounts of Moûtiers' CEA in April and May 1945, see *La Résistance savoyarde,* 19 May 1945.
163 *La Margeride,* 1 November 1944, and *La Résistance savoyarde,* 19 October 1944.
164 *La Margeride,* 10 February 1945, CEA of Paulhenc.
165 F1a 4024, 1–15 January 1945.
166 FIC III 1226, 16 October 1945.
167 *La Margeride,* 15 January 1946.
168 Olga Wormser-Migot, *Le Retour des déportés: Quand les Alliés ouvrirent les portes...,* rev. ed. (Brussels: Editions Complexe, 1985), 174–77.
169 For the possible paths of repatriation, see Cochet, 58–80, and Wieviorka, 81–104, 111–20.
170 Cochet, 141–42.
171 FIC III 1211, 16 April 1945.
172 *Journal officiel de la République française,* ordinances of 5 April 1945, 20 April 1945, 1 May 1945, 11 May 1945, 26 May 1945, 22 June 1945, 5 October 1945, and 18 October 1945; this last provided for a bonus of five thousand francs for certain of the Alsatian *Malgré-nous.*

286   Notes to Chapter Two

173   *Le Cantal libre,* 6 September 1945; F1a 4025 1–15 September 1945, 15–30 November 1945, and 1–15 January 1946; and Cochet, 147.
174   F1a 4028, no. 100, 18 June 1945, CRR Dijon, and F1a 4021 (Dijon), letter from the Minister of PDR to the Minister of the Interior, 27 June 1945.
175   *La Margeride,* 31 March 1945, 28 April 1945, and 2 May 1945. The council voted a thirty-thousand-franc subvention; CM Saint-Flour, 9 June 1945.
176   *La Résistance savoyarde,* 28 April 1945, and *La Liberté de l'Est,* 26 April 1945. See also CM Moûtiers, 10 July 1945.
177   F1a 4022, 15 March–15 April 1945.
178   Of these, six of the Sanflorains, including all the women, returned. Twelve Moutiérains returned in 1945, leaving eight missing at the end of the year.
179   F1a 4028, no. 91, 4 June 1945, CRR Bordeaux.
180   *La Vie nouvelle,* 24 June 1945.
181   For the reception of the third woman, see *La Margeride,* 21 April 1945 and 28 April 1945.
182   *La Voix du Cantal,* 10 February 1945.
183   *La Cantal libre,* 23 May 1945, and *La Margeride,* 19 May 1945 and 26 May 1945.
184   Matard-Bonucci, 61–73. The claim in the same work (163–75) that the news of the camps was softened through information filters may be accurate for news about the Jewish experience in the extermination camps such as Auschwitz but is hard to reconcile with events in the provinces concerning the news from concentration camps like Buchenwald. For the conflict between SHAEF's policy of publicity and the GPRF's policy of censorship, see Wieviorka, 62–64, 78–81.
185   *La Résistance savoyarde,* 8 July 1945. This was an all-too-common tragedy echoed in Rambervillers and Saint-Flour as well as throughout the country. The death rates in some of the concentration camps remained alarmingly high after their liberation because the inmates were so wretchedly malnourished and had been exposed to typhus and other diseases before their liberation. For the depths of illness that could afflict deportees and the emotional shock it caused their families, see Marguerite Duras, *The War: A Memoir,* trans. Barbara Bray (New York: Pantheon, 1986), 5–72.
186   *La Résistance savoyarde,* 2 December 1945.
187   See *La Margeride,* 13 December 1944, and *La Liberté de l'Est,* 7 April 1945. *Le Travailleur vosgien* (15 July 1945) interviewed a survivor of Auschwitz.
188   *La Résistance savoyarde,* 19 May 1945.
189   *La Travailleur vosgien,* 5 August 1945; see also F1a 4029, no. 143, 4 September 1945, CRR Poitiers.
190   F1a 4028, no. 98, 14 June 1945, CRR Rouen. For the prevalence of these images in still and motion pictures, see Maurice Agulhon, *The French Republic 1879–1992,* trans. Antonia Nevill (Oxford: Blackwell, 1993), 323.
191   *La Liberté de l'Est,* 4 August 1945 and 5–6 August 1945. *Le Travailleur vosgien*

Notes to Chapter Two 287

(12 August 1945) complained that the theater showing the film had been covered with pictures of Pétain a year earlier.
192 F1a 4028, no. 88, 31 May 1945, CRR Poitiers.
193 F1a 4022, 15 March–15 April 1945.
194 *Le Cantal libre*, 25 April 1945.
195 The exact figures of death rates are unknown. Wieviorka givens a return rate of 59 percent for deportees and 3 percent for Jewish "racial" deportees (Wieviorka, 20–21, 423–31). See also Lagrou, 192.
196 F1a 4024, 15–31 May 1945.
197 See, for example, F1a 4028, no. 73, 21 April 1945, CRR Châlons-sur-Marne.
198 *Le Réveil des Vosges*, 8 July 1945.
199 *La Résistance savoyarde*, 22 December 1945.
200 *Le Réveil des Vosges*, 8 July 1945.
201 72 AJ 384, 15 May–15 June 1945.
202 In one unusual case, however, the same anger swung in the opposite direction, onto the heads of local resistants whom their neighbors blamed for the deaths of twenty-five men in deportation because their actions had provoked German retaliation; F1a 4024, 15–31 May 1945. For the implications of this reasoning among the Italian peasantry, see Absalom, 184.
203 See Muel-Dreyfus for Vichy's propaganda regarding women. This same reasoning motivated the Nationalists' brutal treatment of Republican women during the Spanish Civil War; see Ripa, "Armes d'hommes," 138–39.
204 The woman did not press charges against her attackers (*La Liberté de l'Est*, 24 May 1945 and 26 May 1945). Another crowd in Epinal hurled bits of glass and roof tiles at women voluntary laborers and followed them to the police station as they were being taken into protective custody (F1a 4029, no. 117, 17 July 1945, Prefect Vosges).
205 He did this, at least in part, out of concern that such actions were making a "deplorable" impression on American soldiers (*La Liberté de l'Est*, 3–4 June 1945).
206 Dodin, 127.
207 *Recueil des actes administratifs. Prefecture de la Savoié*, 30 August 1945, and *La Résistance savoyarde*, 23 June 1945 and 21 July 1945.
208 F1c III 1211, 16 August 1945.
209 F1a 4029, no. 113, 6 July 1945, Prefect Isère, and F1c III 1226, 16 July 1945. See also F1a 4028 and 4029, April–June 1945; *La Liberté de l'Est*, 9 June 1945; and Dodin, 68–69, 178.
210 *Le Cantal libre*, 13 June 1945, and *La Margeride*, 13 June 1945.
211 F1a 4024, 15–31 May 1945.
212 See 72 AJ 384, April–June 1945.
213 The publication of the gendarme's name ensured that he would face community, if not official, censure (*La Liberté de l'Est*, 13 June 1945).

214 *La Margeride*, 28 April 1945, editorial entitled "Espérance."
215 *La Croix de Lorraine*, 24 June 1945.
216 See 72 AJ 384, 15 May–15 June 1945.
217 F1a 4028, no. 100, 16 June 1945, Prefect Jura.
218 For example, *La Liberté de l'Est*, 3 April 1945, and *La Margeride*, 27 June 1945.
219 *La Liberté de l'Est*, 3–4 June 1945. See also F1C III 1211, 16 September 1945. For thank-yous from deportees, see *La Liberté de l'Est*, 19 June 1945, 23 June 1945, and 28 June 1945, and *La Résistance des Vosges*, July 1945.
220 See 72 AJ 384, 16 July–16 August 1945.
221 *Le Travailleur vosgien*, 1 July 1945, and *La Résistance des Vosges*, July 1945; the correspondant complained about the teacher because of the preceived insult to the town's survivors of Buchenwald.
222 See *La Résistance savoyarde*, 14 July 1945, 15 September 1945, and 29 September 1945; *La Liberté de l'Est*, 28 June 1945, 30 August 1945, and 20 November 1945; and *Le Travailleur vosgien*, 26 August 1945. A former POW who returned late in 1945 from Eastern Europe could nevertheless not remember any notice being taken of his homecoming (personal interview with the author, 1991).
223 *La Margeride*, 30 June 1945. Reports of such events can be found in *La Margeride* throughout the summer.
224 F1a 4025, 1–15 August 1945.
225 Dodin, 143.
226 These would be the German fiancées of French POWs or laborers (*La Margeride*, 15 December 1945).
227 Lagrou, 194, and Rousso, *Vichy Syndrome*, 16–18.
228 Lagrou, 194–97, and Matard-Bonucci and Lynch, 115, 164, 174, 216.
229 Matard-Bonnuci and Lynch, 148, 173, 233.
230 F1a 4021 (Dijon), 1–15 July 1945.
231 Fishman, *Wives*, 154.
232 *La Margeride*, 29 November 1944.
233 F1a 4029, no. 129, 7 August 1945, CRR Poitiers.
234 For the use of deportation and repatriation in the PCF/Gaullist skirmishes, see Lagrou, 201–5; Matard-Bonucci and Lynch, 215–30; Cochet, 130–34; and Jean-Pierre Rioux, "'Cette immense joie pleine de larmes': Les Français et le 'jour V,'" in *8 Mai 1945: La Victoire en Europe*, edited by Maurice Vaïsse (Lyon: La Manufacture, 1985), 328.
235 F1a 4029, no. 176, 4 December 1945, Prefect Ariège. Other war victims also grew tired of the government's efforts; in September 1945, 160 sinistrés in Epinal staged a spontaneous demonstration in support of one of their number's right to comandeer an apartment (*La Liberté de l'Est*, 20 September 1945, and also 4 April 1945 and *Le Réveil des Vosges*, 27 January 1946). The Communist press also complained that collaborators were still working in the government's Secours social

(*La Femme d'Auvergne*, 18 November 1944, and *Le Travailleur vosgien*, 24 June 1945).
236 F1a 4029, no. 106, 27 June 1945, CRR Bordeaux, and no. 110, 3 July 1945, CRR Limoges; F1a 4021, 1–15 June 1945, and 72 AJ 384, 16 July–15 August 1945. For more violent expressions of frustration, see *La Liberté de l'Est*, 21 December 1945. See also F1a 4029, no. 103, 22 June 1945, Prefect Finistère.
237 *La Liberté de l'Est*, 12 June 1945.

CHAPTER 3 LEGAL JUSTICE AND THE
PURGE OF COLLABORATORS

1 Novick, 56–59. For a full discussion of the problems associated with determining the numbers of summary executions, see Henry Rousso, "L'Epuration en France, une histoire inachevée," *Vingtième Siècle* 23 (1992): 81–84.
2 For an example of the black legend, see Philippe Bourdrel, *L'Epuration sauvage, 1944–1945*, 2 vols. (Paris: Perrin, 1988–91). For examples of lynchings, see Lottman, 106–31.
3 For a recalcitrant bureaucrat "purged" by early retirement, see F1c III 1211, 16 February 1945 and 16 March 1945.
4 See, for example, *La Résistance savoyarde*, 14 September 1944.
5 For the importance of *"renouvellement"* in the national purge, see Novick, vii.
6 *Le Réveil des Vosges*, 27 May 1945; *La Croix de Lorraine*, 19 November 1944; and *La Résistance savoyarde*, 1 September 1945. See also the prefect's speech in *La Savoie française*, 5 October 1944.
7 Colin Lucas, "The Theory and Practice of Denunciation in the French Revolution," *Journal of Modern History* 68, no. 4 (1996): 768–85.
8 Sheila Fitzpatrick and Robert Gellately, "Introduction to the Practices of Denunciation in Modern European History," *Journal of Modern History* 68, no. 4 (1996): 764.
9 For denunciation as a tool for involving the authorities in the community, see John Connelly, "The Uses of *Volksgemeinschaft:* Letters to the NSDAP Kreisleitung Eisenach, 1939–1940," *Journal of Modern History* 68, no. 4 (1996): 899–930. For "weapons of the weak," see James C. Scott, *Weapons of the Weak: Everyday Forms of Peasant Resistance* (New Haven: Yale University Press, 1985).
10 Burrin, 215.
11 For an eloquent listing of the possibilities, see Dodin, 99.
12 *La Margeride*, 30 December 1944.
13 *La Résistance savoyarde*, 12 January 1946.
14 *La Cantal libre*, 31 December 1944 and 2 January 1945.
15 *La Margeride*, 14 October 1944 and 21 October 1944.
16 Novick explains the legal purge in detail. For the relevant ordinances and laws,

see P. H. Doublet, *La Collaboration: L'Épuration, la confiscation, les réparations aux victimes de l'occupation* (Paris: Librairie générale de droit et de jurisprudence, 1945). The government could employ several approaches to the purge, including bureaucratic procedures leading to dismissal from employment in both the public and private sectors, confiscation of the profits of economic collaboration, fines for minor offenses, and legal procedures against criminal activity. Because the discussion in the provinces in 1944–45 took the government's national purge as the legal purge, only that aspect will be discussed here. Rousso, "Epuration," offers the best overview. For the administrative purge, see François Rouquet, *L'Epuration dans l'administration française* (Paris: Editions du CNRS, 1993), and Singer. For overviews of the purge other than those already cited, see Henri Amouroux, *La Grande Histoire des Français après l'occupation,* vol. 9, "Les Règlements de comptes, septembre 1944–janvier 1945" (Paris: Robert Laffont, 1991), and Marcel Baudot, "L'Épuration: Bilan chiffré," *Bulletin de l'Institut d'histoire du temps présent* 25 (1986): 37–53.

17 For a bitter local commentary, see *La Résistance savoyarde,* 16 June 1945. For these trials, see Louis Noguères, *La Haute Cour de la Libération (1944–1949)* (Paris: Editions de Minuit, 1965).

18 For an illustration of an "ordinary case," see François Rouquet, "Une Affaire ordinarie d'épuration: Le cas A," *Vingtième Siècle* 33 (1992): 118–25.

19 For official clarifications of these unusual procedures, see *La Résistance savoyarde,* 21 December 1944, or *La Croix de Lorraine,* 12–19 August 1945.

20 Novick, 147–48.

21 Novick, 140–56.

22 See the protests against not being consulted by the judiciary issued by the CDL of Cantal in *Le Patriote de Cantal,* 3 March 1945.

23 See F1a 4028, no. 18, 23 December 1944, Prefect Drôme.

24 For example, see the labyrinthine case of an FFI chaplain accused of denouncing two Jews (but acquitted) in *La Margeride,* 5 December 1945.

25 F1a 4024, 15–31 January 1945.

26 F1a 4028, no. 29, 18 January 1945, Prefect Tarn.

27 The judicial system did not enjoy a sterling reputation for impartiality even before the war. See Weber, 132–36.

28 F1c III 1211, 16 May 1945, 16 July 1945, and 16 October 1945.

29 *Le Réveil des Vosges,* 30 September 1945. Similarly, the saying next to the masthead of *La Résistance des Vosges,* July 1945, read: "The collaborators have taken to the maquis . . . of [judicial] procedure."

30 F1c III 1211, 16 November 1945. In contrast, see a unique defense of the courts by a Savoyard juror in *La Résistance savoyarde,* 22 April 1945.

31 F1a 4024, 1–15 March 1945.

32 See CM Rambervillers, 26 May 1945.

33 *La Résistance savoyarde*, 19 October 1944.
34 *La Résistance savoyarde*, 7 April 1945.
35 *La Résistance savoyarde*, 23 June 1945.
36 *Le Réveil des Vosges*, 17 June 1945.
37 *Le Travailleur vosgien*, 22 February 1946.
38 *La Margeride*, 20 January 1945.
39 *La Démocratie savoyarde*, 25 November 1944. See also *La Résistance savoyarde*, 24 March 1945 and 22 December 1945, and *Le Réveil des Vosges*, 25 February 1945.
40 See, for instance, *La Résistance savoyarde*, 2 December 1945, for an audience "resolutely hostile" to the accused, and 26 January 1945 for an audience kindly disposed to the defendant.
41 F1a 4024, 1–15 June 1945.
42 *La Liberté de l'Est*, 4 July 1945.
43 The number of persons constrained by administrative internment is unknown but may fall between 60,000 and 120,000 (Rousso, "Epuration," 102). For the role of administrative internment in restoring public confidence in the government and its purge, and thereby restoring order, see F1a 4028, no. 23, 4 January 1945, CRR Marseille.
44 F1c III 1226, 15 May–15 June 1945.
45 F1a 4021, 15–31 May 1945 and 1–15 June 1945.
46 See Novick, 217–21.
47 De Gaulle explained his decision to pardon 1,303 individuals condemned to death, including all of the women and most minors, as a means of maintaining order and ensuring impartiality in the midst of inflamed passions and calls for revenge. The same considerations led the government to mitigate "the effect of a large number of decisions, particularly in the case of the unfortunate young men who had been lured into the 'Militia,' the 'Legion of French Volunteers,' or the 'African Phalanx.'" De Gaulle did, however, deny the requests for clemency of 768 men condemned to death "whose personal and spontaneous action had caused the death of other Frenchmen or directly aided the enemy" (de Gaulle, *The Complete War Memoirs of Charles de Gaulle*, trans. by Jonathan Griffin and Richard Howard [New York: Simon and Schuster, 1955–60], 789–92).
48 For a comparison with other countries, see Novick, 209–14.
49 Rousso, *Vichy Syndrome*, 16–18. For a fuller discussion of this myth, see chapter 2 above and chapter 5 below.
50 Marcel Baudot, "La Résistance française face aux problèmes de répression et d'épuration," *Revue d'histoire de la deuxième guerre mondiale* 81 (1971): 33. For the use of pardons as a demonstration of mercy designed to reinforce the vertical bonds of paternalism, see Douglas Hay, "Property, Authority and the Criminal Law," in *Albion's Fatal Tree: Crime and Society in Eighteenth-Century England*, ed. Douglas Hay (London: Allen Lane, 1975), 44–48.

51 F1a 4025, 15–30 September 1945.
52 Italics mine. F1c III 1226, 16 June 1945.
53 See the prefect of Cantal's warnings in F1c III 1226, 16 September 1945, and the prefect of the Vosges' public announcement designed to calm the "emotion" provoked by certain judgments and releases in *La Croix de Lorraine*, 12–19 August 1945.
54 F1a 4021, 1–15 June 1945.
55 F1a 4028, no. 83, 8 May 1945, Prefect Hérault.
56 *Le Travailleur vosgien*, 21 December 1945.
57 See Jean-Pierre Azéma, "La Milice," *Vingtième Siècle* 28 (1990): 83–105; Marc O. Baruch, *Servir l'Etat français: L'Administration en France de 1940 à 1944* (Paris: Fayard, 1997), 529–75; Burrin, 444–64; J. Delperrie de Bayac, *Histoire de la Milice*, 2 vols. (Paris: Fayard, 1969).
58 For example, *La Margeride*, 18 October 1945, and *La Résistance savoyarde*, 24 November 1945.
59 *La Résistance savoyarde*, 3 November 1945.
60 *La Margeride*, 3 February 1945; see also 18 October 1944 for another case.
61 F1a 4021, 1–15 March 1945; see also "Des Lecteurs se sont émus," *La Margeride*, 20 January 1945.
62 *La Résistance savoyarde*, 6 October 1945. For similar riots in Chambéry, see F1c III 1226, 15 May–15 June 1945 and 15 June–15 July 1945; *La Résistance savoyarde*, 23 June 1945; and Perry Biddiscombe, "The French Resistance and the Chambéry Incident of June 1945," *French History* 11, no. 4 (1997): 438–60.
63 See AS 9 M III 48, Gendarmerie Albertville, 21 October 1946.
64 See F1a 4021, 1–15 June 1945.
65 Sympathizers with collaboration, of course, also objected to the purge's idea of justice, but on different grounds than those that were publicly expressed in 1944–45.
66 This is the total figure for court activity up to 1951; the numbers for 1944–45 would of course be much lower. It contrasts sharply with the 350,000 dossiers submitted to the courts by the purge committees, police, gendarmerie, and army (Rousso, "Epuration," 92–93, 102). For a breakdown of sentences passed by the courts, see Rousso, "Epuration," 92.
67 F1c III 1211, 16 May 1945.
68 For example, *Le Travailleur vosgien*, 18 March 1945, or *Le Réveil des Vosges*, 31 December 1944.
69 72 AJ 384, 15 November–15 December 1944.
70 F1a 4028, no. 16, 19 December 1944, CRR Angers. See also F1a 4021, 1–15 November 1944.
71 *Le Réveil des Vosges*, 5 November 1944. See also *La Margeride*, 25 October 1944.
72 For head shavings see Brive, "L'Image"; Alain Brossat, *Les Tondues: Un Car-*

naval moche (Levallois-Perret: Manya, 1992); Luc Capdevila, "La 'collaboration sentimentale': Antipatriotism ou sexualité hors-normes? (Lorient, mai 1945)," Cahiers de l'IHTP 31 (1995): 67–82; Corran Laurens, "'La Femme au turban': Les Femmes tondues," in The Liberation of France: Image and Event, ed. H. R. Kedward and Nancy Wood (Oxford: Berg, 1995), 155–79; Fabrice Virgili, "Les 'Tondues' à la Libération: Le Corps des femmes, enjeu d'une réappropriation," Clio 1 (1995): 111–27; and Fabrice Virgili, "Les Tontes de la Libération en France," Cahiers de l'IHTP 31 (1995): 53–66. For an artistic interpretation, see Marguerite Duras, Hiroshima mon amour, trans. Richard Seaver, full text from a film produced by Alain Resnais (New York: Grove, 1961). For an analysis of this movie as a portrayal of head shaving as a crime against love, see Brossat, Tondues, 53–67.

73 La Margeride, 24 November 1945. Such thinking was not specific to France at the liberation; see Ripa, "Armes d'hommes."

74 La Margeride, 21 February 1945.

75 Françoise LeClerc and Michèle Weindling, "La Répression des femmes coupables de collaboration," Clio 1 (1995): 129–50.

76 La Savoie française, 26 August 1944.

77 See AC 1 W 359.

78 La Croix de Lorraine, 29 October 1944. Originally published in Courrier français du témoignage chrétien, 9 September 1944.

79 Les Quatre Vallées d'Albertville, 2 September 1944.

80 Brossat, Tondues, 124.

81 Brossat, Tondues, 202.

82 E. P. Thompson, Customs in Common: Studies in Traditional Popular Culture (New York: The New Press, 1993), 530. Thompson, on p. 524, specifically suggests that the head shavings might prove to be an example of twentieth-century rough music.

83 For this transition in the eighteenth and nineteenth centuries, see Michel Foucault, Discipline and Punish: The Birth of the Prison, trans. Alan Sheridan (New York: Vintage, 1979).

84 Donald Kelley, ed. Versions of History (New Haven: Yale University Press, 1991), 98.

85 Peter Linebaugh, The London Hanged: Crime and Civil Society in the Eighteenth Century (Cambridge: Cambridge University Press, 1992), 281.

86 Lubbock Avalanche-Journal, 8 August 1997.

87 Burrin, 212.

88 The punishment also befell German women who were raped by foreign men; see Martin Kitchen, Nazi Germany at War (New York: Longman, 1995), 69–70. See also Jill Stephenson, "'Emancipation' and Its Problems: War and Society in Württemberg 1939–45," European History Quarterly 17 (1987): 356–57.

Notes to Chapter Three

89 Yannick Ripa, "Armes d'hommes" and "La Tonte purificatrice des républicaines pendant la guerre civile espagnole," *Cahiers de l'IHTP*, 31 (1995): 39–52.

90 The Poles flogged men for similar offenses, Stefan Korbonski, *The Polish Underground State: A Guide to the Underground, 1939-1945*, trans. Marta Erdman (New York: Hippocrene Books, 1978), 76, and Mark Mazower, *Inside Hitler's Greece: The Experience of Occupation 1941-44* (New Haven: Yale University Press), 162, 288.

91 Douglas Botting, *From the Ruins of the Reich: Germany 1945-1949* (New York: Meridian, 1985), 257.

92 No one knows how many French women had German lovers during the occupation. Two figures, however, sketch a rough if unreliable estimate. There were perhaps fifty to seventy-five thousand Franco-German children born to such dangerous liaisons, but some may have been the product of rape and others not German at all. And not every encounter produced a child. Alternatively, ten to twenty thousand women were punished for horizontal collaboration through the legal and professional purges (Burrin, 213).

93 Fishman, *Wives*, 141.

94 *La Margeride*, 4 July 1945.

95 For the association of French women with Marianne and therefore the nation, see Virgili, "Les Tontes de la Libération," 64. For the contemporary understanding of collaboration as a "feminine" surrender to the "masculine" enemy, see Michael Kelly, "The View of Collaboration during the *Après-Guerre*," in *Collaboration in France*, ed. G. Hirschfeld (Oxford: Berg, 1989), 237–51.

96 For a case of two women murdered by vigilantes after the authorities failed to arrest them for collaboration, see F1a 4028, no. 18, 23 December 1944, CRR Rennes.

97 F1a 4021, 1–15 February 1945.

98 *La Margeride*, 31 March 1945.

99 *La Résistance savoyarde*, 24 March 1945, 31 March 1945, and 15 April 1945.

100 Fabrice Virgili has identified five periods of head shaving extending into 1946, a duration of time that this study confirms ("*Les Femmes tondues:* Liberation and the Shame of Collaboration," paper presented at the Contemporary History Conference "After the War Was Over: Reconstructing the Family, Society and the Law in Southern Europe, 1944–1950," University of Sussex, July 1996).

101 *La Résistance savoyarde*, 27 October 1945.

102 See 72 AJ 384, 15 April–15 May 1945, for a national survey of protests against and mob harassments, even lynchings, of individuals discharged from custody.

103 F2 4366, arrondissement de Saint-Flour.

104 Brossat, *Tondues*, 148–55; *Libération*, 22–23 October 1983; *Le Monde*, 22 October 1983.

105 *La Margeride*, 15 November 1944. Another report appears in *La Margeride*, 21 October 1944.

106 *La Margeride*, 18 October 1944. For examples, in a very different context, of how a community can tailor a national purge to the local politics of reputation, see Lynne Viola, "The Second Coming: Class Enemies in the Soviet Countryside, 1927–1935," in *Stalinist Terror: New Perspectives*, ed. J. Arch Getty and Roberta T. Manning (Cambridge: Cambridge University Press, 1993), 65–98.
107 For examples, see *Le Cantal libre*, 6 February 1945, and *Le Démocrate de l'Est*, 8 March 1945.
108 *La Margeride*, 30 December 1944.
109 *La Liberté de l'Est*, 10 July 1945; *La Margeride*, 23 September 1944; *La Résistance des Vosges*, 10 March 1945; and *La Résistance savoyarde*, 28 September 1944.
110 *La Margeride*, 10 February 1945.
111 *Le Cantal libre*, 8 November 1944 and 9 November 1944; also see *La Margeride*, 11 November 1944. In the departmental capital of Aurillac that same week, 150 armed FFIs attacked the prison, presumably either to release comrades arrested by the police or to murder collaborators in police custody (72 AJ 384, 15 October–15 November 1944).
112 See AC 1 W 359, letter from Prefect of Cantal to CRR at Clermont-Ferrand, 9 November 1944.
113 See AC 1 W 359, gendarme report of 31 March 1945, and Inspecteur de police judiciaire à Clermont-Ferrand, 26 April 1945.
114 F1C III 1211, 16 April 1945.
115 *La Margeride*, 26 July 1945.
116 All the sentences in Cantal were commuted. Sentences passed by the departmental Cours de Justice were as follows:

	Cantal	Savoie	Vosges
death	23	93	58
in absentia	18	71	37
forced labor	5	171	109
imprisonment	26	215	248
acquittals	5	95	233

See Martres, *Cantal*, 645; AN F2 4395 (Savoie, 1947), and F2 4403 (Vosges, 1947).
117 *La Margeride*, 4 October 1944.
118 *La Margeride*, 11 November 1944.
119 *La Margeride*, 20 December 1944.
120 *La Voix du Cantal*, 11 November 1944.
121 *Le Cantal ouvrier et paysan*, 7 April 1945.
122 *Le Cantal ouvrier et paysan*, 14 April 1945.
123 Mme. Frachet, "Septembre 1944" (typescript, 1944). The author would like to thank M. Jean-Claude Kempf of Rambervillers for making this and the following unpublished accounts available to her.

124 Mme. Garnier, "La Libération, août–octobre 1944" (typescript, 1944).
125 Jean Vartier, "Rambervillers, son occupation, sa libération" (typescript, 1945).
126 Jean Mueth, "Rapport" (typescript, October 1944).
127 Mario Faivre, "Notes à propos de l'année 1944" (typescript, n.d. [1945?]). For less reliable alternative accounts of the head shavings, see *Le Réveil des Vosges*, 14 December 1944, and *Le Travailleur vosgien*, 15 April 1945 and 20 January 1946.
128 The same interpretation can be found in Novick, 69.
129 Exposés can be found throughout the après-libération press; in one, a correspondent simply printed a letter of denunciation sent to the Vichy authorities in 1942 without any comment (*La Margeride*, 10 February 1945).
130 *Le Réveil des Vosges*, 14 January 1945.
131 See an unusual case in CM Saint-Flour, 30 December 1944, and the MP reports in *La Résistance savoyarde*, 21 September 1944 and 14 December 1944.
132 *Le Réveil des Vosges*, 22 April 1945.
133 *Le Travailleur vosgien*, 13 May 1945.
134 *La Margeride*, 23 December 1944. The rhetoric against black marketeering will be examined more extensively in chapter 4.
135 See an article branding an occupation-era mayor as a coward on dubious grounds in *Le Réveil des Vosges*, 21 January 1945.
136 *Le Travailleur vosgien*, 13 May 1945.
137 *La Liberté de l'Est*, 16 March 1945, and F1a 4024, 15–30 March 1945.
138 F1a 4024, 1–15 June 1945; 72 AJ 384, 15 May–15 June 1945; and *La Liberté de l'Est*, 3–4 June 1945 and 5 June 1945.
139 F1a 4024, 15–31 May 1945.
140 F1a 4028, no. 67, 11 April 1945, Prefect Dordogne. For a "Secret Purge Committee" in Meurthe-et-Moselle, see F1a 4025, 1–15 August 1945.
141 *Le Travailleur vosgien*, 10 June 1945.
142 F1a 4025, 1–15 July 1945.
143 *La Liberté de l'Est*, 1 September 1945; see also Amouroux, 78.
144 *La Liberté de l'Est*, 31 August 1945.
145 The article also reported that the Parisian edition of *Humanité* placed the murders close to Nancy and blamed them on the electoral maneuvering of the Comité des Forges, an absurd concoction in the reporter's eyes (*La Croix de Lorraine*, 9 September 1945).
146 See *La Liberté de l'Est*, 12 June 1945, and *La Croix de Lorraine*, 19 November 1945.
147 F1a 4025, 1–15 September 1945.
148 See, for example, *La Liberté de l'Est*, 11 February 1946.
149 As proclaimed on the Monument to the Tarin Resistance in Moûtiers.
150 *La Résistance savoyarde*, 21 September 1944.
151 *La Résistance savoyarde*, 21 September 1944.

Notes to Chapter Three 297

152 *La Résistance savoyarde*, 21 September 1944, and *L'Echo des vallées d'Albertville*, 30 September 1944.
153 *La Résistance savoyarde*, 21 September 1944.
154 The cases were transferred to the 2ᵉ Bureau because the Cour de Justice had not yet replaced the court-martial (*La Résistance savoyarde*, 23 November 1944).
155 The CRR reported the suppression of all such self-styled *prévôtés* in January 1945 (F1a 4022, 16–31 January 1945).
156 *La Résistance savoyarde*, 14 December 1944.
157 *La Résistance savoyarde*, 21 September 1944; see also 23 November 1944 and 22 April 1945.
158 *La Résistance savoyarde*, 15 April 1945.
159 See AS 346 R7, Affaires diverses, 1941–45, attentats-biens. Also see brief notices in *La Résistance savoyarde*, 30 November 1944, and *La Vie nouvelle*, 10 December 1944.
160 *La Résistance savoyarde*, 16 November 1944.
161 *La Résistance savoyarde*, 19 May 1945, and *La Vie nouvelle*, 3 June 1945. For details about the elections, see chapter 6.
162 *La Résistance savoyarde*, 2 June 1945.
163 *La Résistance savoyarde*, 19 May 1945.
164 *La Résistance savoyarde*, 2 June 1945.
165 Thompson, *Customs*, 530.
166 The law of 30 January 1979 closed most archival records covering 1940–46 to protect the privacy and honor of French citizens. Scholars can request special permission to see particular files, but the complexity of the authorization procedure makes the granting of such permission uncertain. Furthermore, the justice records that presumably hold information about vigilantes are more thoroughly inaccessible through one expedient or another, such as simply neglecting to catalog them. Recent changes in the laws, however, might mean that the relevant documents are now available.
167 F1c III 1226, 16 July 1945.
168 F1a 4029, no. 143, 4 September 1945, CRR Poitiers, and F1a 4028, no. 44, 22 February 1945, CRR Lyon.
169 Luc Capdevila, "Local Uses of Violence after Liberation: Reconstruction and Self-Definition in 'Petite Bretagne,' August 1944–early 1946," paper presented at the Contemporary History Conference "After the War Was Over: Reconstructing the Family, Society and the Law in Southern Europe 1944–1950," University of Sussex, July 1996.
170 For the simultaneous abduction and murder of four men in different parts of Chambéry, see *La Résistance savoyarde*, 7 December 1944.
171 The prefect of Tarn opined that vigilante attacks were "motivated, most of the time, by personal vengeance . . . [or] . . . by quarrels within a village" (F1a 4029, no. 145, 4 September 1945, Prefect Tarn).

Notes to Chapter Three

172 Luca Alessandrini, "The Option of Violence: Partisan Activity in the Bologna Area, 1945–1948," paper presented at the Contemporary History Conference "After the War Was Over: Reconstructing the Family, Society and the Law in Southern Europe 1944–1950," University of Sussex, July 1996.
173 See AS 346 R7, RG Albertville, 21 December 1944.
174 See 72 AJ 384, 15 September–15 October 1945; F1a 4021, 1–15 April 1945.
175 The CRR commented that "if on the whole public opinion disapproves of such gestures, it nonetheless recognizes that the character of the victims, of whom two are dead, does not merit spending more time on this incident" (F1a 4021, 1–15 January 1945).
176 See the regular tally of vigilante activity in 72 AJ 384.
177 See AS 346 R 7, attentats-biens.
178 See 72 AJ 384, 15 January–15 February 1945.
179 And 185 summary executions before its liberation (Rousso, "Epuration," 83).
180 *La Résistance savoyarde,* 7 December 1944 and 9 December 1944, and *L'Echo des vallées d'Albertville,* 9 December 1944 and 16 December 1944.
181 72 AJ 384, 15 January–15 February 1945. There were, however, cases in which local authorities cooperated with the investigation (AS 364 R 7, attentat-biens).
182 Dinan and its hinterland experienced a high level of vigilante violence (Capdevila, "Uses of Violence").
183 *L'Amor libre,* 16 June 1945, and 72 AJ 384, 15 May–15 June 1945. The government's campaign against vigilantes, of which these cases form part, helps explain the extraordinary surge in condemnations for illegal possession of weapons in 1945–50 (Aubusson de Cavarlay, Huré, and Pottier, 89, and 128).
184 *La Vie nouvelle,* 7 January 1945.
185 *La Vie nouvelle,* 14 January 1945.
186 F1a 4022, 16–31 January 1945, and *La Résistance savoyarde,* 1 February 1945.
187 F1c III 1226, 5 February–5 March 1945.
188 F1c III 1226, 16 June 1945.
189 *La Démocratie savoyarde,* 7 April 1945; *La Sasson,* 27 June 1945; and *La Résistance savoyarde,* 19 January 1946 and 26 January 1946.
190 F1c III 1226, Prefect of Savoie to Minister of Interior, 17 May 1945.
191 F1c III 1226, 16 September 1945.
192 F1c III 1226, 16 July 1945.
193 F1c III 1226, Prefect of Savoie to Minister of Interior, 17 May 1945.
194 F1c III 1226, 16 August 1945.
195 See *La Résistance savoyarde,* 15 September 1945 and 29 September 1945.
196 *La Résistance savoyarde,* 8 December 1945.
197 The name has been changed in deference to the French amnesty laws.
198 *La Résistance savoyarde,* 27 October 1945.
199 F1c III 1226, 16 December 1945.

200 *La Résistance savoyarde*, 22 December 1945.
201 *La Résistance savoyarde*, 12 January 1946.
202 *La Résistance savoyarde*, 28 December 1945.
203 Italics mine. *La Résistance savoyarde*, 19 January 1946.
204 FIC III 1226, 16 December 1945.
205 *La Résistance savoyarde*, 12 January 1946.
206 *La Résistance savoyarde*, 26 January 1946.
207 *La Résistance savoyarde*, 2 February 1946 and 9 February 1946.
208 *La Résistance savoyarde*, 2 March 1946.
209 FIC III 1226, 16 December 1945.
210 *La Résistance savoyarde*, 19 January 1946.

CHAPTER 4 SOCIAL JUSTICE AND
THE PROVISIONING CRISIS

1 For a survey of the economic situation see Kramer and also Rioux, *Fourth Republic*, 17–28. For war damage, see Azéma, *From Munich to the Liberation*, 130. For the government and consumer management of the shortages in France, see Veillon, *Vivre*, and the special issue of the *Cahiers de l'IHTP*, Dominique Veillon and Jean-Marie Flonneau, eds., "Le Temps des restrictions en France (1939–1949)," *Cahiers de l'IHTP* 32–33 (1996). For agriculture, see Isabel Boussard, "Etat de l'agriculture française aux lendemains de l'occupation (1944–1948)," *Revue d'histoire de la deuxième guerre mondiale* 116 (1979): 69–106, and Isabel Boussard, "Principaux aspects de la politique agricole française pendant la deuxième guerre mondiale," *Revue d'histoire de la deuxième guerre mondiale* 134 (1984): 1–32.

2 72 AJ 384, 16 August–15 September 1945; see also FIC III 1226, 24 October 1944 and 16 October 1945. The overwhelming preoccupation with provisioning lasted until 1949 (Jean-Marie Flonneau, "Le Loiret," *Cahiers de l'IHTP* 32–33 [1996]: 283).

3 For Cantal, see Eugène Martres, "Le Cantal," *Cahiers de l'IHTP* 32–33 (1996): 119–33. The department did, however, suffer the short-term shortages of bread (April 1945) and meat (October 1945) that were felt throughout the country (72 AJ 384, 16 July–16 August 1945; FIC III 1211, 16 August 1945; and *La Margeride*, 25 November 1945). In Savoie, the military personnel were in the frontier army or in repatriation centers, training camps, or hospitals (FIC III 1226, 16 April 1945).

4 Dodin, 129–50.
5 *La Liberté de l'Est*, 3–4 June 1945.
6 F1a 4025, 15–30 September 1945.
7 See AS Rav 67, September 1944.
8 *La Résistance savoyarde*, 21 September 1944.
9 See AS Rav 466.

10   See CM Rambervillers, 27 July 1945, and CM Saint-Flour, 8 December 1944.
11   The new category meant larger rations of pasta, eggs, and butter (from 225 grams per month to 300 grams per month). *La Résistance savoyarde*, 30 June 1945 and 8 July 1945.
12   *La Margeride*, 3 February 1945, and *Le Cantal libre*, 2 February 1945.
13   See CM Rambervillers, 27 July 1945, and AC R.8.293, CLL Saint-Flour, 8 February 1945.
14   Thompson, "Moral Economy." For the shortages of 1939–49 creating a sense of injustice parallel to that experienced during the French Revolution, see Jean-Marie Guillon, "Le Var. La pénurie, c'est les autres," *Cahiers de l'IHTP* 32–33 (1996), 439–52.
15   John Barber and Mark Harrison, *The Soviet Home Front 1941–1945* (New York: Longman, 1991), 77–93.
16   Richard Lukas, *The Forgotten Holocaust: The Poles under German Occupation 1939–1944* (Lexington: University Press of Kentucky, 1986), 30.
17   Flonneau, "Le Loiret," 43–58.
18   See 72 AJ 384, 15 February–15 March 1945.
19   *La Liberté de l'Est*, 6 May 1945.
20   Veillon, *Vivre*, 114.
21   *La Margeride*, 29 September 1945.
22   For the political ramifications of famine in Greece, see Mazower, *Inside Hitler's Greece*, 23–52. For a lucid discussion of the destabilizing and delegitimizing potential of a badly managed rationing system, see Belinda Davis, "Food Scarcity and the Empowerment of the Female Consumer in World War I Berlin," in *The Sex of Things: Gender and Consumption in Historical Perspective*, ed. Victoria de Grazia (Berkeley: University of California Press, 1996): 287–310. See also Daniel; Barbara Alpern Engel, "Not by Bread Alone: Subsistence Riots in Russia during World War I," *Journal of Modern History* 69 (1997): 696–721; and Gerald D. Feldman, "War Economy and Controlled Economy: The Discrediting of 'Socialism' in Germany during World War I," in *Confrontation and Cooperation: Germany and the United States in the Era of World War I, 1900–1924*, ed. Hans-Jürgen Schröder (Oxford: Berg, 1993): 229–52.
23   Christian Bachelier, "De la pénurie à la vie chère: L'opinion publique à travers les premiers sondages, 1944–1949," *Cahiers de l'IHTP* 32–33 (1996): 486.
24   See Hanna Diamond, "The Everyday Experience of Women during the Second World War in the Toulouse Region," in *War and Society in Twentieth-Century France*, ed. Michael Scriven and Peter Wagstaff (New York: Berg, 1991), 49–62; Laura Frader, "Beyond Separate Spheres: Women, the Family and Protest in Nineteenth- and Twentieth-Century France," in *Public/Private Spheres: Women Past and Present*, ed. Debra Kaufman (Boston: Northeastern Custom Book Program, 1989), 105–27; Donna Ryan, "Ordinary Acts and Resistance: Women in

Street Demonstrations and Food Riots in Vichy France," *Proceedings of the Annual Meeting of the Western Society for French History* 16 (1989): 400–407; and Danielle Tartakowsky, "Manifester pour le pain, novembre 1940–octobre 1947," *Cahiers de l'IHTP* 32–33 (1996): 465–78.

25 *La Résistance savoyarde*, 22 April 1945.
26 *La Résistance savoyarde*, 26 January 1946 and 26 January 1945. See also *Le Cantal ouvrier et paysan*, 2 December 1945.
27 This particular report focused on the "meat crisis" but does not differ qualitatively from many others he wrote (F1a 4024, 15–30 June 1945).
28 72 AJ 384, 15 February–15 March 1945.
29 F1a 4028, no. 69, 13 April 1945, Prefect Isère. See also F1a 4028, no. 47, 1 March 1945, CRR Bordeaux.
30 F1a 4022, 15 February–15 March 1945.
31 *La Résistance savoyarde*, 7 April 1945.
32 *La Margeride*, 30 June 1945.
33 *La Résistance savoyarde*, 1 March 1945.
34 *L'Eveil de la Haute-Loire*, 17 May 1945.
35 *La Résistance des Vosges*, July 1945. See also Guillon, 447.
36 *La Margeride*, 29 August 1945.
37 Weber, 71.
38 F1a 4025, 1–15 October 1945.
39 *La Croix de Lorraine*, 14 January 1945. See also Dodin, 147.
40 His language grew stronger with the passage of the months. See F1a 4024, 15–31 May 1945; F1a 4025, 1–15 October 1945; and *La Croix de Lorraine*, 14 January 1945.
41 F1c III 1226, 16 October 1945.
42 For this and the other governmental price policy errors discussed below, see Michel Margairaz, "L'Etat et les restrictions en France dans les années 1940," *Cahiers de l'IHTP* 32–33 (1996): 38–40.
43 F1a 4028, no. 90, 2 June 1945, CRR Limoges.
44 F1c III 1226, 16 April 1945.
45 *La Margeride*, 30 June 1945.
46 *Le Réveil des Vosges*, 25 November 1945.
47 F1a 4025, 1–15 January 1946.
48 See, for example, Veillon, *Vivre*, 229–75.
49 F1c III 1211, 16 April 1945. Administrative reports from the provinces are full of similar demonstrations of the economic disincentives for delivering all one's crops to the RG.
50 See 72 AJ 384, 16 July–15 August 1945.
51 For example, *La Liberté de l'Est*, 9 August 1945; *La Résistance savoyarde*, 22 December 1945; and *La Margeride*, 10 February 1945.

52 For a discussion of food crime, see Aubusson de Cavarlay, Huré, and Pottier; see also Hélène Chaubin, "L'Hérault," *Cahiers de l'IHTP* 32–33 (1996): 191–93, and Marie-Thérèse Viaud, "La Dordogne," *Cahiers de l'IHTP* 32–33 (1996): 143–49.
53 *La Margeride*, 11 August 1945 and 12 December 1945; see also 17 January 1945 and 30 December 1944.
54 *La Margeride*, 3 October 1945. The scale of such fraud may be guessed from the Saint-Flour ration-ticket scandal discussed in chapter 1.
55 *La Margeride*, 14 October 1944.
56 *Le Cantal libre*, 7 October 1944.
57 *Le Réveil des Vosges*, 11 February 1945, and F1a 4029, no. 133, CRR Laon-Saint-Quentin.
58 *La Résistance savoyarde*, 17 November 1945, and *La Liberté de l'Est*, 11–12 October 1945.
59 *La Résistance savoyarde*, 8 December 1945.
60 *La Margeride*, 26 July 1945 and 20 October 1945.
61 *La Margeride*, 24 March 1945.
62 Lucie Aubrac, *Outwitting the Gestapo*, trans. Konrad Bieber (Lincoln: University of Nebraska Press, 1993), 25.
63 Veillon, *Vivre*, 127–31.
64 See 72 AJ 384, 15 May–15 June 1945. For the similar role of queues during the French Revolution, see René Sédillot, *Histoire des marchés noirs* (Paris: Tallandier, 1985), 72.
65 F1a 4022, 15 March–15 April 1945.
66 *Le Réveil des Vosges*, 28 October 1945. The classic representation of the shopkeeper's war is Jean Dutourd, *Au bon beurre* (Paris: Gallimard, 1952).
67 *La Résistance savoyarde*, 14 October 1945, from the correspondent in Chambéry.
68 *La Liberté de l'Est*, 3–4 June 1945, and *La Résistance savoyarde*, 26 January 1945.
69 *Le Cantal libre*, 20 October 1944, and *La Résistance savoyarde*, 30 June 1945.
70 *La Liberté de l'Est*, 25 July 1945.
71 F1a 4028, no. 79, 29 April 1945, Prefect Indre-et-Loire.
72 See 72 AJ 384, 16 July–15 August 1945.
73 Menchérini, 424.
74 For the possibilities, see Claude Cherrier, "La Seine-et-Marne," *Cahiers de l'IHTP* 32–33 (1996): 260–63; Christian Font, "Une enquête orale menée en Aveyron," *Cahiers de l'IHTP* 32–33 (1996): 513–18; Maïté Frank, "La Seine-et-Oise," *Cahiers de l'IHTP* 32–33 (1996): 233–36; Jean-Louis Panicacci, "Les Alpes-Maritimes," *Cahiers de l'IHTP* 32–33 (1996): 199–204; and Veillon, *Vivre*. See also Manfred J. Enssle, "The Harsh Discipline of Food Scarcity in Postwar Stuttgart, 1945–1948," *German Studies Review* 10, no. 3 (1987): 481–502, and Jill Stephenson, "War and Society in Württemberg, 1939–1945: Beating the System," *German Studies Review* 7, no. 1 (1985): 89–106.

Notes to Chapter Four   303

75 In 1942 both Church and State officially approved family-scale extralegal trading (Veillon, *Vivre*, 180).
76 F1a 4029, no. 103, 22 June 1945, Prefect Côtes-du-Nord.
77 Font, 513, and Veillon, *Vivre*, 164.
78 *La Sasson*, 4 February 1945. Typical ersatz recipes of the time can be found in Veillon, *Vivre*, 340.
79 See, for example, Bachelier, 482, and the rest of this special issue of *Cahiers de l'IHTP*.
80 *La Résistance savoyarde*, 16 November 1944.
81 See, for example, 72 AJ 384, 15 November–15 December 1944 and 16 August–15 September 1945.
82 Veillon, *Vivre*, 131, and Guillon, "Le Var," 452.
83 This analysis of public sentiment appears throughout the gendarmerie reports in 72 AJ 384. For the famine plot, see Steven L. Kaplan, "The Famine Plot Persuasion in Eighteenth-Century France," *Transactions of the American Philosophical Society* 72, n. 3 (1982).
84 *L'Elan syndical*, November 1944.
85 F1a 4028, no. 44, 22 February 1945, CRR Lyon. See also 72 AJ 384, 15 December 1944–15 January 1945 and 15 February–15 March 1945, and *Le Cantal ouvrier et paysan*, 4 August 1945.
86 F1c III 1211, 16 April 1945.
87 F1a 4028, no. 21, 30 December 1944, CRR Dijon.
88 Jean-Marie Flonneau, "Législation et organisation économiques au temps des restrictions (1938–1949)," *Cahiers de l'IHTP* 32–33 (1996): 281; Guillon, 446; Eric D. Kohler, "Inflation and Black Marketeering in the Rhenish Agricultural Economy, 1919–1922," *German Studies Review* 7, no. 1 (1985): 58–59; and Jean-Philippe Marcy, "Le marché noir en Aveyron vu à travers la presse," *Cahiers de l'IHTP* 32–33 (1996): 402.
89 *La Liberté de l'Est*, 7 December 1945.
90 F1a 4022, 15 February–15 March 1945.
91 *La Résistance savoyarde*, 6 October 1945.
92 *La Résistance savoyarde*, 31 March 1945 and 21 July 1945. See also *Le Démocrate de l'Est*, 11–12 February 1945, and *Le Réveil des Vosges*, 14 January 1945.
93 *La Résistance savoyarde*, 21 July 1945. See also *La Résistance savoyarde*, 8 July 1945, and *La Margeride*, 13 January 1945.
94 *La Margeride*, 18 October 1944, 15 November 1944, 6 January 1945, and 8 December 1945, and *Le Cantal ouvrier et paysan*, 13 January 1945. Similar rebuttals of tendentious "rumors" appeared in the Savoyard press.
95 See, for example, *Le Démocrate de l'Est*, 28–29 January 1945, and *La Liberté de l'Est*, 28 January 1946.
96 Parisians and Londoners had required pure white bread since at least the eigh-

teenth century (Steven L. Kaplan, *The Bakers of Paris and the Bread Question, 1700-1775* [Durham, N.C.: Duke University Press, 1996], 33-36, and Roger Wells, *Wretched Faces: Famine in Wartime England 1793-1801* [New York: St. Martin's Press, 1988], 14-15).

97 *Le Travailleur vosgien,* 21 December 1945.
98 *Le Cantal ouvrier et paysan,* 25 August 1945, and *La Margeride,* 13 December 1944.
99 *La Paix,* 19 May 1945.
100 For a discussion of the importance of the production and consumption as well as the purchase of food, see Michael Wildt, "Plurality of Taste: Food and Consumption in West Germany during the 1950s," *History Workshop Journal* 39 (1995): 22-41.
101 F1a 4028, no. 90, 2 June 1945, Prefect Indre.
102 F1a 4021, 15-31 July 1945 and 15-30 September 1945.
103 See AC 1 W 117, Problèmes du ravitaillement 1944-46, original note dated 8 September 1945.
104 F1a 4025, 1-15 November 1945.
105 *La Liberté de l'Est,* 23 October 1945.
106 For the difference, see Charles Tilly, *The Contentious French* (Cambridge, Mass.: Belknap, 1986).
107 Experts on eighteenth-century food riots disagree on the nuances of this interpretation. See, for example, John Bohstedt, *Riots and Community Politics in England and Wales 1790-1810* (Cambridge, Mass.: Harvard University Press, 1983); Cynthia A. Bouton, *The Flour War: Gender, Class, and Community in Late Ancien Régime French Society* (University Park: Pennsylvania State University Press, 1993); Kaplan; Colin Lucas, "The Crowd and Politics between *Ancien Régime* and Revolution in France," *Journal of Modern History* 60, no. 3 (1988): 421-57; Eric Richards, "The Last Scottish Food Riots," *Past and Present,* supp. 6 (1982): 1-59; Louise A. Tilly, "The Food Riot as a Form of Political Conflict in France," *Journal of Interdisciplinary History* 2 (1971): 23-57; Thompson; and Wells.
108 The term "Consumer vigilantes" comes from Steven Kaplan's description of eighteenth-century rioters, but it is particularly apt for 1944-45 when the purge and provisioning were so closely linked in the popular search for justice (Kaplan, "Famine Plot," 27).
109 See 72 AJ 384, 16 August-15 September 1945.
110 F1a 4021, 15-30 September 1945.
111 *La Résistance savoyarde,* 22 April 1945.
112 F1a 4025, 15-31 October 1945.
113 See 72 AJ 384, 16 July-15 August 1945.
114 See 72 AJ 384, 16 August-15 September 1945.
115 See 72 AJ 384, 16 July-15 August 1945.

116 See 72 AJ 384, 16 August–15 September 1945, and F1a 4029, no. 160, 25 September 1945, CRR Poitiers.
117 F1a 4024, 15–30 June 1945.
118 Nor, of course, are these the only examples. See Anthony James Coles, "The Moral Economy of the Crowd: Some Twentieth-Century Food Riots," *Journal of British Studies* 18, no. 1 (1978): 157–76, and Paul Hanson, "The 'Vie Chère' Riots of 1911: Traditional Protests in Modern Garb," *Journal of Social History* 22, no. 3 (1988): 463–81.
119 See 72 AJ 384, 15 November 1944–15 August 1945.
120 See 72 AJ 384, 15 April–15 May 1945.
121 From a protest involving three thousand persons in Chatellerault on 1 September 1945 (F1a 4029, no. 160, 25 September 1945, Prefect Vienne).
122 Taylor argues that occupation-era authorities granted housewives and mothers a special right to protest over food shortages (Lynne Taylor, "Collective Action in Northern France, 1940–1944," *French History* 11, no. 2 [1997]: 190–214).
123 The list does not include Paris at all, and the archival copy is missing some pages. It also betrays some uncertainty about the classification of violent demonstrations such as *entraves* (72 AJ 384, 15 October 1944–15 August 1945).
124 F1a 4029, no. 165, 5 November 1945, Prefect Aisne. See the dramatic account in *La Margeride*, 22 September 1945.
125 See Buton, 196, and Tartakowsky, 471.
126 See the tribute to the town's RG agent in *La Liberté de l'Est*, 3 January 1946.
127 *La Résistance savoyarde*, 30 November 1944.
128 *La Résistance savoyarde*, 28 December 1944; see also 14 December 1944 and 1 March 1945.
129 F1a 4024, 15–30 April 1945, and F1a 4025, 1–15 August 1945.
130 See AS Rav 466 and *La Résistance savoyarde*, 15 April 1945.
131 *La Margeride*, 25 August 1945.
132 See AC 1 W 117, gendarmerie report, 13 September 1945, and police note dated Aurillac, 18 September 1945; *La Margeride*, 15 September 1945; and *Le Cantal ouvrier et paysan*, 22 September 1945.
133 *La Margeride*, 22 September 1945 and 26 September 1945.
134 See AC 1 W 117, police commissioner Saint-Flour to divisional chief of regional security services, 28 September 1945.
135 *La Margeride*, 6 October 1945, and *Le Cantal ouvrier et paysan*, 3 November 1945. See also *Femmes d'Auvergne*, 17 November 1945.
136 See AC 1 W 117, subprefect Saint-Flour to prefect, 29 September 1945, and Director RG to prefect, 28 September 1945.
137 *La Margeride*, 3 November 1945; see also 17 November 1945 and *Le Cantal ouvrier et paysan*, 2 February 1945.

138 F1a 4025, 15–31 August 1945.
139 *La Liberté de l'Est,* 27 September 1945.
140 "*L'anarchie des prix*" was a common phrase at the time (*La Liberté de l'Est,* 16 October 1945).
141 *La Liberté de l'Est,* 17 October 1945.
142 *La Liberté de l'Est,* 20 October 1945.
143 The prefect's letter was dated 19 October 1945 (*La Liberté de l'Est,* 21 October 1945). The CRR gave the credit to the competent authorities (F1a 4025, 15–31 October 1945).
144 See, for example, "Le Scandale de la féculerie," *La Liberté de l'Est,* 22 November 1945.
145 *Le Travailleur vosgien,* 9 November 1945.
146 Some of Primo Levi's memoirs offer eloquent testimony of how black markets flourish in the most desperate times. See his *Survival in Auschwitz: The Nazi Assault on Humanity,* trans. Stuart Woolf, 1958 (New York: Collier, 1993), and his *The Reawakening,* trans. Stuart Woolf, 1965 (New York: Collier, 1993). For the black market, see Marcy; Roger Picard, "La répression du marché noir entre 1941 et 1944: Le camp de Rouillé (Vienne)," *Cahiers de l'IHTP* 32–33 (1996): 411–18 and throughout many of the articles in this special issue; Jörg Roesler, "The Black Market in Post-War Berlin and the Methods Used to Counteract it," *German History* 7, no. 1 (1989): 92–107; Sédillot; Edward Smithies, *The Black Economy in England since 1914* (Dublin: Gill and Macmillan, 1984) 93; and Lynne Taylor, "The Black Market in Occupied Northern France, 1940–44," *Contemporary European History* 6, no. 2 (1997): 153–76.
147 F1c III 1211, 16 May 1945, and 16 July 1945. See also 72 AJ 384, 15 March–15 April 1945.
148 It is, of course, possible that there was a gendered division of black market labor in which women took care of the contacts "at home" within the couple's town and men traveled "in public" on black market expeditions. Anecdotal evidence and the fact that so many mothers had to survive alone while their husbands were in Germany as POWs, laborers, or deportees make this unlikely to have been a hard-and-fast rule, if it was one. See, for example, Aubrac or Heinrich Böll, *The Casualty,* trans. Leila Venniwitz (New York: Farrar, Straus, Giroux, 1986).
149 Flonneau, 279.
150 For the rhetorical eclipse of *résistantes,* see Rita Thalmann, "L'Oubli des femmes dans l'historiographie de la Résistance," *Clio* 1 (1995): 21–35.
151 72 AJ 384, 15 December 1944–15 January 1945.
152 *Le Patriote du Cantal,* 14 July 1945.
153 *La Croix de Lorraine,* 2 December 1945 and 9 December 1945. For other condemnations regarding the possession and resale of American matériel, see *Le Démocrate de l'Est,* 7 March 1945, and *La Liberté de l'Est,* 5 April 1945.

154 This incident in which twelve *transalpins* were captured exposed the Savoyards' anti-Italian sentiment because, to the paper's evident approval, the gendarmes imprisoned the Italian smugglers but sent the French ones to a *chantier de travail* (*La Résistance savoyarde*, 6 October 1945).

155 See AC 8 W 282, Trafic clandestin; 1 W 324, Ravitaillement, besoins immédiats du département; and R.8.293, Director RG to President CDL, 9 February 1945.

156 See AC 8 W 282, reports of Director RG, September 1945–January 1946.

157 *Recueil des actes administratifs du département du Cantal*, 1 October 1944 (eggs) and 5 October 1945 (sugar, meat).

158 F1a 4024, 1–15 March 1945.

159 F1a 4028, no. 48, 3 March 1945, Prefect Haute-Vienne, February 1945, and *La Résistance des Vosges*, December 1944.

160 "Lettre ouverte du Comité d'unité d'action des syndicats CGT et CFTC de Haute-Tarentaise à Monsieur le Préfet de la Savoie," *La Résistance savoyarde*, 31 March 1945.

161 *Le Cantal libre*, 12 January 1945.

162 *La Liberté de l'Est*, 26 October 1945.

163 F1a 4028, no. 57, 22 March 1945, Prefect Loir-et-Cher. The authorities in Puy-de-Dôme uncovered a black market organization tied to Paris that used mailmen who collected cheese in their mail pouches (F1a 4021, 15–28 February 1945).

164 See AC 8 W 280, Fraudes, p.v. de gendarmerie 1944–46, 11 December 1944. In January 1946 the gendarmerie reportedly caught another woman engaged in the same traffic by following "la rumeur publique" (*La Margeride*, 25 January 1946).

165 *La Résistance savoyarde*, 8 September 1945. For similar complaints against vacationers, see F1a 4028, no. 25, 9 January 1945, CRR Rouen; F1a 4029, no. 136, 22 August 1945, Prefect Finistère; no. 132, 13 August 1945, CRR Rouen, and no. 136, 22 August 1945, CRR Rennes; and 72 AJ 384, 16 July–16 August 1945, regarding Loire-Inférieure, Côtes-du-Nord, and Basse-Pyrénées.

166 *La Margeride*, 30 December 1944. Some correspondents, however, did have pity on the hunger trippers, see *La Margeride*, 14 February 1945.

167 See AC 1 W 324.

168 *La Margeride*, 29 September 1945.

169 *La Margeride*, 3 October 1945.

170 The offense of overcharging GIs was magnified by an alleged previous record of *not* overcharging German soldiers (*La Margeride*, 13 December 1944, and *La Résistance des Vosges*, February 1945).

171 *La Vie nouvelle*, 14 October 1945 and 21 October 1945.

172 *L'Espoir du Cantal*, 28 July 1945.

173 See F1a 4021, 6 October 1944, and 15–31 May 1945; F1c III 1211, 16 February 1945, and F1a 4024, 1–15 December 1944.

174 Lukas, 31. See Absalom, 309 and passim, for how the black market enabled escaped British POWs to survive in hiding from 1943 to 1945 in Italy.
175 FIC III 1226, 22 December 1944. For the Resistance's encouragement under the occupation, see Christian Bougeard, "Les Côtes-du-Nord," *Cahiers de l'IHTP* 32–33 (1996): 357–58.
176 *La Résistance savoyarde,* 7 December 1944.
177 *La Résistance savoyarde,* 28 September 1944.
178 *Les Quatre Vallées d'Albertville,* 2 September 1944.
179 "Dernier Avertissement," *La Savoie française,* 13 December 1944. See also *La Margeride,* 13 December 1944.
180 *La Résistance savoyarde,* 21 September 1944 and 28 September 1944.
181 *La Résistance savoyarde,* 14 December 1944.
182 FIC III 1211, 16 July 1945.
183 FIA 4028, no. 18, 23 December 1944, CRR Lyon, radio speech, 9 December 1944.
184 *Les Allobroges,* Editions Savoie, 7 September 1944. Also see *La Margeride,* 31 January 1945.
185 Barber and Harrison, 89, and William Moskoff, *The Bread of Affliction: The Food Supply in the USSR during World War II* (Cambridge: Cambridge University Press, 1990), 171–84.
186 FIA 4021, 15–31 July 1945; FIA 4022, 15 May–15 June 1945; and FIA 4024, 15–30 June 1945.
187 FIC III 1211, 16 July 1945.
188 FIC III 1211, 16 August 1945.
189 FIC III 1226, 16 August 1945.
190 *La Résistance savoyarde,* 12 January 1946. The Algerian also made the local news for trafficking in coffee (*La Résistance savoyarde,* 28 April 1945).
191 *La Liberté de l'Est,* 10 July 1945.
192 *La Margeride,* 7 February 1945.
193 *La Margeride,* 17 October 1945, 28 July 1945, 11 July 1945, and 28 June 1945.
194 The decree of 4 October 1944 authorized administrative internment for black market offenses (FIC III 1211, 16 September 1945).
195 *Le Réveil des Vosges,* 18 March 1945 and 22 March 1945. See also *La Liberté de l'Est,* 16 January 1946 for action against two café owners charged with buying and selling wine for 100 francs per liter when the legal price was 22 francs per liter.
196 FIC III 1221, 16 September 1945 and 16 July 1945.
197 *La Margeride,* 2 May 1945.
198 FIC III 1211, 16 June 1945.
199 FIA 4029, no. 115, 11 July 1945, Prefect Jura, and 72 AJ 384, 16 August 1945–15 September 1945.
200 *La Résistance savoyarde,* 22 September 1945.
201 See CM Moûtiers, 19 October 1945.

202 *La Résistance savoyarde,* 28 September 1944.
203 *La Margeride,* 1 November 1944.
204 *La Margeride,* 11 October 1944.
205 See CM Rambervillers, 26 May 1945.
206 *Le Démocratie savoyarde,* 17 February 1945.

CHAPTER 5   HONORARY JUSTICE AND
THE CONSTRUCTION OF MEMORY

1 *La Résistance savoyarde,* 28 September 1944.
2 *La Résistance des Vosges,* June 1945.
3 *Le Réveil des Vosges,* 23 September 1945.
4 The "ancestral voices" are not those of generational ancestors but of revolutionary or spiritual forerunners who have died for the cause. See O'Brien.
5 *La Margeride,* 13 December 1944.
6 See Mosse; Antoine Prost, *In the Wake of War: 'Les Anciens Combattants' and French Societyk, 1914–1939,* trans. Helen McPhail (Oxford: Berg, 1992); and Jay Winter, *Sites of Memory, Sites of Mourning: The Great War in European Cultural History* (Cambridge: Cambridge University Press, 1995).
7 Or even on the national level, where some women, such as a former liaison agent from near Saint-Flour, received medals for their wartime contributions. See *La Margeride,* 6 October 1945.
8 *Le Travailleur vosgien,* 24 June 1945.
9 For the eclipse of the memory of *résistantes,* see Thalmann.
10 *Le Démocrate de l'Est,* 17 November 1944.
11 For the politics of the Monuments aux Morts and the secular religion of nationalism, see David G. Troyansky, "Monumental Politics: National History and Local Memory in French *Monuments aux Morts* in the Department of the Aisne since 1870," *French Historical Studies* 15, no. 1 (1987): 121–41.
12 *La Margeride,* 21 October 1944.
13 *La Résistance savoyarde,* 14 September 1944. For other examples, see *La Résistance savoyarde,* 9 September 1944, 21 September 1944, 14 December 1944, and 19 May 1945; *Le Patriote du Cantal,* 2 December 1944; and *La Margeride,* 28 October 1944, 4 November 1944, 28 March 1945, and 14 April 1945. These do not include the obituaries for deportees.
14 See, for example, CM Rambervillers, 29 September 1945; *La Croix de Lorraine,* 16 December 1945; *La Liberté de l'Est,* 3 May 1945; *La Résistance savoyarde,* 8 March 1945 and 28 December 1945; and FIC III 1226, 15 November 1945.
15 The author of the article protested that the idea of adding a small plaque to the World War I monument was an insult to the glorious dead of 1939–45 (*Résistance des Vosges,* December 1945).

Notes to Chapter Five

16 *La Résistance savoyarde*, 14 October 1945.
17 For the symbolic meaning of renaming streets, see Daniel Milo, "Le Nom des rues," in *Les Lieux de mémoire*, vol. 2.3, ed. Pierre Nora (Paris: Gallimard, 1986), 283–312.
18 See CM Saint-Flour, 14 September 1944. See also *La Margeride*, 23 September 1944.
19 See CM Saint-Flour, 4 October 1944.
20 *Le Cantal ouvrier et paysan*, 10 March 1945, and *La Margeride*, 28 March 1945.
21 The minutes, unfortunately, give no hint as to the nature of the debate. See CM Moûtiers, 22 September 1944.
22 See CM Rambervillers, 10 December 1944 and 6 January 1945.
23 *Recueil des actes administratifs du département du Cantal*, 14 April 1945.
24 *La Résistance savoyarde*, 30 November 1944 and 5 May 1945, and *La Margeride*, 2 December 1944, and 9 December 1944.
25 *La Liberté de l'Est*, 25 April 1945.
26 F1a 4024, 1–15 May 1945.
27 *La Résistance des Vosges*, 16 June 1945.
28 For a political interpretation of the joint use of republican and Catholic symbolism at the liberation, see Brossat, *Libération*, 106.
29 *La Liberté de l'Est*, 8 May 1945.
30 *La Liberté de l'Est*, 10–11 May 1945; see also 29 May 1945.
31 The reporter found the mock burial "charming, because spontaneous" (*La Margeride*, 26 May 1945).
32 *Le Cantal libre*, 15 May 1945, and *La Margeride*, 16 May 1945. The relevant documents for Moûtiers are unfortunately missing from the archives, but the town apparently celebrated with wild rejoicing, including the firing of guns and throwing of grenades as well as all-night dancing (AS 9 M III 48, gendarmerie report, 10 May 1945). Only Rambûvetais, along with their American guests, celebrated the final end of the war in the Pacific (*La Liberté de l'Est*, 16 August 1945, 17 August 1945, and 18 August 1945). The CRR at Clermont-Ferrand noted little public response to the official decoration of the Monuments aux Morts (F1a 4021, 1–15 August 1945).
33 See 72 AJ 384, 15 April–15 May 1945; F1c III 1226, 16 June 1945; and F1a 4020, Rapports et correspondance du CRR à Châlons-sur-Marne, 16 June 1945.
34 *La Résistance des Vosges*, June 1945.
35 *La Margeride*, 26 May 1945. Most reports of 8 May celebrations do not mention them being spoiled by Vichyites.
36 *La Résistance savoyarde*, 28 July 1945.
37 See John Gillis, ed., *Commemorations: The Politics of National Identity* (Princeton: Princeton University Press, 1994); Patrick H. Hutton, *History as an Art of Memory*

(Hanover, N.H.: University Press of New England, 1993), 124–53; Pierre Nora, *Les Lieux de mémoire*, 3 vols. (Paris: Gallimard, 1984–92), particularly vol. 2.

38 For the Resistencialist myth, see Rousso, *Vichy Syndrome*, 16–18. For the "nationalization of memory," see Lagrou. For the construction and operation of national war myths elsewhere in Europe, see R. J. B. Bosworth: *Explaining Auschwitz and Hiroshima: History Writing and the Second World War, 1945–1990* (New York: Routledge, 1993); Angus Calder, *The Myth of the Blitz* (London: Pimlico, 1991); Tony Judt, "The Past Is Another Country: Myth and Memory in Postwar Europe," *Daedalus* 121, no. 4 (1992): 83–118; István Rév, "Amnesia: The Revised Framework of Hungarian History," *Budapest Review of Books* 4, no. 1 (1994): 2–6; and Nina Tumarkin, *The Living and the Dead: The Rise and Fall of the Cult of World War II in Russia* (New York: Basic Books, 1994).

39 See, for example, *Le Réveil des Vosges*, 23 December 1945, or *La Résistance savoyarde*, 28 September 1944.

40 Nor was the translation of war dead into martyrs and moral exemplars exclusively French; see Tumarkin, 76–81 for the construction of such martyrs in the USSR. For the confluence of nationalism and popular Catholicism in patriotic martyrdom, see O'Brien.

41 See, for example, *La Margeride*, 25 October 1944.

42 The oratorical tradition of ascribing the most patriotic of last thoughts to the dead reaches back to Michelet (Benedict Anderson, *Imagined Communities: Reflections on the Origin and Spread of Nationalism*, rev. ed. [London: Verso, 1991], 198).

43 For redemptive memory, see Herf, 164–66, and Lawrence L. Langer, *Admitting the Holocaust: Collected Essays* (New York: Oxford University Press, 1995), 31–40.

44 The article also warns Paris against returning to its "petites habitudes, à leurs petites combines de ces dernières années" (*La Margeride*, 18 October 1944 and also 24 February 1945).

45 For the fighting in Cantal during the summer of 1944, see Martres, *Cantal*, 347–498. For Oradour-sur-Glane and its fame, see Sarah Farmer, *Oradour: Arrêt sur mémoire*, trans. Pierre Guglielmina (Paris: Calmann-Lévy, 1994).

46 The Germans punished the town of Murat for the deaths of the eight Germans and two collaborators on 24 June by deporting 115 Muratais men and burning part of the town (Martres, *Cantal*, 504–10).

47 *La Margeride*, 2 September 1944.

48 *La Margeride*, 28 October 1944, and *La Voix du Cantal*, 4 November 1944.

49 *La Margeride*, 11 October 1944 and 9 December 1944.

50 *La Margeride*, 7 October 1944.

51 Italics in original. *La Margeride*, 18 October 1944.

52 *La Margeride*, 26 May 1945, 2 June 1945, and 9 June 1945.

53 *La Margeride*, 20 June 1945.

54 See *Le Montagnard*, 13 June 1947. The author would like to thank Mme. Bouteuin of the municipal archives of Saint-Flour for sending her this article.
55 For an eloquent assessment of what the loss of Dr. Mallet meant to the area's peasantry, see *La Margeride*, 13 January 1945.
56 *La Margeride*, 22 November 1944.
57 *La Margeride*, 2 September 1944.
58 *La Margeride*, 1 November 1944. Other villages held ceremonies in November 1944, February 1945, and November 1945.
59 *La Margeride*, 9 December 1944.
60 *La Margeride*, 3 February 1944; *Le Cantal libre*, 24 April 1945; and *La Voix du Cantal*, 28 April 1945.
61 *La Margeride*, 20 June 1945 and 27 June 1945, and *Le Cantal libre*, 28 June 1945.
62 *La Margeride*, 11 July 1945.
63 It is probably not coincidental that René Amarger was also involved in the football league. The raffle receipts of 2,789 francs for a hare and 1,893 francs for a packet of tobacco were considered disappointing and were ascribed to rain (*La Margeride*, 4 October 1944 and 1 November 1944).
64 *La Margeride*, 18 November 1944.
65 For example, *La Margeride*, 29 November 1944 and 21 March 1945. For the bludgeoning potential of shame in a memorial cult, see Tumarkin, 133.
66 *La Margeride*, 7 November 1945; *La Voix du Cantal*, 24 November 1945, and CM Saint-Flour, 12 December 1945. It was inaugurated in 1947; see *Le Montagnard*, 24 June 1947. The author would like to thank Mme. Bouteuin of the municipal archives for sending her this article.
67 It was not yet paid for, however; by August the *office agricole* had collected from its adherents 80,755 francs out of the over 100,000 francs necessary (*La Margeride*, 28 April 1945, 6 June 1945, and 1 August 1945).
68 *La Margeride*, 28 March 1945.
69 Her election, however, was an ambiguous endorsement of the Mallet cult. Out of the 1,133 votes cast in the uncontested race, only 855 were valid and only 669 were for Mme. Mallet. The rebuff may have been aimed at madame's supporter, René Amarger, rather than at the widow herself (*La Margeride*, 26 September 1945, 29 September 1945, 3 October 1945, and 6 October 1945, and *La Voix du Cantal*, 29 September 1945).
70 De Gaulle's absence, however, may be connected to the prefect's warning that events at Mont-Mouchet in June 1944 were sufficiently controversial that the general's reputation might suffer from being associated with them (FIC III 1211, 16 May 1945). For the controversy, see *La Margeride*, 29 September 1945 and 6 October 1945.
71 *La Margeride*, 19 May 1945 and 26 May 1945, and *La Voix du Cantal*, 19 May 1945.

Notes to Chapter Five   313

72 *La Margeride*, 30 June 1945.
73 *La Margeride*, 17 November 1945 and 21 June 1946.
74 The town council voted two thousand francs for the monument at Mont-Valérien. For fund-raising, see *La Margeride*, 26 November 1945, 15 December 1945, and 18 January 1946.
75 *La Margeride*, 14 April 1945.
76 *La Margeride*, 18 July 1945 (Talizat) and 7 July 1945 (Neuvéglise).
77 The two had been honored with public funerals a year earlier (*La Margeride*, 30 June 1945). For an analysis of the liberation as a popular ritual of unity, see Brossat, *Libération*.
78 *La Margeride*, 29 August 1945, and *Le Cantal libre*, 29 August 1945.
79 *La Margeride*, 29 August 1945.
80 *Le Démocrate de l'Est*, 7 October 1944. Such historical lineages were sometimes drawn in other places, although not as persistently as in Rambervillers; see *La Margeride*, 13 October 1945, for Vercingetorix as the founder of the nation's chain of "sacred martyrs."
81 *La Liberté de l'Est*, 30 September–1 October 1945.
82 In March 1946 the municipal council voted to give one thousand francs to the "Comité du monument des fusillés de Portieuse, en souvenir de Gustave Chardot, enfant de Rambervillers." See CM Rambervillers, 23 March 1946.
83 *La Résistance des Vosges*, November 1944.
84 *La Croix de Lorraine*, 7 October 1945; *La Résistance des Vosges*, September 1945 and October 1945, and *La Liberté de l'Est*, 29 August 1945. The author would like to thank Mayor G. Chevrier of Rambervillers for sharing the mayor's speech, the order of the day, and two unidentified press clippings with her.
85 *La Croix de Lorraine*, 7 October 1945.
86 *La Liberté de l'Est*, 30 September–1 October 1945.
87 Brossat, *Libération*, 106.
88 *La Croix de Lorraine*, 21 October 1945.
89 This is the only outright statement of this position found in the documents (*Le Travailleur vosgien*, 24 June 1945).
90 *Le Réveil des Vosges*, 16 December 1945.
91 Jeanménil, four kilometers east of Rambervillers, suffered the deportation of its people and near destruction; in November 1944 the Rambûvetais could watch Saint-Dié burning twenty-seven kilometers to the east (*La Résistance des Vosges*, December 1945).
92 *Le Réveil des Vosges*, 16 December 1945.
93 The author would like to thank M. M. Nicolas of Rambervillers for his help on this point.
94 For a counterexample of a town that placed twentieth-century traumas within its

314 Notes to Chapter Five

own history without distancing itself from Paris, see David Troyansky, "Memorializing Saint-Quentin: Monuments, Inaugurations, and History in the Third Republic," *French History*, 10, no. 1 (1999): 1–29.

95   *La Résistance savoyarde*, 11 January 1945.
96   He was fatally wounded while distributing tracts calling for a protest on 11 November 1942 (*La Résistance savoyarde*, 9 November 1944).
97   *La Résistance savoyarde*, 14 September 1944.
98   *La Résistance savoyarde*, 21 September 1944.
99   *La Résistance savoyarde*, 9 June 1945 and 2 June 1945 (reports from different communes).
100 *Recueil des actes administratifs. Préfecture de la Savoie*, 9 November 1944, Arrêté 152, 24 October 1944.
101 The Irish Martyrs of 1916 offer an example of how popular Catholicism and nationalistic or patriotic martyrdom can merge (O'Brien, 102, 114).
102 *La Résistance savoyarde*, 14 September 1944, and *La Vie nouvelle*, 1 October 1944.
103 *La Résistance savoyarde*, 9 November 1944.
104 See AS 346 R 7, note to prefect, December 1944. See also the warning in *La Margeride*, 30 December 1944, and Matard-Bonucci and Lynch, 163.
105 Mont-Cenis and Petit-Saint-Bernard are the two nearby passes into Italy. *La Résistance savoyarde*, 2 June 1945.
106 *La Résistance savoyarde*, 9 June 1945.
107 *La Résistance savoyarde*, 23 June 1945.
108 *La Résistance savoyarde*, 28 July 1945.
109 Only twenty of the victims rest in Moûtiers; after the ceremonies there, the remains of Abbé Muyard were buried in state in his hometown of Ugine (*La Résistance savoyarde*, 4 August 1945).
110 *La Résistance savoyarde*, 4 August 1945.
111 In December the municipality agreed to pay an undertaker from Bourg-Saint-Maurice twenty-five thousand francs for coffins for eighteen of the hostages. See CM Moûtiers, 21 December 1945 and 31 August 1945.
112 *La Résistance savoyarde*, 28 July 1945, also see 21 September 1944.
113 *La Résistance savoyarde*, 1 September 1945.
114 At the same time, the council turned down a request for funds to board repatriates, although it had honored a similar appeal in 1945; this suggests a shift of emotional focus from the shock of the Return to the desire to memorialize (*La Résistance savoyarde*, 14 October 1945, 21 October 1945, 27 October 1945, 3 November 1945, 2 December 1945, and 19 January 1946; and CM Moûtiers 31 August 1945 and 6 July 1946).
115 The prefect took the opportunity to reiterate the "the notorious insufficiency of the police forces in my department" (FIC III 1226, 16 August 1945).

116 *La Résistance savoyarde,* 10 November 1945.
117 *La Résistance savoyarde,* 28 July 1945 and 4 August 1945. Other towns in Savoie celebrated the anniversary of their liberations in style.
118 *La Résistance savoyarde,* 24 August 1945. Because the paper closed for the summer holiday in August, no issues appeared on 11 or 18 August.
119 *La Résistance savoyarde,* 14 October 1945, and *La Vie nouvelle,* 14 October 1945.
120 See CM Moûtiers, 10 July 1945.
121 See CM Moûtiers, 3 April 1952. The town paid 2,050,000 francs to prepare the square de la Liberté for the new statue. See AS Z 256, Albertville, Moûtiers, monuments.
122 *La Résistance savoyarde,* 21 June 1952, 24 June 1952, and 5 July 1952.
123 *La Résistance savoyarde,* 12 January 1946. See chapter 3 above for the Capella affair.
124 See AN F1c III 1226, 16 June 1945.
125 See Rousso, *Vichy Syndrome,* for the postwar haunting.

CHAPTER 6   POPULAR JUSTICE OR
REPUBLICAN LEGITIMACY?

1 See Foulon, "Prise et exercice."
2 For national summaries of the elections, see Rioux, *Fourth Republic,* 48–62, and *L'Année politique 1944–45,* 201–4; 317–20; 491–510.
3 72 AJ 384, 15 March–15 April 1945; F1a 4021, 1–15 March 1945 and 1–15 April 1945; F1a 4022, 1–15 February 1945, and F1a 4024, 15–28 February 1945. There have been suggestions that the Gaullists did not want the POWs to be able to vote; see Cochet, 157, and Kaspi, 276.
4 F1a 4024, 15–30 April 1945. The same opinion is expressed in F1c III 1226, 15 March 1945.
5 *La Résistance savoyarde,* 8 March 1945. For other protests by local Resistance organizations, see *La Margeride,* 23 December 1944, and F1c III 1226, 22 December 1944.
6 The people in six other communes also refused to vote, and someone stole and destroyed the urns in three others, presumably for similar reasons (F1a 4028, no. 91, 4 June 1945, Prefect Lot-et-Garonne, and 72 AJ 384, 15 April–15 May 1945).
7 72 AJ 384, 15 April–15 May 1945.
8 *La Margeride,* 12 December 1945; F1c III 1211, 16 September 1945, 16 October 1945, and 16 November 1945; and F1a 4021, 1–15 September 1945.
9 72 AJ 384, 15 April–15 May 1945.
10 *La Margeride,* 28 April 1945.
11 F1a 4021, 15–30 April 1945.
12 Brive, "L'Image," 393.

13 *La Margeride*, 10 January 1945.
14 The quotation comes from a complaint that a POW had not been elected despite his martyrdom (*La Margeride*, 12 May 1945).
15 See, for instance, *La Margeride*, 19 May 1945.
16 For the directives of the CDL of Savoie on how to draw up such a list, see F1a 4022, 15 February 1945–15 March 1945.
17 F1c III 1226, 16 March 1945.
18 *La Voix du Cantal*, 28 April 1945.
19 F1a 4028, no. 55, 20 March 1945, CRR Angers, and F1c III 1226, 15 March 1945.
20 F1a 4028, no. 39, 10 February 1945, Prefect Ain.
21 F1a 4021, 15–30 April 1945, and 1–15 May 1945, and F1c III, 16 May 1945.
22 See AC 1 W 359, gendarmerie report, 25 April 1945, and *La Margeride*, 26 July 1945.
23 *La Margeride*, 12 May 1945.
24 F1a 4021, 15–30 April 1945.
25 *La Margeride*, 18 April 1945 and 21 April 1945, and *La Voix du Cantal*, 21 April 1945.
26 Of the seventeen members of the special delegation, all but two ran for election. One did not run for unknown reasons; the other did not because he had been tortured to death by the Gestapo in May 1944, a fact unknown in Saint-Flour in August 1944 when the special delegation was appointed.
27 *La Margeride*, 28 April 1945.
28 Elections divided Saint-Flour into *ville* and *faubourg*. Of the 1,835 electors in the *ville*, 1,440 voted in the first ballot and 1,383 voted in the second. Of the 1,502 electors in the *faubourg*, 1,112 voted in the first ballot and 1,050 in the second. Some of the abstentions may have been due to absence in the armed services or captivity. On the subject of female voters, the prefect saw fit to mention that even the convents of Aurillac and Saint-Flour had not failed in their duty (F1c III 1211, 16 May 1945).
29 The section used her membership as proof of its respectability (*La Margeride*, 24 January 1945).
30 *La Margeride*, 19 May 1945 and 9 May 1945.
31 *La Margeride*, 5 May 1945.
32 *La Margeride*, 19 May 1945.
33 *La Margeride*, 29 August 1945.
34 F1c III 1226, 16 May 1945.
35 *La Résistance savoyarde*, 28 April 1945.
36 See, for example, F1a 4022, 15 February–15 March 1945.
37 The mayor who had presided over the town during its occupation and liberation retired before the elections, to the public regret of his colleagues and the town

paper. Of the 1,558 registered voters, 1,053 cast 1,038 valid ballots in the first poll, and 1,040 cast 1,040 valid ballots in the second (*La Résistance savoyarde,* 5 May 1945 and 19 May 1945).

38 *La Résistance savoyarde,* 5 May 1945.
39 *La Résistance savoyarde,* 19 May 1945, and *La Vie nouvelle,* 3 June 1945.
40 F1a 4024, 15–31 May 1945.
41 *La Croix de Lorraine,* 29 April 1945. For the same message expressed with a great deal more invective, see *Le Réveil des Vosges,* 29 April 1945.
42 Out of 3,400 registered voters, 2,738 voted in the first ballot and 2,386 in the second (*La Liberté de l'Est,* 22 May 1945, and *Le Travailleur vosgien,* 3 June 1945).
43 The results can be found in *La Liberté de l'Est,* 8 May 1945 and 22 May 1945.
44 *Le Travailleur vosgien,* 27 May 1945 and 3 June 1945.
45 F1a 4024, 1–15 May 1945 and 15–31 May 1945.
46 F1c III 1211, 16 November 1945.
47 F1c III 1211, 16 November 1945. *La Voix du Cantal,* 20 October 1945, claimed that *Le Cantal libre* owed Laurens only 1,100 francs.
48 *La Margeride,* 17 October 1945 and 20 October 1945. See also *L'Espoir du Cantal,* 13 October 1945.
49 *L'Espoir du Cantal,* 20 October 1945.
50 *La Margeride,* 17 October 1945.
51 He made the statement during a political rally (F1c III 1211, 16 November 1945).
52 The breakdown was: 984 for the Action Paysanne, 1,062 for the Socialists, 270 for the Communists, and 184 for the Radicals (*La Margeride,* 27 October 1945).
53 Martres, *Cantal,* 9, 30–31, 676–77.
54 F1a 4021, 15–31 October 1945.
55 In Cantal in 1936, 15 to 22.5 percent of voters registered for the combined "extreme left" of the PCF-SFIO and 30 to 37.5 percent for the right (Goguel, 51, 85, and 87).
56 F1c III 1211, 16 November 1945.
57 *La Margeride,* 1 December 1945.
58 *La Margeride,* 5 December 1945, 8 December 1945, and 29 December 1945.
59 *La Résistance savoyarde,* 29 September 1945.
60 There was a 20 percent abstention rate; for an overview, see Rioux, *Fourth Republic,* 58–59.
61 *La Margeride,* 6 October 1945.
62 *Le Réveil des Vosges,* 15 July 1945.
63 See, for example, F1c III 1211, 16 October 1945, and F1a 4025, 1–15 September 1945.
64 F1a 4029, no. 163, 3 October 1945, Prefect Indre.
65 F1a 4029, no. 113, 6 July 1945, Prefect Haute-Savoie.

66 72 AJ 384, 16 July–16 August 1945.
67 *La Résistance savoyarde,* 8 December 1945. See also *La Margeride,* 15 September 1945; F1a 4025, 1–15 August 1945; and F1a 4022, 15 March–15 April 1945.
68 72 AJ 384, 15 February–15 March 1945.
69 72 AJ 384, 16 July–16 August 1945.
70 F1a 4021, 1–15 April 1945, and F1a 4025, 1–15 January 1946.
71 F1c III 1211, 16 November 1945, and F1a 4021, 1–15 November 1945.
72 F1c III 1226, 16 September 1945.
73 *La Résistance savoyarde,* 29 September 1945.
74 *La Résistance savoyarde,* 6 October 1945.
75 *La Vie nouvelle,* 23 September 1945 and 30 September 1945. The Conseil général elected in 1937 had twenty Radicals, three Socialists, four members from the right, and one Republican-Socialist. The 1945 council had nine Radical-Socialists, seven SFIO, five PCF, two Union des Gauches, three Jeune République, one République de Gauche, one Independent, and one MRP (*La Résistance savoyarde,* 6 October 1945).
76 *Femmes d'Auvergne,* 6 October 1945.
77 *La Résistance savoyarde,* 10 November 1945.
78 *La Résistance savoyarde,* 3 November 1945.
79 *La Liberté de l'Est,* 28 November 1945.
80 For the government's view of the episode, see Kramer, 42–43.
81 See Kaplan, *Bakers,* 23–26, and Bouton. The Fifth Republic cracked down on *"faux baguettes"* in 1996.
82 See, for instance, Kaplan, *Bakers,* 458–520.
83 Kaplan, *Bakers,* 2.
84 For example, F1a 4025, 15–31 August 1945, and F1c III 1211, 16 October 1945.
85 F1c III 1226, 16 October 1945.
86 72 AJ 384, 16 August–15 September 1945, and F1a 4025, 1–15 October 1945.
87 F1a 4025, 1–15 August 1945.
88 F1a 4025, 1–15 August 1945, 1–15 September 1945, and 15–30 September 1945.
89 *La Résistance savoyarde,* 3 November 1945, and *La Vie nouvelle,* 4 November 1945.
90 *La Résistance savoyarde,* 2 December 1945.
91 Ordinance of 19 October 1945, *La Résistance savoyarde,* 17 November 1945, and *La Margeride,* 27 October 1945, and the prefect's warning in the 14 November 1945 issue.
92 The "overconsumption" rate rose significantly in rural areas (F1c III 1211, 16 November 1945, and F1a 4022, 24 December 1945).
93 F1a 4025, 1–15 December 1945.
94 *La Croix de Lorraine,* 16 December 1945.
95 *La Liberté de l'Est,* 22–23 December 1945; *La Croix de Lorraine,* 30 December 1945; and F1a 4025, 15–31 December 1945.

96 *Le Travailleur vosgien,* 28 December 1945.
97 F1a 4025, 1–15 January 1946.
98 *La Liberté de l'Est,* 28 December 1945. See a similar protest from the textile syndicate of Champ-du-Pin in *La Liberté de l'Est,* 22–23 December 1945.
99 *La Liberté de l'Est,* 1–2 January 1946.
100 *La Liberté de l'Est,* 28 January 1946.
101 *La Liberté de l'Est,* 1–2 January 1946.
102 *Le Travailleur vosgien,* 18 January 1946.
103 Quoted from the newspaper *Déliverance* in F1a 4025, 1–15 January 1946.
104 *La Margeride,* 19 December 1945.
105 *La Résistance savoyarde,* 5 January 1946.
106 *La Démocratie savoyarde,* 5 January 1946.
107 *La Résistance savoyarde,* 19 January 1946.

CONCLUSION

1 F1a 4025, 1–15 January 1946.
2 *La Démocratie savoyarde,* 5 January 1946.
3 *La Résistance savoyarde,* 19 January 1946.
4 *La Démocratie savoyarde,* 5 January 1946. See also *Le Réveil des Vosges,* 6 January 1946, and *Le Travailleur vosgien,* 22 February 1946.
5 *La Liberté de l'Est,* 1–2 January 1946.
6 *L'Elan syndical,* November 1944. Pierre Laborie dates the disenchantment of the public with the Resistance (and its government) from the end of 1944 (Laborie, "Opinion et représentations: La Libération et l'image de la Résistance," *Revue d'histoire de la deuxième guerre mondiale et des conflits contemporains* 33, no. 131 [1983]: 77).
7 For the role of bread in the old regime, see the notes in chapter 4.
8 For an account of the amnesties, see Lottman, 276–84. For the process of forgetting and repressed remembering, of which the amnesties were a part, see Rousso, *Vichy Syndrome.*
9 For postwar pessimism, see Richard Kuisel, *Seducing the French: The Dilemma of Americanization* (Berkeley: University of California Press, 1993), 30–36, and Laurence Wylie, *Village in the Vaucluse,* 3d ed. (Cambridge, Mass.: Harvard University Press, 1974).
10 Historians have begun to chart these hauntings that Henri Rousso frames as a neurotic syndrome in works such as Bosworth; Judt; Rousso, *Vichy Syndrome;* Michael C. Steinlauf, *Bondage to the Dead: Poland and the Memory of the Holocaust* (Syracuse: Syracuse University Press, 1997); and Tumarkin.
11 For a discussion of this subject, see Judt and Rév.

BIBLIOGRAPHY

NEWSPAPERS

Les Allobroges: Organe clandestin du Front national de février 1942 au 22 août 1944. Provisoirement organe commun du Front national et du Mouvement national de Libération. Editions Savoie (September 1944–September 1945).
L'Amor libre: Hebdomadaire d'informations locales (Dinan, June 1945).
L'Aurore du Cantal: Organe départemental du Parti radical-socialiste (July 1945–November 1945).
Le Cantal libre: Organe du CDL (September 1944–February 1946).
Le Cantal ouvrier et paysan: Organe hebdomadaire régional du Parti communiste français (September 1944–February 1946).
La Croix de Lorraine: Hebdomadaire de défense des idées sociales et chrétiennes (October 1944–February 1946).
Le Démocrate de l'Est: Journal républicain quotidien (October 1944–March 1945).
La Démocratie savoyarde: Hebdomadaire d'action laique, démocratique et sociale (November 1944–February 1946).
L'Echo des vallées d'Albertville: Journal d'annonces industrielles, commerciales, judiciaires et légales (September 1944–February 1946).
L'Elan syndical: Organe mensuel du Comité d'unité d'action CGT et CFTC de Savoie et de Haute-Savoie (October 1944–February 1945).
L'Espoir du Cantal: Organe de la fédération Socialiste (SFIO) (July 1945–February 1946).
L'Eveil de la Haute-Loire (Le Puy, May–June 1945).
La Femme d'Auvergne: Organe du Comité national des Femmes de France (September 1944–December 1944). Changed to *Femmes d'Auvergne: Organe de l'Union des femmes françaises (section du Cantal)* (December 1944–February 1946).
La Libération en armes. (Angoulême, March–June 1945).
La Liberté de l'Est (March 1945–February 1946).
La Margeride: Organe du MLN (September 1944–February 1946).

La Paix: Organe d'union par la verité (Romans, May–June 1945).
Le Patriote du Cantal: Organe du FN du Cantal (September 1944–February 1946).
Les Quatre Vallées d'Albertville (September 1944).
La Résistance des Vosges: Journal bi-mensuel de "Ceux de la Résistance," CDLR, ayant paru dans la clandestinité (November 1944–February 1946).
La Résistance savoyarde: Organe provisoire du Comité de Libération (September 1944–April 1946).
Le Réveil des Vosges: Organe du Front national de lutte pour la Libération et l'indépendance de la France (October 1944–February 1946).
La Sasson: Organe bi-mensuel savoisien de l'Union des Femmes de France (February 1945–December 1945).
La Savoie française: Organe quotidien du CDL (September 1944–January 1946).
Le Travailleur vosgien: Organe de la Fédération socialiste des Vosges (November 1944–February 1946).
La Vie nouvelle: Hebdomadaire savoisien d'information et d'action catholique et sociale (September 1944–March 1946).
La Voix du Cantal (November 1944–December 1945).
Le Volontaire des Alpes: Supplément de France d'Abord: Organe des FTPF, FFI, Front national. Edition savoyarde (September 1944–January 1945).
Vosges nouvelles: Organe hebdomadaire du Parti communiste des Vosges ayant paru dans la clandestinité (December 1944–February 1946).

GOVERNMENT DOCUMENTS

Bulletin officiel du département des Vosges, République française (October 1944–March 1946).
Journal officiel de la République française (August 1944–March 1946).
Recueil des actes administratifs du département du Cantal, République française (August 1944–February 1946).
Recueil des actes administratifs. Préfecture de la Savoie (September 1944–February 1946).

BOOKS AND ARTICLES

Absalom, Roger. *A Strange Alliance: Aspects of Escape and Survival in Italy, 1943–1945.* Florence: Leo S. Olschki, 1991.
"L'Agriculture et le ravitaillement depuis la Libération." *Etudes et conjonctures,* série Union française, nos. 5–6 (1946–47): 67–113.
Agulhon, Maurice. *The French Republic, 1879–1992.* Translated by Antonia Nevill. Oxford: Blackwell, 1993.
Alessandrini, Luca. "The Option of Violence: Partisan Activity in the Bologna Area, 1945–1948." Paper presented at the Contemporary History Conference "After the

War Was Over: Reconstructing the Family, Society and the Law in Southern Europe 1944–1950," University of Sussex, July 1996.

Amouroux, Henri. *La grande Histoire des Français après l'Occupation*. Vol. 9, *Les règlements de comptes, septembre 1944–janvier 1945*. Paris: Robert Laffont, 1991.

Anderson, Benedict. *Imagined Communities: Reflections on the Origin and Spread of Nationalism*. Rev. ed. London: Verso, 1991.

Andrieu, Clarie. *Le Programme commun de la Résistance, des idées dans la guerre*. Paris: Editions de l'Erudit, 1984.

L'Année politique, 1944–1945: Revue chronologique des principaux faits politiques, économiques et sociaux de la France, de la Libération de Paris au 31 Décembre 1945. Paris: Editions du grand siècle, 1946.

Aubrac, Lucie. *Outwitting the Gestapo*. Translated by Konrad Bieber. Lincoln: University of Nebraska Press, 1993.

Aubusson de Cavarlay, Bruno, Marie-Sylvie Huré, and Marie-Lys Pottier. "La justice pénale en France. Résultats statistiques (1934–1954)." *Cahiers l'IHTP*, série "Justice," no. 23 (1993).

Azéma, Jean-Pierre. *From Munich to the Liberation, 1938–1944*. Translated by Janet Lloyd. 1979. Cambridge: Cambridge University Press, 1984.

———. "La Milice." *Vingtième Siècle* 28 (1990): 83–105.

Azéma, Jean-Pierre, and François Bédarida, eds. *La France des années noires*. 2 vols. Paris: Editions du Seuil, 1993.

Bacque, James. *Other Losses: An Investigation into the Mass Deaths of German Prisoners at the Hands of the French and Americans after World War II*. Toronto: Stoddart, 1989.

Barber, John, and Mark Harrison. *The Soviet Home Front, 1941–1945*. New York: Longman, 1991.

Baruch, Marc O. *Servir l'Etat français: L'Administration en France de 1940 à 1944*. Paris: Fayard, 1997.

Baudot, Marcel. "L'Epuration: Bilan chiffré." *Bulletin de l'IHTP* 25 (1986): 37–53.

———. "Etat des recherches sur la répression de la collaboration à la libération." *Bulletin de l'IHTP* 4 (1981): 19–23.

———. "La Résistance française face aux problèmes de répression et d'épuration." *Revue d'histoire de la deuxième guerre mondiale* 81 (1971): 23–47.

Becker, Jean-Jacques. *Le Parti communiste veut-il prendre le pouvoir? La stratégie du PCF de 1930 à nos jours*. Paris: Editions du Seuil, 1981.

Bellanger, Claude, Jacques Godechot, Pierre Guiral, and Fernand Terrou, eds. *Histoire générale de la presse française*. Vol. 3, *de 1940 à 1958*. Paris: Presses universitaires de France, 1975.

Bendjebbar, André. *Libérations rêvées, Libérations vécues, 1940–1945*. Paris: Hachette, 1994.

Bernd, Martin, and Alan Milward, eds. *Agriculture and Food Supply in the Second World War*. Ostfildern, West Germany: Scripta Mercaturae, 1985.

Bessel, Richard. *Germany after the First World War*. Oxford: Clarendon, 1993.

Biddiscombe, Perry. "The French Resistance and the Chambéry Incident of June 1945." *French History* 11, no. 4 (1997): 438–60.

Bischof, Günter, and Stephen E. Ambrose, eds. *Eisenhower and the German POWs: Facts against Falsehood*. Baton Rouge: Louisiana State University Press, 1992.

Bloch, Marc. "Réflexions d'un historien sur les fausses nouvelles de la guerre." *Revue de synthèse historique* 33 (1921): 13–35.

Bohstedt, John. *Riots and Community Politics in England and Wales, 1790–1810*. Cambridge, Mass.: Harvard University Press, 1983.

Böll, Heinrich. *The Casualty*. Translated by Leila Venniwitz. New York: Farrar, Straus, Giroux, 1986.

Bosworth, R. J. B. *Explaining Auschwitz and Hiroshima: History Writing and the Second World War, 1945–1990*. New York: Routledge, 1993.

Botting, Douglas. *From the Ruins of the Reich: Germany, 1945–1949*. New York: Meridian, 1985.

Boulard, Fernand. *Premiers itinéraires en sociologie religieuse*. Paris: Editions ouvrières, économie et humanisme, 1954.

Bourdrel, Philippe. *L'Epuration sauvage, 1944–1945*. 2 vols. Paris: Perrin, 1988–91.

Boussard, Isabel. "Etat de l'agriculture française aux lendemains de l'occupation (1944–1948)." *Revue d'histoire de la deuxième guerre mondiale* 16 (1979): 69–106.

———. "Principaux aspects de la politique agricole française pendant la deuxième guerre mondiale." *Revue d'histoire de la deuxième guerre mondiale* 134 (1984): 1–32.

Bouton, Cynthia A. *The Flour War: Gender, Class, and Community in Late Ancien Régime French Society*. University Park: Pennsylvania State University Press, 1993.

Brêche, Yves. "Moûtiers: Le grand destin d'une petite cité alpine." *L'Histoire en Savoie* 59 (1980): 1–32.

Bridgman, Jon. *The End of the Holocaust: The Liberation of the Camps*. Portland, Oreg.: Areopagitica Press, 1990.

Brive, Marie-France. "L'Image des femmes à la Libération." In *La Libération dans le Midi de la France*, edited by Rolande Trempé, 389–402. Toulouse: Eché Editions, 1986.

———. "Les Résistantes et la Résistance," *Clio* 1 (1995): 57–66.

Brossat, Alain. *Libération, fête folle: 6 juin 44–8 mai 45: Mythes et rites ou le grand théâtre des passions populaires*. Série mémoires, no. 30. Paris: Editions Autrement, April 1994.

———. *Les Tondues: Un carnaval moche*. Levallois-Perret: Editions Manya, 1992.

Burrin, Philippe. *La France à l'heure allemande, 1940–1944*. Paris: Editions du Seuil, 1995.

Buton, Philippe. *Les Lendemains qui déchantent: Le Parti communiste français à la Libération*. Paris: Presses de la Fondation nationale des sciences politiques, 1993.

Calder, Angus. *The Myth of the Blitz*. London: Pimlico, 1991.

Capdevila, Luc. "La 'Collaboration sentimentale': Antipatriotisme ou sexualité hors-normes? (Lorient, mai 1945)." *Cahiers de l'IHTP*, 31 (1995): 67–82.

———. "Local Uses of Violence after Liberation: Reconstruction and Self-Definition

in 'Petite Bretagne,' August 1944–early 1946." Paper presented at the Contemporary History Conference "After the War Was Over: Reconstructing the Family, Society and the Law in Southern Europe, 1944–1950," University of Sussex, July 1996.
Certeau, Michel de. *The Practice of Everyday Life*. Translated by Steven Rendall. Berkeley: University of California Press, 1984.
Chabert, Louis. *Les Grandes Alpes industrielles de Savoie: Évolution économique et humaine*. Saint-Alban Leysse: Imprimerie Gaillard, 1978.
Clause, Georges. "Reims autour du 7 mai 1945." In *8 Mai 1945: La victoire en Europe: Actes du colloque international de Reims, 1985*, edited by Maurice Vaïsse, 383–419. Lyon: La Manufacture, 1985.
Cobb, Richard. *French and Germans, Germans and French: A Personal Interpretation of France under Two Occupations, 1914–1918/1940–1944*. Hanover, N.H.: Brandeis University Press, 1983.
Cochet, François. *Les Exclus de la victoire: Histoire des prisonniers de guerre, déportés et STO (1945–1985)*. Paris: Editions SPM et Kronos, 1992.
Coles, Anthony James. "The Moral Economy of the Crowd: Some Twentieth-Century Food Riots." *Journal of British Studies* 18, no. 1 (1978): 157–76.
Comité d'histoire de la deuxième guerre mondiale. *La Libération de la France: Actes du colloque international tenu à Paris du 28 au 31 octobre 1974*. Paris: Editions du CNRS, 1976.
Connelly, John. "The Uses of *Volksgemeinschaft:* Letters to the NSDAP Kreisleitung Eisenach, 1939–1940." *Journal of Modern History* 68, no. 4 (1996): 899–930.
Daniel, Ute. *The War from Within: German Working-Class Women in the First World War*. Translated by Margaret Ries. Oxford: Berg, 1997.
Davis, Belinda. "Food Scarcity and the Empowerment of the Female Consumer in World War I Berlin." In *The Sex of Things: Gender and Consumption in Historical Perspective*, edited by Victoria de Grazia, 287–310. Berkeley: University of California Press, 1996.
Debû-Bridel, Jacques. *Histoire du marché noir (1939–1947)*. Paris: La Jeune Parque, 1947.
Delarue, Jacques. *Trafics et crimes sous l'occupation*. Paris: Fayard, 1968.
Delperrie de Bayac, J. *Histoire de la Milice*. 2 vols. Paris: Fayard, 1969.
Diamond, Hanna. "The Everyday Experience of Women during the Second World War in the Toulouse Region." In *War and Society in Twentieth-Century France*, edited by Michael Scriven and Peter Wagstaff, 49–62. New York: Berg, 1991.
———. "Gaining the Vote: A Liberating Experience?" *Modern and Contemporary France*, n.s. 3, no. 2 (1995): 129–48.
———. "Libération! Quelle Libération? L'expérience des femmes toulousaines." *Clio* 1 (1995): 89–109.
Dictionnaire des communes. Nancy: Editions Berger-Levrault, 1949.
Dodin, Robert. *Les Vosges de 1939 à 1945*. Epinal: Editions du Sapin d'Or, 1990.

Doublet, P. H. *La Collaboration: L'Épuration, la confiscation, les réparations aux victimes de l'occupation.* Paris: Librairie générale de droit et de jurisprudence, 1945.

Douzou, Laurent. "La Résistance, une affaire d'hommes?" *Cahiers de l'IHTP,* 31 (1995): 11–24.

Duchen, Claire. "Une Femme nouvelle pour une France nouvelle?" *Clio* 1 (1995): 151–64.

———. *Women's Rights and Women's Lives in France, 1944-1968.* London: Routledge, 1994.

Duras, Marguerite. *Hiroshima mon amour.* Translated by Richard Seaver. Full text from a film produced by Alain Resnais. New York: Grove, 1961.

———. *The War: A Memoir.* Translated by Barbara Bray. New York: Pantheon, 1986.

Dutourd, Jean. *Au bon beurre.* Paris: Gallimard, 1952.

Engel, Barbara Alpern. "Not by Bread Alone: Subsistence Riots in Russia during World War I." *Journal of Modern History* 69 (1997): 696–721.

Enssle, Manfred J. "The Harsh Discipline of Food Scarcity in Postwar Stuttgart, 1945–1948." *German Studies Review* 10, no. 3 (1987): 481–502.

Farcy, Jean-Claude, and Henry Rousso. "Justice, répression et persécution en France (fin des années 1930–début des années 1950). Essai bibliographique." *Cahiers de l'IHTP,* série "Justice," no. 24 (1993).

Farmer, Sarah. *Oradour: Arrêt sur mémoire.* Translated by Pierre Guglielmina. Paris: Calmann-Lévy, 1994.

———. "Oradour-sur-Glane: Memory in a Preserved Landscape." *French Historical Studies,* 19, no. 1 (1995): 27–48.

———. "Oradour-sur-Glane: "Village Martyr" in the Landscape of Memory, 1944–1991." Ph.D. diss., University of California at Berkeley, 1992.

Feldman, Gerald D. "War Economy and Controlled Economy: The Discrediting of 'Socialism' in Germany during World War I." In *Confrontation and Cooperation: Germany and the United States in the Era of World War I, 1900-1924,* edited by Hans-Jürgen Schröder, 229–52. Oxford: Berg, 1993.

Fishman, Sarah. "Grand Delusions: The Unintended Consequences of Vichy France's Prisoner of War Propaganda." *Journal of Contemporary History* 26 (1991): 229–54.

———. *We Will Wait: Wives of French Prisoners of War, 1940-1945.* New Haven: Yale University Press, 1991.

Fitzpatrick, Sheila. "Signals from Below: Soviet Letters of Denunciation of the 1930s." *Journal of Modern History* 68, no. 4 (1996): 831–66.

Fitzpatrick, Sheila, and Robert Gellately. "Introduction to the Practices of Denunciation in Modern European History." *Journal of Modern History* 68, no. 4 (1996): 747–67.

Flonneau, Jean-Marie. "Crise de vie chère et mouvement syndical, 1910–1914." *Mouvement Social* 72 (1970): 49–81.

Foucault, Michel. *Discipline and Punish: The Birth of the Prison*. Translated by Alan Sheridan. New York: Vintage, 1979.

Foulon, Charles-Louis. "L'Opinion, la résistance et le pouvoir en Bretagne à la Libération." *Revue d'histoire de la deuxième guerre mondiale* 117 (1980): 75–100.

———. *Le Pouvoir en province à la Libération: Les Commissaires de la République, 1943–1946*. Paris: Presses de la Fondation nationale des sciences politiques, 1975.

———. "Prise et exercice du pouvoir en province à la libération." In *La Libération de la France: Actes du colloque international tenu à Paris du 28 au 31 octobre 1974*. Comité d'histoire de la deuxième guerre mondiale, 501–57. Paris: Editions du CNRS, 1976.

Frader, Laura. "Beyond Separate Spheres: Women, the Family and Protest in Nineteenth- and Twentieth-Century France." In *Public/Private Spheres: Women Past and Present*, edited by Debra Kaufman, 105–27. Boston: Northeastern Custom Book Program, 1989.

Frank, Dana. "Housewives, Socialists, and the Politics of Food: The 1917 New York Cost-of-Living Protests." *Feminist Studies* 11 (1985): 255–85.

Gaulle, Charles de. *The Complete War Memoirs of Charles de Gaulle*. Translated by Jonathan Griffin and Richard Howard. New York: Simon and Schuster, 1955–60.

Gildea, Robert. *The Past in French History*. New Haven: Yale University Press, 1994.

Gillis, John, ed. *Commemorations: The Politics of National Identity*. Princeton: Princeton University Press, 1994.

Goguel, François. *Géographie des élections françaises de 1870 à 1951*. Paris: Armand Colin, 1951.

Gregory, Adrian. *The Silence of Memory: Armistice Day, 1919–1946*. Oxford: Berg, 1994.

Guéraiche, William. "Les Femmes politiques de 1944 à 1947: Quelle libération?" *Clio* 1 (1995): 165–86.

Guglielmi, Jean-Louis, and Marguerite Perrot. *Salaires et revendications sociales en France, 1944–1952*. Paris: Colin, 1953.

Guillon, Jean-Marie. "La Libération du Var: Résistance et nouveaux pouvoirs." *Cahiers de l'IHTP* 15 (1990).

Halls, W. D. *Politics, Society and Christianity in Vichy France*. Oxford: Berg, 1995.

Hanson, Paul. "The 'vie chère' Riots of 1911: Traditional Protests in Modern Garb." *Journal of Social History* 22, no. 3 (1988): 463–81.

Hay, Douglas. "Property, Authority and the Criminal Law." In *Albion's Fatal Tree: Crime and Society in Eighteenth-Century England*, edited by Douglas Hay et al., 17–63. London: Allen Lane, 1975.

Heilbronner, A. "Le ravitaillement en France." *Revue d'économie politique* 6 (1947): 1644–82.

Heineman, Elizabeth. "The Hour of the Woman: Memories of Germany's 'Crisis Years' and West German National Identity." *American Historical Review* 101, no. 2 (1996): 354–95.

Herf, Jeffrey. *Divided Memory: The Nazi Past in the Two Germanys.* Cambridge, Mass.: Harvard University Press, 1997.

Hillel, Marc. *Vie et mœurs des G.I.s en Europe, 1942–1947.* Paris: Bulland, 1981.

Hirschfeld, Gerhard, and Patrick Marsh, eds. *Collaboration in France: Politics and Culture during the Nazi Occupation, 1940–1944.* Oxford: Berg, 1989.

Hoffmann, Stanley. *Decline or Renewal? France since the 1930s.* New York: Viking, 1974.

———. "Paradoxes of the French Political Community." In *In Search of France: The Economy, Society and Political System in the Twentieth Century,* 1–117. New York: Harper and Row, 1965.

Höhn, Maria, "Frau im Haus und Girl im *Spiegel:* Discourse on Women in the Interregnum Period of 1945–1949 and the Question of German Identity." *Central European History* 26, no. 1 (1993): 57–90.

Hostache, René. *Le Conseil national de la Résistance: Les institutions de la clandestinité.* Paris: Presses universitaires de France, 1958.

Hudry, François M. *Histoire des communes savoyardes.* Vol. 4, *Albertville et son arrondissement.* Roanne le Coteau: Editions Horvath, 1982.

Husson, Jean-Pierre. "Le retentissement de la victoire dans la Marne." In *8 Mai 1945: La victoire en Europe: Actes du colloque international de Reims, 1985,* edited by Maurice Vaïsse, 365–81. Lyon: La Manufacture, 1985.

Hutton, Patrick H. *History as an Art of Memory.* Hanover, N.H.: University Press of New England, 1993.

Ingrand, Henri. *Libération de l'Auvergne.* Paris: Hachette, 1974.

Institut d'Histoire du Temps Présent. "Les pouvoirs en France à la Libération: Colloque de 13 et 14 décembre 1989." Photocopy.

Institut national de la statistique et des études économiques. *Annuaire statistique.* Vol. 58, 1951. Paris: Imprimerie nationale, 1952.

———. *Mouvement économique en France de 1938 à 1948 (mis à jour pour 1949).* Paris: Imprimerie nationale; Presses universitaires de France, 1950.

———. *Mouvement économique en France de 1944 à 1957.* Paris: Imprimerie nationale; Presses universitaires de France, 1958.

Judt, Tony. "The Past Is Another Country: Myth and Memory in Postwar Europe." *Daedalus* 121, no. 4 (1992): 83–118.

Kaplan, Steven L. *The Bakers of Paris and the Bread Question, 1700–1775.* Durham, N.C.: Duke University Press, 1996.

———. "The Famine Plot Persuasion in Eighteenth-Century France." *Transactions of the American Philosophical Society* 72, n. 3 (1982).

Kaplan, Temma. "Female Consciousness and Collective Action: The Case of Barcelona, 1910–1918." *Signs* 7 (1982): 545–66.

Kaspi, André, ed. *La Libération de la France, juin 1944–janvier 1946.* Paris: Perrin, 1995.

Kater, Michael. "Forbidden Fruit? Jazz in the Third Reich." *American Historical Review* 94, no. 1 (1989): 11–43.

Kedward, H. R. *In Search of the Maquis: Rural Resistance in Southern France, 1942–1944.* Oxford: Clarendon, 1993.

———. "The Maquis and the Culture of the Outlaw (with Particular Reference to the Cévennes)." In *Vichy France and the Resistance: Culture and Ideology,* edited by H. R. Kedward and R. Austin, 232–51. London: Croom Helm, 1985.

———. "Patriots and Patriotism in Vichy France." *Transactions of the Royal Historical Society,* 5th ser., 32 (1982): 175–92.

———. *Resistance in Vichy France.* Oxford: Oxford University Press, 1978.

———. "The Vichy of the Other Philippe." In *Collaboration in France,* edited by G. Hirschfeld, 32–46. Oxford: Berg, 1989.

Kedward, H. R., and Nancy Wood, eds. *The Liberation of France: Image and Event.* Oxford: Berg, 1995.

Kelley, Donald, ed. *Versions of History.* New Haven: Yale University Press, 1991.

Kelly, Michael. "The View of Collaboration during the '*Après-Guerre*'." In *Collaboration in France,* edited by G. Hirschfeld, 239–51. Oxford: Berg, 1989.

Kitchen, Martin. *Nazi Germany at War.* New York: Longman, 1995.

Kohler, Eric D. "Inflation and Black Marketeering in the Rhenish Agricultural Economy, 1919–1922." *German Studies Review* 7, no. 1 (1985): 43–64.

Koos, Cheryl A. "Gender, Anti-individualism, and Nationalism: The Alliance Nationale and the Pronatalist Backlash against the *Femme moderne,* 1933–1940." *French Historical Studies* 19, no. 3 (1996): 699–724.

Korbonski, Stefan. *The Polish Underground State: A Guide to the Underground, 1939–1945.* Translated by Marta Erdman. New York: Hippocrene Books, 1978.

Koreman, Megan. "The Collaborator's Penance: The Local Purge of Collaborators, 1944–1945." *Contemporary European History* 6, no. 2 (1997): 177–92.

———. "From War to Peace: Three French Towns in 1944–45." Ph.D. diss., University of California at Berkeley, 1993.

———. "A Hero's Homecoming: The Return of the Deportees to France, 1945." *Journal of Contemporary History* 32, no. 1 (1997): 9–22.

Kramer, Steven Philip. "La crise économique de la Libération." *Revue d'histoire de la deuxième guerre mondiale* 111 (1978): 25–44.

Kritz, Neil, ed. *Transitional Justice: How Emerging Democracies Reckon with Former Regimes.* 3 vols. Washington, D.C.: United States Institute of Peace Press, 1995.

Kuisel, Richard F. *Seducing the French: The Dilemma of Americanization.* Berkeley: University of California Press, 1993.

Kupferman, Fred. *Les Premiers beaux jours, 1944–1946.* Paris: Calmann-Lévy, 1985.

Laborie, Pierre. "Opinion et représentations: La Libération et l'image de la Résistance." *Revue d'histoire de la deuxième guerre mondiale et des conflits contemporains* 33, no. 131 (1983): 65–91.

———. *L'Opinion française sous Vichy.* Paris: Editions du Seuil, 1990.

Lagrou, Pieter. "Victims of Genocide and National Memory: Belgium, France and the Netherlands, 1945–1965." *Past and Present* 154 (1997): 181–222.

Lake, Marilyn. "Female Desires: The Meaning of World War II." In *Feminism and History*, edited by Joan Wallach Scott, 429–49. Oxford: Oxford University Press, 1996.

Langer, Lawrence L. *Admitting the Holocaust: Collected Essays*. New York: Oxford University Press, 1995.

Larkin, Maurice. *France since the Popular Front: Government and People, 1936–1986*. Oxford: Clarendon, 1988.

Laurens, Corran. "'La femme au turban': Les femmes tondues." In *The Liberation of France: Image and Event*, edited by H. R. Kedward and Nancy Wood, 155–79. Oxford: Berg, 1995.

LeClerc, Françoise, and Michèle Weindling. "La Répression des femmes coupables de collaboration." *Clio* 1 (1995): 129–50.

Levi, Primo. *The Reawakening*. Translated by Stuart Woolf, 1965. New York: Collier, 1993.

———. *Survival in Auschwitz: The Nazi Assault on Humanity*. Translated by Stuart Woolf, 1958. New York: Collier, 1993.

Lewis, Norman. *Naples '44*. New York: Pantheon, 1978.

Linebaugh, Peter. *The London Hanged: Crime and Civil Society in the Eighteenth Century*. Cambridge: Cambridge University Press, 1992.

Lottman, Herbert R. *The People's Anger: Justice and Revenge in Post-Liberation France*. London: Hutchinson, 1986.

Lucas, Colin. "The Crowd and Politics between *Ancien Régime* and Revolution in France." *Journal of Modern History* 60, no. 3 (1988): 421–57.

———. "The Theory and Practice of Denunciation in the French Revolution." *Journal of Modern History* 68, no. 4 (1996): 768–85.

Lukas, Richard. *The Forgotten Holocaust: The Poles under German Occupation, 1939–1944*. Lexington: University Press of Kentucky, 1986.

Lynch, Frances M. B. *France and the International Economy: From Vichy to the Treaty of Rome*. London: Routledge, 1997.

Marrus, Michael R. *The Unwanted: European Refugees in the Twentieth Century*. Oxford: Oxford University Press, 1985.

Marrus, Michael R., and Robert Paxton. *Vichy France and the Jews*. New York: Basic Books, 1981.

Martres, Eugène. *Le Cantal de 1939 à 1945: Les troupes allemandes à travers le Massif Central*. Cournon d'Auvergne: Editions de Borée, 1993.

———. "La 'République de Mauriac' (mai–août 1944)." *Revue d'histoire de la deuxième guerre mondiale* 99 (1975): 73–90.

Matard-Bonucci, Marie-Anne, and Edouard Lynch, eds. *La Libération des camps et le Retour des déportés*. Brussels: Editions complexe, 1995.

Mazower, Mark. *Inside Hitler's Greece: The Experience of Occupation, 1941–44*. New Haven: Yale University Press, 1993.

Milo, Daniel. "Le Nom des rues." In *Les Lieux de mémoire*. Vol. 2.3, edited by Pierre Nora, 283–312. Paris: Gallimard, 1986.

Milward, Alan S. *War, Economy, and Society, 1939–1945*. Berkeley: University of California Press, 1977.

Moeller, Robert G. "War Stories: The Search for a Usuable Past in the Federal Republic of Germany." *American Historical Review* 101, no. 4 (1996): 1008–1048.

Moore, Barrington, Jr. *Injustice: The Social Bases of Obedience and Revolt*. White Plains, N.Y.: M. E. Sharpe, 1978.

Moskoff, William. *The Bread of Affliction: The Food Supply in the USSR during World War II*. Cambridge: Cambridge University Press, 1990.

Mosse, George. *Fallen Soldiers: Reshaping the Memory of the World Wars*. Oxford: Oxford University Press, 1990.

Muel-Dreyfus, Francine. *Vichy et l'éternel féminin: Contribution à une sociologie politique de l'ordre des corps*. Paris: Editions du Seuil, 1996.

Noguères, Louis. *La Haute Cour de la Libération (1944–1949)*. Paris: Editions de Minuit, 1965.

Nora, Pierre, ed. *Les Lieux de mémoire*. Vol. 2.3, *La Nation*. Paris: Gallimard, 1986.

Novick, Peter. *The Resistance versus Vichy: The Purge of Collaborators in Liberated France*. New York: Columbia University Press, 1968.

O'Brien, Conor Cruise. *Ancestral Voices: Religion and Nationalism in Ireland*. Chicago: University of Chicago Press, 1994.

Ophuls, Marcel. *Le Chagrin et la pitié*. Productions Télévision Rencontre, 1969.

Palluel-Guillard, André, ed. *La Savoie de la Révolution à nos jours, XIXe–XXe siècle*. Rennes: Ouest-France, 1986.

Paxton, Robert O. *Vichy France: Old Guard and New Order, 1940–1944*. New York: Columbia University Press, 1972.

Pickles, Dorothy. *France between the Republics*. London: Redhill, Love & Malcolmson, 1946; Ann Arbor, Mich.: University Microfilms, 1969.

Pollard, Miranda. "Women and the National Revolution." In *Vichy France and the Resistance: Culture and Ideology*, edited by H. R. Kedward and Roger Austin, 36–47. Totowa, N.J.: Barnes & Noble Books, 1985.

Prost, Antoine. *In the Wake of War: "Les anciens combattants" and French Society, 1914–1919*. Translated by Helen McPhail. Oxford: Berg, 1992.

Rév, István. "Amnesia: The Revised Framework of Hungarian History." *Budapest Review of Books* 4, no. 1 (1994): 2–6.

Richards, Eric. "The Last Scottish Food Riots." *Past and Present*, supp. 6 (1982): 1–59.

Rickard, Charles. *La Savoie dans la Résistance: Haute-Savoie—Savoie*. Rennes: Ouest-France, 1986.

Rioux, Jean-Pierre. "'Cette immense joie pleine des larmes': Les Français et le 'jour V.'"

In *8 mai 1945: La victoire en Europe,* edited by Maurice Vaïsse, 313–35. Lyon: La Manufacture, 1985.

———. "L'Épuration en France." In *Etudes sur la France de 1939 à nos jours,* 162–79. Paris: Editions du Seuil, 1985.

———. *The Fourth Republic, 1944-1958.* Translated by Godfrey Rogers. Cambridge: Cambridge University Press, 1987.

———. "Les Mauvais rêves de la République." *Le Monde,* 14 December 1990.

Ripa, Yannick. "Armes d'hommes contre femmes désarmées: De la dimension sexuée de la violence dans la guerre civile espagnole." In *De la Violence et des femmes,* edited by Cécile Dauphin, 131–45. Paris: Albin Michel, 1997.

———. "La Tonte purificatrice des républicaines pendant la guerre civile espagnole." *Cahiers de l'IHTP* 31 (1995): 39–52.

Roberts, Mary Louise. *Civilization without Sexes: Reconstructing Gender in Postwar France, 1917-1927.* Chicago: University of Chicago Press, 1994.

Roesler, Jörg. "The Black Market in Post-War Berlin and the Methods Used to Counteract It." *German History* 7, no. 1 (1989): 92–107.

Rouquet, François. "Une Affaire ordinaire d'épuration: Le cas A." *Vingtième Siècle* 33 (1992): 118–25.

———. *L'Épuration dans l'administration française.* Paris: Editions du CNRS, 1993.

Rouquet, François, and Danièle Voldman, eds. "Identités féminines et violences politiques (1936-1946)." *Cahiers de l'IHTP* 31 (1995).

Rousso, Henry. "L'Epuration en France: Une histoire inachevée." *Vingtième Siècle* 33 (1992): 78–105.

———. *The Vichy Syndrome: History and Memory in France since 1944.* 1987. Translated by Arthur Goldhammer. Cambridge, Mass.: Harvard University Press, 1991.

Ryan, Donna. *The Holocaust and the Jews of Marseille: The Enforcement of Anti-Semitic Policies in Vichy France.* Urbana: University of Illinois Press, 1996.

———. "Ordinary Acts and Resistance: Women in Street Demonstrations and Food Riots in Vichy France." *Proceedings of the Annual Meeting of the Western Society for French History* 16 (1989): 400–407.

Sauber, Marianna. "Traces fragiles: Les plaques commémoratives dans les rues de Paris" *Annales économies, sociétés, civilisations* 48, no. 3 (1993): 715–28.

Sauvy, Alfred. *La Vie économique des Français de 1939 à 1945.* Paris: Flammarion, 1978.

Schwartz, Paula. "*Partisanes* and Gender Politics in Vichy France." *French Historical Studies* 16 (1989): 126–51.

———. "Redefining Resistance: Women's Activism in Wartime France." In *Behind the Lines: Gender and the Two World Wars,* edited by Margaret Higonnet, 141–53. New Haven: Yale University Press, 1987.

———. "La Répression des femmes communistes (1940-1944)," *Cahiers de l'IHTP* 31 (1995): 25–38.

———. "Résistance et différence des sexes: Bilan et perspectives," *Clio* 1 (1995): 67–88.

Scott, James C. *Domination and the Arts of Resistance: Hidden Transcripts.* New Haven: Yale University Press, 1990.

———. *Weapons of the Weak: Everyday Forms of Peasant Resistance.* New Haven: Yale University Press, 1985.

Sédillot, René. *Histoire des marchés noirs.* Paris: Tallandier, 1985.

Shennan, Andrew. *Rethinking France: Plans for Renewal, 1940-1946.* Oxford: Clarendon, 1989.

Singer, Claude. *L'Université libérée, l'université épurée (1943-1947).* Paris: Les Belles Lettres, 1997.

Smithies, Edward. *The Black Economy in England since 1914.* Dublin: Gill and Macmillan, 1984.

Stark, Gary D. "All Quiet on the Home Front: Popular Entertainments, Censorship and Civilian Morale in Germany, 1914-1918." In *Authority, Identity and the Social History of the Great War,* edited by Frans Coetzee and Marilyn Shevin-Coetzee, 57-80. Providence, R.I.: Berghahn, 1995.

Steinlauf, Michael C. *Bondage to the Dead: Poland and the Memory of the Holocaust.* Syracuse, N.Y.: Syracuse University Press, 1997.

Stephenson, Jill. "'Emancipation' and Its Problems: War and Society in Württemberg, 1939-45." *European History Quarterly* 17 (1987): 356-57.

———. "War and Society in Württemberg, 1939-1945: Beating the System." *German Studies Review* 7, no. 1 (1985): 89-106.

Sweets, John. *Choices in Vichy France: The French under Nazi Occupation.* New York: Oxford University Press, 1986.

———. *The Politics of Resistance in France, 1940-1944: A History of the Mouvements Unis de la Résistance.* Dekalb: Northern Illinois University Press, 1976.

Taylor, Lynne. "The Black Market in Occupied Northern France, 1940-1944." *Contemporary European History* 6, no. 2 (1997): 153-76.

———. "Collective Action in Northern France, 1940-1944." *French History* 11, no. 2 (1997): 190-214.

Thalmann, Rita. "L'Oubli des femmes dans l'historiographie de la Résistance." *Clio* 1 (1995): 21-35.

Thébaud, Françoise. "Résistances et Libérations." *Clio* 1 (1995): 11-19.

Thompson, E. P. *Customs in Common: Studies in Traditional Popular Culture.* New York: The New Press, 1993.

———. "The Moral Economy of the English Crowd in the Eighteenth Century." *Past and Present* 50 (1971): 76-136.

Tilly, Charles. *The Contentious French.* Cambridge, Mass.: Bellknap, 1986.

———. "Food Supply and Public Order in Modern Europe." In *The Formation of National States in Western Europe,* edited by Charles Tilly, 380-455. Princeton: Princeton University Press, 1975.

Tilly, Louise A. "The Food Riot as a Form of Political Conflict in France." *Journal of Interdisciplinary History* 2 (1971): 23–57.
Todorov, Tzvetan. *A French Tragedy: Scenes of Civil War, Summer 1944*. Translated by Mary Byrd Kelly. Hanover, N.H.: University Press of New England, 1996.
Troyansky, David G. "Memorializing Saint-Quentin: Monuments, Inaugurations, and History in the Third Republic." *French History* 10, no. 1 (1999): 1–29.
———. "Monumental Politics: National History and Local Memory in French *Monuments aux Morts* in the Department of the Aisne since 1870." *French Historical Studies* 15, no. 1 (1987): 121–41.
Tumarkin, Nina. *The Living and the Dead: The Rise and Fall of the Cult of World War II in Russia*. New York: Basic Books, 1994.
Turner, Victor. *The Forest of Symbols: Aspects of Ndembu Ritual*. Ithaca, N.Y.: Cornell University Press, 1967.
———. "Social Dramas and Stories about Them." In *On Narrative*, edited by W. J. T. Mitchell, 137–64. Chicago: University of Chicago Press, 1980.
Veillon, Dominique. *Vivre et survivre en France, 1939-1947*. Paris: Histoire Payot, 1995.
Veillon, Dominique, and Jean-Marie Flonneau, eds. "Le Temps des restrictions en France (1939–1949)." *Cahiers de l'IHTP* 32–33 (1996).
Vercors. *Le Silence de la mer*. Paris: Editions de Minuit, 1944.
Viola, Lynne. "The Second Coming: Class Enemies in the Soviet Countryside, 1927–1935." In *Stalinist Terror: New Perspectives*, edited by J. Arch Getty and Roberta T. Manning, 65–98. Cambridge: Cambridge University Press, 1993.
Virgili, Fabrice. "*Les Femmes tondues:* Liberation and the Shame of Collaboration." Paper presented at the Contemporary History Conference "After the War Was Over: Reconstructing the Family, Society and the Law in Southern Europe, 1944–1950," University of Sussex, July 1996.
———. "Les 'Tondues' à la Libération: Le corps des femmes, enjeu d'une réappropriation." *Clio* 1 (1995): 111–27.
———. "Les Tontes de la Libération en France." *Cahiers de l'IHTP* 31 (1995): 53–66.
Voldman, Danièle. *Attention mines, 1944-1947*. Paris: Editions France-Empire, 1985.
———. "Les Bombardements aériens: Une mise à mort du "guerrier"? (1914–1945)." In *De la violence et des femmes*, edited by Cécile Dauphin, 146–58. Paris: Albin Michel, 1997.
———, ed. "Images, discours et enjeux de la reconstruction des villes françaises après 1945." *Cahiers de l'IHTP* 5 (1987).
Weber, Eugen. *The Hollow Years: France in the 1930s*. New York: Norton, 1994.
Wells, Roger. *Wretched Faces: Famine in Wartime England, 1793-1801*. New York: St. Martin's Press, 1988.
Wieviorka, Annette. *Déportation et génocide: Entre la mémoire et l'oubli*. Paris: Plon, 1992.
Wildt, Michael. "Plurality of Taste: Food and Consumption in West Germany during the 1950s." *History Workshop Journal* 39 (1995): 22–41.

Wilkinson, James D. "Remembering World War II: The Perspective of the Losers." *The American Scholar* 54 (1985): 329–43.
Winter, Jay. *Sites of Memory, Sites of Mourning: The Great War in European Cultural History*. Cambridge: Cambridge University Press, 1995.
Wormser-Migot, Olga. *Le Retour des déportés: Quand les Alliés ouvrirent les portes* . . . Rev. ed. Brussels: Editions Complexe, 1985.
Wylie, Laurence. *Village in the Vaucluse*. 3d ed. Cambridge, Mass.: Harvard University Press, 1974.
Zaretsky, Robert. *Nîmes at War: Religion, Politics, and Public Opinion in the Gard, 1938–1944*. University Park: Pennsylvania State University Press, 1995.
Zuccotti, Susan. *The Holocaust, the French, and the Jews*. New York: Basic Books, 1993.

INDEX

Absents, 73–75, 230–32, 235. *See also* Deportees; Prisoners of War; Resistencialist myth; War victims

Administrative internment, 101, 102, 113, 126, 185

Amarger, René, 16–17, 19–20, 121, 197, 200, 205, 211

Americans. *See* U.S. Army

Anciens de l'Armée secrète (AAS), 26, 28, 70–71, 134, 225

Anti-Italian sentiment, 21–22, 226

Atrocities, 31, 32. *See also* Pont de Soubizergues; Twenty-One Hostages

Black market, 4, 7, 26, 59, 63, 80, 148, 152, 156, 158, 162–64, 168, 174, 176–88, 250, 254; public opinion of, 53, 64–65; and purge, 108, 117, 125–26, 131–33, 138, 142; as threat to government, 176, 187; and U.S. Army, 41–42, 177

Bread, 156, 159, 164, 166, 251–55, 258–59, 261

Capella Affair, 143–46, 227

Catholics: and popular piety, 45–46, 215–17; and relations with resistants, 16–17, 28, 45–47, 216–17

Chambres civiques, 96–97, 101, 105, 113, 245. *See also* Purge courts

Charities, 26, 52, 76–79, 87. *See also* Dancing

CNR Charter, 4–5, 240, 261

Commisaires régional de la République, 9. *See also* Administrative internment

Communism, 18, 262. *See also* Parti communiste français

Cour de Justice, 94, 96–100, 103. *See also* Purge courts

Crime, 48, 58, 61, 71, 137, 157–59, 185. *See also* Ration ticket fraud

Dancing, 68–72, 95, 190, 207, 223

De Gaulle, Charles, 1, 3, 38–39, 195, 210, 247–48, 261, 312 n.70. *See also* Pardons

Denunciation, 93–95, 113, 116–17, 130, 183, 268 n.12

Deportees, 36, 45, 65, 74, 79–80, 86, 127–28, 144, 220, 230–31, 244–46. *See also* Absents; Mallet: Mme.; Return

Displaced persons, 72–75

Economy, 2, 57–64. *See also* Food shortages; Free market; Inflation; Shortages

Elections, 229–30, 255–57, 261; munici-

Elections (*continued*)
pal, 7, 30, 209, 230–43; national, 172, 175, 243–46, 252

Faux-maquis, 49, 136, 139. *See also* Crime
Fifth column, 50–51, 93, 119, 139, 146–47, 164–66, 242, 245
First anniversary of liberation: of Moûtiers, 223–25; of Rambervillers, 213–14; of Saint-Flour, 211–12
Food protests, 154–56, 160, 163, 166–73, 184
Food shortages, 6, 14, 24, 32, 35, 37, 41, 148–88, 253, 261; and politics, 153, 173–76, 248, 251–52; and the purge, 133–34. *See also* Black market; Bread; Crime; Food protests; Free market; Rationing system
Forces françaises de l'intérieur (FFI), 12, 14, 22, 25–26, 31, 49, 51, 135, 139–41, 189, 193, 195, 212, 225
Free market, 155–156, 168, 251–254, 256

Gender roles, 65–68, 111. *See also* Women

Head shaving, 15, 94, 108–11, 113–14, 116, 122–24, 127, 130, 135, 137, 146–47. *See also* Horizontal collaboration; Vigilantes
Horizontal collaboration, 101, 108–14, 127. *See also* Head shaving

Inflation, 61–64, 156, 258

Jews. *See* Return
Justice: definitions of, 4–7, 107, 124, 148, 189, 260–62

Land mines, 37, 42
Laurens, Camille. *See* Elections: national
Liberation: of Moûtiers, 23–26, 130, 220–22; of Rambervillers, 31–35, 38–39, 122–24, 212; of Saint-Flour, 14–15, 116, 210; as transfer of power, 8–10. *See also* Head shaving
Liberation committees, 9, 16, 27; and elections, 238, 241; and food, 149–50, 155, 158, 182–83; and the purge, 97–98, 100, 103, 140, 142, 144. *See also* Liberation
Lissorgues, Abbé, 17, 19, 121, 233, 243–46

Mallet family, 204–6; Dr. Louis, 194, 205–8, 210; Mme., 81, 203–6, 208–9, 211, 235–37; Pierre, 200–203, 205–6
Martyrs, 189, 192–94, 198–99, 200–204, 206, 210–11, 219, 234–36, 239–40. *See also* Mallet family; Pont de Soubizergues
Memory, 20, 189–228; and the purge, 130, 136, 143. *See also* Mallet family; Pont de Soubizergues; Resistencialist myth
Milice, 22–23, 65, 104–6, 118, 142–43, 145–46, 218–19, 225, 227
Milices patriotiques, 15, 28, 52–53, 130–32, 182, 183, 259
Ministry of Prisoners, Deportees, and Refugees, 75–76, 79–80, 88, 221. *See also* Return
Mont-Mouchet, 14, 200–201, 209–11
Monuments, 192–94, 204, 207–8, 217, 223–27
Moral hierarchy, 45, 55, 64–65, 81, 87, 151–52, 189, 235, 244–45
Municipal government: of Moûtiers, 26–30; of Rambervillers, 38–39; of Saint-Flour, 15–16

National degradation, 96–97. *See also* Chambres civiques; Purge

Pardons, 101–3, 129, 141–46, 227, 256, 258, 260

Parti communiste français (PCF), 64, 194, 237, 239, 243, 245, 247; and food, 167, 170, 171–72, 188; of Moûtiers, 28–29, 134; of Saint-Flour, 18, 121, 202, 233, 236. *See also* Communism
Place names, 193–95, 214
Police, 48–50, 118, 138, 183–84
Pont de Soubizergues, 14, 15, 117, 120, 194, 197, 200–203, 205, 210
Prisoners of war: American treatment of German, 54–55; French, 73, 75, 78, 89–90, 254; German, 37–38, 54–57. *See also* Absents; Return
Protests, 90–91. *See also* Food protests; Strikes
Purge, 92–147; and food, 164, 170; sympathy for accused, 17–18, 105, 120, 126. *See also* Administrative internment; Black market; Head shaving; Horizontal collaboration; Pardons; Vigilantes
Purge Commission: of Moûtiers, 28, 130–33; of Saint-Flour, 116–17
Purge courts: disillusionment with, 98–100. *See also* Chambres civiques; Cour de Justice; Purge

Rationing system, 55, 148, 150–57, 160, 168. *See also* Food shortages; Ration ticket fraud; Ravitaillement général; Shopping
Ration ticket fraud, 19–20, 158–59, 185
Ravitaillement général (RG), 149, 157–67, 169, 173–74, 178–79
Refugees, 35, 39, 72, 77. *See also* Charities; War victims
Remembrance Committee, 16, 200, 203, 207
Resistencialist myth, 3, 74, 190, 198–200, 209–11, 214–15, 217–18, 227–28, 260, 262; and Absents, 88–90; opposition to, 4, 260–61; and the purge, 101–2

Return, the, 49, 79–88, 220–21; and elections, 230–32, 241; and food, 151; of Jews, 65, 74; and the purge, 85–86, 101, 102, 137, 186. *See also* Deportees; Ministry of Prisoners, Deportees, and Refugees; Prisoners of war; Voluntary laborers
Rumors, 32, 50–51, 76, 83, 118, 121, 132, 139, 164–65, 180–81, 186, 220–21, 255

Shopkeepers, 124–25, 160–61, 167
Shopping, 160–62
Shortages, 58–61. *See also* Black market; Food shortages; Protests
Strikes, 59, 63–64, 169

Twenty-One Hostages, 23, 220–24

Union de femmes françaises (UFF), 18, 29, 170–73, 209, 230–31, 250
U.S. Army, 37, 39–44, 67, 79; relations with French, 43–44, 53–55, 214–15. *See also* Black market; Prisoners of war; Victory celebrations

Victory celebrations, 195–97
Vigilantes, 6, 118–19, 126–29, 133–35, 137–47, 190, 224, 240–41; attempts to stop, 120–21, 134, 139–42, 146–47; and the black market, 161, 177–78; and public opinion, 128–29, 138, 140–41; and the purge, 104, 105, 114–15
Violence. *See* Black market; Crime; Faux-maquis; Food protests; Head shaving; Vigilantes; Voluntary laborers
Voluntary laborers, 73–74, 83–85, 99, 109, 127

War victims, 24, 36, 39. *See also* Absents; Deportees; Refugees; Return
Women: and politics, 29, 153, 232, 236, 238–39, 243, 248–50; in public mem-

Women: and politics (*continued*) ory, 190–91; and the purge, 94–95, 108–14, 136–37; and the vote, 66–68, 230. *See also* Food protests; Gender roles; Head shaving; Horizontal collaboration; Shopping

MEGAN KOREMAN was, most recently, Associate Professor of History at Texas Tech University.

Library of Congress Cataloging-in-Publication Data
Koreman, Megan.
The expectation of justice : France, 1944–1946 / Megan Koreman.
p. cm.
ISBN 0-8223-2352-4 (cl. : alk. paper) ISBN 0-8223-2373-7 (pa. : alk. paper)
1. World War, 1939–1945 — France.   2. World War, 1939–1945 — Collaborationists — France Case studies.   3. Social justice — France — History Case studies.   4. France — History — 1945–   Case studies.   I. Title.
D802.F8   K65   1999
944.082 — dc21   99-25936   CIP

www.ingramcontent.com/pod-product-compliance
Lightning Source LLC
Chambersburg PA
CBHW061343300426
44116CB00011B/1968